The Monarchs of the Main

The Monarchs of the Main
A Classic Account of the Buccaneers & Pirates of the Great Age of Sail

Walter Thornbury

The Monarchs of the Main: a Classic Account of the Buccaneers & Pirates of the Great Age of Sail
by Walter Thornbury

Originally published in three volumes, this Leonaur edition contains the complete text of the original editions.

Leonaur is an imprint of Oakpast Ltd

Material original to this edition and presentation of the text in this form copyright © 2012 Oakpast Ltd

ISBN: 978-0-85706-886-6 (hardcover)
ISBN: 978-0-85706-887-3 (softcover)

http://www.leonaur.com

Publisher's Notes

The views expressed in this book are not necessarily those of the publisher.

Contents

Preface	7
History of Tortuga	11
Manners of the Hunters	26
The Flibustiers or Sea Rovers	60
Peter the Great—the First Buccaneer	79
Lolonnois the Cruel	95
Alexandre Bras-de-Fer & Montbars the Exterminator	130
Sir Henry Morgan	147
Conquest of Panama	202
The Companions & Successors of Morgan	230
The Cruises of Sawkins & Sharp	242
Dampier's Voyages	270
Ravenau de Lussan	289
The Last of the Buccaneers	337
Fall of the Floating Empire	361
The Pirates of New Providence & the Kings of Madagascar	364

Preface

I claim for this book, at least originality. But this originality, unfortunately, if it attaches interest to an author's labours, adds also to his responsibilities.

The history of the buccaneers has hitherto remained unwritten. Three or four forgotten volumes contain literally all that is recorded of the wars and conquests of these extraordinary men. Of these volumes two are French, one Dutch, and one in English. The majority of our readers, therefore, it is probable, know nothing more of the freebooters but their name, confound them with the mere pirates of two centuries later, and derive their knowledge of their manners from those dozen lines of the Abbé Reynal, that have been transferred from historian to historian, and from writer to writer, for the last two centuries.

The chief records of buccaneer adventurers are drawn literally from only three books. The first of these is Oexmelin's *Histoire des Aventuriers*. Oexmelin was a Frenchman, who went out to St. Domingo as a planter's apprentice or *engagé*, and eventually became surgeon in the buccaneer fleet—knew Lolonnois, and accompanied Sir Henry Morgan to Panama. The second is Esquemeling's *Zee Roovers*. A book constantly mistaken by booksellers and in catalogues for Oexmelin. Esquemeling was a Dutch *engagé* at St. Domingo, and his book is an English translation from the Dutch. The writer appears of humbler birth than Oexmelin, but served also at Panama.

The third is Ringrose's *History of the Cruises of Sharpe, &c.* This man, who served with Dampier, seems to have been an ignorant sailor, and a mere log-keeper.

The fourth is Ravenau de Lussan's *Narrative*. De Lussan was a young French officer of fortune, who served in some of Ringrose's cruises. This is a book written by a vivacious and keen observer, but is less complete than Oexmelin's, but equally full of anecdote, and very amusing.

For secondary authorities we come to the French Jesuit historians of the West Indian Islands, diffuse Rochefort, the gossiping *bon vivant* Labat; Tertre, dry and prejudiced; Charlevoix, careful, condensed, and entertaining; and Raynal, polished, classical, second-hand, and declamatory.

The English secondaries are, Dampier, with his companions, Wafer and Cowley. Several old pamphlets contain quaint versions of Morgan's conquest of Panama; and in 1817, Burney, in his "History of Discoveries in the South Sea," devotes many chapters to a dry but very imperfect abridgment of buccaneer adventure, omitting carefully everything that gives either life or colour. Captain Southey, in his "History of the West Indies," supplies many odd scraps of old voyages, and presents many scattered figures, but attempts no picture.

Nor has modern fiction, however short of material, discovered these new and virgin mines. Mrs. Hall has a novel, it is true, called *The buccaneer*, the scene of which is, however, laid in England; and Angus B. Reach has skimmed the same subject, but has evidently not even read half the three existing authorities. Dana, the American poet, has a poem called the buccaneer, but this is merely a collection of lines on the sea. Sir Walter Scott's Bertram, although he had been a buccaneer, is a mere ruffian, who would do for any age, and Scott himself places Morgan's conquest of Panama in the reign of Charles I., when it actually took place in that of Charles II., fifty years later.

Defoe himself, little conscious of the rich region he was treading, sketched a buccaneer sailor when he re-christened Alexander Selkirk Robinson Crusoe, and condensed all the spirit of Dampier into a book still read as eagerly by the man as by the boy.

When I find a writer of Scott's profundity of reading and depth of research placing the great event of buccaneer history fifty years before its time, booksellers mistaking a Dutch for a French writer, and living historians confounding the *flibustiers* of

Tortuga, who attacked only the Spaniards, with their degraded successors the pirates of New Providence, who robbed all nations and even their own without mercy, I think I have proved that my book is not a superfluity.

It is seldom that an author can invite the whole reading world to peruse the self-rewarding labour of his student life. Mine is no book for a sect, a clique, a profession, or a trade. It brings new scenes and new creations to the novel reader, jaded with worn-out types of conventional existence. It supplies the historian with a page of English, French, and Spanish history that the capricious muse of history has hitherto kept in MS. It traces the foundation of our colonial empire. To the psychologist it furnishes deep matter for thought, while the philosopher may see in these pages humanity in a new aspect, and man's soul exposed to new temptations.

What Dampier has described and Defoe drawn materials from, no man can dare to assert is wanting in interest. The readers to whom these books are new will be astonished to find the adventures of Xenophon paralleled in De Lussan's retreat over the Isthmus, and Swift forestalled in his conception of some of the oddest customs of Lilliput. Oexmelin, I may boldly assert, is a much more amusing writer than half our historians, a keen and enlightened observer, who looked upon buccaneering as a chivalrous life, in which the sea knight got equally hard knocks as the land hero, but more money.

If my characters are not so grand as those of history, I can present to my reader men as greedy of gold, ambitious and sagacious as Pizarro or Cortes, and as reckless as Alexander, and as cruel as Caesar. If the buccaneers were but insects, bred from the putrefactions of a decaying empire, their plans were at least gigantic, and their courage unprecedented.

Anomalous beings, hunters by land and sea, scaring whole fleets with a few canoes, sacking cities with a few grenadiers, devastating every coast from California to Cape Horn, they only needed a common principle of union to have founded an aggressive republic, as wealthy as Venice and as warlike as Carthage. One great mind and the New World had been their own.

But from the first Providence sowed amongst them the seeds of discord—difference of religion and difference of race. Never settling, their race had its ranks renewed, not by descendants, but by fresh recruits, men with new interests and lower aims. In less than a century the Brotherhood had passed away, their virtues were forgotten and their vices alone remembered.

The buccaneers were robbers, yet they sought something beyond gold. Mansvelt took the island of St. Catherine, and planned a republic, and Morgan contemplated the destruction of the Bravo Indians. They were outlaws, and yet religious robbers, yet generous and regardful of the minutest delicacies of honour; lovers of freedom, yet obeying the sternest discipline; cruel, yet tender to their friends.

All the light and shade of the darkest fiction look poor beside the adventures of these men. Catholics, Protestants, Puritans, gallants, officers, common seamen, farmers' sons, men of rank, hunters, sailors, planters, murderers, fanatics, Creoles, Spaniards, negroes, astrologers, monks, pilots, guides, merchants—all pass before us in a motley and ever-changing masquerade. The backgrounds to these scenes are the wooded shores of the West Indian Islands, woods sparkling at night with fire-flies, broad savannahs dark with wild cattle, the volcanic islands peopled by marooned sailors, stormy promontories, the lonely sand "keys" of Jamaica, and the rocky fastnesses of Tortuga.

CHAPTER 1

History of Tortuga

Drake, Cavendish, and Oxenham, indeed all the naval heroes of Elizabeth's reign, were the precursors of the buccaneers. The captains of those "tall ships" that sailed from Plymouth Sound, and the green nooks of the sunny coast of Devon, to capture stately carracks laden deep with silks, spices, pearls, and precious stones, the treasure of Potosi and Peru, were but buccaneers under another name, agreeing with them in the great principle of making war on none but Spaniards, but on Spaniards unceasingly. "No peace beyond the line" was the motto on the flag of both Drake and Morgan.

Sir John Hawkins, who began the slave trade, and who was Drake's earliest patron, took the town of Rio de la Hacha, and struggled desperately with the galleons in the port of St. Juan d'Ulloa. Drake sacked Nombre de Dios, and, passing across the isthmus, stormed Vera Cruz. He destroyed St. Domingo and Carthagena, burnt La Rancheria, and attacked Porto Rico. But still more truly a buccaneer was John Oxenham, one of Drake's followers, who, cruising about Panama, captured several bullion vessels; but was at last slain, with all his men, having fallen in love with a Spanish captive, and liberated her son, who surprised him with reinforcements from Nombre de Dios. Then came Raleigh, more chivalrous than them all—looser in principle, but wiser in head. He planned an attack on Panama, and ravaged St. Thomas's.

The first buccaneers were poor French hunters, who, driven by the Spaniards out of Hispaniola, fled to the neighbouring island of Tortuga, and there settled as planters.

This buccaneer colony of Tortuga arose rather by accident than by the design of any one ambitious mind. The French had established a colony in the almost deserted island of St. Christopher's, which had begun to flourish when the Spaniards, alarmed at a hostile power's vicinity to their mines, to which their thoughts then alone tended, put a stop to the prosperity of the French settlements by frequent attacks made by their fleets on their way to New Spain. From the just hatred excited by these unprovoked forays sprang the first impulse of retaliation. These injuries provoked the French, as they had done the Dutch, to fit out privateers. But a still more powerful motive soon became paramount. A spirit of cupidity arose, which was stimulated by the heated imaginations of men poor and angry. Before them lay regions of gold, timidly guarded by a vindictive but feeble enemy; and Spain became to these pioneer settlers what a bedridden miser is to the dreams of a needy bravo.

The report of the Dutch successes spread through all the ports of France. Sailors were the ready bearers of wild tales they had themselves half invented. Some hardy adventurers of Dieppe fitted out vessels to carry on a warfare that retaliation had now rendered just, war made legal, and chance rendered profitable. The sailor who was today munching his onion on the quays of Marseilles might, a few weeks hence, be lord of Carthagena, or rolling in the treasures of a Manilla galleon, clothed in Eastern silks, and delighted with the perfumes of India. Finding their enterprise successful, but St. Kitt's too distant to form a convenient depot for their booty, they began to look about for some nearer locality. At first they found their return voyages to the West Indian islands frequently occupying three months, which seemed years to men hurrying to store up old plunder, and to sally forth for new. In search of an asylum, these privateersmen touched at Hispaniola, hoping to find some lonely island near its shores; but as soon as they had landed, and saw the great forests full of game, and broad savannahs alive with wild cattle, and finding it abandoned by the Spaniards, and the Indians nearly all dead or emigrated, they determined to settle at a place so full of advantages, where they could revictual their ships, and remain secure and unobserved. The sight of Tortuga, a small neighbouring island, rocky, and yet not without a harbour, convinced them that nature had constructed for their growing empire at once a magazine, a citadel, and a fortress. They had now a sanctuary and a haven, shelter for their booty, and food for their men.

The Spaniards, although not occupying the island, were anxious that it should not be occupied by others. They had long had a foreboding that this island would become a resort for pirates, and had just garrisoned it with an *alfarez* and twenty-five men. The French had, however, little difficulty in getting rid of this small force, the soldiers being enraged at finding themselves left by their countrymen, without provisions or reinforcements, upon a barren rock.

Once masters of the heap of stones, the French began to deliberate by what means they could retain it. The sight of buildings already begun, and the prospect of more food than they could get at St. Christopher's, determined these restless men to settle on the spot they had won. Part of them returned to Hispaniola to kill oxen and boars, and to salt the flesh for those who would remain to plant; and those men who determined to build assured the sailors that stores of dry meat should always be ready to revictual their ships.

The adventurers, having a nucleus for their operations, began to widen their operations. They became now divided into three distinct classes, always intermingling, and never very definitely divided, but still for the main part separate: the *sea rovers*, or *flibustiers*; the *planters*, or *habitans*; and the *hunters*, or buccaneers. For the first class, there were many names: the English, following an Indian word, called them buccaneers, from the Indian term *boucan* (dried meat); the Dutch denominated them *zee roovers*, and the French *flibustiers*, or *aventuriers*. A fourth class, growing by degrees either into the buccaneers or the planters, were the apprentices, or *engagés*.

A few French planters could not have retained the island had not their numbers been swelled by the addition of many English. In a short time, French vessels touched at the island, to trade for the booty that now arrived more frequently, unintermittingly, and in greater quantities. The trade grew less speculative and uncertain. French captains found it profitable to barter not only for hides and meat with the buccaneers, but with the *flibustiers* for silver-plate and pieces of eight. The high prices paid for wine and brandy soon rendered the commerce with Bordeaux a matter worthy the attention of the French Government. In a few days of buccaneer excess more was spent in barter than could have been realised in months of average traffic with the more cautious.

The Spaniards, fully alive to the danger of this planter settlement, determined to destroy it at a single blow. The design was easy of accomplishment, for the buccaneers had grown careless from long impunity, and had long since crowned themselves undisputed kings of Hispaniola and its dependencies. Taking advantage of a time when the English corsairs were at sea and the French buccaneers hunting on the mainland, the Spanish General of the Indian Fleet landed with a handful of soldiers and retook the island in an hour. The few planters were overpowered before they could run together, the hunters before they could seize their arms. Some were at once put to the sword, and others hung on the nearest trees. The larger portion, however, taking advantage of well-known lurking places, waited for the night, and then escaped to the mainland in their canoes. The Spaniards, satisfied with the terror they had struck, left the island un-garrisoned, and returned exultingly to St. Domingo. Hearing, however, that there were a great many buccaneers still settled as hunters in Hispaniola, and that the wild cattle were diminishing by their ravages, the general levied some troops to put them down. To these men, who were known as the Spanish *fifties*, we shall hereafter advert.

The Spanish fleet was scarcely well out of sight before the buccaneers, angry but unintimidated, flocked back to their now desolated island, full of rage at the sight of the bodies of their companions and the ashes of their ruined houses. The English returned headed by a buccaneer named Willis, who gave an English character to the new colony. The French adventurers, jealous of English interference, and fearful that the island would fall into the possession of England, left Tortuga, and, going to St. Christopher's, informed the Governor, the Chevalier de Poncy, of the ease with which it could be conquered. De Poncy, alive to the scheme and jealous for French honour, fitted out an expedition, and entrusted the command to M. Le Vasseur, a brave soldier and good engineer, just arrived from France, who levied a force of forty French Protestants, and agreed to conquer the island for De Poncy and to govern in his name, as well as to pay half the expenses of the conquest. In a few days he dropped anchor in

Port Margot, on the north side of Hispaniola, about seven leagues from Tortuga. He instantly collected a force of forty French buccaneers from the woods and the savannahs, and, having arranged his plans, made a descent upon the island in the month of April, 1640. As soon as he had landed, he sent a message to the English Governor to say that he had come to avenge the insults received by the French flag, and to warn him that if he did not leave the island with all those of his nation in twenty-four hours, he should lay waste every plantation with fire and sword. The English, feeling their position untenable, instantly embarked in a vessel lying in the road, without (as Oexmelin, a French writer, says) striking a blow in self-defence. The French population of the island then, rising in arms, welcomed the invaders as friends.

Le Vasseur, the bloodless conqueror of this new Barataria, was received with shouts and acclamations. He at once visited every nook of the island that needed defence, and prepared to insure it against reconquest either by the Spaniards or the English. He found it inaccessible on three sides; and on the unprotected quarter built a fort, on a peak of impregnable rock, rising 600 feet above the narrow path which it commanded. The summit of this rock was about thirty feet square, and could only be ascended by steps cut in the stone or by a moveable iron ladder. The fort held four guns. A spring of water completed the advantages of the spot, which was surrounded with walls and fenced in with hedges, woods, precipices, and every aid that art or nature could furnish. The only approach to this steep was a narrow avenue in which no more than three men could march abreast.

The buccaneers now flocked to Tortuga in greater numbers than before, some to congratulate the new governor on his victory, and others to enrol themselves as his subjects: all who came he received with promises of support and protection. The Spaniards, in the meanwhile, determined to crush this wasp's nest, fitted out at St. Domingo a new armament of six vessels, having on board 500 or 600 men. They at first anchored before the fort, but, receiving a volley, moored two leagues lower down, and landed their troops. In attempting to storm the fort by a *coup de main*, they were beaten off with the loss of 200 men, the garrison sallying out and driving them back to their ships.

The now doubly victorious governor was hailed as the defender and saviour of Tortuga. The news of victory soon reached the ears of M. de Poncy, at St. Christopher's, who, at first rejoiced at the success, became soon afraid of the ambition of his new ally. Fearing that he would repudiate the contract, and declare himself an independent sovereign, he took the precaution of testing his sincerity. He sent two of his relations to Tortuga to request land as settlers, but really to act as spies. Le Vasseur, subtle and penetrating, at once detected their object. He received the young men with great civility, but took care to secure their speedy return to St. Christopher's. Having now attained the summit of his wishes, he became, as many greater men have been, intoxicated with power. His temper changed, and he grew severe, suspicious, intolerant, and despotic. He not only bound his subjects in chains, but delighted to clank the fetters, and remind them of their slavery. He ill-used the planters, loaded the merchants with taxes, punished the most venial faults, and grew as much hated as he had been once beloved. He went so far in his tyranny as to forbid the exercise of the Catholic religion, to burn the churches and expel the priests. The murder of such a persecutor has always been held a sin easily forgiven by the confessor, and lust and superstition soon gave birth to murder.

Charlevoix relates an amusing instance of the governor's contumacy. De Poncy, informed that his vessels had taken a silver idol (a Virgin Mary) from some Spanish cathedral, wrote to demand its surrender. Le Vasseur returned a wooden image by the messenger, desiring him to say, that for religious purposes, wood or silver was equally good. One of his most cruel inventions Le Vasseur called his "hell." It seems to have resembled the portable iron cages in which Louis XI. used to confine his state prisoners.

M. de Poncy, informed of the extraordinary change in the character of Le Vasseur, endeavoured to beguile him by promises, threats, and entreaties. Justice gave him now a pretext of enforcing what self-interest had long meditated. The toils were growing closer round the doomed man, but Heaven sent a speedier punishment. Le Vasseur, still waiving all openings for formal complaint, was exulting in all the glory of a small satrapy, when two nephews conspired against his life. Cupidity inspired the crime, and they easily persuaded themselves that God and man alike demanded the expiation. One writer calls them simply captains, "companions of fortune," and another, the nephews of Le Vasseur.

These ungrateful men had already been declared his heirs, but they had quarrelled with him about a mistress he had taken from them, and one fault in a friend obliterates the remembrance of many virtues. They believed that the inhabitants, rejoiced at deliverance from such tyranny, would appoint them joint governors in the first outburst of their gratitude. They shot him from an ambush as he was descending from the rock fort to the shore, but, only wounding him slightly, were obliged to complete the murder with a poignard. The wounded man called for a priest, and declared himself, with his last breath, a steadfast Catholic. He seems to have been a dark, wily man, of strong passions, tenacious ambition, and ungovernable will.

While this crime was perpetrating, De Poncy, determined to recover possession of at least his share of Tortuga, and weary and angry at the subterfuges of Le Vasseur, had resolved upon a new expedition. The leader was a Chevalier de Fontenoy, a soldier of fortune, who, attracted by the sparkle of Spanish gold, had just arrived at St. Kitt's in a French frigate. Full of chivalry, he at once proposed to sail, although informed that the place was impregnable, and could only be taken by stratagem. While the armament was fitting up, he made a cruise round Carthagena, on the look out for Spanish prizes, and joined M. Feral, a nephew of the general, at Port de Paix, a rendezvous twelve leagues from Tortuga. Informed there of the murder of Le Vasseur, they at once sailed for the harbour, and landed 500 men at the spot where the Spaniards had formerly been repulsed. The two murderers immediately capitulated, on condition of being allowed to depart with all their uncle's treasure. The Chevalier was proclaimed governor, and received with as many acclamations as Le Vasseur had been before him. The old religion was restored, and commerce patronized and protected, by royal edict. Two bastions were added to the fort, and more guns mounted. The buccaneers crowded back in greater numbers than even on Le Vasseur's arrival. Before they had only imagined the advantages of this conquest, but now they had tasted them. The Chevalier hailed all buccaneers as friends and brothers, and even himself fitted out privateers. The Spanish ships could scarcely venture out of port, and one merchant alone is known to have lost 300,000 crowns' worth of merchandise in a single year.

It is easier to conquer than to retain a conquest, and vigilance grows blunted by success. The Chevalier, too confident in his strength, allowed half his population to embark in cruisers. The sick, the aged, the maimed, laboured in the plantations with the slaves. The Spaniards, informed of this, landed in force, without resistance. The few buccaneers crowded into the fort, which the enemy dared not approach. Discovering, however, a mountain that commanded the rock, precipitous, but still accessible, they determined to plant a battery upon it, and drive the buccaneers from their last foothold. With infinite vigour and determination they hewed a road to the mountain between two rocks. Making frames of wood, they lashed on their cannons, and forced the slaves and prisoners to drag them to the summit, and, with a battery of four guns, suddenly opened a fire upon the unguarded fort. The Chevalier, not expecting this enterprise, had just deprived himself of his last defence, by cutting down the large trees that grew round the walls. In spite of all the threats and expostulations of the governor, the garrison, galled by this plunging fire, at once capitulated. They left the island in twenty-four hours, with arms and baggage, drums beating, colours flying, and match burning, and set sail in two half-scuttled vessels lying in the road, having first given hostages not to serve against Spain for a given time. In another vessel, but alone, set sail the two murderers, who, being short of food, consummated their crimes by leaving the women and children of their company on a desert island.

The Spanish general, repairing the fort, garrisoned it with sixty men, whom he supplied with provisions. Fontenoy, repulsed in an attempt to recover the island, soon afterwards returned to France.

In 1655, when Admiral Penn appeared off St. Domingo with Cromwell's fleet, the Spaniards, to increase their forces in Hispaniola, recalled the troop which had held Tortuga eighteen months— the commander first blowing up the fort, burning the church, the houses, and the magazines, and devastating the plantations. Not long afterwards, an English refugee of wealth, Elias Ward (or, as the

French call him, *Elyazouärd*), came from Jamaica, with his family and a dozen soldiers, and with an English commission from the general, and was soon joined by about 120 French and English adventurers.

The treaty of the Pyrenees, in 1659, brought no repose to the hunters of Hispaniola from Spanish inroads. The planters were compelled to work armed, and to keep watch at night for fear of being murdered in their beds. In 1667 the war recommencing, let the bloodhounds, who had long been straining in the leash, free to raven and devour. De Lisle again plundered St. Jago, and obtained 2,500 *piastres* ransom, each of his adventurers secured 300 crowns, the Spaniards abandoning the defiles and carrying off their treasure to Conception.

This was the golden age of buccaneering. Vauclin, Ovinet, and Tributor, plundered the towns of Cumana, Coro, St. Martha, and Nicaragua. Le Basque, with only forty men, surprised Maracaibo by night. He seized the principal inhabitants and shut them in the cathedral, and threatened to instantly cut off their heads if the citizens ventured to rise in arms. Daylight discovering his feeble force, he could obtain no ransom. The *flibustiers* then retreated, each man driving a prisoner before him, a pistol slung in one hand and a naked sabre raised over the Spaniard's head in the other. These hostages were detained twenty-four hours, and released at the moment the French departed. This is the same Le Basque whom Charlevoix describes as cutting out the Margaret from under the cannon of Portobello, and winning a million *piastres*. At another time, they retreated laden with booty and carrying with them the governor and the principal citizens of St. Jago; but the Spaniards, rallying, placed themselves, 1,000 in number, in an ambuscade by the way, trusting to their numbers and expecting an easy victory. The French, turning well, scarcely missed a shot, and in a short time killed 100 of the enemy's men, and, wounding a great many more, drove them off after two hours' fighting. They rallied and returned in a short time, determined to conquer or die; but the French, showing the prisoners, declared that if a shot was fired by the enemy they would kill them before their eyes, and would then sell their own lives dearly. This menace frightened the Spaniards, and the *flibustiers* continued their retreat unmolested. Having waited some time in vain on the coast for the ransom, they left the prisoners unhurt, and returned gaily to Tortuga.

In 1663, Spain, finding that France in secret encouraged the buccaneers of Hispaniola, gave orders to exterminate every Frenchman in the island, promising recompense to those who distinguished themselves in the war. An old Flemish officer, named Vandelinof, who had served with distinction in the Low Country wars, took the command. His first stratagem was to attempt to surprise the chief French *boucan*, at Gonaive, on the Brûlé Savannah, with 800 men. The hunters, observing them, gave the alarm, and, collecting 100 "brothers," advanced to meet them in a defile where the Spanish numbers were of no avail. The Fleming was killed at the first volley, and after an obstinate struggle the Spaniards fled to the mountains.

The enemy, after this defeat, returned to their old and safer plan of night surprises—which frequently succeeded, owing to the negligent watch kept by the buccaneers. The hunters, much harassed by the constant sense of insecurity, began to retire every night to the small islands round St. Domingo, and seldom went alone to the chase. Some *boucans*, such as those at the port of Samana, grew rapidly into towns. Near this excellent harbour the cattle were unusually abundant, and in a few hours the *flibustier* could carry his hides to his market at Tortuga. Gradually French and Dutch vessels began to visit the port to buy hides and to trade.

Every morning before starting to the savannah, the hunters climbed the highest hill to see if any Spaniards were visible. They then agreed on a rendezvous for the evening, arriving there to the moment. If any one was missing he was at once known to be taken or killed, and no one was permitted to return home till their *comerade*'s death had been avenged. One evening the hunters of Samana, missing four of the band, marched towards St. Jago, and, discovering from some prisoners that their companions had been massacred, entered a Spanish village and slew every one they met.

The Spaniards too had sometimes their revenge. "The river of massacre" near Samana was so called from thirty buccaneers who were slain there while fording the river laden with hides. Another band of hunters, led by Charles Tore, had been hunting at a place called the Bois-Brûlé Savannah, and having completed the number of skins the merchants had contracted for, returned to Samana. Crossing a savannah they were surprised by an overwhelming force of Spaniards, and, in spite of a desperate resistance, slain to a man. The buccaneers, irritated by these losses, began to think of revenge. When the Spaniards destroyed the wild cattle, some turned planters about Port de Paix, others became *flibustiers*.

The death of De Poncy threw the French colonies into some disorder, and Tortuga was for awhile forgotten both by the home and colonial government. During this interval a gentleman of Perigord, named Rossy, a retired buccaneer, resolved to resume his old profession. Returning to St. Domingo, he was hailed as a father by the hunters, who proposed to him to recover Tortuga. Rossy, knowing that fidelity is the last virtue that forsakes the heart, accepted their proposal with the enthusiasm of a gambler accustomed to such desperate casts. He was soon joined by five hundred refugees, burning for conquest and revenge. They assembled in canoes at a rendezvous in Hispaniola, and agreed to land one hundred men on the north side of the island and surprise the mountain fort. The Spaniards in the town, not even entrenched, were soon beaten into the fort. The garrison of the rock were rather astonished to be awoke at break of day by a salute from the neighbouring mountain, when they could see the enemy still quietly encamped below. Sallying out, they could discern no opponents, but before they could regain the fort were all cut to pieces or made prisoners. The survivors were at once thrust into a boat and sent to Cuba, and Rossy declared governor. He soon after received a commission from the French king, together with a permission to levy a tax, for the support of his dignity, of a tenth of all prizes brought into Tortuga. Rossy governed quietly for some years, and eventually retired to his native country to die, and La Place, his nephew, reigned in his stead.

In 1664, the French West India Company became masters of Tortuga and the Antilles, and appointed M. D'Ogeron, a gentleman of Anjou who had failed in commerce, as their governor. He proved a good administrator, and built magazines and storehouses for his grateful and attached people. D'Ogeron soon established order and prosperity in the island, which became a refuge for the red flag and the terror of the Spaniards. He colonised all the north side of Hispaniola, from Port Margot, where he had a house, to the three rivers opposite Tortuga. He attracted colonists from the Antilles, and brought over women from France, in order to settle his nomadic and mutinous population. In 1661, the West India Company, dissatisfied with the profits of their merchandize, resolved to relinquish the colony and call in their debts; and it was in the St. John, sent out for this purpose, that the buccaneer historian Oexmelin, whom we shall have frequently to quote, first visited Tortuga. D'Ogeron, determined not to relinquish a settlement already beginning to flourish, hastened to France, and persuaded some private merchants to continue the trade. They promised to fit out twelve vessels annually, if he would supply them with back freight. He on his part agreed to provide the colonists with slaves and to destroy the wild dogs, which were committing great ravages among the herds of Hispaniola. This new company did not answer. The inhabitants suffered by the monopoly, and grew discontented at only being allowed to trade with certain vessels, and being obliged to turn their backs on better bargains or cheaper merchandize. An accident lit the train. M. D'Ogeron attempted to prevent their trading with some Dutch merchants, and they rose in arms. Shots were fired at the governor, and the revolters threatened to burn out the planters who would not join their flag. But succours from the Antilles soon brought them to their senses, and, one of their ringleaders being hung, they surrendered at discretion. The governor, alarmed even at an outbreak that he had checked, made in his turn concessions. He permitted all French merchants to trade upon paying a heavy harbour due, and the number of ships soon became too numerous for the limited commerce of the place. M. D'Ogeron next procured colonists from Brittany and Anjou, and eventually, after some further exploits, very daring but always unfortunate, he was succeeded in command by his nephew M. De Poncy.

There are several Tortugas. There is one in the Caribbean sea, another near the coast of Honduras, a third not far from Carthagena, and a fourth in the gulf of California; they all derived their names from their shape, resembling the turtle which throng in these seas.

The buccaneer fastness with which we have to do is the Tortuga of the North Atlantic Ocean, a small rocky island about 60 leagues only in circumference, and distant barely six miles from the north coast of Hispaniola. This Tortuga was to the refugee hunters of the savannahs what New Providence became to the pirates, and the

Galapagos islands to the South Sea adventurers of half a century later. It had only one port, the entrance to which formed two channels: on two sides it was iron-bound, and on the other defended by reefs and shoals, less threatening than the cliffs, but not less dangerous. Though scantily supplied with spring water—a defect which the natives balanced by a free use of "the water of life"—the interior was very fertile and well wooded. Palm and sandal wood trees grew in profusion; sugar, tobacco, aloes, resin, China-root, indigo, cotton, and all sorts of tropical plants were the riches of the planters. The cultivators were already receiving gifts from the earth, which—liberal benefactor—she gave without expecting a return, for the virgin soil needed little seed, care, or nourishment. The island was too small for savannahs, but the tangled brushwood abounded in wild boars.

The harbour had a fine sand bottom, was well sheltered from the winds, and was walled in by the Coste de Fer rocks. Round the habitable part of the shore stretched sands, so that it could not be approached but by boats. The town consisted of only a few store-houses and wine shops, and was called the *Basse Terre*. The other five habitable parts of the island were Cayona, the Mountain, the Middle Plantation, the Ringot, and Mason's Point. A seventh, the Capsterre, required only water to make it habitable, the land being very fertile. To supply the want of springs, the planters collected the rain water in tanks. The soil of the island was alternately sand and clay, and from the latter they made excellent pottery. The mountains, though rocky, and scarcely covered with soil, were shaded with trees of great size and beauty, the roots of which clung like air plants to the bare rock, and, netting them round, struck here and there deeper anchors into the wider crevices. This timber was so dry and tough that, if it was cut and exposed to the heat of the sun, it would split with a loud noise, and could therefore only be used as fuel.

This favoured island boasted all the fruits of the Antilles: its tobacco was better than that of any other island; its sugar canes attained an enormous size, and their juice was sweeter than elsewhere; its numerous medicinal plants were exported to heal the diseases of the Old World. The only four-footed animal was the wild boar, originally transplanted from Hispaniola. As it soon grew scarce, the French governor made it illegal to hunt with dogs, and required the hunter to follow his prey single-handed and on foot. The wood-pigeons were almost the only birds in the island. They came in large flocks at certain periods of the year; Oexmelin says that, in two or three hours, without going eighty steps from the road, he killed ninety-five with his own hand. As soon as they eat a certain berry their flesh became bitter as our larks do when they move from the stubbles into the turnips. A Gascon visitor, once complaining of their sudden bitterness, was told by a buccaneer as a joke that his servant had forgot to remove the gall. Fish abounded round the island, and crabs without nippers; the night fishermen carrying torches of the candle-wood tree. The shell fish was the food of servants and slaves, and was said to be so indigestible as to frequently produce giddiness and temporary blindness; the turtle and manitee, too, formed part of their daily diet. The planters were much tormented by the white and red land-crabs, or *tourtourons*, which lived in the earth, visited the sea to spawn, and at night gnawed the sugar-canes and the roots of plants. Their only venomous reptile was the viper, which they tamed to kill mice; in a wild state, it fed on poultry or pigeons. From the stomach of one Oexmelin drew seven pigeons and a large fowl, which had been swallowed about three hours before, and cooked them for his own dinner, verifying the old proverb of "robbing Peter to pay Paul." In times of scarcity these snakes were eaten for food. Besides chameleons and lizards, there were small insects with shells like a snail. These were considered good to eat and very nourishing. When held near the fire, they distilled a red oily liquid useful as a rheumatic liniment. Though the scorpions and *scolopendrias* were not venomous, nature, always just in her compensations, covered the island with poisonous shrubs. The most fatal of these was the noxious *mançanilla*. It grew as high as a pear tree, had leaves like a wild laurel, and bore fruit like an apple; this fruit was so deadly, that even fish that ate of it, if they did not die, became themselves poisonous, and were known by the blackness of their teeth. The only antidote was olive oil. The Indian fishermen used, as a test, to taste the heart of the fish they caught, and if it proved bitter they knew at once that it had been poisoned, and threw it away. The very rain-drops that fell from the leaves were deadly to man and beast, and it was as dangerous to sleep under its shadow as under the *upas*. The friendly boughs invited the traveller (as vice does man) to rest under their shade; but when he awoke he found himself sick and faint, and covered with feverish sores. New-comers were too frequently tempted by the sight and odour of the fruit, and the only remedy for the rash son of Adam was to bind him down, and, in spite of heat and pain, to prevent him drinking for two or three days. The body of the sufferer became at first "red as fire, and his tongue black as ink," then a great torment of thirst and fever came upon him, but slowly passed away. Another poisonous shrub resembled the pimento; its berries were used by the Indians to rub their eyes, giving them, as they believed, a keener sight, and enabling them to see the fish deeper in the water and to strike them at a greater distance with the harpoon. The root of this bush was a poison, so deadly that the only known antidote for it was its own berries, bruised and drunk in wine. Of another plant, Oexmelin relates an instance of a negro girl being poisoned by a rejected lover, by merely putting some of its leaves between her toes when asleep.

Chapter 2

Manners of the Hunters

The hunters of the wild cattle in the savannahs of Hispaniola were known under the designation of buccaneers as early as the year 1630.

They derived this name from *boucan*,[1] an old Indian word which their luckless predecessors, the Caribs, gave to the hut in which they smoked the flesh of the oxen killed in hunting, or not unfrequently the limbs of their persecutors the Spaniards. They applied the same term, from the poverty of an undeveloped language, to the *barbecue*, or square wooden frame upon which the meat was dried. In course of time this hunters' food became known as *viande boucan*ée, and the hunters themselves gradually assumed the name of buccaneers.

Their second title of *flibustiers* was a mere corruption of the English word freebooters—a German term, imported into England during the Low Country wars of Elizabeth's reign. It has been erroneously traced to the Dutch word *flyboat*; but the Jesuit traveller, Charlevoix, asserts that, in fact, this species of craft derived its title from being first used by the *flibustiers*, and not from its swiftness. This, however, is evidently a mistake, as Drayton and Hakluyt use the word; and it seems to be of even earlier standing in the French language. The derivation from the English word freebooter is at once seen when the *s* in *flibustier* becomes lost in pronunciation.

In 1630, a party of French colonists, who had failed in an attack on St. Christopher's, finding, as we have shown, Hispaniola almost deserted by the Spaniards, who neglected the Antilles to push their

---

1. Charlevoix's *Histoire de l'Ile Espagnole*, p. 6, vol. II

conquests on the mainland, landed on the south side and formed a settlement, discovering the woods and the plains to be teeming with wild oxen and wild hogs. The Dutch merchants promised to supply them with every necessary, and to receive the hides and tallow that they collected in exchange for lead, powder, and brandy. These first settlers were chiefly Normans, and the first trading vessels that visited the coast were from Dieppe.

The origin of the buccaneers, or hunters, and the *flibustiers*, or sea rovers, as the Dutch called them, was contemporaneous. From the very beginning many grew weary of the chase and became corsairs, at first turning their arms against all nations but their own, but latterly, as strict privateersmen, revenging their injuries only on the Spaniards, with whom France was frequently at war, and generally under the authority of regular or forged commissions obtained from the Governor of St. Domingo or some other French settlement. Between the buccaneers and *flibustiers* no impassable line was drawn; to chase the wild ox or the Spaniard was the same to the greater part of the colonists, and on sea or land the hunter's musket was an equally deadly weapon.

Two years after the French refugees from St. Christopher's had landed on the half-deserted shores of Hispaniola, the *flibustiers* seized the small adjoining island of Tortuga, attracted by its safe and well-defended harbour, its fertility, and the strength of its natural defences. The French and English colonists of St. Christopher's began now to cultivate the small plantations round the harbour, encouraged by the number of French trading vessels that visited it, and by the riches that the *flibustiers* captured from the Spaniards. These vessels brought over young men from France to be bound to the planters for three years as *engagés*, by a contract that legalized the transitory slavery.

There were thus at once established four classes of men—*buccaneers*, or hunters; *planters*, or inhabitants; *engagés*, who were apprenticed to either the one or the other; and *sea-rovers*. They governed themselves by a sort of democratic compact—each inhabitant being monarch in his own plantation, and every *flibustier* king on his own deck. But the latter was not unfrequently deposed by his crew; and the former, if cruel to his *engagés*, was compelled to submit to the French governor's interference. Before giving any history of the various revolutions in Tortuga, or the wars of the Spaniards in Hispaniola, we will describe the manners of each of the three classes we have mentioned.

And first of the buccaneers, or hunters, of Hispaniola.

These wild men fed on the bodies of the cattle they killed in hunting, and by selling their hides and tallow obtained money enough to buy the necessaries and even the luxuries of life,—for the gambling table and the debauch. While the *flibustiers* called each other "brothers of the coast," the buccaneers were included in the generic term *gens de la côte*, and in time the names of buccaneer and *flibustier* were used indiscriminately.

The hunter's dress consisted of a plain shirt, or blouse (Du Tertre calls it a sack), belted at the waist with a bit of green hide. It was soon dyed a dull purple with the blood of the wild bull, and was always smeared with grease. "When they returned from the chase to the *boucan*," says the above-named writer, "you would say that these are the butcher's vilest servants, who have been eight days in the slaughterhouse without washing." As they frequently carried the meat home by cutting a hole in the centre, and thrusting their heads through it, we may imagine the cannibals that they must have looked. They wore drawers, or frequently only tight moccasins, reaching to the knee; their sandals were of bull's hide or hog skin, fastened with leather laces.

In Oexmelin's *Histoire des aventuriers*, the hunter is represented with bare feet, but this could not have been usual, when we remember the danger of chigoes, snakes, and scorpions, not to speak of prickly pear coverts and thorny brakes. From their leather waist belt hung a short, heavy *machete* or sabre, and an alligator skin case of Dutch hunting knives. On their heads they wore a leather skull-cap, shaped like our modern jockey's, with a peak in front. They wore their hair falling wildly on their shoulders, and their huge beards increased the ferocity of their appearance. Oexmelin particularly mentions the beard, although no existing engraving of the buccaneer chiefs represents them with this grim ornament. According to Charlevoix, some of them wore a shirt, and over this a sort of brewer's apron, or coarse sacking tunic, open at the sides. From this shirt being always stained with blood, perhaps sometimes purposely dipped into it, the Abbé Reynal supposes that such a shirt was the necessary dress of the buccaneer. Oexmelin says that as his vessel approached St. Domingo:

> ...a buccaneers' canoe came off with six men at the paddles, whose appearance excited the astonishment of all those on board, who had never before been out of France. They wore a small linen tunic and short drawers, reaching only half down the thigh. It required one to look close to see if the shirt was linen or not, so stained was it with the blood which had dripped from the animals they kill and carry home. All of them had large beards, and carried at their girdle a case of cayman skin, in which were four knives and a bayonet." Like the Canadian trappers, or, indeed, sportsmen in general, they were peculiarly careful of their muskets, which were made expressly for them in France, the best makers being Brachie of Dieppe, and Gelu of Nantes. These guns were about four feet and a half long, and were known everywhere as "buccaneering pieces."

The stocks were square and heavy, with a hollow for the shoulder, and they were all made of the same calibre, single barrel, and carrying balls sixteen to the pound. Every hunter took with him fifteen or twenty pounds of powder, the best of which came from Cherbourg. They kept it in waxed calabashes to secure it from the damp, having no shelter or hut that would keep out the West Indian rains. Their bullet pouch and powder horn hung on either side, and their small tents they carried, rolled up tight like bandoliers, at their waist, for they slept wherever they halted, and generally in their clothes.

We have no room and no colours bright enough to paint the chief features of the Indian woods, the cloven cherry, that resembles the arbutus, the cocoa with its purple pods, the red *bois immortel*, the stunted bastard cedar, the logwood with its sweet blossom and hawthorn-like leaf, the cashew with its golden fruit, the oleander, the dock-like yam, and the calabash tree.

What Hesperian orchards are those where the citron, lemon, and lime cling together, and the pine-apple grows in prickly hedges, soft custard apples hang out their bags of sweetness, and the avocada swings its pears big as pumpkins; where the bread-fruit with its gigantic leaves, the glossy star apple, and the golden shaddock, drop their masses of foliage among the dewy and fresh underwood of plantains, far below the tall and graceful cocoa-nut tree.

Michael Scott depicts with photographic exactness and brilliancy every phase of the West Indian day, and enables us to imagine the light and shade that surrounded the strange race of whom we write. At daybreak, the land wind moans and shakes the dew from the feathery palms; the fireflies grow pale, and fade out one after the other, like the stars; the deep croaking of the frog ceases, and the lizards and crickets are silent; the monkeys leave off yelling; the snore of the tree toad and the wild cry of the tiger-cat are no more heard; but fresh sounds arise, and the woods thrill with the voices and clatter of an awaking city; the measured tap of the woodpecker echoes, with the clear, flute-like note of the *pavo del monte*, the shriek of the macaw, and the chatter of the parroquet; the pigeon moans in the inmost forest, and the gabbling crows croak and scream.

At noon, as the breeze continues, and the sun grows vertical, the branches grow alive with gleaming lizards and coloured birds, noisy parrots hop round the wild pine, the cattle retreat beneath the trees for shelter, to browse the cooler grass, and the *condouli* and passion flowers of all sizes, from a soup plate to a thumb ring, shut their blossoms; the very humming-birds cease to drone and buzz round the orange flowers, and the land-crab is heard rustling among the dry grass. In the swamps the hot mist rises, and the wild fowl flock to the reeds and canes in the muddy lagoons, where the strong smell of musk denotes the lurking alligator; the feathery plumes of the bamboos wave not, and the cotton tree moves not a limb.

The rainy season brings far different scenes: then the sky grows suddenly black, the wild ducks fly screaming here and there, the carrion crows are whirled bodingly about the skies, the smaller birds hurry to shelter, the mountain clouds bear down upon the valleys, and a low, rushing sound precedes the rain. The torrents turn brown and earthy, all nature seems to wait the doom with fear. The low murmur of the earthquake is still more impressive, with the distant thunder breaking the deep silence, and the trees bending and groaning though the air is still. Besides the rains and the earthquakes, the tornadoes are still more dreadful visitors, when the air in a moment grows full of shivered branches, shattered roofs, and uptorn canes.

The great features of the West Indian forests are the fireflies and the monkeys. At night, when the wind is rustling in the dry palm leaves, the sparkles of green fire break out among the trees like sparks blown from a thousand torches; the gloom pulses with them as the flame ebbs and flows, and the planters' chambers are filled with these harmless incendiaries. The yell of the monkeys at daybreak has been compared to a devils' holiday, to distant thunder, loose iron bars in a cart in Fleet Street, bagpipes, and drunken men laughing.

To Coleridge we are indebted for word pictures of the cabbage tree, and the silk cotton tree with their buttressed trunks; the banyan with its cloistered arcades; the wild plantain with its immense green leaves rent in slips, its thick bunches of fruit, and its scarlet pendent seed; the mangroves, with their branches drooping into the sea; the banana, with its jointed leaves; the fern trees, twenty feet high; the gold canes, in arrowy sheaves; and the feathery palms. Nor do we forget the *figuera*, the *bois le Sueur*, or the wild pine burning like a topaz in a calix of emerald. Beneath the broad roof of creepers, from which the oriole hangs its hammock nest, grow, in a wild jungle of beauty, the scarlet *cordia*, the pink and saffron flower fence, the *plumeria*, and the white *datura*. The flying fish glided by us, says H. N. Coleridge, speaking of the Indian seas, bonitos and *albicores* played around the bows, dolphins gleamed in our wake, ever and anon a shark, and once a great emerald-coloured whale, kept us company. Elsewhere he describes the silver strand, fringed with evergreen drooping mangroves, and the long shrouding avenues of thick leaves that darkly fringe the blue ocean. By the shore grow the dark and stately *manchineel*, beautiful but noxious, the white wood, and the bristling sea-side grape, with its broad leaves and bunches of pleasant berries. The sea birds skim about the waves, and the red flamingoes stalk around the sandy shoals, while the alligators wallow on the mud banks, and the snowy pelicans hold their councils in solemn stupidity.

Leaving the sea and the shore we wander on into the interior, for the West Indian vegetation has everywhere a common character, and see delighted the forest trees growing on the cliffs, knotted and bound together with luxuriant festoons of evergreen creepers, connecting them in one vast network of leaves and branches, the wild pine sparkling on the huge limbs of the wayside trees, beside it the dagger-like Spanish needle, the quilted *pimploe*, and the maypole aloe shooting its yellow flowered crown twenty feet above the traveller, or amid the dark foliage, twines of purple wreaths or lilac jessamine; and the woods ringing with the song of birds, interrupted at times by strange shrieks or moanings of some tropic wanderer; we see with these the snowy amaryllis, the gorgeous hibiscus with its crown of scarlet, the quivering limes and dark glossy orange bushes; we rest under the green tamarind or listen to the mournful creaking of the sand box tree.

The buccaneers went in pairs, every hunter having his *camerade* or *matelot* (sailor), as well as his *engagés*. They had seldom any fixed habitation, but pitched their tents where the cattle were to be found, building temporary sheds, thatched with palm leaves, to defend them from the rain and to lodge their stock of hides till they could barter it with the next vessel for wine, brandy, linen, arms, powder, or lead. They would return three leagues from the chase to their huts, laden with meat and skins, and if they ate in the open country it was always with their musket cocked and near at hand for fear of surprise. With their *matelots* they had everything in common. The chief occupation of these voluntary outlaws was the chase of the wild ox, that of the wild boar being at first a mere amusement, or only followed as the means of procuring a luxurious meal; at a later period, however, many Frenchmen lived by hunting the hog, whose flesh they *boucaned* and sold for exportation, its flavour being superior to that of any other meat.

The buccaneers sometimes went in companies of ten or twelve, each man having his Indian attendant besides his apprentices. Before setting out they arranged a spot for rendezvous in case of attack. If they remained long in one place, they built thatched sheds under which to pitch their tents. They rose at daybreak to start for the chase, leaving one of the band to guard the huts. The masters generally went first and alone (sometimes the worst shot was left in the tent to cook), and the *engagés* and the dogs followed; one hound, the *venteur*, went in front of all, often leading the hunter through wood and over rock where no path had ever been. When the quarry came in sight the dogs barked round it and kept it at bay till the hunters could come up and fire. They generally aimed at the breast of the bull, or tried to hamstring it as soon as possible. Many hunters ran down the wild cattle in the savannah and attacked it with their dogs. If only wounded the ox would rush upon them and gore all he met. But this happened very seldom, for the men were deadly shots, seldom missed their *coup*, and were always sufficiently active, if in danger, to climb the tree from behind which they had fired. The *venteur* dog had a peculiar short bark by which he summoned the pack to his aid, and as soon as they heard it the *engagés* rushed to the rescue. When the beast was half flayed, the master took out the largest bone and sucked the hot marrow, which served him for a meal, giving a bit also to the *venteur*, but not to any other dogs, lest they should grow lazy in hunting; but the last lagger in the pack had sometimes a bit thrown him to incite him to greater exertion. He then left the *engagés* to carry the skin to the *boucan*, with a few of the best joints, giving the rest to the carrion crows, that soon sniffed out the blood. They continued the chase till each man had killed an ox, and the last returned home, laden like the rest with a hide and a portion of raw meat. By this time the first comer had prepared dinner, roasted some beef, or spitted a whole hog. The tables were soon laid; they consisted of a flat stone, the fallen trunk of a tree, or a root, with no cloth, no napkin, no bread, and no wine; pimento and orange juice were sufficient sauce for hungry men, and a contented mind and a keen appetite never quarrelled with rude cooking. This monotonous life was only varied by a conflict with a wounded bull, or a skirmish with the Spaniards. The grand fete days were when the hunter had collected as many hides as he had contracted to supply the merchant, and carried them to Tortuga, to Cape Tiburon, Samana, or St. Domingo, probably to return in a week's time, weary of drinking or beggared from the gambling table, tired of civilization, and restless for the chase.

The wild cattle of Hispaniola—the oxen, hogs, horses, and dogs—were all sprung from the domestic animals originally brought from Spain. The dogs were introduced into the island to chase the Indians, a cruelty that even the mild Columbus practised. Esquemeling says, those first conquerors of the New World made use of dogs...

...to range and search the intricate thicket of woods and forests for those their implacable and unconquerable enemies; thus they forced them to leave their old refuge and submit to the sword, seeing no milder usage would do it. Hereupon they killed some of them, and, quartering their bodies, placed them on the highways, that others might take a warning from such a punishment. But this severity proved of ill consequence, for, instead of frighting them and reducing them to civility, they conceived such horror of the Spaniards that they resolved to detest and fly their sight for ever; hence the greatest part died in caves and subterraneous places of the woods and mountains, in which places I myself have often seen great numbers of human bones. The Spaniards, finding no more Indians to appear about the woods, turned away a great number of dogs they had in their houses; and they, finding no masters to keep them, betook themselves to the woods and fields to hunt for food to preserve their lives, and by degrees grew wild.

The young of these maroon dogs the hunters were in the habit of bringing up. When they found a wild bitch with whelps, they generally took away the puppies and brought them to their tents, preferring them to any other sort of dog. They seem to have been between a greyhound and a mastiff. The Dutch writer whom we have just quoted mentions the singular fact, that these dogs, even in a wild state, retained their acquired habits. The *venteur* always led the way, and was allowed to dip the first fangs into the victim. The wild dogs went in packs of fifty or eighty, and were so fierce that they would not scruple to attack a whole herd of wild boars, bringing down two or three at once. They destroyed a vast number of wild cattle, devouring the young as soon as a mare had foaled or a cow calved. Says Esquemeling:

> One day a French buccaneer showed me a strange action of this kind. Being in the fields hunting together, we heard a great noise of dogs which had surrounded a wild boar. Having tame dogs with us we left them in custody of our servants, being desirous to see the sport. Hence my companion and I climbed up two several trees, both for security and

prospect. The wild boar, all alone, stood against a tree, defending himself with his tusks from a great number of dogs that enclosed him, killed with his teeth and wounded several of them. This bloody fight continued about an hour, the wild boar meanwhile attempting many times to escape. At last flying, one dog leaped upon his back; and the rest of the dogs, perceiving the courage of their companion, fastened likewise on the boar, and presently killed him. This done, all of them, the first only excepted, laid themselves down upon the ground about the prey, and there peaceably continued till he, the first and most courageous of the troop, had eaten as much as he could. When this dog had left off, all the rest fell in to take their share till nothing was left.

In 1668, the Governor of Tortuga, finding these dogs were rendering the wild boar almost extinct, and alarmed lest the hunters should leave a place where food was growing scarce, sent to France for poison to destroy these mastiffs, and placed poisoned horse flesh in the woods. But although this practice was continued for six months, and an incredible number were killed, yet the race soon appeared almost as numerous as before.

The wild horses went in troops of about two or three hundred. They were awkward and misshapen, small and short-bodied, with large heads, long necks, trailing ears, and thick legs. They had always a leader, and when they met a hunter, stared at him till he approached within shot, then galloped off all together. They were only killed for their skins, though their flesh was sometimes smoked for the use of the sailors. These horses were caught by stretching nooses along their tracks, in which they got entangled by the neck. When taken, they were quickly tamed by being kept two or three days without food, and were then used to carry hides. They were good workers, but easily lamed. When a buccaneer turned them adrift from want of food to keep them through the winter, they were known to return ten months after, or, meeting them in the savannah, begin to whine and caress their old masters, and suffer themselves to be recaptured. They were also killed for the sake of the fat about the neck and belly, which the hunters used for lamp oil.

The wild oxen were tame unless wounded, and their hides were generally from eleven to thirteen feet long. They were very strong and very swift, in spite of their short and slender legs. In the course of a single century from their introduction, they had so increased, that the French buccaneers, when they landed, seldom went in search of them, but waited for them near the shore, at the salt pools where they came to drink. The herds fed at night on the savannahs, and at noon retired to the shelter of the forests. A wounded bull would often blockade, for four hours, a tree in which a hunter had taken refuge, bellowing round the trunk and ploughing at the roots with his horns. The French hunters generally shot them; but the Spanish *hocksers* rode them down on horseback, and hamstrung them with a crescent-shaped spear, in form something like a cheese-knife with a long handle.

The wild boars, when much pressed, adopted the same military stratagem as the oxen. They threw themselves into the form of a hollow square, the sows in the rear and the sucking pigs in the middle, the white sabre tusks of the boars gleaming outwards towards the foe. The dogs always fastened upon the defenceless sow in preference to the ferocious male, whom they seldom attacked if it got at bay under a tree, though it might be alone, glaring before the red jaws of eighty yelping dogs. The wild boar hunting was less dangerous than that of the wild oxen, and less profitable. The hogs soon grew scarce, a party of hunters sometimes killing 100 in a day, and only carrying home three or four of the fattest. It was not uncommon for solitary hunters or *engagés* who had lost their way in the woods to amuse themselves by training up the young hogs they found basking under the trees, and teaching them to track their own species and pull them down by tugging at their long leathery ears. Oexmelin, the most intelligent of the few buccaneer writers, relates his own success in training four pigs, whom he taught to follow at his heels like dogs, to play with him, and obey his orders. When they saw a herd of boars they would run forward and decoy them towards him. On one occasion, one of them escaped into the plains, but returned three days after, very complacently heading a herd of hogs, of which his master and his *matelot* killed four. It is not many years since that an English gamekeeper brought up a pig to get his own bread as a pointer.

At first, when the green savannahs were spotted black with cattle, the hunters were so fastidious that they seldom ate anything but the udders of cows, considering bull meat too tough. Many a herd was killed, as at present in Australia or California, for the hide and tallow. If the first animal killed in the day's hunt was a cow, an *engagé* was instantly sent to the tent with part of the flesh to cook for the evening. When the *engagés* had each gone home with his joint and his hide, the buccaneer followed with his own load, his dogs, tired and panting, lagging at his heels. If on his way back he met a boar, or more oxen, he threw down his fardel, slew a fresh victim, and, flaying it, hung the hide on a tree out of reach of the wild dogs, and came back for it on the morrow.

On returning to the *boucan*, each man set to work to stretch (*brochéter*) his hide, fastening it tightly out with fourteen wooden pegs, and rubbing it with ashes and salt mixed together to make it dry quicker. When this was done, they sat down to partake of the food that the first comer had by this time cooked. The beef they generally boiled in the large cauldron which every hunter possessed, drawing it out when it was done with a wooden skewer. A board served them for a dish. With a wooden spoon they collected the gravy in a calabash; and into this they squeezed the juice of a fresh picked lemon, a crushed citron, or a little pimento, which formed the hunter's favourite sauce, *pimentado*. This being done with all the care of a Ude, they seized their hunting knives and wooden skewers, and commenced a solemn attack upon the ponderous joint. The residue they divided among their dogs. Père Labat, an oily Jesuit if we trust to his portrait, describes, with great gusto, a buccaneer feast at which he was present, and at which a hog was roasted whole. The *boucaned* meat was used in voyages, or when no oxen could be met with.

When they wanted to *boucan* a pig, they first flayed it and took out all the bones. The meat they cut in long slips, which they placed in mats, and there left it till the next day, when they proceeded to smoke it. The *boucan* was a small hut covered close with palm-mats, with a low entrance, and no chimney or windows: it contained a wooden framework seven or eight feet high, on which the meat was placed, and underneath which a charcoal fire was lit. The fire they always fed with the animal's own skin and bones, which made the smoke thick and full of ammonia. The volatile salt of the bones being more readily absorbed by the meat than the mere ligneous acid of wood, the result of this process was an epicurean mouthful far superior to our Westphalia hams, and more like our hung beef. Oexmelin waxes quite eloquent in its praise. He says it was so exquisite that it needed no cooking; its very look, red as a rose, not to mention its delightful fragrance, tempted the worst appetite to eat it, whatever it might be. The only misfortune was that six months after smoking, the meat grew tasteless and unfit for use; but when fresh, it was thought so wholesome that sick men came from a distance to live in a hunter's tent and share his food for a time. The first thing that passengers visiting the West Indies saw was a buccaneers' canoe bringing dry meat for sale. The *boucaned* meat was sold in bales of sixty pounds' weight, and their pots of tallow were worth about six pieces of eight.

Labat—no ordinary lover of good cheer, if we may judge from his portrait, which represents him with cheeks as plump as a pulpit cushion, and with fat rolls of double chin—describes the buccaneer fare with much unction, having gone to a hunter's feast,—a corporeal treat intended as a slight return for much spiritual food. Each buccaneer, he says, had two skewers, made of clean peeled wood, one having two spikes. The *boucan* itself was made of four stakes as thick as a man's arm, and about four feet long, struck in the ground to form a square five feet long and three feet across. On these forked sticks they placed cross bars, and upon these the spit, binding them all with withes. The wild boar, being skinned and gutted, was placed whole upon this spit, the stomach kept open with a stick. The fire was made of charcoal, and put on with bark shovels. The interior of the pig was filled with citron juice, salt, crushed pimento, and pepper; and the flesh was constantly pricked, so that this juice might penetrate. When the meat was ready, the cooks fired off a musket twice, to summon the hunters from the woods, while banana leaves were placed round for plates. If the hunters brought home any birds, they at once picked them and threw them into the stomach of the pig, as into a pot. If the hunters were novices, and brought home nothing, they were sent out again to seek it; if they were veterans, they were compelled to drink as many cups as the best hunter had that day killed deer, bulls, or boars. A leaf served to hold the pimento sauce, and a calabash to drink from, while bananas were their substitute for bread. The *engagés* waited on their masters, and one of the penalties for clumsy serving was to be compelled to drink off a calabash full of sauce.

The English "cow killers" and the French hunters were satisfied with getting as many hides as they could in the shortest possible time, but the Spanish *matadores* gave the trade an air of chivalrous adventure by rivalling the feats of the Moorish bull-fighters of Granada. They did not use firearms, but carried lances with a half-moon blade, employing dogs, and, being generally men of wealth and planters, had servants on foot to encourage them to the attack. When they tracked an ox in the woods, they made the hounds drive him out into the prairie, where the *matadors* could spur after him, and, wheeling round the monster, hamstring him or thrust him through with a lance. Dampierre describes minutely the Spanish mode of *hocksing*. The horses were trained to retreat and advance without even a signal. The *hocksing*-iron, of a half-moon shape, measuring six inches horizontally, resembled in form a gardener's turf-cutter. The handle, some fourteen feet long, was held like a lance over the horse's head, a *matador's* steed being always known by its right ear being bent down with the weight of the shaft. The place to strike the bull was just above the hock; when struck the horse instantly wheeled to the left, to avoid the charge of the wounded ox, who soon broke his nearly severed leg, but still limped forward to avenge himself on his formidable enemy. Then the *hockser*, riding softly up, struck him with his iron again, but this time into a fore leg, and at once laid him prostrate, moaning in terror and in pain. Then, dismounting, the Spaniard took a sharp dagger and stabbed the beast behind the horns, severing the spinal marrow. This operation the English called "polling." The hunter at once remounted, and left his skinners to remove the hide.

The stately Spaniard delighted in this dangerous chase, with all its stratagems, surprises, and hair-breadth escapes, when life depended on a turn of the bridle or the prick of a spur. However pressed for food or endangered by enemies, he practised it with all the stately ceremonies of the Madrid arena. The fiery animal, streaming with blood and foam, bellowing with rage and pain, frequently trampled and gored the dogs and slew both horse and rider. Oexmelin mentions a bull at Cuba which killed three horses in the same day, the lucky rider making a solemn pilgrimage to the shrine of Our Lady of Guadaloupe when he had given his victim the *coup de grace.*

These Spanish hunters did not rough it like the buccaneers, and kept horses to carry their bales. They were particular in their food, and ate bread and cassava with their beef; drank wine and brandy; and were very choice in their fruit and preserves. Gay in their dress, they prided themselves on their white linen. Every separate hunting field had its own customs. At Campeachy, where the ground was swampy, the logwood-cutters frequently shot the oxen from a canoe, and were sometimes pursued by a wounded beast, who would try to sink the boat. When the woodmen killed a bull, they cut it into quarters, and, taking out all the bones, cut a hole in the centre of each piece large enough to pass their heads through, and trudged home with it to their tents on the shore. If they grew tired or were pursued, they cut off a portion of the meat and lightened their load.

The Spaniards, less poor, greedy, and thoughtless than the English and French adventurers, killed only the bulls and old cows, and left the younger ones to breed. The French were notorious for their wanton waste, using oxen merely as marks for their bullets, and as utterly indifferent to the future as Autolycus, who "slept out the thought of it." About 1650 the wild cattle of Jamaica were entirely destroyed, and the Governor procured a fresh supply from Cuba.

Whenever the oxen grew scarce, they became wilder and more ferocious. In some places no hunter dared to fire at them if alone, nor ever ventured into their pastures unattended. All animals grow shy if frequently pursued, and no fish are so unapproachable as those of a much frequented stream. Dampierre says that at Beef Island the old bulls who had once been wounded, when they saw the hunters or heard their muskets, would instantly form into a square, with their cows in the rear and the calves in the middle, turning as the hunters turned, and presenting their horns like a cluster of bayonets. It then became necessary to beat the woods for stragglers. A beast mortally wounded always made at the hunter; but if only grazed by the bullet it ran away. A cow was thought to be more dangerous than a bull, as the former charged with its eyes open, and the latter with them closed. The danger was often imminent. One of Dampierre's messmates ventured into the savannah, about a mile from the huts, and coming within shot of a bull wounded it desperately. The bull, however, had strength enough to pursue and overtake the logwood-cutter before he could load again, to trample him, and gore him in the thigh. Then, faint with loss of blood, it reeled down dead, and fell heavily beside the bleeding and groaning hunter. His *comerade*, coming the next morning to seek for the man, found him weak and almost dying, and, taking him on his back, bore him to his hut, where he was soon cured. The rapidity of such cures is peculiar to savages, or men who devote their whole life to muscular exertion; for the flesh of the South Sea Islanders is said to close upon a sword as India-rubber does upon the knife that cuts it. Often, in the heat and excitement of these pursuits, the solitary hunter, and still more often, from want of experience and from youthful rashness, the *engagé*, would lose his way in the woods, or, falling into a forest pool, become a prey of the lurking cayman, if not alarmed by the premonitory odour of musk that indicated its dangerous vicinity. Nature is full of these warnings: and the vibrating rattle of the Indian snake has saved the life of many a buccaneer.

Besides an unceasing supply of beef on shore, and salted turtle at sea, the buccaneers ate the flesh of deer and of *peccavy*. On the mainland wild turkeys were always within shot, and fat monkeys and plump parrots were resources for more hungry and less epicurean men. The rich fruits of the West Indies, needing no cultivation to improve their flavour, grew around their huts, and were to be had all the year round for the picking. The parched hunters delighted in the resinous-flavoured mango and the luscious guava as much as our modern sailors. In such a country every one is a vegetarian; for when dinner is over, to be a fruit eater needs no hermit-like asceticism. The plantain and the yam served them instead of the bread-fruit of the Pacific, or the potato of Virginia, and the custard-apple took the place of pastry; but the great dainty which all their chroniclers mention was the large avocado pear, which they supposed to be an aphrodisiac. This prodigious lemon-coloured fruit was allowed to mellow, its soft pulp was then scooped out and beaten up in a plate with orange and lime juice; but hungry and more impatient men ate it at once, with a little salt and a roast plantain. A buccaneer never touched an unknown fruit till he had seen birds pecking it on the tree. No bird was ever seen to touch the blooming but poisonous apples of the *manchineel*, which few animals but crabs could eat with impunity; as this tree grew by the sea-shore, even fish were rendered poisonous by feeding on the fruit that fell into the water. The verified stories of the *manchineel* excel the fables related of the *upas* of Batavia. The very dew upon its branches poisoned those upon whom it dropped. Esquemeling says: "One day, being hugely tormented with mosquitoes or gnats, and being as yet unacquainted with the nature of this tree, I cut a branch to serve me for a fan, but all my face was swelled the next day, and filled with blisters as if it were burnt, to such a degree that I was blind for three days."

The hunters tormented by mosquitoes and sand flies used leafy branches for fans, and anointed their faces with hog's grease to defend themselves from the stings. By night in their huts they burned tobacco, without which smoke they could not have obtained sleep. The mosquitoes were of all sorts, the buzzing and the silent, the tormentors by day and night; but they dispersed when the land breeze rose, or whenever the wind increased. The common mosquito was not visible by day, but at sunset filled the woods with its ominous humming. Oexmelin describes on one occasion his lying for eight hours in the water of a brook to escape their stings; sitting on a stone or on the sand, and keeping his face, which was above water, covered with leaves to protect him from the fiery stings.

The buccaneers made their pens of reeds, and their paper of the leaves of a peculiar sort of palm, the outer cuticle of which was thin, white, and soft; their ink was the black juice of the juniper berries, letters written with which turned white in nine days. They kept harmless snakes in their houses to feed on the rats and mice, just as we do cats, or the Copts did the ichneumons. They frequently used a handful of fire-flies instead of a lantern: Esquemeling, himself a buccaneer, says, that with three of these in his cottage at midnight he could see to read in any book, however small the print.

The buccaneers carried in their tobacco pouches the horn of an immense sort of spider, which Esquemeling describes as big as an egg, with feet as long as a crab, and four black teeth like a rabbit, its bite being sharp but not venomous. These teeth or horns they used either as toothpicks or pipe-cleaners; they were supposed to have the property of preserving the user from toothache. They are described as about two inches long, black as jet, smooth as glass, sharp as a thorn, and a little bent at the lower end.

Their favourite toy, the dice, they cut from the white ivory-like teeth of the sea-horse. Great observers of the use of things, and well lessoned in the bitter school of experience, they turned every new natural production they met with to some useful purpose, uniting with the keen sagacity of the hunter the shrewd instinct of the savage. Their horsewhips they formed from the skin of the back of a wild bull or sea-cow. The lashes were made of slips of hide, two or three feet long, of the full thickness at the bottom, and cut square and tapering to the point. These thongs they twisted while still green, and then hung them up in a hut to dry; in a few weeks they shrank and became hard as wood, and tough as an American cowhide, an Abyssinian scourge, or the far-famed Russian knout. From the skin of the manitee they cut straps, which they used in their canoes instead of the ordinary *tholes*.

The wild boar hunters frequently lived in huts four or five together, and remained for months, frequently a year, in the same place, supplying the neighbouring planters by contract. The most perfect equality reigned between the *matelots*; and if one of them wanted powder or lead, he took it from the other's store, telling him of the loan, and repaying it when able.

When a dispute arose between any of them, their associates tried to reconcile the difference. A dispute about a shooting wager, or the smallest trifle, might give rise to deadly feuds between such lawless and vindictive exiles, unaccustomed to control, and ready to resort to arms. If both still determined to have revenge, the musket was the impassive arbiter appealed to. The friends of the duellists decided at what distance the combatants should stand, and made them draw lots for the first fire. If one fell dead, the bystanders immediately held a sort of inquest, at which they decided whether he had been fairly dealt with, and examined the body to see that the death-shot had been fairly fired in front, and not in a cowardly or treacherous manner, and handled his musket to see whether it was discharged and had been in good order. A surgeon then opened the orifice of the wound, and if he decided that the bullet had entered behind, or much on one side, they declared the survivor a murderer; Lynch law was proclaimed, they tied the culprit to a tree, and shot him with their muskets. In Tortuga, or near a town, this rude justice was never resorted to, and, even in the wilder places, was soon abandoned as the hunters grew more civilized. These duels generally took place on the sea beach if the *flibustiers* were the combatants.

As these men took incessant exercise, were indifferent to climate, and fed chiefly on fresh meat, they enjoyed good health. They were, however, subject to flying fevers that passed in a day, and which did not confine them even to their tents.

With the Spanish Lanceros, or *fifties* as they were called by the buccaneers, the hunters were perpetually at war, their intrepid infantry being generally successful against the hot charges of these yeomanry of the savannahs. There were four companies of them in Hispaniola, with a hundred spearmen in each company; half of these were generally on the patrol, while the remainder rested, and from their number they derived their nickname. Their duty was to surprise the isolated hunters, to burn the stores of hides, make prisoners of the *engagés*, and guard the Spanish settlers against any sudden attack. At other times they were employed in killing off the herds of wild cattle that furnished the buccaneers with food, and drew fresh bands to the plains where they abounded. In great enterprises the whole corps cried "boot and saddle," and they took with them at all times a few muleteers on foot, either to carry their baggage, or to serve as scouts in the woods, where the cow-killers built their huts. But, in spite of Negro foragers and Indian spies, the keener-eyed buccaneers generally escaped, or, if met with, broke like raging wolves through their adversaries' toils. Accustomed to the bush, inured to famine and fatigue, and more indifferent than even the Spaniards to climate, the buccaneers were seldom taken prisoners. Unerring marksmen, with a spice of the wild beast in their blood, they preferred death to flight or capture.

It is probable that even for this toilsome and dangerous pursuit the Spaniards easily obtained recruits. Constant sport with the wild cattle, abundant food, and a spirit of adventure would prove an irresistible bait to the bravos of Carthagena, or the *matadors* of Campeachy. The hangers-on of the wineshops and the *pulque* drinkers of Mexico would readily embark in any campaign that would bring them a few *pistoles*, and give them good food and gay clothing.

Oexmelin relates several instances of the daring escapes of the buccaneer hunters from the blood-thirsting pursuit of the *fifties*. It was their custom, directly that news reached the tents that the Lanceros were out, to issue an order that the first man who caught sight of the horsemen should inform the rest, in order to attack the foe by an ambuscade, if they were too numerous to meet in the open field. The great aim, on the other hand, of the Lanceros, was to wait for a night of rain and wind, when the sound of their hoofs could not be heard, and to butcher the sleepers when their fire-arms were either damp or piled out of reach. Frequently they surrounded the hunters when heavy after a debauch, and when even the sentinels were asleep at the tent doors.

The following anecdote conveys some impression of these encounters. A French buccaneer going one day into the savannahs to hunt, followed by his *engagé*, was suddenly surrounded by a troop of shouting Lanceros. He saw at once that the *fifties* had at last trapped him. He was surrounded, and escape from their swift pursuit, with no tree near, was hopeless. But he would not let hope desert him so long as the spears were still out of his heart. His *engagé* was as brave as himself, and both determined to stand at bay and sell their lives dearly. The hunter of mad oxen, and the tamer of wild horses, need not fear man or devil. The master and man put themselves back to back, and, laying their common stock of powder and bullets in their caps between them, prepared for death. The Spaniards, who only carried lances, kept coursing round them, afraid to narrow in, or venture within shot, and crying out to them with threats to surrender. They next offered them quarter, and at last promised to disarm but not hurt them, saying they were only executing the orders of their general. The two Frenchmen replied mockingly, that they would never surrender, and wanted no quarter, and that the first lancer who approached would pay dear for his visit. The Spaniards still hovered round, afraid to advance, none of them willing to be the first victim, or to play the scapegoat for the rest. "*C'est le pre-*

mier pas qui coute," and the first step they made was backward. After some consultation at a safe distance, they finally left the buccaneers still standing threateningly back to back, and spurred off, half afraid that the Tartars they had nearly caught might turn the tables, and advance against them.

The steady persistency of the buccaneer infantry was generally victorious over the impetuous but transitory onslaught of the Spanish cavalry.

Another time a wild buccaneer while hunting alone was surprised by a similar party of mounted pikemen. Seeing that there was some distance between him and the nearest wood, and that his capture was certain, he bethought himself of the following *ruse*. Putting his gun up to his shoulder he advanced at a trot, shouting exultingly, "*à moi, à moi!*" as if he was followed by a band of scattered companions who had been in search of the Spaniards. The cavaliers, believing at once that they had fallen into an ambush, took flight, to the joy of the ingenious hunter, who quickly made his escape, laughing, into the neighbouring covert.

The Spaniards were worn out at last with this border warfare, unprofitable because it was waged with men who were too poor to reward the plunderer, and dangerous because fought with every disadvantage of weapon and situation. In the savannahs the Spaniards were formidable, but in the woods they became a certain prey to the musketeer. Unable to drive the plunderers out of the island, the Spaniards at last foolishly resolved to render the island not worth the plunder. Orders came from Spain to kill off the wild cattle that Columbus had originally brought to the island, and particularly round the coast. If the trade with the French vessels and the barter of hides for brandy could once be arrested, the hunters would be driven from the woods by starvation, or perish one by one in their dens. They little thought that this scheme would succeed, and what would be the consequence of such success. The hunters turned sea crusaders, and the sea became the savannah where they sought their human game. Every creek soon thronged with men more deadly than the Danish Vikinger: wrecked on a habitable shore, they landed as invaders and turned hunters as before; driven to their boats, they became again adventurers. In this name and in that of "soldiers of fortune" they delighted: a more honest and less courteous age would have termed them pirates. By the year 1686, the change from buccaneer to *flibustier* had been almost wholly effected.

The buccaneers' *engagés* led a life very little better than those white slaves whom the glittering promises of the planters had decoyed from France. The existence of the former was, however, rendered more bearable by their variety of adventure, by better food, and by daily recreation. If all day in the hot sun he had to toil carrying bales of skins from his master's hut towards the shore, we must remember that American seamen still work contentedly at the same labour in California for a sailor's ordinary wages. Mutual danger produced necessarily, except in the most brutal, a kind of fellowship between the master and the servant of the *boucan*. Up at daybreak, the *engagé* sweltered all day through the bush, groaning beneath his burden of loathsome hides, but the good meal came before sunset, and then the pipes were lit, and the brandy went round, and the song was sung, and the tale was told, while the hunters shot at a mark, or made wagers upon the respective skill of their *matelots* or their *engagés*.

We hear from Charlevoix, that young prodigals of good family had been known to prefer the canvas tent to the tapestried wall, and to have grasped the hunter's musket with the hand that might have wielded the general's baton or the marshal's staff.

The buccaneer's life was not one of mere revelry and ease; no luxurious caves or safe strongholds served at once for their treasure house, their palace, and their fortress. They were wandering outlaws; hated both by the Spaniards and the Indians, they ate with a loaded gun within their reach. The jaguar lurked beside them, the coppersnake glared at them from his lair. If their foot stumbled, they were gored by the ox or ripped up by the boar; if they fled they became a prey to the cayman of the pool; they were swept away as they forded swollen rivers; they were swallowed up by that dreadful foretype of the Judgment, the earthquake. The shark and the sea monster swam by their canoe, the carrion crow that fed today upon the carcase they had left, too often fed tomorrow on the slain hunter. The wildest transitions of safety and danger, plenty and famine, peace and war, health and sickness, surrounded their daily life. Today on the savannah dark with the wild herds, tomorrow compelled to feast on the flesh of a murdered *comerade*; today surrounded by revelling friends, tomorrow left alone to die.

The present system of hide curing practised in California seems almost identical with that employed by the buccaneers. The following extract from Dana's "Three Years Before the Mast" will convey a correct impression of what constituted the greater portion of an *engagé*'s labour. He describes the shore piled with hides, just out of reach of the tide; each skin doubled lengthwise in the middle, and nearly as stiff as a board, and the whole bundles carried down on men's heads from the place of curing to the stacks. "When the hide is taken from the bullock, holes are cut round it, near the edge, and it is staked out to dry, to prevent shrinking. They are then to be cured, and are carried down to the shore at low tide and made fast in small piles, where they lie for forty-eight hours, when they are taken out, rolled up in wheelbarrows, and thrown into vats full of strong brine, where they remain for forty-eight hours. The sea water only cleans and softens them, the brine pickles them. They are then removed from the vats, lie on a platform twenty-four hours, and are then staked out, still wet and soft; the men go over them with knives, cutting off all remaining pieces of meat or fat, the ears, and any part that would either prevent the packing or keeping. A man can clean about twenty-five a-day, keeping at his work. This cleaning must be done before noon, or they get too dry. When the sun has been upon them for a few hours they are gone over with scrapers to remove the fat that the sun brings out; the stakes are then pulled up and the hides carefully doubled, with the hair outside, and left to dry. About the middle of the afternoon, they are turned upon the other side, and at sunset piled up and turned over. The next day they are spread out and opened again, and at night, if fully dry, are thrown up on a long horizontal pole, five at a time, and beaten with flails to get out the dust; thus, being salted, scraped, cleaned, dried, and beaten, they are stowed away in the warehouses."

The buccaneer's life was not spent in quaffing *sangaree* or basking under orange blossoms—not in smoking beside mountains of flowers, where the humming-birds fluttered like butterflies, and the lizards flashed across the sunbeams, shedding jewelled and enchanted light. No Indian in the mine, no Arab pearl-diver, no worn, pale children at an English factory, no galley-slave dying at the oar, led such a life as a buccaneer *engagé* if bound to a cruel master. Imagine a delicate youth, of good but poor family, decoyed from a Norman country town by the loud-sounding promises of a St. Domingo agent, specious as a recruiting sergeant, voluble as the projector of bubble companies, greedy, plausible, and lying. He comes out to the El Dorado of his dreams, and is at once taken to the hut of some rude buccaneer. The first night is a revel, and his sleep is golden and full of visions. The spell is broken at daybreak. He has to carry a load of skins, weighing some twenty-six pounds, three or four leagues, through brakes of prickly pear and clumps of canes. The pathless way cannot be traversed at greater speed than about two hours to a quarter of a league. The sun grows vertical, and he is feverish and sick at heart. Three years of this purgatory are varied by blows and curses. The masters too often loaded their servants with blows if they dared to faint through weakness, hunger, thirst, or fatigue. Some hunters had the forbearance to rest on a Sunday, induced rather by languor than by piety; but on these days the *engagé* had to rise as usual at daybreak, to go out and kill a wild boar for the day's feast. This was disembowelled and roasted whole, being placed on a spit supported on two forked stakes, so that the flames might completely surround the carcase.

Most buccaneers, even if they rested on Sunday, required their apprentices to carry the hides down as usual to the place of shipment, fearing that the Spaniards might choose that very day to burn the huts and destroy the skins. An *engagé* once complained to his master, and reminded him that it was not right to work on a Sunday, God himself having said to the Jews, *"Six days shalt thou labour and do all thou hast to do, for the seventh day is the Sabbath of the Lord thy God."*

"And I tell you," said the scowling buccaneer, striking the earth with the butt-end of his gun and roaring out a dreadful curse, "I tell you, six days shalt thou kill bulls and skin them, and the seventh day thou shalt carry them down to the beach," beating the daring remonstrant as he spoke.

There was no remedy for these sufferers but patience. Time or death alone brought relief. Three years soon run out. The mind grows hardened under suffering as flesh does under the lash. Nature, where she cannot heal a wound, teaches us where to find unfailing balms. Some grew reckless to blows, or learned to ingratiate themselves with their masters by their increasing daring or sturdy industry. An apprentice whose bullet never flew false, or who could run down the wild ox on the plain, acquired a fame greater than that of his master. They knew that in time they themselves would be buccaneers, and could inflict the very cruelties from which they now suffered. There were instances where acts of service to the island, or feats of unusual bravery, raised an *engagé* of a single year to the full rank of hunter. An apprentice who could bring in more hides than even his master, must have been too valuable an acquisition to have been lost by a moment of spleen. That horrible cases of cruelty did occur, there can be no doubt. There were no courts of justice in the forest, no stronger arm or wiser head to which to appeal. But there are always remedies for despair. The loaded gun was at hand, the knife in the belt, and the poison berries grew by the hut. There was the unsubdued passion still at liberty in the heart—there was the will to seize the weapon and the hand to use it. Providence is fruitful in her remedies of evils, and preserves a balance which no sovereignty can long disturb. No tyrant can shut up the volcano, or chain the earthquake. There were always the mountains or the Spaniards to take refuge amongst, though famine and death dwelt in the den of the wild beasts, and, if they fled to the Spaniards, they were often butchered as mere runaway slaves before they could explain, in an unknown language, that they were not spies. But still the very impossibility of preventing such escapes must have tended to temper the severity of the masters. A *flibustier*, anxious for a crew, must have sometimes carried off discontented *engagés* both from the plantations and the *ajoupas*. The following story illustrates the social relations of the buccaneer master and his servant.

A buccaneer one day, seeing that his apprentice, newly arrived from France, could not keep up with him, turned round and struck him over the head with the lock of his musket. The youth fell, stunned, to the ground; and the hunter, thinking he was dead, stripped him of his arms, and left his body where it had fallen and weltering in the blood flowing from the wound. On his return to his hut, afraid to disclose the truth, he told his companions that the lad, who had always skulked work, had at last *marooned* (a Spanish word applied to runaway negroes). A few curses were heaped upon him, and no more was thought about his disappearance.

Soon after the master was out of sight the lad had recovered his senses, arisen, pale and weak, and attempted to return to the tents. Unaccustomed to the woods, he lost his way, got off the right track, and finally gave himself up as doomed to certain death. For some days he remained wandering round and round the same spot, without either recovering the path or being able to reach the shore. Hunger did not at first press him, for he ate the meat with which his master had loaded him, and ate it raw, not knowing the Indian manner of procuring fire, and his knives being taken from his belt. Ignorant of what fruits were safe to eat, where animals fit for food were to be found, and not knowing how to kill them unarmed, he prepared his mind for the dreadful and lingering torture of starvation. But he seems to have been of an ingenious and persevering disposition, and hope did not altogether forsake him. He had too a companion, for one of his master's dogs, which had grown fond of his playmate, had remained behind with his body, licking the hand that had so often fed him.

At first he spent whole days vainly searching for a path. Very often he climbed up a hill, from which he could see the great, blue, level sea, stretching out boundless to the horizon, and this renewed his hope. He looked up, and knew that God's sky was above him, and felt that he might be still saved. At night he was startled by the screams of the monkeys, the bellowing of the wild cattle in the distant savannah, or the unearthly cry of some solitary and unknown bird. Superstition filled him with fears, and he felt deserted by man, but tormented by the things of evil. The tracks of the wild cattle led him far astray. Long ere this his faithful dog, driven by hunger, had procured food for both. Sometimes beneath the spreading boughs of the river-loving *yaco*-tree, they would surprise a basking sow, surrounded by a wandering brood of voracious sucklings. The dog would cling to the sow, while the boy aided him in the pursuit of the errant progeny. When they had killed their prey, they would lie down and share their meal together. The boy learned to like the raw meat, and the dog had acquired his appetite long before.

Experience soon taught them where to capture their prey in the quickest and surest manner. He caught the puppies of a wild dog, and trained them in the chase; and he even taught a young wild boar that he had caught alive to join in the capture of his own species. After having led this life for nearly a year, he one day suddenly came upon the long-lost path, which soon brought him to the seashore. His master's tents were gone, and, from various appearances, seemed to have been long struck.

The lad, now grown accustomed to his wild life, resigned himself to his condition, feeling sure that, sooner or later, he should meet with a party of buccaneers. His deliverance was not long delayed. After about twelve months' life in the bush, he fell in with a troop of skinners, to whom he related his story. They were at first distrustful and alarmed, as his master had told them that he had *marooned*, and had joined the Indians. His appearance soon convinced them that his story was true, and that he was neither a *maroon* nor a deserter, for he was clothed in the rags of his *engagé*'s shirt and drawers, and had a strip of raw meat hanging from his girdle. Two tame boars and three dogs followed at his heels, and refused to leave him. He at once joined his deliverers, who freed him from all obligations to his master, and gave him arms, powder, and lead to hunt for himself, and he soon became one of the most renowned buccaneers on that coast. It was a long time before he could eat roasted meat, which not only was distasteful, but made him ill. Long after, when flaying a wild boar, he was frequently unable to restrain himself from eating the flesh raw.

When an apprentice had served three years, his master was expected to give him as a reward a musket, a pound of powder, six pounds of lead, two shirts, two pairs of drawers, and a cap. The *valets*, as the French called them, then became *comerades*, and ceased to be mere *engagés*. They took their own *matelots*, and became, in their turn, buccaneers. When they had obtained a sufficient quantity of hides, they either sent or took them to Tortuga, and brought from thence a young apprentice to treat him as they themselves had been treated.

The planters' *engagés* led a life more dreadful than that of their wilder brethren. They were decoyed from France under the same pretences that once filled our streets with the peasants' sons of Savoy, and the peasants' daughters from Frankfort, or that now lure children from the pleasant borders of Como, to pine away in a London den. The want of sufficient negroes led men to resort to all artifices to obtain assistance in cultivating the sugar-cane and the tobacco plant. In the French Antilles they were sold for three years, but often resold in the interim. Amongst the English they were bound for seven years, and being occasionally sold again at their own request, before the expiration of this term, they sometimes served fifteen or twenty years before they could obtain their freedom. At Jamaica, if a man could not pay even a small debt at a tavern, he was sold for six or eight months. The planters had agents in France, England, and other countries, who sent out these apprentices. They were worked much harder than the slaves, because their lives, after the expiration of the three years, were of no consequence to the masters. They were often the victims of a disease called "coma," the effect of hard usage and climate, and which ended in idiotcy. Père Labat remarks the quantity of idiots in the West Indies, many of whom were dangerous, although allowed to go at liberty. Many of these worse than slaves were of good birth, tender education, and weak constitutions, unable to endure even the debilitating climate, and much less hard labour. Esquemeling, himself originally an *engagé*, gives a most piteous description of their sufferings. Insufficient food and rest, he says, were the smallest of their sufferings. They were frequently beaten, and often fell dead at their masters' feet. The men thus treated died fast: some became dropsical, and others scorbutic. A man named Bettesea, a merchant of St. Christopher's, was said to have killed more than a hundred apprentices with blows and stripes. "This inhumanity," says Esquemeling, "I have *often seen* with great grief." The following anecdote of human suffering equals the cruelty of the Virginian slave owner who threw one slave into the vat of boiling molasses, and baked another in an oven:

> A certain planter (of St. Domingo) exercised such cruelty towards one of his servants as caused him to run away. Having absconded for some days in the woods, he was at last taken, and brought back to the wicked Pharaoh. No sooner had he got him but he commanded him to be tied to a tree; here he gave him so many lashes on his naked back as made his body

run with an entire stream of blood; then, to make the smart of his wounds the greater, he anointed him with lemon-juice, mixed with salt and pepper. In this miserable posture he left him tied to the tree for twenty-four hours, which being past, he began his punishment again, lashing him as before, so cruelly, that the miserable creature gave up the ghost, with these dying words, 'I beseech the Almighty God, Creator of heaven and earth, that He permit the wicked spirit to make thee feel as many torments before thy death as thou hast caused me to feel before mine.'

A strange thing, and worthy of astonishment and admiration: scarce three or four days were past, after this horrible fact, when the Almighty Judge, who had heard the cries of that tormented wretch, suffered the evil one suddenly to possess this barbarous and inhuman homicide, so that those cruel hands which had punished to death the innocent servant were the tormentors of his own body, for he beat himself and tore his flesh after a miserable manner, till he lost the very shape of a man, not ceasing to howl and cry without any rest by day or night. Thus he continued raving till he died.

It was by the endurance of such sufferings as these that the early buccaneers were hardened into fanatical monsters like Montbars and Lolonnois.

In the early part of his book, Esquemeling gives us his own history. A Dutchman by birth, he arrived at Tortuga in 1680, when the French West India Company, unable to turn the island into a depot, as they had intended, were selling off their merchandise and their plantations. Esquemeling, as a bound *engagé* of the company, was sold to the lieutenant-governor of the island, who treated him with great severity, and refused to take less than three hundred pieces of eight for his freedom. Falling sick through vexation and despair, he was sold to a *chirurgeon*, for seventy pieces of eight, who proved kind to him, and finally gave him his liberty for 100 pieces of eight, to be paid after his first *flibustier* trip.

Oexmelin was probably sold almost at the same time as Esquemeling, and was bought by the commandant-general. Not allowed to pursue his own profession of a surgeon, he was employed in the most laborious and painful work, transplanting tobacco, or thinning the young plants, grating cassava, or pressing the juice from the banana. Overworked and under fed, associating with slaves, and regarded with hatred and suspicion, he scarcely received money enough to procure either food or clothing; his master refusing, even for the inducement of two crowns a-day, to allow him to practise as physician. A single year of toil at the plantations threw him into dangerous ill health; for weeks sheltered only under an outhouse, he was kept alive by the kindness of a black slave, who brought him daily an egg. Feeble as he was, the great thirst of a tropical fever compelled him often to rise and drag himself to a neighbouring tank, that he might drink, even though to drink were to die. Recovering from this fever, a wolfish hunger was the first sign of convalescence, but to appease this he had neither food, nor money to buy it. In this condition he devoured even unripe oranges, green, hard, and bitter, and resorted to other extremities which he is ashamed to confess. On one occasion as he was descending from the rock fort, where his master lived, into the town, he met a friend, the secretary of the governor, who made him come and dine with him, and gave him a parting present of a bottle of wine; his master, who had seen what had passed, by means of a telescope, from his place of vantage, when he returned, took away the wine, and threw him into a dungeon, accusing him of being a spy and a traitor. This prison was a cellar, hollowed out of the rock, full of filth and very dark. In this he swore Oexmelin should rot in spite of all the governors in the world. Here he was kept for three days, his feet in irons, fed only by a little bread and water that they passed to him through an aperture, without even opening the door. One day, as he lay naked on the stone, and in the dark, he felt a snake twine itself, cold and slimy, round his body, tightening the folds till they grew painful, and then sliding off to its hole. On the fourth day they opened the door and tried to discover if he had told the governor anything of his master's cruelties; they then set him to dig a plot of ground near the Fort. Finding himself left unguarded, he resolved to go and complain to the governor, having first consulted a good old Capuchin, who took compassion on his pale and famished aspect. The governor instantly took pity on the wretched runaway, fed and clothed him, and on his recovery to health placed him with a celebrated surgeon of the place, who paid his value to his master; the governor being unwilling to take him into his own service, for fear he should be accused to the home authorities of taking away slaves from the planters.

The *engagés* were called to their work at daybreak by a shrill whistle (as the negroes are now by the hoarse conch shell); and the foreman, allowing any who liked to smoke, led them to their work. This consisted in felling trees and in picking or lopping tobacco; the driver stood by them as they dug or picked, and struck those who slackened or rested, as a captain would do to his galley slaves. Whether sick or well they were equally obliged to work. They were frequently employed in picking *mahot*, a sort of bark used to tie up bales. If they died of fatigue they were quietly buried, and there an end. Early in the morning one of the band had to feed the pigs with potato leaves, and prepare his *comerades'* dinner. They boiled their meat, putting peas and chopped potatoes into the water. The cook worked with the gang, but returned a little sooner to prepare his messmates' dinner, while they were stripping the tobacco stalk. On feast-days and Sundays they had some indulgences. Oexmelin relates an instance of a sick slave being employed to turn a grindstone on which his master was sharpening his axe; being too weak to do it well, the butcher turned round and clove him down between the shoulders. The slave fell down, bleeding profusely, and died within two hours; yet this master was one of a body of planters deemed very indulgent in comparison to those of some other islands. One planter of St. Christopher, named Belle Tête, who came from Dieppe, prided himself on having killed 200 *engagés* who would not work, all of whom, he declared, died of sheer laziness. When they were in the last extremities he was in the habit of rubbing their mouths with the yolk of an egg, in order that he might conscientiously swear he had pressed them to take food till the very last. Upon a priest one day remonstrating with him on his brutality, he replied, with perfect effrontery, that he had once been a bound *engagé*, and had never been treated better; that he had come all the way to that shore to get money, and provided he could get it and see his children roll in a coach, he did not care himself if the devil carried him off.

The following anecdote shows what strange modifications of crime this species of slavery might occasionally produce. There was a rich inhabitant of Guadaloupe, whose father became so poor that he was obliged to sell himself as an *engagé*, and by a singular coincidence sold himself to a merchant who happened to be his son's agent. The poor fellow, finding himself his son's servant, thought himself well off, but soon found that he was treated as brutally as the rest. The son, finding the father was old and discontented, and therefore unable to do much work, and afraid to beat him for the sake of the scandal, sold him soon after to another planter, who treated him better, gave him more to eat, and eventually restored him to liberty. Of the ten thousand Scotch and Irish whom Cromwell sent to the West Indies, many became *engagés*, and finally buccaneers. Many of the old Puritan soldiers, who had served in the same wars, were enrolled in the same ranks.

The same principle of brotherhood applied to the planters as to the ordinary buccaneers. They called each other *matelots*, and, before living together, signed a contract by which they agreed to share everything in common. Each had the power to dispose of his companion's money and goods, and an agreement signed by one bound the other also. If the one died, the survivor became the inheritor of the whole, in preference even to heirs who might come from Europe to claim the share or attempt to set up a claim. The engagement could be broken up whenever either wished it, and was often cancelled in a moment of petulance or of transitory vexation. A third person was sometimes admitted into the brotherhood on the same conditions. By this singular custom, friendships were formed as firm as those between a Highlander and his foster-brother, a Canadian trapper and his *comerade*, or an English sailor and his messmate.

The *matelotage*, or *compagnon à bon lot*, being thus formed, the two planters would go to the governor of the island and request a grant of land. The officer of the district was then sent to measure out what they required, of a specified size in a specified spot. The usual grant was a plot, two hundred feet wide and thirty feet long, as near as possible to the sea-shore, as being most convenient for the transport of goods, as well as for the ease of procuring salt water, which they used in preparing the tobacco leaf. When the sea-shore was covered with cabins the planters built their huts higher up and four deep, those nearest to the beach being obliged to allow a roadway to those who were the furthest back. Their lodges, or *ajoupas*, were raised upon ground cleared from wood, the thicket being first burnt with the lower branches of the larger trees. The trunks, too large to remove, were cut down to within two or three feet of the earth, and allowed to dry and rot for several summers, and finally also consumed by fire. The savages, on the other hand, cut down all the trees, let them dry as they fell, and then, setting the whole alight, reduced it at once to ashes, without any clearing, lopping, or piling. When about thirty or forty feet of ground was thus cleared, they began to plant vegetables and cultivate the ground—peas, potatoes, manioc, banana, and figs being the daily necessaries of their lives. The banana they planted near rivers, no planter residing in a place where there was not some well or spring. Their *casa*, or chief lodge, was supported by posts fifteen or sixteen feet high, thatched with palm branches, rushes, or sugar-canes, and walled either with reeds or palisades. Inside, they had *barbecues*, or forms rising two or three feet from the ground, upon which lay their mattresses stuffed with banana leaves, and above it the mosquito net of thin white linen, which they called a *pavillon*. A smaller lodge served for cooking or for warehousing. Friends and neighbours always assisted in building these cabins, and were treated in return with brandy by the planter. The laws of the society obliged the settlers to help each other, and this kindness was never refused. The same system of mutual support originated the Scotch penny weddings and the English friendly custom of ploughing a young farmer's fields.

Now the *ajoupa* was built, the tobacco ground had to be dug. An enclosure of two thousand plants required much care, and was obliged to be kept clean and free from weeds. They had to be lopped, and transplanted, and irrigated, and finally picked and stored. The people of Tortuga, the buccaneers' island, exchanged their tobacco with the French merchants for hatchets, hoes, knives, sacking, and above all for wine and brandy.

From potatoes, which the planters ate for breakfast, they extracted maize, a sour but pleasant beverage. The cassava root they grated for cakes, making a liquor called *veycon* of the residue. From the banana they also extracted an intoxicating drink.

With the wild boar hunters they exchanged tobacco leaf for dried meat, often paying away at one time two or three hundred weight of tobacco, and frequently sending a servant of their own to the savannahs to help the hunter and to supply him with powder and shot.

CHAPTER 3

The Flibustiers or Sea Rovers

The *flibustiers* first began by associating together in bands of from fifteen to twenty men. Each of them carried the buccaneer musket, holding a ball of sixteen to the pound, and had generally pistols at his belt, holding bullets of twenty or twenty-four to the pound, and besides this they wore a good sabre or cutlass. When collected at some preconcerted rendezvous, generally a key or small island off Cuba, they elected a captain, and embarked in a canoe, hollowed out of the trunk of a single tree in the Indian manner. This canoe was either bought by the association or the captain. If the latter, they agreed to give him the first ship they should take. As soon as they had all signed the charter-party, or mutual agreement, they started for the destined port off which they were to cruise. The first Spanish vessel they took served to repay the captain and recompense themselves. They dressed themselves in the rich robes of Castilian *grandees* over their own blooded shirts, and sat down to revel in the gilded saloon of the galleon. If they found their prize not seaworthy, they would take her to some small sand island and careen, while the crew helped the Indians to turn turtle, and to procure bull's flesh. The Spanish crew they kept to assist in careening, for they never worked themselves, but fought and hunted while the unfortunate prisoners were toiling round the fire where the pitch boiled, or the turtle was stewing. The *flibustiers* divided the spoil as soon as each one had taken an oath that nothing had been secreted. When the ship was ready for sea, they let the Spaniards go, and kept only the slaves. If there were no negroes or Indians, they retained a few Spaniards to wait upon them. If the prisoners were men of consequence, they detained them till they could obtain a ransom. Every *flibustier* brought a certain supply of powder and ball for the common stock. Before starting on an expedition it was a common thing to plunder a Spanish hog-yard, where a thousand swine were often collected, surrounding the keeper's lodge at night, and shooting him if he made any resistance. The tortoise fishermen were often forced to fish for them gratuitously, although nearly every ship had its Mosquito Indian to strike turtle and seacow, and to fish for the whole boat's crew. "No prey, no pay," was the buccaneers' motto. The charter-party specified the salary of the captain, surgeon, and carpenter, and allowed 200 pieces of eight for victualling. The boys had but half a share, although it was either their duty or the surgeon's, when the rest had boarded, to remain behind to fire the former vessel, and then retire to the prize.

The buccaneer code, worthy of Napoleon or Justinian, was equal to the statutes of any land, insomuch as it answered the want of those for whom it was compiled, and seldom required either revision or enlargement. It was never appealed from, and was seldom found to be unjust or severe.

The captain was allowed five or six shares, the master's mate only two, and the other officers in proportion, down to the lowest mariner. All acts of special bravery or merit were rewarded by special grants. The man who first caught sight of a prize received a hundred crowns. The sailor who struck down the enemy's captain, and the first boarder who reached the enemy's deck, were also distinguished by honours. The surgeon, always a great man among a crew whose lives so often depended on his skill, received 200 crowns to supply his medicine chest. If they took a prize, he had a share like the rest. If they had no money to give him, he was rewarded with two slaves.

The loss of an eye was recompensed at 100 crowns, or one slave.
The loss of both eyes with 600 crowns, or six slaves.
The loss of a right hand or right leg at 200 crowns, or two slaves.
The loss of both hands or legs at 600 crowns, or six slaves.
The loss of a finger or toe at 100 crowns, or one slave.
The loss of a foot or leg at 200 crowns, or two slaves.
The loss of both legs at 600 crowns, or six slaves.
Nothing but death seems to have been considered as worth

recompensing with more than 600 crowns. For any wound, which compelled a sailor to carry a *canulus*, 200 crowns were given, or two slaves. If a man had not even lost a member, but was for the present deprived of the use of it, he was still entitled to his compensation as much as if he had lost it altogether. The maimed were allowed to take either money or slaves.

The charter-party drawn up by Sir Henry Morgan before his famous expedition, which ended in the plunder and destruction of Panama, shows several modifications of the earlier contract.

To him who struck the enemy's flag, and planted the buccaneers', fifty *piastres*, besides his share.

To him who took a prisoner who brought tidings, 100 *piastres*, besides his share.

For every grenade thrown into an enemy's port-hole, five *piastres*.

To him who took an officer of rank at the risk of his life, proportionate reward.

To him who lost two legs, 500 crowns, or fifteen slaves.

To him who lost two arms, 800 *piastres*, or eighteen slaves.

To him who lost one leg or one arm, 500 *piastres*, or six slaves.

To him who lost an eye, 100 *piastres*, or one slave.

For both eyes, 200 *piastres*, or two slaves.

For the loss of a finger, 100 *piastres*, or one slave. A *flibustier* who had a limb crippled, received the same pay as if it was lost. A wound requiring an issue, was recompensed with 500 *piastres*, or five slaves. These shares were all allotted before the general division. If a vessel was taken at sea, its cargo was divided among the whole fleet, but the crew first boarding it received 100 crowns, if its value exceeded 10,000 crowns, and for every 10,000 crowns' worth of cargo, 100 went to the men that boarded. The surgeon received 200 *piastres*, besides his share.

The Mosquito Indians were the helots of the buccaneers; they employed them to catch fish, and their vessels had generally a small canoe, kept for their use, in which they might strike tortoise or manitee. These Indians used no oars, but a pair of broad-bladed paddles, which they held perpendicularly, grasping the staff with both hands and putting back the water by sheer strength, and with very quick, short strokes. Two men generally went in the same boat, the one sitting in the stern, the other kneeling down in the head.

They both paddled softly till they approached the spot where their prey lay; they then remained still, looking very warily about them, and the one at the head then rose up, with his striking-staff in his hand. This weapon was about eight feet long, almost as thick as a man's arm at the larger end, at which there was a hole into which the harpoon was put; at the other extremity was placed a piece of light (bob) wood, with a hole in it, through which the small end of the staff came. On this bob wood a line of ten or twelve fathoms was neatly wound—the end of the one line being fastened to the wood, and the other to the harpoon, the man keeping about a fathom of it loose in his hand. When he struck, the harpoon came off the shaft, and, as the wounded fish swam away, the line ran off from the reel. Although the bob and line were frequently dragged deep under water, and often caught round coral branches or sunk wreck, it generally rose to the surface of the water. The Indians struggled to recover the bob, which they were accustomed to do in about a quarter of an hour.

When the sea-cow grew tired and began to lie still, they drew in the line, and the monster, feeling the harpoon a second time, would often make a maddened rush at the canoe. It then became necessary that the steersman should be nimble in turning the head of the canoe the way his companion pointed, as he alone was able to see and feel the way the manitee was swimming. Directly the fish grew tired, they hauled in the line, which the vexed creature drew out again a dozen times with ferocious but impotent speed. When its strength grew quite exhausted, they would drag it up the side of their boat and knock it on the head, or, pulling it to the shore, made it fast while they went out to strike another. From the great size of a sea-cow it was always necessary to go to shore in order to get it safely into their boats; hauling it up in shoal water, they upset their canoes, and then rolling the fish in righted again with the weight. The Indians sometimes paddled one home, and towed the other after them. Dampierre says he knew two Indians, who every day for a week brought two manitee on board his ship, the least not weighing less than six hundred pounds, and yet in so small a canoe that three Englishmen could row it.

If the fishermen struck a sea-cow that had a calf they generally captured both—the mother carrying the young under her side fins, and always regarding their safety before her own; the young, moreover, would seldom desert their mother, and would follow the canoe in spite of noise and blows. The least sound startled the manitee, but the turtles required less care. These fish had certain islands near Cuba which they chose to lay their eggs in. At certain seasons they came from the gulf of Honduras in such vast multitudes, that ships, which had lost their latitude, very often steered at night, following the sound of these clattering shoals. When they had been about a month in the Caribbean sea they grew fat, and the fishing commenced. Salt turtle was the buccaneers' healthiest food, and was supposed to free them from all the ailments of debauchery. The Indians struck the turtle with a short, sharp, triangular-headed iron, not more than an inch long, which fitted into a spear handle. The lance head was loose and had the usual line attached. Their lines they made of the fibrous bark of a tree, which they also used for their rigging.

The manitee, or sea-cow, was a favourite article of food with these wandering seamen. It was a monster as big as a horse, and as unwieldy as a walrus, with eyes not much larger than peas, and a head like a cow. Its flesh was white, sweet, and wholesome. The tail of a young fish was a dainty, and a young sucking-calf, roasted, was an epicure's morsel. The head and tail of older animals were tough, yet the belly was frequently eaten.

Dampierre speaks of his companions feasting on pork and peas, and beef and dough-boys, and this nautical coarseness was generally found associated with occasional tropical luxuriousness. In cases of necessity, wrecked sailors fed on sharks, which they first boiled and then squeezed dry, and stewed with pepper and vinegar. The oil of turtle they used instead of butter for their dumplings. The best turtle were said to be those that fed on land; those that lived on sea-weed, and not on grass, being yellow and rank. The larger fish needed two men to turn them on their backs. The *flibustiers* also ate the iguanas, or large South American lizards. Vast flocks of doves were found in many of the islands, sometimes in such abundance that a sailor could knock down five or six dozen of an afternoon.

The buccaneers' history is a singular example of how evil generates evil. The Spaniards destroyed the wild cattle, and the hunters turned freebooters. Spain discontinued trading to prevent piracy, and the adventurers, starved for want of gold, made descents upon the mainland. The evil grew by degrees till the worm they had at first trod upon arose in their path an indestructible and devastating monster of a hundred heads. First single ships, then fleets, were swept off by these locusts of the deep; first, islands were burnt, then villages sacked, and at last cities conquered. First the North and then the South Pacific were visited, till the whole coast from Panama to Cape Horn trembled at the very flutter of their flag. The first *flibustier*, Lewis Scott, scared Campeachy with a few canoes. Grognet grappled the Lima fleet with a whole squadron of pirate craft. The buccaneer spirit arose from revenge, and ended in robbery and murder. At first fierce but merciful, they grew rapacious, loathsome, and bloody. Their early chivalry forsook them—they sank into the enemies of God and all mankind, and the last refuse of them expired on the gallows of Jamaica, children of Cain, unpitied by any, their very courage despised, and their crimes detested. At their culminating point, united under the sway of one great mind, they might have formed a large empire in South America, or conquered it as tributaries to France or England. Always thirsty for gold, they were often chivalrous, generous, intrepid, merciful, and disinterested.

A greater evil soon cured the lesser. The Spaniards, dreading robbery worse than death, ceased in a great measure to trade. The poorer merchants were ruined by the loss of a single cocoa vessel; the richer waited for the convoy of the plate fleets, or followed in the wake of the galleon, hoping to escape if she was captured, as the chickens do when the hen goes cackling up in the claws of the kite. For every four vessels that once sailed not more than one could be now seen. What with the war of France on Holland, and England on France, and all on Spain, there was little safety for the poor trader. Yet those who could risk a loss still made great profits. This cessation of trade was a poor remedy against the sea robber: it was to rob oneself instead of being robbed, to commit suicide for fear of murder. It was a remedy that saved life, but rendered life hateful. The buccaneers, starving for want of prey, remained moodily in the rocky fastnesses of Tortuga, like famished eagles looking down on a country they have devastated. To accomplish greater feats they united in bodies, and made forays on the coast. They had before remained at the threshold—they now rushed headlong into the sanctuary, and they got *their* bread, or rather other people's bread, by daring dashes and surprises of towns, leaving them only when wrapped in flames or swept by the pestilence that always followed in their train.

We may claim for our own nation the first pioneer in this new field of enterprise. Lewis Scott, an Englishman, led the way by sacking the town of St. Francisco, in Campeachy, and, compelling the inhabitants to pay a ransom, returned safely to Jamaica. Where the carcase is there will the eagles be gathered together, for no sooner had his sails grown small in the distance than Mansweld, another buccaneer, made several successful descents upon the same luckless coast, unfortunate in its very fertility. He then equipped a fleet and attempted to return by the kingdom of New Granada to the South Sea, passing the town of Carthagena. This scheme failed in consequence of a dispute arising between the French and English crews, who were always quarrelling over their respective share of provisions; but in spite of this he took the island of St. Catherine, and attempted to found a buccaneer state.

John Davis, a Dutchman, excelled both his predecessors in daring. Cruising about Jamaica he became a scourge to all the Spanish mariners who ventured near the coasts of the Caraccas, or his favourite haunts, Carthagena and the Boca del Toro, where he lay wait for vessels bound to Nicaragua. One day he missed his shot, and having a long time traversed the sea and taken nothing—a failure which generally drove these brave men to some desperate expedient to repair their sinking fortunes—he resolved with ninety men to visit the lagoon of Nicaragua, and sack the town of Granada. An Indian from the shores of the lagoon promised to guide him safely and secretly; and his crew, with one voice, declared themselves ready to follow him wherever he led. By night he rowed thirty leagues up the river, to the entry of the lake, and concealed his ships under the boughs of the trees that grew upon the banks; then putting eighty men in his three canoes he rowed on to the town, leaving ten sailors to guard the vessels. By day they hid under the trees; at night they pushed on towards the unsuspecting town, and reached it on the third midnight—taking it, as he had expected, without a blow and by surprise. To a sentinel's challenge they replied that they were fishermen returning home, and two of the crew, leaping on shore, ran their swords through the interrogator, to stop further questions which might have been less easily answered. Following their guide they reached a small covered way that led to the right of the town, while another Indian towed their canoes to a point to which they had agreed each man should bring his booty.

As soon as they arrived at the town they separated into small bands, and were led one by one to the houses of the richest inhabitants. Here they quietly knocked, and, being admitted as friends, seized the inmates by the throat and compelled them, on pain of death, to surrender all the money and jewels that they had. They then roused the sacristans of the principal churches, from whom they took the keys and carried off all the altar plate that could be beaten up or rendered portable. The *pixes* they stripped of their gems, gouged out the jewelled eyes of virgin idols, and hammered up the sacramental cups into convenient lumps of metal.

This quiet and undisturbed pillage had lasted for two hours without a struggle, when some servants, escaping from the adventurers, began to ring the alarm bells to warn the town, while a few of the already plundered citizens, breaking into the marketplace, filled the streets with uproar and affright. Davis, seeing that the inhabitants were beginning to rally from that panic which had alone secured his victory, commenced a retreat, as the enemy were now gathering in armed and threatening numbers. In a hollow square, with their booty in the centre, the buccaneers fought their way to their boats, amid tumultuous war-cries and shouts of derision and exultation. In spite of their haste, they were prudent enough to carry with them some rich Spaniards, intending to exchange them for any of their own men they might lose in their retreat. On regaining their ships they compelled these prisoners to send them as a ransom 500 cows, with which they revictualled their ships for the passage back to Jamaica. They had scarcely well weighed anchor before they saw 600 mounted Spaniards dash down to the shore in the hopes of arresting their retreat. A few broadsides were the parting greetings of these unwelcome visitors.

This expedition was accomplished in eight days. The booty consisted of coined money and bullion amounting to about 40,000 crowns. Esquemeling computes it at 4,000 pieces of eight, and in ready money, plate, and jewels to about 50,000 pieces of eight more.

Thus concluded this adventurous raid, in which a town forty leagues inland, and containing at least 800 well-armed defenders, was stormed and robbed by eighty resolute sailors. Davis reached Jamaica in safety with his plunder, which was soon put into wider circulation by the aid of the dice, the tavern keepers, and the courtesans. The money once expended, Davis was roused to fresh exertion. He associated himself with two or three other captains, who, superstitiously relying on his good fortune, chose him as admiral of a small flotilla of eight or nine armed gunboats. The less fortunate rewarded him with boundless confidence. His first excursion was to the town of St. Christopher, in Cuba, to wait for the fleet from New Spain, in hopes to cut off some rich unwieldy straggler. But the fleet contrived to escape his sentinels and pass untouched. Davis then sallied forth and sacked a small town named St. Augustine of Florida, in spite of its castle and garrison of 100 men. He suffered little loss; but the inhabitants proved very poor, and the booty was small.

In making war against Spain, the hunters were mere privateersmen cruising against a national enemy; but in their endurance, patience, and energy, they stood alone. In their onset—rushing, singing, and dancing through fire and flame—they resembled rather the old Barsekars or the first levies of Mohammed. But in one point they were very remarkable; that they did more, and were yet actuated by a lower motive. Almost devoid of religion, they fought with all the madness of fanaticism against a people themselves constitutionally fanatic, but already enervated by climate, by sudden wealth, and a long experience of contaminating luxury. The galleons of Manilla were their final aim, as they gradually passed from the devastated shores of South America to the Philippine Islands and the coasts of Guinea. They had been the instrument of Providence, and knew themselves so, to avenge the wrongs of the Indian upon the Spaniard; they were soon to become the first avengers of the Negro. Long years of plunder had made the Spaniard and the

Creole as secretive as the Hindu. At the first intelligence of some terrified fisherman, the frightened townsman threw his *pistoles* into wells, or mortared them up in the wall of his fortresses. Laden mules were driven into the interior; the women fled to the nearest plantation; the old men barred themselves up in the church. Their first thought was always flight; their second, to turn and strike a blow for all they loved, valued, and revered.

The debauchery of the buccaneers was as unequalled as their courage. Oexmelin relates a story of an Englishman who gave 500 crowns to his mistress at a single revel. This man, who had earned 1,500 crowns by exposing himself to desperate dangers, was, within three months, sold for a term of three years to a planter, to discharge a tavern debt which he could not pay. A conqueror of Panama might be seen tomorrow driven by the overseer's whip among a gang of slaves, cutting sugar canes, or picking tobacco.

Another buccaneer, a Frenchman, surnamed Vent-en-Panne, was so addicted to play that he lost everything but his shirt. Every *pistole* that he could earn he spent in this absorbing vice—so tempting to men, who longed for excitement, were indifferent to money, and daily risked their lives for the prospect of gain. On one occasion he lost 500 crowns, his whole share of some recent prize-money, besides 300 crowns which he had borrowed of a *comerade* who would now lend him no more. Determined to try his fortune again, he hired himself as servant at the very gambling-house where he had been ruined, and, by lighting pipes for the players and bringing them in wine, earned fifty crowns in two days. He staked this, and soon won 12,000 crowns. He then paid his debts and resolved to lose no more, shipping himself on board an English vessel that touched at Barbadoes. At Barbadoes he met a rich Jew who offered to play him. Unable to abstain, he sat down, and won 1,300 crowns and 100,000 lbs. of sugar already shipped for England, and, in addition to this, a large mill and sixty slaves. The Jew, begging him to stay and give him his revenge, ran and borrowed some money, and returned and took up the cards. The buccaneer consented, more from love of play than generosity; and the Jew, putting down 1,500 *jacobuses*, won back 100 crowns, and finally all his antagonist's previous winnings—stripping him even to the very clothes he wore. The delighted winner allowed him for very shame to retain his clothes, and gave him money enough to return, disconsolate and beggared, to Tortuga. Becoming again a buccaneer, he gained 6,000 or 7,000 crowns. M. D'Ogeron, the governor, treating him as a wayward child, taking away his money, sent him back to France with bills of exchange for the amount. Vent-en-Panne, now cured of his vice, took to merchandise; but, always unfortunate, was killed in his first voyage to the West Indies, his vessel being attacked by two Ostende frigates, of twenty-four or thirty guns each, which were eventually, however, driven off by the dead man's crew of only thirty buccaneers.

When the pleasures of Tortuga or Jamaica had swallowed up all the hard-earned winnings of these men, they returned to sea, expending their last *pistoles* in powder and ball, and leaving heavy scores still unsettled with the *cabaretiers*. They then hastened to the quays, or small sandy islands off Cuba, to careen their vessels and to salt turtle. Sometimes they repaired to Honduras, where they had Indian wives; latterly, to the Galapagos isles, to the Boca del Toro, or the coast of Castilla del Oro.

Some buccaneers, Esquemeling says, would spend 3,000 *piastres* in a night, not leaving themselves even a shirt in the morning. He adds:

> My own master would buy a whole pipe of wine, and, placing it in the street, would force every one that passed by to drink with him, threatening also to pistol them in case they would not do it. At other times he would do the same with barrels of ale or beer; and very often with both his hands he would throw these liquors about the street, and wet the clothes of such as walked by, without regard whether he spoiled their apparel or not, or whether they were men or women.

Port Royal was a favourite scene for such carousals.

Even as late as 1694, Montauban gives us some idea of the wild debaucheries committed by the buccaneers even at Bourdeaux. He says:

> My freebooters who had not seen France for a long time, finding themselves now in a great city where pleasure and plenty reigned, were not backward to refresh themselves after the fatigues they had endured while so long absent from

their native country. They spent a world of money here, and proved horribly extravagant. The merchants and their hosts made no scruple to advance them money, or lend them as much as they pleased, upon the reputation of their wealth and the noise there was throughout the city of the valuable prizes whereof they had a share. All the nights they spent in such divertisements as pleased them best; and the days, in running up and down the town in masquerade, causing themselves to be carried in chairs with lighted flambeaux at noon—of which debauches some died, while four of my crew fairly deserted me.

This, it must be remembered, was at a time when buccaneering had sunk into privateering—the half-way house to mere piracy. The distinguishing mark of the true buccaneer was, that he attacked none but Spaniards.

Of the buccaneers' estimation of religion, Charlevoix gives us some curious accounts. He says:

> ... there remained no traces of it in their heart, but still, sometimes, from time to time, they appeared to meditate deeply. They never commenced a combat without first embracing each other, in sign of reconciliation. They would at such times strike themselves rudely on the breast, as if they wished to rouse some compunction in their hearts, and were not able. Once escaped from danger, they returned headlong to their debauchery, blasphemy, and brigandage. The buccaneers, looking upon themselves as worthy fellows, regarded the *flibustiers* as wretches, but in reality there was not much difference. The buccaneers were, perhaps, the less vicious, but the *flibustiers* preserved a little more of the externals of religion; *with the exception of a certain honour among them, and their abstinence from human flesh, few savages were more wicked, and a great number of them much less so.*

This passage shows a very curious jealousy between the hunters and the corsairs, and a singular distinction as to religious feeling. Père Labat, however, speaks of the *flibustiers* as attending confession immediately after a sea-fight with most exemplary devotion.

A more important distinction than that made by Charlevoix was that between the Protestant and Roman Catholic adventurers, the latter being as superstitious as the former were irreverent. Ravenau de Lussan always speaks with horror of the blasphemy and irreligion of his English *comerades*, one of whom was an old trooper of Cromwell's; and Grognet's fleet eventually separated from the English ships, on account of the latter crews lopping crucifixes with their sabres, and firing at images with their pistols. A *flibustier* captain, named Daniel, shot one of his men in a Spanish church for behaving irreverently at mass; and Ringrose gives an instance of an English commander who threw the dice overboard, if he found his men gambling on a Sunday.

We find Ravenau de Lussan's troop singing a *Te Deum* after victories, and Oexmelin tells us that prayers were said daily on board *flibustier* ships.

It is difficult to say from what class of life either the buccaneers or the *flibustiers* sprang. The planters often became hunters, and the hunters sailors, and the reverse. Morgan was a Welsh farmer's son, who ran away to sea; Montauban, the son of a Gascon gentleman; D'Ogeron had been a captain in the French marines; Von Horn, a common sailor in an Ostende smack; Dampierre was a Somersetshire yeoman, and Esquemeling a Dutch planter's apprentice. Charlevoix says:

> Few could bear for many years a life so hard and laborious, and the greater part only continued in it till they could gain enough to become planters. Many, continually wasting their money, never earned sufficient to buy a plantation; others grew so accustomed to the life, and so fond even of its hardships and painful risks, that, though often heirs to good fortunes, they would not leave it to return to France.

The life of M. D'Ogeron, the governor of Tortuga, is an example of another class of buccaneers, and of the causes which led to the choice of such a profession. At fifteen, he was captain of a regiment of marines, and in 1656, joining a company intending to colonize the Matingo River, he embarked in a ship, fitted out at the expense of 17,000 *livres*. Disappointed in this bubble, he tried to settle at Martinique, but deceived by the governor, who withdrew a grant of land, he determined to settle with the buccaneers of St. Domingo. Embarking in a rickety vessel, he ran ashore on Hispaniola, and lost all his merchandise and provisions. Giving his *engagés* their liberty, he joined the hunters, and became distinguished as well for courage as virtue. His goods sent from France were sold at a loss, and he returned to his native country a poor man. Collecting his remaining money, he hired *engagés*, and loaded a vessel with wine and brandy. Finding the market glutted, he sold his cargo at a loss, and was cheated by his Jamaica agent. Returning again to France, he fitted out a third vessel, and finally settled as a planter in Hispaniola. At this juncture the French West India Company fixed their eyes upon him, and in 1665 made him governor of their colony.

Ravenau de Lussan illustrates the motives that sometimes led the youth of the higher classes to turn buccaneers. He commences his book with true French vanity, by saying, that few children of Paris, which contains so many of the wonders of the world (ten out of the eight, we suppose), seek their fortune abroad. From a child he was seized with a passionate disposition for travel, and would steal out of his father's house and play truant when he was yet scarce seven. He soon reached La Vilette and the suburbs, and by degrees learnt to lose sight of Paris. With this passion arose a desire for a military life. The noise of a drum in the street transported him with joy. He made a friend of an officer, and, offering him his sword, joined his company, and witnessed the siege of Condé, ending his campaign, still unwearied of his new form of life. He then became a cadet in a marine regiment. The captain drained him of all his money, and his father, at a great expense, bought him his discharge. Under the Count D'Avegeau he entered the French Guards, and fought at the siege of St. Guislain. Growing, on his return, weary of Paris, he embarked again on sea, having nothing but voyages in his head; the longest and most dangerous appearing to his imagination, he says, the most delightful. Travelling by land seemed to him long and difficult, and he once more chose the sea, deeming it only fit for a woman to remain at home ignorant of the world. His affectionate parents tried in vain to reason him out of this gadding humour, and finding him only grow firmer and more inflexible, they desisted.

Not caring whither he went, so he could get to sea, he embarked in 1697 from Dieppe for St. Domingo. Here he remained for five months *engagé* to a French planter, "more a Turk than a Frenchman." He says:

> But what misery soever I have undergone with him, I freely forgive him, being resolved to forget his name, which I shall not mention in this place, because the laws of Christianity require that at my hand, though as to matters of charity he is not to expect much of that in me, since he, on his part, has been every way defective in the exercise thereof upon my account.

But his patience at last worn out, and weary of cruelties that seemed endless, De Lussan applied to M. de Franquesnay, the king's lieutenant, who himself gave him shelter in his house for six months. He was now in debt, and thinking it "honest to pay his creditors," he joined the freebooters in order to satisfy them, not willing to apply again for money to his parents. "These borrowings from the Spaniards," he says, "have this advantage attending them, that there is no obligation to repay them," and there was war between the two crowns, so that he was a legal privateersman. Selecting a leader, De Lussan pitched on De Graff, as a brave corsair, who happened to be then at St. Domingo, eager to sail. Furnishing himself with arms, at the expense of Franquesnay, he joined De Graff. He says:

> We were in a few hours satisfied with each other, and became such friends as those are wont to be who are about to run the same risk of fortune, and apparently to die together.

The 22nd of November, the day he sailed from Petit Guave, seemed the happiest of his life.

Dampierre mentions an old buccaneer, who was slain at the taking of Leon.

> He was a stout, grey-headed old man, aged about eighty-four, who had served under Oliver Cromwell in the Irish rebellion; after which he was at Jamaica, and had followed privateering ever since. He would not accept the offer our men made him to tarry ashore, but said he would venture as far as the best of them; but when surrounded by the Spaniards he refused to take quarter, but discharged his gun amongst

them, keeping a pistol still charged; so they shot him dead at a distance. His name was Swan (*rara avis*). He was a very merry, hearty old man, and always used to declare he would never take quarter.

When the adventurers were at sea, they lived together as a friendly brotherhood. Every morning at ten o'clock the ship's cook put the kettle on the fire to boil the salt beef for the crew, in fresh water if they had plenty, but if they ran short in brine; meal was boiled at the same time, and made into a thick porridge, which was mixed with the gravy and the fat of the meat. The whole was then served to the crew on large platters, seven men to a plate. If the captain or cook helped themselves to a larger share than their messmates, any of the republican crew had a right to change plates with them. But, notwithstanding this brotherly equality, and in spite of the captain being deposable by his crew, there was maintained at all moments of necessity the strictest discipline, and the most rigid subordination of rank. The crews had two meals a day. They always said grace before meat: the French Catholics singing the canticles of Zecharias, the *Magnificat*, or the *Miserere*; the English reading a chapter from the New Testament, or singing a psalm.

Directly a vessel hove in sight, the *flibustiers* gave chase. If it showed a Spanish flag, the guns were run out, and the decks cleared; the pikes lashed ready, and every man prepared his musket and powder, of which he alone was the guardian (and not the gunner), these articles being generally paid for from the common stock, unless provided by the captain.

They first fell on their knees at their quarters (each group round its gun), to pray God that they might obtain both victory and plunder. Then all lay down flat on the deck, except the few left to steer and navigate—proceeding to board as soon as their musketeers had silenced the enemy's fire. If victorious, they put their prisoners on shore, attended to the wounded, and took stock of the booty. A third part of the crew went on board the prize, and a prize captain was chosen by lot. No excuse was allowed; and if illness prevented the man elected taking the office, his *matelot*, or companion, took his place.

On arriving at Tortuga, they paid a commission to the governor, and before dividing the spoil, rewarded the captain, the surgeons, and the wounded. The whole crew then threw into a common heap all they possessed above the value of five *sous*, and took an oath on the New Testament, holding up their right hands, that they had kept nothing back. Any one detected in perjury was marooned, and his share either given to the rest, to the heirs of the dead, or as a bequest to some chapel. The jewels and merchandise were sold, and they divided the produce. Says Oexmelin:

> It was impossible to put any obstacle in the way of men who, animated simply by the hope of gain, were capable of such great enterprises, having *nothing but life* to lose and all to win. It is true that they would not have persisted long in their expeditions if they had had neither boats nor provisions. For ships they never wanted, because they were in the habit of going out in small canoes and capturing the largest and best provisioned vessels. For harbours they could never want, because everybody fled before them, and they had but to appear to be victorious.

This intelligent and animated writer concludes his book by expressing an opinion that a firm and organized resistance by Spain at the outset might have stopped the subsequent mischief; but this opinion he afterwards qualifies in the following words, which, coming from such a writer so well acquainted with those of whom he writes, speaks volumes in favour of buccaneer prowess: "*Je dis peut-être, car les aventuriers sont de terribles gens.*"

Charlevoix describes the first *flibustiers* as going out in canoes with twenty-five or thirty men, without pilot or provisions, to capture pearl-fishers and surprise small cruisers. If they succeeded, they went to Tortuga, bought a vessel, and started 150 strong, going to Cuba to take in salt turtle, or to Port Margot or Bayaha for dried pork or beef—dividing all upon the *compagnon à bon lot* principle. They always said public prayer before starting on an expedition, and returned solemn thanks to God for victory. A Jesuit writer says:

> They were at first so crowded in their boats that they had scarcely room to lie down; and, as they practised no economy in eating, they were always short of food. They were also

night and day exposed to the inclemency of the weather, and yet loved so much the independence in which they lived, that no one murmured. Some sang when others wished to sleep, and all were by turns compelled to bear these inconveniences without complaint. But one may imagine men so little at their ease spared no pains to gain more comforts; that the sight of a larger and more convenient vessel gave them courage sufficient to capture it; and that hunger deprived them of all sense of the danger of procuring food. They attacked all they met without a thought, and boarded as soon as possible. A single volley would have sunk their vessels; but they were skilful in manoeuvre, their sailors were very active, and they presented to the enemy nothing but a prow full of fusiliers, who, firing through the portholes, struck the gunners with terror. Once on board, nothing could prevent them becoming masters of a ship, however numerous the crew. The Spaniards' blood grew cold when those whom they called, and looked upon as, demons came in sight, and they frequently surrendered at once in order to obtain quarter. If the prize was rich their lives were spared; but if the cargo proved poor, the buccaneers often threw the crew into the sea in revenge.

Their favourite coasts were the Caraccas, Carthagena, Nicaragua, and Campeachy, where the ports were numerous and well frequented. Their best harbours at the Caraccas were Cumana, Canagote, Coro, and Maracaibo; at Carthagena, La Rancheria, St. Martha, and Portobello. Round Cuba they watched for vessels going from New Spain to Maracaibo. If going, they found them laden with silver; if returning, full of cocoa. The prizes to the Caraccas were laden with the lace and manufactures of Spain; those from Havannah, with leather, Campeachy wood, cocoa, tobacco, and Spanish coin.

The dress of the buccaneer sailors must have varied with the changes of the age. Retaining their red shirts and leather sandals as the working dress of their brotherhood, we find them donning all the splendour rummaged from Spanish cabins, now wearing the plumed hat and laced sword-belt of Charles the Second's reign, and now the tufts of ribbons of the perfumed court of Louis Quatorze.

Sprung from all nations and all ranks, some of them prided themselves upon the rough beard, bare feet, and belted shirt of the rudest seaman, while others, like Grammont and De Graff, flaunted in the richest costumes of their period. They must have passed from the long cloak and loose cassock of the Stuart reign to the jack-boots and Dutch dress of William of Orange; from the laced and flowing Steenkirk to the fringed cock-hat and deep-flapped waistcoat of Queen Anne. In the English translation of Esquemeling, Barthelemy Portugues, one of the earliest sea-rovers, is represented as having his long, lank hair parted in the centre and falling on his shoulders, and his *moustachios* long and rough. He wears a plain embroidered coat with a neck-band, and carries in his arms a short, broad sabre, unsheathed, as was the habit with many buccaneer chiefs. Roche Braziliano appears in a plain hunter's shirt, the strings tying it at the neck being fastened in a bow. Lolonnois has the same shirt, showing at his neck and puffing through the openings of his sleeve, and he carries a naked broadsword with a shell guard. In the portrait of Sir Henry Morgan we see much more affectation of aristocratic dress. He has a rich coat of Charles the Second's period, a laced cravat tied in a fringed bow with long ends, and his broad sword-belt is stiff with gold lace. The hunter's shirt, however, still shows through the slashed sleeves.

CHAPTER 4

Peter the Great— the First Buccaneer

The date of the first organized buccaneer expedition is uncertain. We only know that about the year 1654, a large party of buccaneers, French and English, joined in an expedition to the continent. They ascended, in canoes, a river on the Mosquito Shore, a small distance on the south side of Cape Gracias à Dios, and after labouring for a month against a strong stream, full of torrents, left their boats and marched to the town of Nueva Segovia, which they plundered, and then returned down the river.

It is difficult to trace the exact beginning of the *flibustiers*, or, as they were soon called, the buccaneers. According to most writers, the first successful adventurer known at Tortuga was Pierre-le-Grand (Peter the Great). He was a native of Dieppe, and his greatest enterprise was the capture of the vice-admiral of the Spanish *flota*, while lying off Cape Tiburon, on the west side of Hispaniola. This he accomplished in a canoe with only twenty-eight companions. Setting out by the Carycos he surprised his unwieldy antagonist in the channel of Bahama, which the Spaniards had hitherto passed in perfect security. He had been now a long time at sea without obtaining any prize worth taking, his provisions were all but exhausted, and his men, in danger of starving, were almost reduced to despair. While hanging over the gunwale, listless and discontented, the buccaneers suddenly spied a large vessel of the Spanish fleet, separated from the rest and fast approaching them. They instantly sailed towards her to ascertain her strength, and though they found it to be vastly superior to theirs, partly from despair and partly from cupidity they resolved at once to take it or die in the attempt. It was but to die a little quicker if they failed, and the blood in their veins might as well be shed in a moment as slowly stagnate with famine. If they did not conquer they would die, but if they did not attack, and escaped notice, they would also perish, and by the most painful and lingering of deaths. Being now come so near that flight was impossible, they took a solemn oath to their captain to stand by him to the last, and neither to flinch nor skulk, partly hoping that the enemy was insufficiently armed, and that they might still master her. It was in the dusk of the evening, and the coming darkness facilitated their boarding, and concealed the disadvantage of numbers. While they got their arms ready they ordered their *chirurgeon* to bore a hole in the sides of the boat, in order that the utter hopelessness of their situation might impel them to more daring self-devotion, that they might be forced to attack more vigorously and board more quickly. But their courage needed no such incitement. With no other arms than a sword in one hand and a pistol in the other, they immediately climbed up the sides of the Spaniard and made their way pell-mell to the state cabin. There they found the captain and his officers playing at cards. Setting a pistol to their breasts, they commanded them to deliver up the ship. The Spaniards, surprised to hear the buccaneers below, not having seen them board, and seeing no boat by which they could have arrived (for the surgeon had now sunk it, and rejoined his friends through a porthole), cried out, in an agony of superstitious fear, "Jesu, bless us, these are devils!" thinking the men had fallen from the clouds, or had been shaken from some shooting star. In the mean time Peter's kinsfolk fought their way into the gunroom, seized the arms, killed a few sailors who snatched up swords, and drove the rest under hatches.

That very morning some of the Spanish sailors had told their captain that a pirate boat was gaining upon them, but when he came up to see, and beheld so small a craft, he laughed at their fears of a mere cockle shell, and went down again, despising any vessel, though it were as big and strong as their own. Upon a second alarm, late in the day, when his lieutenant asked him if he should not get a cannon or two ready, he grew angry, and replied,

"No, no, rig the crane out, and hoist the boat aboard." Peter, having taken this rich prize, detained as many of the Spanish seamen as he needed, and put the rest on shore in Hispaniola, which was close at hand. The vessel was full of provisions and great riches, and Pierre steered at once for France, never returning to resume a career so well begun.

The news of this capture set Tortuga in an uproar. The planters and hunters of Hispaniola burned to follow up a profession so glorious and so profitable. It had been discovered now that a man's fortune could be made by one single scheme of daring and enterprise. Not being able to purchase or hire boats at Tortuga, they set forth in their canoes to seek them elsewhere. Some began cruising about Cape de Alvarez, carrying off small Spanish vessels that carried hides and tobacco to the Havannah. Returning with their prizes to Tortuga, they started again for Campeachy or New Spain, where they captured richer vessels of greater burden. In less than a month they had brought into harbour two plate vessels, bound from Campeachy to the Caraccas, and two other ships of great size. In two years no less than twenty buccaneer vessels were equipped at Tortuga, and the Spaniards, finding their losses increase and transport becoming precarious, despatched two large men-of-war to defend the coast.

The next scourge of the Spaniard in these seas was Pierre François, a native of Dunkirk, whose combinative, far-seeing genius and dauntless heart soon raised him above the level of the mere footpads of the ocean. His little brigantine, with a picked crew of twenty-six men—hunters by sea and land—cruised generally about the Cape de la Vela, waiting for merchant ships on their way from Maracaibo to Campeachy. Pierre had now been a long time afloat and taken no prize, the usual prelude to great enterprises amongst these men, who defied all dangers and all enemies. The provisions were running short, the boat was leaky, the captain moody and silent, and the crew half mutinous. To return empty-handed to Tortuga was to be a butt for every sneerer, a victim to unrelenting creditors; to the men beggary, to Pierre a loss of fame and all future promotion. But, there being a perfect equality in these boats, the crews seldom rose in open rebellion; and as every one had a voice in the proposal of a scheme, there was no one to rail at if the scheme failed. At last, amid this suspense, more tedious than a tropic calm, one more daring or more far-seeing than the rest stood up and suggested a visit to the pearl-fishings at the Rivière de la Hache. History, always drowsy at critical periods, does not say if François was the proposer of this scheme or not. We may be sure he was a sturdy seconder, and that the plan was carried amid wild cheering and waving of hats and guns and swords enough to scare the sharks floating hungrily round the boat, and frighten the glittering flying-fish back into the sea. These Rancheria fishings were at a rich bank of pearl to which the people of Carthagena sent annually twelve vessels, with a man-of-war convoy, generally a Spanish *armadilla* with a crew of 200 men, and carrying twenty-four pieces of cannon. Every vessel had two or three Negro slaves on board, who dived for the pearls. These men seldom lived long, and were frequently ruptured by the exertion of holding breath a quarter of an hour below the waves. The time for diving was from October till May, when the north winds were lulled and the sea calm.

The large vessel was called the *Capitana*, and to this the proceeds of the day were brought every night, to prevent any risk of fraud or theft. Rather than return unsuccessful, Pierre resolved to swoop down upon this guarded covey, and carry off the ship of war in the sight of all the fleet; a feat as dangerous as the abduction of an Irish heiress on the brink of marriage. He found the fishing boats riding at anchor at the mouth of the River de la Hache, and the man-of-war scarcely half a league distant. In the morning he approached them, and they, seeing him hovering at a distance like a kite above a farmyard, ran under shelter of their guardian's guns, like chickens under the hen's wing. Keeping still at a distance, they supposed he was afraid to approach, and soon allowed their fears to subside. The captain of the *armadilla*, however, took the precaution of sending three armed men on board each boat, believing the pearls the object of the buccaneer, and left his own vessel almost defenceless. The hour had come. Furling his sails, Pierre rowed along the coast, feigning himself a Spanish vessel from Maracaibo, and when near the pearl bank, suddenly attacked the vice-admiral with eight guns and sixty men, and commanded him to surrender. The Spaniards, although surprised, made a good defence, but at last surrendered after half an-hour's hand-to-hand fight, before the almost unmanned *armadilla* could approach to render assistance. Pierre now sank his own boat, which had only been kept afloat by incessant working at the pumps. Many men would have rested satisfied with such a prize, but Pierre knew no Capua, and "thought naught done while aught remained to do." He at once resolved, by a stratagem, to capture the *armadilla*, and then the whole fleet would be his own. The night being very dark, and the wind high and favourable, he weighed anchor, forcing the prisoners to help his own crew. The man-of-war, seeing one of its fleet sailing, followed, fearing that the sailors were absconding with the pearls. As soon as it approached, Pierre made all the Spaniards, on pain of instant death, shout out "*Victoria, victoria!* we have taken the *ladrones*," upon which the man-of-war drew off, promising to send for the prisoners in the morning. Laughing in his sleeve, Pierre gave orders for hoisting all sail, and stood away for the open sea, putting forth all his strength to get out of sight by daybreak. But the blood of the murdered Spaniards, yet hot upon the deck, was crying to heaven against him, and he was pursued. He had not got a league before the wind fell, and his ship lay like a log on the water, just within sight of his pursuers, who kept a long way off, burning with impatience and shame, and fretting like hounds in leash when the boar breaks out. About evening the wind rose, after much invocatory whistling, many prayers, many curses. Pierre, ignorant of the power of his prize, and what canvas she could bear, hoisted at random every stitch of sail and ran for his life, pursued by the *armadilla*, wrathful, white-winged, and swift. Like many a fleet runner, Pierre stumbled in his very eagerness for speed. He overloaded his vessel with sail. The wind grew higher, and howled like an avenging spirit, and his mainmast fell with the crash of a thunder-split oak. But Pierre held firm; he threw his prisoners into the hold, nailed down the hatches, and, trusting to night to escape, stood boldly at bay. He despaired of meeting force by force, having only twenty-two sound men, the rest being, before long, either killed or wounded. All in vain; the great bird of prey bore down upon him like a hawk upon a throstle, gaining, gaining every moment. Pierre defended himself courageously, and at last surrendered on condition. The Spanish captain agreed that the buccaneers should not be employed in carrying, building-stones for three or four years like mere negroes, but should be set safe on dry land. As yet, the deep animosity of the two races had not sprung up. The prize they so nearly bore off contained above 100,000 pieces of eight in pearls, besides provisions and goods. At first the captain would have put them all to the sword, but his crew persuaded him to keep his word. The Frenchmen were then thrust down with curses into the same dark hold from whence the imprisoned Spaniards were now released; so "*the whirligig of time brings about its revenge.*" When the crestfallen buccaneers were brought before the governor of Carthagena, an outcry arose among the populace that the robbers should all be hung, to atone for an *alfarez* whom they had killed, and who, they said, was worth the whole French nation put together. The governor, however, though he did not put them to death, ungenerously broke the terms of his agreement, and compelled his prisoners to work at the fortifications of St. Francisco, in his own island. After about three years of this painful slavery, amid the jeers and contumely of the very negroes, they were sent to Spain, and from thence escaping one by one to France, made their way back to the Spanish main, more eager than ever to revenge their wrongs at the hands of a nation whose riches furnished a ready means of expiation, and whose cowardice rendered them incapable of frequent retaliation.

The third hero on our stage, equally bold and no less memorable, was Barthelemy Portugues, a native of Portugal, as his name implied. Roused by the rumours of adventures which insured gold and glory, Barthelemy (no saint, and certainly more ready to flay others than to submit to flaying) sought out a small vessel at Jamaica, and fitted it up at his own expense. As only his most remarkable enterprises are recorded it is probable, from his having money, that he was already known as a successful *flibustier*. This boat he armed with four three-pounders, and embarked with a crew of thirty men. Leaving Kingston with a good wind at his back, he set sail to cruise off Cape de Corriente, which he knew was the high road where he should meet vessels coming from the Caraccas or Carthagena, on their way to Campeachy, New Spain, or the Havannah. He had not been long beating about the Cape—a point rounded with as much care by a Spanish merchantman, afraid of buccaneers, as Cape St. Vincent was by the European captain, dreading the Salee rovers—

before a great vessel, bound from Maracaibo and Carthagena to the Havannah, hove in sight. It had a crew of seventy men, and carried twenty guns, and many passengers and marines. The *flibustiers*, thinking a Spaniard so well armed and manned to be more than their match, held one of their republican councils round the mast, and refused to attack unless the captain wished. He decided that no opportunity should be lost, for that nothing in any part of the world could be won without risk. They instantly gave chase to the vessel that quietly awaited their approach, as astonished at the attack as a swallow would be if it were pursued by a gnat. Receiving one flaming broadside, noisy but harmless, the half-stripped rovers instantly threw themselves on board, but were repulsed by the Spaniards, who were numerous, hopeful, and brave. Returning to their vessel and throwing down their cutlass for the musket, they kept up a close fire of small arms for five hours without ceasing. Every gunner and every reefer was picked off, the decks were red, the return fire grew slack as the defence grew weaker, and the foe's proud courage cooled; the buccaneers again threw themselves on board, and made themselves masters of the ship, with the loss of only ten men and four wounded. They had now only fifteen men left to navigate a vessel containing nearly forty prisoners. This number was all that were left alive, and of these many were maimed with shot wounds or gashed with sword cuts. The conquerors' first act was to throw the dead overboard, officer and sailor, just as they fell, stripping off the jewels and ransacking pockets for the dead men's doubloons. The living Spaniards, wounded and dying, they drove into one small boat, and gave them their liberty, afraid to keep them as prisoners and unwilling to shed their blood. They then set to work to splice the rigging and piece the sails, and lastly, to rummage for the plunder. They found the value of their prize to be 75,000 crowns, besides 120,000 pounds of cocoa, worth about 5,000 additional. Having refitted the shattered vessel, they would have sailed round the island of Jamaica, but a contrary wind and current obliged them to steer to Cape St. Anthony, the west extremity of Cuba, where they landed and took in water, of which they were in great want.

They had scarcely hoisted sail to resume their course, probably intending to return to port to sell their spoil before starting afresh, when they unexpectedly fell upon three large vessels coming from New Spain to the Havannah, who gave chase, as certain of victory as three greyhounds bounding after a single hare. The *flibustiers*, heavy laden with plunder, and unable to make way, were almost instantly retaken, falling as easy a prey as a gorged wolf does to the hunter. In a few hours the buccaneers were under hatches, stripped of even their very clothes, and counting the moments before execution—the Puritan doling out his hymns, the Catholic muttering his Miserere, and the rude cow-killer vowing vengeance if he could but escape. Two evenings after a storm arose and separated the leash of armed merchantmen.

The vessel containing the luckless Portugues arrived first at St. Francisco, Campeachy. Barthelemy, who spoke Spanish, had been well treated by the captain, who did not know what a prize he had taken. The news of the capture soon ran through the town, the captain became a public man, the bells rang, the people flocked to see the caged lions, and the principal merchants of the place crowded to congratulate him on his success. Among the curious and timid visitors was one who recognised Barthelemy, in spite of all his oaths and denials, and demanded his surrender. No hate can match the hate of injured avarice and frustrated cupidity.

"This is Barthelemy the Portuguese," he told every one, "the most wicked rascal in the world, and who has done more harm to Spanish commerce than all the other pirates put together."

He ran everywhere and declared they had at last got hold of the man so famous for the many insolences, robberies, and murders he had committed on their coast, and by whose cruel hands many of their kinsmen had perished. The captain, rather distrustful—somewhat favourable to Barthelemy, perhaps, considering him as a brother seaman, worth any ten land-lubbers, and annoyed at the arrogance of the merchant's demand—refused to surrender the Portuguese, or to send him on shore. The enraged merchant upon this proceeded to the governor, who, listening to his complaint, sent to demand the buccaneers in the king's name. He was instantly arrested, spite of the captain's entreaties, and placed on board another vessel, heavily ironed, for fear he should escape, as he had done on a former occasion. A gibbet was erected, and the next day it was resolved to lead him at once from his cabin to the place of execution, without the hypocritical and useless ceremony of even a prejudged trial. For some time Portugues remained uncertain of his fate, till a Spanish sailor (for he seems to have had the power of winning friends) told him that the gibbet was already putting together, and the rope was ready noosed. In that delay was his safety; that very night he resolved to escape, or perish by a quicker or less disgraceful death. No doubt, with that strange mixture of religion remaining in the minds of most buccaneers, he prayed to God or the saints to aid him.

He soon freed himself from his irons. Discovering in his cabin two of those large earthen jars in which wine was brought from Spain to the Indies, he closed over the orifices, and hung them to his side with cords, being probably unable to swim, and the distance too far to the shore. Finding that he could not elude the vigilance of the sleepless sentinel that paced at his door, he stabbed him with a knife he had secretly purchased, and let himself noiselessly down, from the mainchains into the water, floating to land without the splash that a swimmer would have made in still water. Once on land he concealed himself in a wood, prepared to bear any danger, and glad at heart to endure starvation rather than suffer a public and shameful death. He was too cunning to set off at once on a route that would be explored, but hid himself among trees half covered with water, in order to prevent the possibility of his being tracked by the maroon bloodhounds—a common stratagem with the moss-troopers, who found the sound of running water drown the noise of their movements and the murmur of their breathing, and destroy all traces of their track. Bruce and Wallace had long before escaped by the artifice that now saved a robber and a murderer. His must have been anxious nights, varied by the shouts of negroes, the deep bay of the dogs, the oaths of the Spaniards, the discharge of fire-arms, the toll of the alarm bell, the glare of beacons; and the flash of torches. For these three days he lived on yams and other roots growing around him. From a tree in which he sometimes harboured he had the satisfaction of seeing his pursuers search the wood in vain, and finally relinquish the pursuit.

Believing that the danger had now in some degree decreased, the lion-hearted sailor determined to push for the Golpho Triste, forty leagues distant, where he hoped to find a buccaneer ship careening. He arrived there after fourteen days of incredible endurance. He started in the evening from the seashore, within sight of the lit-up town where a black gibbet was still standing bodingly against the sky. His forced marches were full of terrible dangers and perils. He had no provisions with him, and nothing but a small calabash of water hung at his side. Hunger and thirst strode beside him, the wild beast glared in his path, the Spanish voices seemed to pursue him. His subsistence was the raw shell-fish that he found washed among the rocks upon the shore, fresh or putrid he had no time to consider. He had streams to ford, dark with caymans, and he had to traverse woods where the jaguars howled. Whenever he came to a stream unusually dark, deep, and dangerous, and where no ford was visible (for he could not swim), he threw in large stones as he waded to scare away the crocodiles that lurked round the shallows. In one spot he travelled five or six leagues swinging like a sloth from bough to bough of a pathless wood of mangroves, never once setting foot upon the ground. His day's progress was often scarcely perceptible. At one river more than usually deep he found an old plank, which had drifted ashore when the seaman was washed off, and from this he obtained some large rusty nails. Extracting these nails, he sharpened them on a stone with great labour, and used them to cut down some branches of trees, which he joined together with osiers and pliable twigs, and slowly constructed a raft. Hunger, thirst, heat, and fear beset him round; and the voice of the sea, always on his right hand, came to him like the hungry howl of death. In these fourteen nights he must have literally tasted death, and anticipated the horrors of hell.

"*Fortune favours the brave.*" He found a buccaneer vessel in the gulf, and he was saved. The crew were old companions of his, newly arrived from Jamaica and from England. He related to them his adversities and his misfortunes. All listened eagerly to adventures that might tomorrow be their own. He thought alone of revenge, and told them that if they chose he would give them a ship worth a whole fleet of their canoes. He desired their help. He only asked for one boat and thirty men. With these he promised to return to Campeachy and capture the vessel that had taken him but fourteen days before. They soon granted his request, the boat was at once equipped, and he sailed along the coast, passing for a smuggler bringing contraband goods. In eight days he arrived at Campeachy, undauntedly and without noise boarding the vessel at midnight. They were challenged by the sentinel. Barthelemy, who spoke good Spanish, replied, in a low voice, "We are part of the crew returning with goods from land, on which no duty has been paid."

The sentinel, hoping for a share, or at least some hush-money, did not repeat the question. Allowing him no time to detect the trick, they stabbed him, and, rushing forward, overpowered the watch. Cutting the cable, they surprised the sleepers in their cabins, and, weighing anchor, soon compelled the Spaniards, by a resolute attack, to surrender; and, setting sail from the port, rejoined their exulting comrades, unpursued by any vessel. Great was the joy of the adventurers in becoming possessors of so brave a ship. Portugues was now again rich and powerful, though but lately a condemned prisoner in the very vessel upon whose deck he now stood the lord of all. With this cargo of rich merchandise Barthelemy intended to achieve enterprises, for though the Spaniards' plate had been all disembarked at Campeachy, the booty was still large. But let no hunter halloo till he is out of the wood, and no sailor laugh till he gets into port. While he was making his voyage to Jamaica, and already counting his profits as certain, a terrible storm arose off the isle of Pinos, on the south of Cuba, which drove his prize against the Jardine rocks, where she went to pieces. Portugues and his companions escaped in a canoe to Jamaica, and before long started on new adventures. What eventually became of him we know not, but we are told that "*he was never fortunate after.*" Whether he swung on the Campeachy gibbet after all, became a prey to the Darien man-eater, was pierced by the Greek bullet, or was devoured by the sea, long expecting its victim, we shall never know. He sails away from Kingston with colours flying, and wanders away into unknown deeps.

Of this wild man's end nothing was ever known. He was living at Jamaica when Esquemeling left for England. His bones, perhaps, still whiten on some Indian bay, with the sea moaning around that nameless dust for ever—doomed to destroy man, but lamenting the very desolation it occasions.

This Roche Braziliano (or Roc, the Brazilian, as the English adventurers called him,) was born at Groninghen, in East Friezeland;

and his own name being forgotten, he was called the Brazilian, because his parents had been Dutch settlers in the Brazils. Roche was taught the Indian and Portuguese languages at an early age, and, when the latter nation retook the Brazils, removed with his parents to the French Antilles, where he learned French. Disliking the nation, he passed into Jamaica. Here he learned to speak English, and, settling among our more congenial race, became attached to the country of his adoption. But he had lingered too long in the desert to have much taste for even Goshen. He had already acquired the Arab's love for wandering, and poverty combined to lead him into an adventurer's ship. Into this mode of life all restless talent and love of enterprise was now driven.

After only three voyages, Roche became commander of a brig whose crew had mutinied from their captain and offered him the command. In a few days, this almost untried man had the good fortune to capture a large vessel coming from New Spain with a great quantity of plate on board. On his arrival in Jamaica, Roc became at once the acknowledged leader of all the Vikinger of the Spanish main—their first sailor, their hero, and their model. He soon grew so terrible that the Spanish mothers used his name as a hush-word to their children.

Roc is described as having a stalwart and vigorous body. He was of ordinary height, but stout and muscular. His face was wide and short, his cheek-bones prominent, and his eyebrows bushy and of unusual size. He was skilful in the use of all Indian and Catholic (Spanish) arms, a good hunter, a good fisherman, and a good shot—as skilful a pilot as he was a brave soldier. He generally carried a naked sabre resting on his arm, and made no scruple of cutting down any of his crew who were idle, mutinous, or cowardly. He was much dreaded even in Jamaica, and particularly when drunk, says his candid biographer. At those times he would frequently run a-muck through the streets, beating and wounding any one he met, especially if they dared to oppose or resist him. In his sober moments he was esteemed and feared, but he too often abandoned himself to every sort of debauchery.

In Roc we see the first indication of a new phase of buccaneering life—*a fanatical hatred of the Spaniard*. The sailor, at first a mere privateersman at sea, and a hunter on shore, was now a legal robber, with a spice of the crusader: a chivalrous Vendetta feeling had become superadded to the mere love of booty. A thirst for gold had proved irresistible: what would it be now when it became heightened by a thirst for blood?

To the Spaniards Roc was always very barbarous and cruel, out of an inveterate hatred to that nation. He seldom gave them quarter, and treated them with untiring ferocity. He taxed his invention for new modes of torture, revenging upon them by a rather indirect mode of retaliation the wrongs inflicted upon his parents by the Portuguese. He is said to have even roasted alive some of his prisoners on wooden spits, like *boucaned* boars, because they refused to disclose the hog-yards where he might victual his ships. By the Spaniards he was reported to be really an apostate outlaw of their own nation, this being the only way in which they could account for his needless and useless cruelties.

On one occasion, as he was cruising on the coast of Campeachy, a dismal tempest, says the chronicler, "surprised him so violently" that his ship was wrecked, himself and his crew only escaping with their muskets, a little powder, and a few bullets, much more useful, however, than gold on such a coast. They reached shore not far from Golpho Triste, the scene of Barthelemy's escape. Roc was not the man to be cast down by an accident no more regarded by true adventurers than the upsetting of a coach by an ordinary traveller. Getting ashore in a canoe, he determined to march quickly along the coast, and repair to the gulf, a well-known haunt of the members of their craft. Roc bade his men be of good heart, and he would bring them safe out of every danger, and, giving them hope, the promise was already half accomplished. Getting on the main road, they proceeded on their march through a hostile country, with the air of men who had conquered the whole Indies. They had already reached a desert track, and were grown fatigued, hungry, and thirsty, when some Indians gave the alarm, and the Spaniards were soon down upon them, to the number of one hundred well-armed and well-mounted horsemen, while the buccaneers were but thirty men.

As soon as Roc saw the enemy, the Brazilian cried out, "Courage, *mes frères*, we are hungry now, but, Caramba, you shall soon have a dinner if you follow me," and then, perceiving the imminent danger, he encouraged his men, telling them they were better soldiers than the Spaniards, and that they ought rather to die fighting under their arms as became men of courage, than to surrender, and have their lives pressed out by the extremest torments. Seeing their commander's courage, the wrecked men resolved to attack, instead of waiting tamely for the enemy's approach, and, facing the Spaniards, they at once discharged their guns so dexterously, that they killed a horseman with almost every shot. After an hour's hot fighting, the Spaniards fled. The adventurers lost only two men, two more being lamed. Stripping the dead, they took from them every valuable, and despatched the wounded with the butt-end of their muskets. They then feasted on the wine and brandy they found in their knapsacks, or at their saddle bows, and declared themselves ready to attack as many again; and having finished their meal, they mounted on the stray horses, and proceeded on their march.

The victors had not gone more than two days' journey before they caught sight of a well-manned Spanish vessel, lying off the shore beneath. It had come to protect the boats which landed the men who cut the Campeachy dyewood. Roc saw that the poultry-yard knew nothing of the kite that was hovering near. He instantly concealed his band, and went with six *comerades* into a thicket near the beach to watch. Here they passed the night. At daybreak the Spaniards, pulling to shore in their canoe, were received in a courteous but unexpected manner by the buccaneers. Roc instantly summoned his men, boarded and took the vessel. The little man-of-war contained little plate, but, what was of equal use, two hundred weight of salt, with which he salted down a few of the horses which he killed. The remaining horses he gave to his Spanish prisoners, telling them laughingly, that the beasts were worth more than the vessel, and that once on their backs on dry land no rascal need fear drowning.

A buccaneer's first thought on obtaining one prize was to gain another as soon as possible. Roc had still twenty-six man by him, and a good vessel to move in. He soon took a ship, bound to Maracaibo from New Spain, laden with merchandise and money designed to buy a cargo of cocoa-nuts. With this they repaired to Jamaica, letting the vessel scorch in harbour till their money was all gone. Having spent all, Braziliano put out to sea again, impatient of poverty and resolved to trust to fortune, for he was her favourite child. He sailed for the rendezvous at Campeachy, and after fifteen days started in a canoe to hover round the port, beating about like a hawk in search of prey.

He was soon after captured and taken with his men before a Spanish governor, who cast them into a dungeon, intending to hang them every one. But fortune only hid her smiles for a moment, and had not deserted him. Roc, as subtle as he was intrepid, had not yet exhausted his wiles. He was at bay and the dogs were gathered round, but they had not yet got him by the throat. He made friends with the slave who brought him food, and promised to give him money to buy his freedom if he would aid his scheme. He did not wish to compromise the slave: he only wished him to be the bearer of a letter to the governor. The slave told the governor that he had been put on shore in the bay by some buccaneers and had been ordered to deliver the letter. The letter was an angry threat, supposed to be indicted by the captain of a French vessel lying in the offing. It advised the governor "to have a care how he used those persons he had in his custody, for in case he should do them any harm, they did swear unto him, they would never give quarter unto any person of the Spanish nation that should fall into their hands." The governor, lifting up his eyes and twisting his *moustachios* at the threat, was intimidated, and became anxious to get rid as soon as possible of such dangerous prisoners, for Campeachy had already been taken once by the adventurers, and he feared what mischief the companions who visited Spanish towns might do. He began now to treat his prisoners with greater kindness, and on the first opportunity sent for them, and, exacting a simple oath that they would abandon piracy, shipped them on board the galleon fleet bound for Spain. Roc, with his usual versatility, soon made himself so much beloved that the Spanish captain offered to take him as a sailor, and he accepted the offer. During this single voyage to Spain he made a sum of no less than 500 crowns by selling the officers fish that he struck in the Indian manner with arrows and harpoons from the main-chains. His *comerades*, whom he never forgot, were treated with consideration on his account.

On his arrival in Spain, Roc, in spite of his oath, which had been exacted by fear of death, and therefore absolvable by any priest, lost no time in getting back to Jamaica, where he arrived without a vessel to call his own, but in other respects in better circumstances than when he left. He joined himself at once to two French adventurers.

The chief of these, named Tributor, was an old buccaneer of great experience. They determined to land upon the peninsula of Yucatan, in hopes of taking the town of Merida. Roc, who had been there before as a prisoner, and had doubtless proposed the scheme, served as guide, but some Indians got upon their trail and alarmed the Spaniards, who fortified the place and prepared for an attack. On the buccaneers' arrival they found the town well garrisoned and defended, and while they were still debating whether to advance or retreat, the question was abruptly decided for them by a body of the enemy's horsemen who fell upon their rear, cut half of them to pieces, and made the rest prisoners. The wily Roc, never taken much by surprise, contrived to escape, but old Tributor and his men were all captured. Oexmelin expresses his wonder at Roc's escape, because he had always held it vile cowardliness to allow another man to strike before himself. "Hitherto he had been the last to yield, even when he was overborne by enemies, and had been heard to say that he preferred death to dishonour." *Nemo mortalium, &c.*

CHAPTER 5

Lolonnois the Cruel

The Spanish ships now decreased in number, merchants relinquishing a trade so uncertain and perilous. The consequence of this was that the buccaneers, finding their sea cruises grow less profitable, began to venture upon the mainland, and attack towns and even cities.

The first buccaneer who distinguished himself in this wider field of action was Francis Lolonnois. He was born among the sands of Olonne, in Poictou, and drew his *nom de guerre* from that wild and fitting birthplace. He quitted France in early life, and embarked at Rochelle as an *engagé* for the Caribbean Islands, where he served the customary slavery of three years. Having heard much during this servitude of the hunters of Hispaniola, he sailed for that island as soon as his apprenticeship had expired, and he was again a free adventurer. He first bound himself as a valet to a hunter, and finally became himself a buccaneer, having now passed through all the usual experiences of a young West Indian colonist. Spending some time upon the savannahs, he became restless and tired of shore, and desirous of enlisting as a freebooter under the red flag. Repairing to Tortuga, the head-quarters of *flibustier* enterprise, he enrolled himself among the rovers of the sea, with whom he made many voyages as simple mariner or companion. From the first day he trod plank he is said to have shown himself destined to attain high distinction, surpassing all the "brothers" in adroitness, agility, and daring.

In these floating republics talent soon rose to the surface. Lolonnois was elected master of a vessel, with which he took many prizes, but at last lost everything by a storm which wrecked his ship, drowned his men, sank his cargo, and cast him bleeding and naked upon a savage shore. His courage and conduct, however, had won the admiration of the Governor of Tortuga, M. de la Place, whose island he had enriched by the frequent sale of prizes, and who launched him again in a new ship to encounter once more all the fury of the sea, the hurricane, and the Spaniard. Fortune was at first favourable to him, and he acquired great riches. His name became so dreaded by the Indians and the Spaniards that they chose rather to die or drown than surrender to one who never knew the word mercy. He never learned how to chain fortune to his mast, and was soon a second time wrecked at Campeachy. The men were all saved, but on reaching land were pursued and killed by the Spaniards. Lolonnois, himself severely wounded, saved his life by a stratagem. Mixing the sand of the shore with the blood flowing from his wounds, he smeared his face and body, and hid himself dexterously under a heap of dead, remaining there till the Spaniards had carried off one or two of his less severely wounded companions into Campeachy. As soon as they were gone he arose with a grim smile from his lurking place among the slain, and betook himself to the woods. He then washed his now stiffened wounds in a river, and bound up his gashes as he could. As soon as they were healed (the flesh of these men soon healed), he put on the dress of a slain Spaniard, and made his way boldly into the neighbouring city. In the suburbs he entered into conversation with some slaves he met, whom he bribed by an offer of freedom if they would obey him and follow his guidance.

They listened to his proposal, and, stealing their master's canoe, brought it to the sea-shore, where Lolonnois lay concealed. But before this the disguised buccaneer had gone rambling fearlessly through the enemy's town, witnessing the rejoicings made at his own supposed death; for his companions, who were kept close prisoners in a dungeon, had been asked what had become of their captain, to which they had always replied that he was dead, upon which the Spaniards lit up bonfires in their open squares, thanking God for their deliverance from so cruel a pirate.

The flames of these fires were red upon the bay when Lolonnois and the slaves pushed off their canoe and made haste to escape. They reached Tortuga in safety, and Lolonnois kept his promise, and set the slaves at liberty—although, if he had been base and worthless enough, he could have refitted his boat with the profits of their sale. He now thought only of revenging himself on the Spaniards for their cruelty in murdering the survivors of a wreck. He spent whole days in considering how he could capture a vessel and restore himself to his former reputation for skill and fortune. By some extraordinary plan, Esquemeling—who writes always with affected horror of the men amongst whom he lived—says, with "craft and subtlety," he soon obtained a third ship, with a crew of twenty-one men and a surgeon. Being well provided with arms and necessaries—how provided by a penniless man it is impossible to guess—he resolved to visit De Los Cayos, a village on the south side of Cuba, where he knew vessels from the Havannah passed to the port of Boca de Estera, where they purchase tobacco, sugar, and hides, coming generally in small boats, for the sea ran very shallow. At this place meat was also obtained to victual the Spanish fleets.

Here Lolonnois was very sanguine of booty, but some fishermen's boats, observing him, alarmed the town. One of these canoes they captured, and, placing in it a crew of eleven men, proceeded to coast about the Bayes du Nord. The buccaneers kept at some distance from each other, in hopes of sooner surrounding their prey, for each of their crews was strong enough to capture any merchant vessel that had not more than fifteen or sixteen unarmed men on board. They remained some months beating off and on Cuba, but caught nothing, although this was the very height of the commercial season. After a long delay of wonder and vexation, they learned the cause of their failure from the crew of a fishing-boat which they captured, who told them that the people of Cayos would not venture to sea because they knew that they were there. It would be dangerous for them to remain, they added, for the chief merchants of the port had instantly despatched a "vessel overland" to the Governor of Havannah, telling him that Lolonnois had come in two canoes to destroy them, and begging him to send and destroy the "*ladrones*." The governor could with difficulty at first be persuaded to listen to the petition, because he had just received letters from

Campeachy bidding him rejoice at the death of that pirate; but, aroused by the continued importunities of his angry petitioners, he at last sent a ship to their relief.

This ship carried ten guns, and had a crew of ninety young, vigorous, and well-armed men, to whom he gave at parting an express command that they should not return into his presence without having first destroyed those pirates. He sent with them a negro hangman, desiring him to kill on the spot all they should take, except Lolonnois, the captain, who was to be brought alive in triumph to the Havannah. The ship had scarcely arrived at Cayos when the pirate, advertised of its approach, came to seek it at its moorings in the river Estera. Lolonnois cried out, when he saw it loom in the distance, "Courage, *mes camarades!* courage, *mes bons frères!* we shall soon be well mounted." Capturing some fishermen busy with their nets, he forced them at night to show him the entrance of the port.

Rowing very quietly in the shadow of the trees that bordered the river's banks and hid their approach, they arrived under the vessel's side a little after two o'clock in the morning—not long before daybreak. The watch on board the ship hailed them, and asked them whence they came and if they had seen any pirates? They made one of the fishermen who guided them reply in Spanish that they had seen no pirates or anything else; and this made the Spaniards believe that Lolonnois had fled at their approach. The buccaneers instantly began to open fire on both sides from their canoes. The Spaniards, who kept good guard, returned the fire, but without much effect, for their enemies lay down flat in their boats, and the trees served them as gabions. The Spaniards fought bravely, in spite of the suddenness and vigour of the attack, and made some use of their great guns. The combat lasted from dawn till midday, the crew of the vessel discharging ineffectual volleys of musketry, which seldom injured the assailants, whose bullets, on the other hand, killed or wounded every moment some of the Havannah youth. When the firing began to slacken, Lolonnois pulled his canoes out into the stream, and boarded the vessel, which almost instantly surrendered.

Those who survived were beaten down under the hatches, while the wounded on the decks received the *coup de grace*. When this had been done, Lolonnois commanded his men to bring up the prisoners one by one from the hold, cutting off their heads as they came up with his own hand, and tasting their blood. The negro hangman, seeing the fate of his predecessors, threw himself passionately at the feet of the buccaneer chief, and exclaimed in Spanish, "If you will not kill me I will tell you the truth." Lolonnois, supposing he had some secret to tell, bade him speak on. But he refused to open his lips further till life were promised him; upon the promise being made, the trembling wretch exclaimed, "Senor *capitan*, *Monsieur*, the governor of the Havannah, not doubting but that this well-armed frigate would have taken the strongest of your vessels, sent me on board to serve as executioner, and to hang all the prisoners that his men took, in order to intimidate your nation, so that they should not dare ever to approach a Spanish vessel."

Esquemeling, who always exaggerates the cruelty of his quondam companions, says, Lolonnois, making the black confess what he thought fit, commanded him to be murdered with the rest; but Oexmelin gives a more probable version. At the negro's mention of his being a hangman he grew furious, and but for his words, "I give thee quarter and even liberty because I promised it thee," would certainly have put him to death. He then slew all the rest of the crew but one man, whom he spared in order to send him back with a letter to the governor of the Havannah. The letter ran thus:

> I have returned your kindness by doing to your men what they designed to do to me and my companions. I shall never henceforward give quarter to any Spaniard whatsoever, and I have great hopes of executing upon your own person the very same punishment I have done upon those you sent against me. It would be better for you to cut your throat than to fall into my power.

The governor, enraged at the loss of his ship and crew, and exasperated by the insolent daring of the letter, swore in the presence of many that he would not grant quarter to any pirate who fell into his hands. Furious that two canoes, with twenty-two half-naked men, should be able to deride the might of Spain in his person, he instantly sent round word to the neighbouring Indian forts to hang all their French and English prisoners, instead of, as usual, embarking them for Spain. The citizens of Havannah, hearing of this imprudent bravado, sent a deputation to the governor to represent to him that, for one Englishman or Frenchman that the Spaniards captured, the buccaneers took every day a hundred of their people, that the men of Havannah were obliged to get their living by trading, that life was far dearer to them than mere money, which was all the buccaneers wanted; and lastly, that all their fishermen would be daily exposed to danger, the buccaneers having frequent opportunity for reprisal. Upon this the angry governor was at last persuaded to bridle his passion and remit the severity of his oath.

Lolonnois, now provided with a good ship, resolved to cruise from port to port to obtain provisions and men. Off Maracaibo he surprised a ship laden with plate, outward-bound to buy cocoa-nuts, and with this prize returned to Tortuga, much to his own satisfaction and the general joy of that strange colony of runaway slaves, disbanded soldiers, hunters, privateersmen, pirates, puritans, and papists. He had not been long in port before he planned an expedition to Maracaibo, joining another adventurer in equipping a body of five hundred men. In Tortuga he found prisoners for guides, and disbanded adventurers resolute enough to be his companions. His partner was Michael le Basque, a buccaneer who had retired very rich, and was now major of the island. He had done great actions in Europe, and bore the repute of being a good soldier. Lolonnois was to rule by sea and Le Basque by land.

Le Basque knew all the avenues of Maracaibo, and had lately taken in a prize two Indians, who knew the port well and offered to act both as pilots and guides. Le Basque had consented to join Lolonnois, struck by the daring and comprehension of his plans, and Lolonnois was overjoyed at the alliance of so tried a man. Notice was instantly given to all the unemployed buccaneers that they were planning a great expedition with much chance of booty. All who were willing to join them were to come by a certain day to the rendezvous either at Tortuga or Bayala, on the north side of Hispaniola; at the latter place he revictualled his fleet, took some French hunters as volunteers into his company, careened his vessels, and procured beef and pork by the chase.

His fleet consisted of eight small ships, of which his own, the largest, carried only twenty pieces of cannon; his crews amounted altogether to about four hundred men. Setting sail from Bayala the last day in July, while doubling Ponta del Espada (Sword Point), the eastern cape of Hispaniola, Lolonnois overtook two Spanish vessels coming from Porto Rico to New Spain, and one of these Lolonnois insisted on capturing with his own hand, sending in his fleet to Savona. The Spaniards, although they had an opportunity for two whole hours, refused to fly, and, being well armed, prepared for a desperate resistance; the combat lasted for three hours. The ship carried sixteen guns, and was manned by fifty fighting men. They found in her a cargo of 120,000 pounds' weight of cocoa, 40,000 pieces of eight, and the value of 10,000 more in jewels. Lolonnois instantly sent this prize back to Tortuga to be unloaded, with orders to return to the rendezvous at Savona. On their way to this place, his vanguard had also been in luck, having met with a Spanish vessel bringing military stores and money from Cumana for the garrisons of Hispaniola. In this vessel, which they took without any resistance, though armed with eight guns, they found 7,000 pounds' weight of powder, a great number of muskets and other arms, together with 12,000 pieces of eight.

These successes encouraged the adventurers, and to superstitious men seemed like promises of good fortune and success. The generosity of the governor of Tortuga also tended to heighten their spirits. M. D'Ogeron, the French governor, had been greatly delighted at the early arrival of so rich a prize, worth, at the lowest calculation, 180,000 *livres*, and threw open all his store-houses for the use of the prize crew. Ordering her to be quickly unloaded, he sent her back to Lolonnois full of provisions and necessaries. Many persons who had come from France with the governor now joined an expedition which had begun so auspiciously, desirous of gaining a fortune with the same rapidity as the older colonists. By hazarding a little money a planter could obtain a chance of sharing in the plunder of a distant city without moving from under the shadow of his tamarind tree, and the governor's approval threw an air of legal government patronage over the expedition. D'Ogeron even sent his two nephews on board, young gallants newly arrived from France, and one of whom afterwards ruled the island in the room of his uncle. With a fleet recruited with men in room of those killed by the fever or the Spaniards, and full of hope and spirits, Lolonnois sailed for Maracaibo. His own vessel he gave to his comrade Anthony du Puis, and went himself on board the *Cacaoyere*, as the largest prize was called.

Before sailing, he reviewed his little invincible armada. His own new frigate carried sixteen guns and 120 men. His vice-admiral, Moses Vauclin, had ten guns and ninety men; and his *matelot*, Le Basque, sailed in a vessel called *La Poudrière*, because it contained all the powder, the ammunition, and the money for the sailors' pay. It carried twenty pieces of cannon and ninety men. Pierre le Picard steered a brigantine with forty men. Moses had equipped another of the same size, and the two other smaller vessels were each managed by a crew of thirty men. Every sailor was armed with a good musket, a brace of pistols, and a strong sabre. At this review Lolonnois first disclosed his whole plan, which was to visit Maracaibo, in the province of New Venezuela, and to pillage all the towns that border the lake. He then produced his guides, one of whom had been a pilot over the bar at Maracaibo, and who vouched for the ease with which the attack could be made. Shouts and clamour announced the universal satisfaction at the proposal. They all agreed to follow him, and took an oath that they would obey him implicitly on the penalty of being mulcted of their booty. The usual *chasse-partie*, or buccaneers' agreement, was then drawn up, specifying the exact share that each one should receive of the spoil, from the captain down to the boys of the ships, and not forgetting the wounded and the guides.

Venezuela, or "little Venice," derived its name from its being very low land, and only preserved from frequent inundation by artificial means. At six or seven leagues' distance from the Bay of Maracaibo, or Gulf of Venezuela, are two small islands—the island of the Watch Tower and the island of the Pigeons. Between these two islands runs a channel of fresh water—as wide across as an eight-pound shot can carry, about sixty leagues long, and thirty broad—which empties itself into the sea. On the Isla de las Vigilias stood a hill surmounted by a watch-tower; on the Isla de las Palombas a fort to impede the entrance of vessels, which were obliged to come very near, the channel being narrowed by two sand-banks, which left only fourteen feet water. The sand-drifts were very numerous; some of them, particularly one called El Tablazo, not having more than six feet water. Says Esquemeling:

> West hereof is the city of Maracaibo, very pleasant to the view, its houses being built along the shore, having delightful prospects all round. The city may contain three or four thousand persons, slaves included, all which make a town of reasonable bigness. There are judged to be about 800 persons able to bear arms, all Spaniards. Here are one parish church, well built and adorned, four monasteries, and one hospital. The city is governed by a deputy-governor, substituted by the governor of the Caraccas. The trade here exercised is mostly in hides and tobacco. The inhabitants possess great numbers of cattle and many plantations, which extend thirty leagues in the country, especially towards the great town of Gibraltar, where are gathered great quantities of cocoa nuts, and all other garden fruits, which serve for the regale and sustenance of the inhabitants of Maracaibo, whose territories are much drier than those of Gibraltar. Hither those of Maracaibo send great quantities of flesh, they making returns in oranges, lemons, and other fruits; for the inhabitants of Gibraltar want flesh, not being capable of feeding cows and sheep.

The inner lake within the great bar, so difficult to cross, was fed by upwards of seventy streams, of which several were navigable. The two capes on either side of the gulf were named respectively Cape St. Roman and the Cape of Caquibacoa. The east side, though frequently flooded, was unhealthy, but very fertile, something resembling the Maremma, where, according to an Italian proverb, a man gets rich in six months and dies in seven.

In the bay itself, ten or twelve leagues from the lake, are the two islands of Onega and Las Monges. On the east side, near the *embouchure*, there was a fishermen's village called Barbacoa, where the Indians lived in trees to escape the floods; for, after great rains, the lands were often overflowed in broad tracts of two or three leagues. A few miles from this was the town of Gibraltar, where the best cocoa in the Indies was grown, as well as the celebrated "priests' tobacco." Beyond this twenty leagues of jurisdiction, rose mountains perpetually covered with snow, contrasting remarkably with the swampy fields and the rich tropical vegetation of the well-irrigated district below. On the other side of these mountains lay the mother city of Merida, between which, during the summer alone, mules carried merchandise to Gibraltar; the cocoa and tobacco of Merida being exchanged for Peruvian flour and the fruits of Gibraltar. Near this latter town were rich plantations and wooded districts, abounding with the tall cedars from which the Indians scooped out solid *piraguas*, or canoes, capable of carrying thirty tons, which were rigged with one large sail.

The territory of Gibraltar was flat, and naturally fertile, watered by rivers and brooks, besides being artificially irrigated by small channels, necessary in the frequent droughts. Everything desirable for food and pleasant to the sight grew here in abundance, the air was filled with birds as beautiful as wandering blossoms, and the rivers teemed with many-coloured fish. But into this Indian Paradise death had entered, and these swamps were the lairs of the deadliest fevers that devastate humanity. In the rainy season the merchants left Gibraltar, just as the rich do Rome, and retired to Merida or Maracaibo to escape the pestilence that walked not merely in darkness but even in the bright noon. At six leagues from this town and its 1,500 inhabitants, ran a river navigable by vessels of fifty tons' burthen.

Maracaibo itself had a spacious and secure port, and was well adapted for building vessels, owing to the abundance of timber in the neighbourhood. In the small island of Borrica were fed great numbers of goats, which were bred chiefly for their skins. In curious contradistinction to all this bustle of commerce, life, and wealth, on the south-east border of the lake lived the Bravo-Indians, a savage race, who had never been subdued by the Spaniard. They also, like the fishermen, dwelt in huts built in the branches of the mangrove trees at the very edge of the water, safe from the floods, and from the equally annoying, though less fatal, visitation of the mosquitoes. Beyond them to the west spread a dry and arid country—where nothing but cacti and stunted, bitter shrubs grew, so thorny as to be almost impassable by the traveller—waste and barren. Here the Spaniards pastured a few flocks, and the only houses were the huts of the armed shepherds who tended the lonely herds. These cattle were killed chiefly for their fat and hides, the flesh being left for the flocks of merchant birds—a sort of vulture, four or five of whom would pick an ox to the bone in a day or two.

Lolonnois, arriving at one of the islands in the gulf, landed and took in provisions, not wishing to arrive at the bar till daybreak, in hopes of surprising the fort; and anchoring, out of sight of the watch-tower weighed anchor in the evening from the island of Onega, and sailed all night, but was seen by the sentinels, who immediately made signals to the fort, which discharged its cannon and announced the approach of an enemy.

Mooring off the bar, Lolonnois lost no time in landing to attack the fort that guarded the very door through which he must pass. The batteries consisted of simple gabions or baskets masked with turf, and concealing fourteen pieces of cannon and 250 men, with flanking earthworks thrown up to protect the gunners. Lolonnois and Le Basque landed at a league from the fort, and advanced at the head of their men. The governor, seeing them land, had prepared an ambuscade, in hopes of attacking them at the same time in flank and rear. The buccaneers, discovering this, got before the Spaniards, and routed them so utterly that not a single man returned to the fort, which was instantly attacked "with the usual desperation of this sort of people," says Esquemeling. The fighting continued for three hours. The buccaneers, aiming with hunters' precision, killed so many of the Spaniards, and reduced their numbers so terribly, that the survivors could not prevent the savage swordsmen storming the embrasures, slaying half the survivors, and taking the rest prisoners. A few survivors are said by one writer to have fled in confusion into Maracaibo, crying, "The pirates will presently be here with 2,000 men."

The rest of the day Lolonnois spent in destroying the fort he had captured, first signalling his ships to come in as the danger was over. His men levelled the earth ramparts, spiked the guns, buried the dead, and sent the wounded on board the fleet. The next day, very early in the morning, the ships weighed anchor and directed their course, in close-winged phalanx, like a flock of locusts, towards the doomed city of Maracaibo, now only six leagues distant. They made but slow way, in spite of all their impatience, for there was very little wind; and it was not till the next morning that they drew in sight of the town, standing pleasantly on the cool shore, with its galleries of shaded balconies, its towers and steeples—the goal to which they steered.

Suspicious of ambuscades after the danger at the bar, Lolonnois put his men into canoes, and pulled to shore under protection of salvos from his great guns, which he ordered to be pointed at the woods which lined the beach. Half the men went in the canoes, and half remained on board; but these furious discharges were thrown away, the Spaniards having long since fled. To their great astonishment, the town itself was deserted. The people, remembering the horrors of a former buccaneer descent, when Maracaibo had been "sacked to the uttermost," had escaped to Gibraltar in their boats and canoes, taking with them all the jewels and money they could carry.

To the alarmed friends who received them, they said that the fort of the bar had been taken, and nothing been saved, nor any soldiers escaped. At Gibraltar they believed themselves safe, thinking the buccaneers would pillage the unfortunate and defenceless town and then retreat over the bar.

The hungry sailors, who had lived scantily for four weeks, found the deserted houses well provided with flour, bread, pork, poultry, and brandy, and with these they made good cheer. The warehouses were brimming with merchandise, the cellars were flowing with Spanish wine. The more prudent fell to plunder, the more thoughtless to revel. The former class probably embraced the older, and the latter the younger men. Each party abused the vice from which he abstained, and gave himself up without scruple to his own more favourite indulgence. But soon the man weary of wine began to plunder, and the man loaded with pieces of eight began to drink. The moment that plunder ceased, waste began, and prudence and folly alike ended the day,—poor and drunk. The commanders at once seized on the best houses, indulging their natural love of order and justice, by placing sentinels at the larger shops and warehouses.

The great monastery of the Cordeliers served them as a guardhouse, for a long time the abode of thieves, yet never so manifestly as now; for a long time the shrine of mammon, yet now for the first time filled by his avowed worshippers. Had the town not been deserted, that night would have heard the groans of the victim of cruelty; as it was, it echoed only with the songs and shouts of debauchery. The buccaneer had reached his Capua, but there were no Judiths ready to slay these Holofernes in their drunken sleep. Perhaps a night surprise would have failed. These men were still the vigilant hunters and the watchful sailors; sunken rocks and lurking Spaniards, breakers and wild bulls, reefs and wild panthers had taught them never to sleep unguarded and unwatched.

The next day a fresh source of plunder was opened. Lolonnois—for Le Basque's command, even by land, seems to have been secondary—sent a body of 160 men to reconnoitre the neighbouring woods, where some of the inhabitants were, it was supposed, concealed. They returned the same night, discharging their guns, and dragging after them a miserable weeping train of twenty prisoners, men, women, and children; and, besides this, a sack of 20,000 pieces of eight, and many mules, laden with household goods and merchandise.

Some of the prisoners were at once racked, to make them confess where they had hidden their riches, but neither pain nor fear could extort their secret. Lolonnois, who valued not murdering, though in cold blood, ten or twelve Spaniards, drew his cutlass and hacked one of them to pieces before all his companions; and while the pale, tortured men were still writhing and groaning by his side, declared, "If you do not confess and declare where you have the rest of your goods, I will do the like to all your companions."

In spite of all these horrible cruelties and inhuman threats, only one was found base enough to offer to conduct the buccaneers to a place where the rest of the fugitives were hidden. When they arrived there, they found their coming had been announced, the riches had been removed to another place, and the Spaniards had fled. The exiles now changed their hiding-places daily, and, amid the universal danger and distrust, a father would not even rely on his own son.

After fifteen days "taking stock" at Maracaibo, Lolonnois marched towards Gibraltar, intending afterwards to sack Merida, as at these places he expected to find the wealth transported from the City of the Lake. Several of his prisoners offered to serve as guides, but warned him that he would find the place strong and fortified.

"No matter," cried the buccaneer, "the better sign that it is worth taking."

Gibraltar was already prepared. The inhabitants, expecting Lolonnois, had entreated aid from the governor of Merida, a stout old soldier who had served in Flanders. He sent back word, that they need take no care, for he hoped in a little while to exterminate the pirates. He had soon after this hopeful bravado entered the town at the head of 400 well-armed men, and was soon joined by an equal number of armed townsmen, whom he at once enrolled. On the side of the town towards the sea he raised with great rapidity a battery, mounting twenty guns, well protected by baskets of earth, and flanked by a smaller traverse of eight pieces. He lastly barricaded a narrow passage to the town, through which the pirates, he knew, must pass, and opened another path leading to a swampy wood that was quite impassable.

Three days after leaving Maracaibo Lolonnois approached Gibraltar, and, seeing the royal standard hung out, perceived there were breakers ahead, and called a general council, one of those republican gatherings that distinguished the buccaneer armies, and remind us of the less unanimous consultations that Xenophon describes. He confessed that the difficulty of the enterprise was great, seeing the Spaniards had had so much time to put themselves in a state of defence, and had now got together a large force and much ammunition; "but have a good courage," said he, "we must either defend ourselves like good soldiers or lose our lives with all the riches we have got. Do as I shall do, who am your captain. At other times we have fought with fewer men than we have now, and yet have overcome a greater number of enemies than can be in this town; *the more they are the more riches we shall gain.*"

His men all cried out, with one voice, that they would follow and obey him.

"'Tis well," he replied, "but know ye, the first man who will show any fear or the least apprehension thereof, I will pistol him with my own hands."

The buccaneers cast anchor near the shore, about three-quarters of a league from the town, and the next day before sunrise landed to the number of 380 determined men, each armed with a cutlass, a brace of pistols, and thirty charges of powder and bullets. On the shore they all shook hands with one another, many for the last time, and began their march, Lolonnois exclaiming, "Come, *mes frères*, follow me and have good courage."

Their guide, ignorant of what the governor of Merida had done, led them in all good faith up the barricaded way, where, to his surprise, he found the paths in one place blocked up with large trees, newly cut, and in another swamped so that the soft mud reached up above their thighs.

Lolonnois, seeing the passage hopeless, attempted the narrow way, which had been carefully cleared as a trap for them. Here only six men could go abreast, and the shots of the town ploughed incessantly down the path. At the same time the Spaniards, in a small terraced battery of six guns, beat their drums and hung out their silk flags. The adventurers, harassed by the fire that they could not return, and slipping on the swampy path, grew vexed and impatient.

"Courage, my brothers," cried their leader, "we must beat these fellows or die; follow me, and if I fall don't give in for that."

With these words he ran full butt, with head down like a mad bull, against the Spaniards, followed by all his men, as daring but less patient than himself. Cutting down boughs they made a rude pathway, firm and sure, over the deep mud. When within about a pistol shot from the entrenchments, they began again to sink up to their knees, and the enemy's grape-shot fell thick and hot upon the impeded ranks. Many dropped, but their last words were always, "Courage, never flinch, *mes frères*, and you'll win it yet." All this time they could scarce see or hear, so blinded and deafened were they by the thunder and fire.

In the midst of this discomfiture the Spaniards suddenly broke through the gloom, just as they got out of the wood and trod upon firmer ground, and drove them back by a furious onslaught, many of them being killed and wounded. They then attempted the other passage again, but without success, and finding the Spaniards would not sally out, and the gabions too heavy to tear up by hand, Lolonnois resorted to the old stratagem, so successful at Hastings, by which the very impatience of courage is made to prove fatal to an enemy.

At a preconcerted signal the buccaneers began to retreat, upon which the defenders of the battery, exclaiming, "They fly, they fly;

follow, follow," sallied forth in disorder to the pursuit, shouting and firing like an undisciplined rabble. Once out of gun-shot of the batteries, the pursued turned into pursuers, and falling on the foe, sword in hand, slew about 200. Fighting their way through those who survived, the buccaneers soon became masters of all the fortifications. Not more than 100 out of the 600 defenders remained alive, and these, as Falstaff says, would have to limp to the town-end and beg for life. The brave old governor lay dead among his foremost men.

The survivors who could crawl or run hid themselves in the woods, impeded in their flight by the very obstructions they had themselves raised. The men in the battery surrendered, and obtained quarter. Neither Lolonnois nor Le Basque was scratched, but forty of their companions perished, and eighty were grievously wounded. The greater part of these died through the fevers and subsequent pestilence. 500 dead Spaniards were found, but many more had hidden themselves, to die alone in peace.

The buccaneers, now masters of Gibraltar, pulled down the Spanish colours from tower and steeple, and hoisted their own red or black flag. Making prisoners of all they met, they shut them up under guard in the chief church, where they erected a battery of great guns, in case the Spaniards should attempt to rally in a fit of despair. They then collected the dead bodies of the Spaniards, and, piling them up, scarred and gashed, in two large canoes, towed them out a quarter of a league to sea, and scuttled them. They then gathered from every house, rich or poor, all the plate, merchandise, and household stuff, which was not too hot or too heavy to carry off, as rapacious as the borderer who stopped wistfully opposite the hay-stack, wishing it had but four legs, that he might make it "gang awa' wi' the rest."

The Spaniards having buried their treasure, as usual, armed parties were sent into the surrounding woods to search for buried money, and to bring in hunters and planters as prisoners to torture. Hung up by the beard, or burnt with gun-matches, the wretched sufferers were forced to confess the hiding-places.

Lolonnois soon turned the fertile country into a smoking black desert, and, still insatiable for money and blood, planned an expedition over the snow mountains to Merida, but reluctantly relinquished it when he found his men unwilling to risk what they had got for the mere uncertainly of getting more, though Merida was only forty leagues distant. They had now 150 prisoners, besides 500 slaves, and many women and children, many of whom were dying daily of famine, so short were provisions already in a city in which the small army had been encamped only eighteen days.

When they had spent six weeks in the town, Lolonnois determined to return, nothing now being left to pillage. Disease and famine were worse enemies than the Spaniard or the Indian, and cared for neither steel nor lead. A pestilential disease appeared in consequence of the numerous dead bodies left in the woods exposed to the wild beasts and the birds. Those that lay nearest to the walls had been strewn over with earth, the rest were left to taint the air, and slay the living—a putrid fever broke out; the Spaniards killed more of the enemy after their death than they had done in their life. The Frenchmen's wounds, already closing, began now to re-open, the sick died daily, and the strongest pined and sickened; all longed to return, even plunder grew distasteful to them without health, and once more at sea they hoped soon to be well.

Men who had been revelling in the plenty of two captured cities, could not return without impatience to the restraints of a time of scarcity. Gibraltar always depending upon Maracaibo for its meat, and not well supplied with flour, was, in fact, like a miser dying for want of a loaf, while his storehouses were brimmed over with gold. The little meat and flour were quickly consumed by the buccaneers, who left their prisoners to shift for themselves. The cattle they soon appropriated, giving the mules' and asses' flesh to those Spaniards whose hunger was strong enough to conquer their disgust. A few of the women were allowed better fare, and many who had become the mistresses of their captors were well treated by their lovers. Some of these were mere slaves, others were voluntary concubines, but the greater part had been compelled, by poverty and fear, to abandon their fathers and husbands.

Lolonnois, sending four of his prisoners into the woods, demanded a ransom of 80,000 pieces of eight within two days, threatening the fugitives to burn the town to ashes if his desire was not acceded to. The Spaniards, already half-beggared, disagreed about the ransom; the bolder and the more avaricious refused to pay a *piastre*, the old, the timid, and the more generous preferred poverty to such a loss. Some said it would serve as a mere bribe to allure a third adventurer, and others declared it was the only means of saving Merida. While they were thus disputing the two days passed, and the debate was put an end to by the sight of flame ascending above the roofs. The city was already fired in two or three places, when the inhabitants, promising to bring the ransom, persuaded the buccaneers to assist in quenching the flames, not, however, till the chief houses were burned, and the chief monastery was ruined.

Oexmelin merely says that Lolonnois set fire to the four corners of the town, and in six hours reduced the whole to ashes. Palm-thatch and cedar walls burn quick, and the sea-breeze was there to fan the flames, while the buccaneers were learned in the art of destruction. Lolonnois then collected his men by beat of drum, and embarked his booty. Before he sailed, he sent two of his prisoners again into the woods, to tell the inhabitants that all the prisoners in his hands would be at once put to death if the ransom were not paid. All prisoners who had not paid their ransom he took with him, even the slaves being valued at so much, and having put on board all riches that were movable, and a large sum of money as a ransom for what was immovable, the buccaneer fleet returned to Maracaibo. The city, now partly repeopled, was thrown again into disorder, nor much lessened when three or four prisoners came to the governor, bearing a demand from Lolonnois to pay at once 30,000 pieces of eight down upon his deck, or to expect a second sack, and the fate of Gibraltar. While these terms were under concession, and the Spanish merchants were chaffering with the sailors, as a lowland farmer might have done with a highland *cateran*, a party of well-inclined *flibustiers*, unwilling to waste their time, rowed on shore, and stripped the great church of its pictures, images, carvings, clocks, and bells, even to the very cross on its steeple, piously desiring to erect a chapel at Tortuga, where there was much need of spiritual instruction. The Spaniards at last agreed to pay for their ransom and liberty 20,000 *piastres*, 10,000 pieces of eight, and 500 cows, provided the fleet would do no further injury, and depart at once, and the blessing of Maracaibo with them.

We can imagine the trembling and suppressed joy with which

the people of Maracaibo must have beheld the fleet sail slowly out of their harbour, all eyes on board bent onward to the horizon and the golden future—none looking back with a moment's regret upon the misery and the black ruin left behind. How many orphans must have cursed them as they sailed, and how many widows! Three days after the embarkation, to the horror of the city, a vessel with a red flag at its masthead was seen re-entering the harbour, but only, as it soon appeared, to demand a pilot to take the fleet over the bar.

On their way to Hispaniola, Lolonnois touched at the Isle de la Vacca, intending to stay there and divide the spoil. This island was inhabited by French buccaneers, who sold the flesh of the animals they killed to vessels in want of victual. But a dispute arising here, the fleet again set out to disband the crew at Gouaves in Hispaniola.

They arrived in two months, and, unlading the whole "*cargazon* of riches," proceeded to make a dividend of their prizes and their gains. Lolonnois and the other captains began by taking a solemn oath in public, that they had concealed and held back no portion of the spoil, but had thrown all without reserve into the public stock. The ceremony of this oath must have been an imposing sight: wild groups of half-stripped sailors, wounded men, and female captives, negroes and Indians, Spanish soldiers and mulatto fishermen, and in the middle piled bales of silks, heaps of glittering coin, and rich stuffs streaming over scattered arms and costly jewels, while, looking on, perhaps wistfully, leaning on their muskets, a few hunters fresh from the savannahs, bull's-hide sandals on their feet, and long knives hanging from their belts. After the captains had taken the oath, the common *matelots*, down even to the cabin boys, took the vow that they had given up all their spoil, to be shared equally by those who had equally ventured their lives to win it.

After an exact calculation, the total value of their profits in jewels and money was discovered to be 260,000 crowns, not including 100,000 crowns' worth of church furniture and a cargo of tobacco. On the final division every man received money, silk, and linen to the value of about 100 pieces of eight. The surgeon and the wounded were as usual paid first. The slaves were then sold by auction, and their purchase-money divided among the various crews. The uncoined plate was weighed, and sold at the rate of ten pieces of eight to a pound; the jewels were sold at false and fanciful prices, and were generally undervalued, owing to the ignorance of the arbitrators. A buccaneer always preferred coin to jewels, and jewels, as being portable, to heavy merchandise, which they often threw overboard or wantonly destroyed. The adventurers then all took the oath a second time, and proceeded to apportion the shares of such as had fallen, handing them to the *matelots*, or messmate, to forward to their heirs or nearest relations. We do not know whether, in peculiar cases, a *matelot* became his *camarade*'s heir.

The dividend over, they returned to Tortuga, amid the general rejoicing of all over whom love or cupidity had any power. Says Oexmelin:

> For three weeks, while their money lasted probably an eye witness of the scene, "there was nothing but dances, feasts, and protestations of unceasing friendship.

The *cabaretiers* and the gambling-house keepers soon revenged the cruelties of Maracaibo. The proud captors of that luckless city in a few weeks were hungry beggars, basking on the quay of Tortuga, straining their eyes to catch sight of some vessel that might take them on board, and relieve them from that reaction of wretchedness. They were jeered at as mad spendthrifts by the very men who had urged them to their folly. The love of courtesans grew colder as the pieces of eight diminished, and men were refused charity by the very wretches whom their foolish generosity had lately enriched. No doubt watches were fried and bank-bills eaten as sandwiches, just as they were during the war at Portsmouth or at Dover. The prudent were those who made the money spin out a day longer than their fellows, and the wildest were those who had found out that two dice-boxes and two fiddlers ran through the burdensome money a little faster than only one dice-box and one fiddler.

Some of the buccaneers, skilful with the cards, added to their store and returned at once to France, resolved to turn merchants, and trade with the Indies they had wasted. The extravagant prices paid by these men for wine, and particularly brandy, rendered that trade a source of great profit. Just before the return of the fleet two

French vessels had arrived at Tortuga laden with spirits, which at first sold at very moderate rates, but ultimately, from the great demand and the limited means of supply, reached an exorbitant price, a gallon selling for as much as four pieces of eight.

The tavern-keepers and the *filles de joie* obtained most of the money so dearly earned, and lavished it as those from whom they won it had done. Cards and dice helped those who had not struck a blow at the Spaniard, to now quietly spoil the captors. The story of Sampson and Delilah was daily acted. Even the governor hastened to benefit by the expedition. He bought a cargo of cocoa of the buccaneers, and shipped it at once to France in Lolonnois' vessel, giving scarcely a twentieth part of its value, and realising a profit of £120,000. The adventurers did not grudge him this bargain, as he had risked everything for Tortuga, and had suffered considerable losses. Says Oexmelin, with some *naïveté*:

> M. D'Ogeron aimait les 'honnêtes gens,' les obligeait sans cesse, et ne les laissait jamais manquer de rien.

Neither Lolonnois' talent, rank, nor courage kept him further from the tavern door than the meanest of his crew. The poor drudge of a negro that served as a butt to the sailors could not give way to baser debauchery. It was the voice of the cannon alone that roused him to great actions. On land he was a Caliban, at sea a Barbarossa. In spite of his great booty, in a few short weeks he was poorer than his crew. Tortuga was to him the Circe's island that transformed him into a beast. As soon as his foot trod the plank, he became again the wily and the wise Ulysses: the first in daring or in suffering, ready to endure or to attack, above his fellow men in patience and impatience. His expenses were large, and when the prizes ceased to come in he was soon reduced to live upon his capital, and that quickly melted away in open-house feasting and entertainments given to the governor. He had been before he returned, moreover, so burdened with debts that even his prize-money could not have defrayed them. There was but one means of release—another expedition. Let the Spanish mother clasp her child closer to her breast, for she knows not how soon she may have to part with it for ever. Is there no comet that may warn an unprepared and a doomed people?

Lolonnois had now acquired great repute at Tortuga. He was known to be brave, and, what is a rare combination, prudent. Under his guidance men who had forgot his previous misfortunes, thought themselves secure of gold, and without glory gold is not to be won. He needed now no entreaties to induce men to fill his ships; the difficulty was in selecting from the volunteers. Those who had before stayed behind now determined to venture; those who had once followed him were already driven by mere poverty to enlist. The privations of land were intolerable to men who had just revelled in riches—the privations of sea could be endured by the mere force of habit. The planters threw by their hoes, and quitted the hut for the cabin.

The towns of Nicaragua were now to share the fate of those of Venezuela. About 700 men and six ships formed the expedition. Lolonnois himself sailed in a large "flute" which he had brought from Maracaibo with 300 men; the other adventurers embarked in five smaller vessels. Having careened and revictualled at Bayala, in Hispaniola, he steered for Matamana, a port on the south side of Cuba. He here informed his companions of the plan of the expedition, and produced an Indian of Nicaragua who had offered to serve as guide. He assured them of the riches of the country, and expressed his belief that they could surprise the place before the inhabitants had secreted their money. His proposal was received with the usual unhesitating applause.

At Matamana, Lolonnois collected by force all the canoes of the tortoise fishermen, much to their grief and dismay, these poor men having no other means of subsistence but fishing. These boats he needed to take him up the channel of Nicaragua, which was too shallow for vessels of any larger burthen. While attempting to round Cape Gracias à Dios, the fleet was arrested by what the Spanish sailors call a "furious calm"—a sad and tedious imprisonment to men to whom every delay involved the success of their enterprise.

In spite of all their endeavours, they were carried by the current into the Gulf of Honduras. Both wind and tide being against them, the smaller vessels—better sailors and more manageable than that of Lolonnois—made more way than he could do; but were obliged to wait for him, and stay for his orders, being quite powerless without him and his 300 men.

They spent nearly a month in trying to recover their path, but all in vain, losing in two hours what they gained in two days, and, their provisions running short, put ashore to revictual.

Touching at the first land they could reach, they sent their canoes up the river Xagua—their guides bringing them to the villages of the "long-eared Indians," a race tributary to Spain, whose traders bartered knives and mirrors with them for cocoa. The buccaneers burned their huts and carried off their millet, hogs, and poultry, loading the canoes with all the food they could bring away to their impatient *comerades*, who determined to remain here till the unfavourable weather had passed, and burn and pillage along the whole borders of the gulf. The Indian provisions proved but scanty for so numerous a band, but were divided equally among the ships that were seeking food like locusts, and moving daily on to new pastures.

A council of war was now held to discuss their position. Some were for discontinuing the expedition, since the provisions ran so short. The oldest and most experienced proposed plundering round the gulf till the bad season had passed; and this plan was decided on. Having rifled a few villages, they came to Puerto Cavallo, a place where Spanish ships frequently anchored, and which contained two storehouses full of cochineal, indigo, hides, &c., from Guatimala. There happened then to be lying in the port a Spanish vessel of twenty-four guns and sixteen *patarerros*. Its cargo, however, was nearly all unloaded and carried up into the interior to be exchanged in barter with the Indians. This ship was instantly seized; and Lolonnois, landing without any resistance, burned the magazines and all the houses, and made many prisoners. The Spaniards he put to the torture to induce them to confess. If any refused to answer, he pulled out their tongues, or cut them to pieces with his hanger, "desiring," says Esquemeling, "to do so to every Spaniard in the world." Many, terrified by the rack, promised to confess, really having nothing to disclose. These men were always cruelly put to death in revenge. One mulatto was bound hand and foot and thrown alive into the sea to intimidate the rest, and to induce two survivors to show the French chief the nearest road to the neighbouring town of San Pedro.

For this expedition Lolonnois selected 300 men, leaving his

lieutenant, Moses Vauclin, to govern in his absence, and despatching a few of his small flotilla to help him by a diversion on the coast. Before starting, he told his companions that he would never refuse to march at their head, but that he should kill with his own hand "the first who turned tail." San Pedro was only ten leagues distant. He had not proceeded three before he fell into an ambuscade.

The Spaniards' favourite scheme of attack was the treacherous surprise—a mere sort of attempt at wholesale assassination—seldom successful, and always exasperating the enemy to greater cruelties. They had now entrenched themselves behind gabions in a narrow road, impassable on either side with trees and strong thickets. Lolonnois instantly striking down the guides, whether innocent or guilty, charged the enemy with desperate courage, and put them to flight after a long encounter, ending in a total rout. They killed a few buccaneers and left many of their own men dead upon the ground. The wounded Spaniards, being first questioned as to the distance from San Pedro, and the best way to get there, were instantly beheaded. The prisoners informed him that some runaway slaves, escaped from Porto Cavallo, had told them of the intended attack on San Pedro. Determined to prevent this, they had planned the ambuscade, and two other still stronger earthworks which awaited him further on. To prevent connivance, or any possible treachery, Lolonnois then had the Spaniards brought before him one by one, and demanded of each in turn if there was no means of getting into another and less guarded road. On their each denying that there was, he grew frenzied and almost mad at the thoughts of such inevitable danger, and had them all murdered but two; and then, in ungovernable passion, he ripped open with his cutlass the breast of one of these survivors, who was bound to a tree. Esquemeling asserts that he even tore out his heart and gnawed it "like a ravenous wolf," swearing and shouting that he would serve them all alike if they did not show him another way. The miserable survivor, willing to save his life at any risk, his memory or invention quickened by the imminent danger, conducted him into another path, but so bad a one that Lolonnois preferred to return to the old one in spite of all its perils, so difficult, slow, and laborious was the march. He now seems to have grown almost fevered with rage, anxiety, and vexation. "*Mon Dieu*," he growled, "*les Espagnols me le payeront*," and he cursed the delay that kept him from the enemy.

There is no doubt that in these men a fanatical and almost superstitious hatred of the enemy had sprung up, inflamed by mutual cruelties, for forgiveness was not the chief virtue of the victorious Spaniard. To the buccaneer the Spaniard seemed cruel, cowardly, treacherous, and degraded; to the Spaniard the buccaneer seemed a monster scarcely human—bloody, voluptuous, faithless, and rapacious.

That same evening the chief fell into a second ambuscade, which, says Esquemeling, "he assaulted with such horrible fury" that in less than an hour's time he routed the Spaniards and killed the greater part of them, the rest flying to the third ambush, which was planted about two leagues from the town. The Spaniards had thought, by these repeated attacks, to destroy the enemy piecemeal, and for this object, which they did not attain, frittered their forces into small and useless detachments.

Lolonnois and his people, weary with fighting and marching, and half-fainting with hunger and thirst, lay down in the wood that night, and slept till the morning, the *matelots* keeping good watch and ward, and guarding their sleeping companions. At daybreak they resumed their journey, with confidence increased by the clear light and with bodies invigorated by rest. The third ambuscade was stronger and more advantageously placed than even the two preceding. They attacked it with showers of fireballs, and drove out the enemy, slaying without mercy, and giving no quarter. "No quarter, no quarter," cried their ferocious leader, still thirsty for human blood, when they would have stayed their hands, from exhaustion rather than from pity. "The more we kill here, the less we shall meet in the town," was his war-cry. Very few of the enemy escaped to San Pedro, the greater part being either slain or wounded.

Before they ventured to make the final attack, the buccaneers rested to look to their arms and prepare their ammunition. In vain they attempted to discover a second approach. There was but one, and that was well barricaded, and planted all round with thorny shrubs, which the best shod traveller could not pass, much less barefooted men, clad only in a shirt and drawers. These thorns, Oexmelin says, were more dangerous than those crow's-feet used in Europe to annoy cavalry.

Lolonnois, seeing that no other way was left, and that delay would imply fear in his own men, and excite hope in the enemy, resolved to storm the works, in spite of the rage and despair of a well-armed and superior force, sheltered from shot and commanding his approach. Says Esquemeling:

> The Spaniards posted behind the said defences, seeing the pirates come, began to ply them with their great guns; but these, perceiving them ready to fire, used to stoop down, and then the shot was made to fall upon the defendants with fire-balls and naked swords, killing many of the town.

Driven back for a time, they renewed the attack with fewer men; husbanding their shot, for they were now short of powder; never shooting at a long distance; and seldom firing but with great deliberation when an enemy's head appeared above the rampart; and occasionally giving a general discharge, in which nearly every bullet killed an enemy. Several times the buccaneers advanced to the very mouths of the guns, and, throwing down fire-balls into the works, leaped after them, sword in hand, through the embrasures; but only to be again driven back.

This obstinate combat, so eager on both sides, had lasted about four hours, and night was fast approaching, when Lolonnois, ordering a last furious attack, put the now weakened Spaniards to flight, a great number of them being killed as soon as they turned their backs. The citizens then hung out a white flag, and, coming to a parley, agreed to surrender the town on condition of receiving two hours' respite. During this time, Lolonnois found that he had lost about thirty men, ten more being wounded. This demand of two hours was employed by the towns-people in loading themselves with their riches and preparing for flight—the buccaneers virtuously abstaining from any molestation till the time had duly expired, and then pursuing the fugitives and plundering them of every *maravedi*. But neither their self-denial nor their vigilance was well rewarded, for fortune gave them nothing but a few leather sacks full of indigo, the rest, even in that short time, having been buried or destroyed—a disappointment which, we think, no reasonable person can regret. Lolonnois had particularly ordered that not only all the goods should be seized, but that every fugitive should be made prisoner.

The buccaneer chief, having stayed a few days at San Pedro, and "committed most horrid insolences," was anxious to send for a new reinforcement, and attack the town of Guatimala—a place a long way distant, and defended by 400 men. On his men as usual refusing to accede to an apparently rash project, Lolonnois contented himself by pillaging San Pedro, intending to impress a recollection of his visit upon the grateful inhabitants by burning their town. He obtained no great booty, for the inhabitants were a poor people, trading in nothing but dyes. If he had chosen to carry away their stores of indigo, he might have realised more than 40,000 crowns; but the buccaneers cared for nothing but coin and bullion, and were too ignorant, too lazy, and too improvident to stop their debauches by loading their vessels with a perishable cargo of uncertain value.

Having remained now eighteen days in San Pedro without obtaining much, for the West Indian Spaniard had already learned to hide as skilfully as the Hindoo *ryot*, Lolonnois called together his prisoners, and demanded from them a ransom as the condition of sparing their town. They doggedly answered, with all the insolence of despair, that he had taken from them all they had, and that they had nothing more to give; that they could not coin without gold, and that, as far as they went, he might do what he liked to the town.

Lolonnois then reduced the town to ashes, and, marching to the sea-side to rejoin his companions, found that they had been employing their time, innocently and usefully, in capturing the fishing-boats of Guatimala. Some Indians, newly taken, informed him that a *hourque*, a vessel of 800 tons, bringing goods from Spain to the Honduras, was then lying in the great river of Guatimala. Resolving to careen and victual at the islands on the other side of the gulf, they left two canoes at the mouth of the river to give notice when the vessel should venture forth.

The time spent in thus watching outside the covert, they devoted to turtle fishing, dividing themselves into parties, each having his own station to prevent disputes. Their nets they made of the bark of the *macoa* tree; a natural pitch or bitumen for their boats they found in fused heaps upon the shore. The formation of this pitch, or "wax," as Esquemeling calls it, the sailors attributed to wild bees; the hollow trees in which they built being torn down by storms and swept down into the sea. The rest of their time—which never seems to have been wearisome, unless the subsequent mutiny indicates it, for these men had the tenacity of a slot-hound in the pursuit of blood—was spent in cruises among those Indians of the coast of Yucatan, who seek for amber on the shore. These tribes were the willing serfs of Spain, having served them without resistance for a full century. The Spaniards had, as they believed, converted the whole nation to Christianity by sending a priest to them once a-week, but, on their sudden return to idolatry, had begun to persecute them, angry at their own failure.

According to the buccaneers' account, these Indian chiefs worshipped each a peculiar spirit, to whom they offered sacrifices of fire, burning incense of sweet-scented gums. They had a singular custom of carrying their new-born children into their temples, and leaving them for a night in a hole filled with wood-ashes, generally in an open place, untended, and where wild beasts could enter. Leaving the child here they found in the morning the footprints of some wild beast on the ashes. To this animal, whatever it might be, jaguar, snake, or cayman, they dedicated the child, whose patron god it became. To this animal the child prayed for vengeance against its enemies, and to it he offered sacrifices.

Their marriages were accompanied by a very beautiful and simple ceremony. A young man, having satisfied his intended bride's father as to his fitness to manage a plantation, was presented with a bow and arrow. He then visits the maiden, and puts on her head a wreath of green leaves and sweet-smelling flowers, taking off the crown usually worn by virgins. A meeting of her relations is then called, the maize juice is drunk, and the day after marriage the bride's garland is torn to pieces with cries and lamentations.

In these islands the buccaneers found canoes of the Aregues Indians, which must have drifted 600 leagues. They had remained turtle-fishing and amber-seeking about three months, when the welcome tidings came that the enemy's vessel had ventured out. All hands were now employed in preparing the careening ships. It was, however, at last agreed to wait for its return, when, as they expected, it would not only contain merchandise but money. They therefore sent their canoes to observe her motions, and, hearing of the ambuscade, the Spaniards returned to port. Lolonnois, as weary of delay as a greyhound is vexed by a hare's repeated doubling, determined to do what Mahomet did when the mountain would not go to him; since the Spaniards would not come to him, he went himself to the Spaniards. Informed of their approach by spies, Indians or fishermen, the vessel was prepared to receive him. The decks were cleared, the boarding-nettings up, and the guns double-shotted. The Spaniard carried fifty-six pieces of cannon, and the crew were well provided with hand grenades, torches, fusees, and fire-balls, especially on the quarter-deck and bows, and a crew of some 130 men stood armed and threatening at their quarters. But Lolonnois cared for none of these things, and the rich cargo shone, to his eye, through the ship's transparent sides. With his small craft of twenty-two guns, with a single fly-boat as his only ally, he boldly attacked the enemy, but was at first beaten off.

To the buccaneer a slight check was almost a certain precursor of victory; waiting till about sixty of the Spanish sailors had fallen from the fire of his deadly musketry, when their courage slackened, and the smoke of their powder lay in a dark mist round the bulwarks, hiding his movements, he boarded with four canoes, well manned. In spite of the brave defence, the buccaneers fought with such fury that they forced the Spaniards to surrender.

Lolonnois then sent his boats up the river to secure a small *patache*, which they knew lay near at hand, laden with plate, indigo, and cochineal. But the inhabitants, alarmed at the capture of the larger vessel, swept away from under their very eyes, saved the *patache* by preventing her departure.

The booty of the prize was much less than was expected, the vessel being already almost entirely unladen. Its cargo consisted of iron and paper, and it still contained 20,000 reams of paper, and 100 tons of iron bars, which had served as ballast. The few bales of merchandise were nothing but linens, serges, and cloth, thread, and a few jars of wine. In the return cargo there would have been at least a million in specie. These heterogeneous articles were of no use to men who wanted nothing but coin or jewels, lead or powder. Dividing the paper, they used it for napkins, and other useless trifles, and several jars of almond and olive-oil were wasted in the same reckless manner.

Having now accomplished their purpose, without much return for their three months' patience, Lolonnois called a general council of the fleet, and declared his intention of going to Guatimala. Upon this announcement a division arose in the assembly, and the hoarse murmurs of a coming tempest were heard around the speaker. Many of the adventurers, new to the trade, could no longer conceal their weariness and their disappointment. They had set sail from Tortuga with the feeling with which a country boy comes to London. They had believed that pieces of eight grew on the trees like pears, and had overlooked the dragons that guarded the Hesperian trees. Having seen their predecessors return home laden with the plunder of Maracaibo, many had overlooked the toil and dangers by which it was won, in the sight of the joy and prodigality with which it was lavished; they had seen only the rich pearls, and forgotten the stormy seas from which they had been gathered. They were weary of the hardships, and mutinous for want of food. The mere seeker for gold could not endure what was submitted to by those who were desirous of earning distinction. The older hands laughed at their pinings, derided their complaints, and swore that they would rather die and starve there, than return home with empty purses, to be the scorn and laughing-stock of all Hispaniola. The majority of the experienced men, foreseeing that the voyage to Nicaragua would not succeed, and was "little to their purpose," separated from Lolonnois, and set sail secretly in the swift sailing vessel that Moses Vauclin had captured in the port of Cavallo, and which he now commanded, boasting, with reason, that it was the swiftest sailing vessel that had been seen in the West Indies for fifty years. With Moses Vauclin went Pierre le Picard, who, seeing others desert Lolonnois, resolved to do the same.

Steering homewards, the fugitives coasted along the whole continent till they came to Costa Rica, where they landed a good party, marched up to Veraguas, and burnt the town, pillaging the Spaniards, who made a stout resistance, carrying off a few prisoners, and obtaining a scanty booty of some seven or eight pounds' worth of gold, which their slaves washed from the mud of the rivers. Alarmed at the multitude of Spaniards that began to gather round them, the marauders abandoned their design of attacking the town of Nata, on the south sea-coast, although many rich merchants lived there, whose slaves worked in the gold-washings of Veraguas. Returning to Tortuga, these undisciplined men, impatient of poverty, united themselves under the flag of a noble adventurer, the Chevalier du Plessis, who had just arrived in the Indies, poor and proud, and prepared to cruise against the Spaniard in those seas. Vauclin being an experienced pilot, well acquainted with the turtle islands, and every key and reef the surf washed from California to Cape Horn, was taken into favour by the titled privateersman, who promised him the first prize he captured, if he would sail in his company. But a serious difficulty arose in the execution of this liberal promise, for the Chevalier was soon after shot through the head while grappling with a Spanish ship of thirty-six guns, and Moses was elected captain in his stead. In his first cruise, the brave deserter was fortunate enough to take a cocoa vessel from the Havannah, with a cargo valued at 150,000 *livres*.

During this time, Lolonnois and his men remained alone and deserted in the gulf of Honduras. He was now in some distress, short of provisions, and in a vessel too "great to get out at the reflux of those seas." His 300 men had no food but that which they contrived to kill daily on shore, living chiefly on the flesh of parrots and monkeys. By day they generally fished or hunted, by night, taking advantage of the land breeze, they sailed painfully on till they rounded Cape Gracias à Dios, and slowly the Pearl Islands hove in sight. Staunch and inexorable, Lolonnois, amid all the tedium of this enervating idleness, still nourished the project of making a swoop down upon Nicaragua, intending to leave his cumbrous vessel behind, and row up the river St. John in canoes, until he reached the lake. But the same reason that made his vessel lag behind those of his companions, now drove it ashore in a shallow near Cape Gracias, where it drew too much water to be extricated. In vain he unloaded his guns and iron, and used every means that experience and ingenuity could suggest to lighten the ship, and float her again into deep water. Always firm and resolute, Lolonnois at once determined to break her to pieces on the sand-shoal, and with her planks and nails to construct a boat.

His men, with perfect *sang froid*, not even impatient at the loss, much less afraid of danger, escaping to land, began to build Indian *ajoupas*, or huts. Lolonnois, accustomed to such reverses, concealed his chagrin, if he even felt any. Regardless of himself, he adjured his men to lose no courage, for he knew of a means of escape, and, what was more, a way to make their fortune yet, before they returned to Tortuga. Prepared for every emergency, and even for the longest delay, part of the crew were at once employed in planting peas and other vegetables, the remainder in fishing and hunting, all but the few who worked busily at the boat in which Nicaragua was to be visited. In spite of desertion, failure, wreck, and famine, Lolonnois held on to the plan of the expedition, which he deemed cowardly and shameful to abandon. The men, confident in the sagacity and courage of their leader, surrendered themselves like children to his guidance.

The Indians of the Perlas Islands, on which they had struck, were a fierce and untameable race, strong and agile, swift as horses, hardy divers, brave but cruel, warlike, and man-eaters. Their wooden clubs were jagged with crocodiles' teeth; they had no bows or arrows, but used lances a fathom and a-half long. They built no huts, and lived on fruits grown in plantations cleared from the forest. Fishers and swimmers, they were so dexterous as to be able to bring up with a rope an anchor of 600 cwt. from a rock, a feat which Esquemeling himself saw a few of them perform. The seamen in vain attempted to propitiate these wild freemen, to serve them as guides or hunters. At last, finding a great number together, and pursuing the fugitives, they tracked five men and four women to a cave, and took much pains to propitiate them. The captives remaining obstinately silent, as if from fear, in spite of the food that was given them, were dismissed with presents of knives and beads. They left, promising to return; "but soon forgot their *benefactors*," says Esquemeling, disgustfully. The sailors believed that at night all the Indians swam to a neighbouring island, as they never saw either boat or Indian again.

Some time before this the Frenchmen's terror had been excited by the discovery that these Indians were cannibals. Two buccaneers, a Frenchman and a Spaniard, had straggled into the woods in search of game. Pursued by a troop of savages, the latter, after a desperate struggle, was captured, and heard of no more; the former, the swifter footed of the two, escaped. A few days after, an armed party of a dozen *flibustiers*, led by this survivor, went into the same part of the forest to see if they could find any traces of the Indian encampment. Near the place where the Spaniard had fallen into the ambush they discovered the ashes of a fire, still warm, and among the embers some human bones, well scraped, and a white man's hand with two fingers half roasted, but still unconsumed.

For six months, till the long-boat was completed, the buccaneers lived on Spanish wheat, bananas, and on the fruits and green crops which they had sown on landing. Their bread they baked in portable ovens saved from the wreck.

Lolonnois now once more prepared to carry out his unabandoned project. With part of his crew he resolved to row up the river of Nicaragua, to capture some canoes, and return to fetch away those whom the new boat would not hold. The men cast lots for the choice of sailing with him. He took about one-half of the shipwrecked crew with him, part in the long-boat and part in a skiff which had been saved when the larger vessel drove on the bank. They arrived in a few days at Desaguadera, near Nicaragua, but attacked on the beach by an overpowering number of Spaniards and Indians, they were driven back to their boats, with the loss of many men, and escaped with difficulty, beaten and desponding.

Lolonnois, now fairly at bay with fortune, still resolved neither to return to Tortuga ragged and penniless, nor to rejoin his *comerades* till he had obtained a sufficient number of canoes to embark his companions. In order the better to obtain provisions he divided his men into two bands. The one party proceeded to the Cape Gracias à Dios, where they were well received; the other sailed to Boca del Toro, on the coast of Carthagena, where adventurers frequently repaired for turtle and other provisions, intending to embark in the first friendly vessel that should arrive.

Nicaragua was still destined to remain unscathed. "God Almighty," says Esquemeling, who writes with some bitterness, and probably much hypocrisy, "the time of His divine justice being now come, had appointed the Indians of Darien to be the instruments and executioners thereof." Landing at a place called the La Pointe à Diegue to obtain fresh water, Lolonnois and his men, weary of "wave, and wind, and oar," drew their canoes to land, and threw up entrenchments, knowing that they were now in the neighbourhood of the Bravo Indians, the most savage race known on the mainland—as cruel as sharks, and as numerous and greedy of blood as the vultures. He himself and a few others, passing the river, near the Gulf of Darien, landed in order to sack a town and obtain provisions. Here this modern Ulysses found a termination to his troubles and his life, for, being taken prisoner by the Indians, he was killed, chopped to pieces, and devoured. Many of his companions were also burnt alive, and but a few escaped to Tortuga, by the detail of their horrors to check for a few days the love of adventure in the minds of its restless and impetuous adventurers.

Esquemeling, or his English translator—who generally considers it necessary to conclude his chapters with a sanctimonious moral, a snuffle of the nose, and a lifting up of the eyes—says:

> Hither Lolonnois came (brought by his evil conscience that cried for punishment), thinking to act his cruelties; but the Indians, within a few days after his arrival, took him prisoner, throwing his body limb by limb into the fire, and his ashes into the air (*virtuous indignation*), that no trace or memory might remain of such an infamous, inhuman creature....Thus ends the history, the life, and the miserable death of that infernal wretch, Lolonnois, who, full of horrid, execrable, and enormous deeds, and debtor to so much innocent blood, died by cruel and butcherly hands, such as his own were in the course of his life.

Towards the conclusion of his malediction Esquemeling's wrath unfortunately gets much the better of his grammar.

The men left behind in the island de las Perlas, after long waiting for their companions—who had only escaped Scylla to run into Charybdis—were taken off by an English adventurer, who, collecting a body of 500 men, resolved on an expedition to the mainland. Ascending the river Moustique, near Cape Gracias, he sailed on, expecting to find some inlet to the lake of Nicaragua, round which Lolonnois' men still hovered. The expedition started full of hope, for the shipwrecked men were rejoiced at ending ten months of suffering, anxiety, and privation.

The result was worse than mere disappointment. In fifteen days they reached no Spanish town, but only some poor Indian villages, which they found deserted by the natives, who, aware of their coming, had fled, carrying off all the produce of their plantations. These they burnt in their rage, and marched recklessly onwards. They had carried no provision with them, expecting to find everywhere sufficient; and, to render their condition worse, had brought all their 500 men, except five or six who were left to guard each vessel. "These their hopes," says Esquemeling—turning up as usual the whites of his eyes—who looks with great contempt on all unsuccessful attempts at thieving, "were found totally vain, *as not being grounded.*" In a few days the hope of plunder, which had first animated them, grew clouded by despondency. Scarcity rapidly became want, and they were reduced to such extreme necessity and hunger that they gathered the plants that grew on the river's bank for food. In a fortnight their courage and vigour had entirely gone; their hearts sank, and their bodies were wasted by famine.

Leaving the river they took to the woods, seeking for Indian villages where they might obtain food. Ranging up and down the woods for some days in a fruitless search, they returned to the river, now their only guide, and struck back towards the point of coast where their ships lay. In this laborious journey they were reduced to much extremity—eating their shoes, their leather belts, and the very sheaths of their knives and swords. They grew at last so ravenous as to resolve to kill and devour the first Indian they could meet; but they could not obtain one either for food or as a guide. Some fell sick, and, fainting by the wayside, were left to perish. Many were killed and eaten by the Indians, and others died of starvation. At last they reached the shore, and, finding some comfort and relief to their present miseries, at once set sail to encounter more. After remaining some time on land, they reembarked, but a quarrel arising between the French and English buccaneers, who seldom kept long friends, they separated into small parties, and engaged in fresh expeditions.

CHAPTER 6

Alexandre Bras-de-Fer & Montbars the Exterminator

We now come to a class of buccaneers who lived at we scarcely know what period, although they were probably contemporaries of Oexmelin. Their adventures, though on a narrower scale, are perhaps more interesting than those that had subsequently taken place, and are valuable as illustrations of manners.

Oexmelin relates, in his usual shrewd and vivacious manner, the singular exploits of Alexandre Bras-de-Fer, a French adventurer, with whom he was acquainted, and who, unlike his contemporaries, never joined in large expeditions, preferring the promptitude of a single swift cruiser, with none to share his risks or subtract from his booty. His life seems to have been crowded with romantic and strange incidents. His character appears to have been a strange combination of bravery and chivalry, a love of rapine, and a fantastic vanity. Oexmelin says naïvely, that this modern Alexander was as great a man among the adventurers of Tortuga as the ancient Alexander was among the conquerors of the East. Nor does he see much difference between the two worthies, except that the Macedonian was the adventurer upon the larger scale.

Our Alexandre was vigorous in body and handsome in feature—so, at least, vouches Oexmelin, who, a surgeon by profession, once cured him of a severe wound that he had received—a cure which, if Alexandre had been generous (which he was not, in this instance at least), might have made the doctor's fortune.

Bras-de-Fer displayed as great judgment in the conception of his enterprises as he did courage in the carrying them out. His head and hand worked well together, and he seldom had to fight his way out of dangers into which his own incautiousness had led him. The vessel which he commanded he called the *Phoenix*, because it was of such a unique and peculiar structure that it was said to be among vessels what the phoenix was fabled to be among birds.

Alexandre always went alone, in preference to crowding in a fleet. His pride or his prudence may have given him a fondness for solitary cruises, for the *Phoenix* was a bird of prey. A picked crew and a single swift vessel had many advantages over a rebellious flotilla—and subordinate captains were often mutinous if not treacherous. If solitude increased his risk, it also increased his probability of success.

Oexmelin, the only writer who mentions Alexandre, relates but one of his adventures, which he took down, as he tells us, from the hero's own lips. The rest of his exploits he suppresses, either from a fear of being tedious or a dread of being considered a mere romancer.

On the occasion of which he speaks, Alexandre was bound upon an expedition of great consequence—which, however, as it did not succeed, the narrator, with a wise modesty, does not think worth mentioning. After lying some time imprisoned in a tedious calm, his prayers for a change of weather were answered by a great storm, that blew up the sea into mountains—wind and fire seeming to struggle together in the air for the possession of the helpless ship and its pale crew. The furious thunder drowned the very roar of the sea, and the masts soon went by the board. The lightning, striking its burning arrows through the deck, set fire to the powder-magazine, and blew up the part of the vessel in which it was stored. Half of the crew were hurled into the air, and were killed before they reached the boiling sea that eagerly waited for their fall. The remainder of the crew, finding the vessel going down by the head, took to swimming, and soon reached dry land: Alexandre—strong and brawny, brave, but desirous of life, and always awake to the means of its preservation—by no means the last, setting an example at once of prudence, coolness, and decision. On shaking the brine from their limbs and looking around, the wrecked men found that they had been thrown upon a tract of land as much to be dreaded by the buccaneer as the realm of

Polyphemus was by the wise Ulysses. They stood upon an island near the Boca del Drago (Dragon's Mouth), inhabited by a tribe of Indians, fierce and cruel cannibals. Remaining for some time upon the shore, they exerted themselves in recovering what they could from the scorched driftings of the wreck. Amongst other things they saved—what was more valuable than food, because they presented the means of saving their lives for the present and for the future—a number of their hunters' muskets, sufficient to arm all their number, together with a quantity of powder and lead for bullets. Without either of the three requisites the other two had been useless. They now gathered courage from the possibility of escape, and determined to secure themselves from the Indians, reconnoitre the place for fear of surprise, and after that remain patiently encamped till some friendly vessel should arrive.

One day, while some of the band were smoking, singing, and talking, their past dangers already half forgotten in the desire of escaping the present by encountering fresh in the future, the sentinels on the look-out hill gave the signal of an approaching vessel. On all rushing to the spot, the keener eyes detected a large ship, dark against the grey horizon. It presently discharged a gun at the shore, and in the direction in which they stood. Preparing for the worst, Alexandre and his men hid themselves in a wooded hollow and held a council of war. Some were of opinion that they should wait for the stranger's arrival, and then quietly beg the captain to take them on board. The more impatient and lawless, less pacific in such an emergency, believed that such a plan would lead, if the vessel proved, as it probably would, a Spaniard, to their all being taken prisoners, and at once strung from the yard-arm, without inquiry, as Frenchmen and pirates. Bras-de-Fer spoke last, and crushed all opposition by his voice and gesture. He was for war to the death, and escape at any risk. Better Spanish rope than Indian fire, better pistol shot than starvation. Quick in decision and firm in execution, he had at once determined not merely to stand on the defensive, but at all risks to assume the aggressive. The adventurers yielded as if an angel had spoken, for Alexandre had more than the usual ascendancy of a leader over them. Both his mind and body were of a more athletic bulk and iron mould. He could dare and suffer more. His active and his passive, his moral and physical courage, were greater than theirs. They loved him because he shared their dangers, and did not humiliate them by the assumption of his real superiority. He wore the crown, but he was not always dazzling their eyes with its oppressive glitter. They respected him, because he could control both his own passions and those of the men whom he led to victory and never to defeat. The success of his victories he doubled by the prudence with which they were followed up, and the skill with which he conducted a retreat rendered his very defeats in themselves successes.

The vessel, which proved to be a Spanish merchant ship, with war equipments, approached nearer, standing off and on, attracted by the fruit and flowers whose perfume spread over the level sea, and allured by that fragrance, a sure proof of the existence of good water not far from the shore. The boats were lowered, and a well-armed party landed with much caution. The captain marched at their head, followed by his best soldiers, dreading an ambuscade of the Indians of that coast, who were known to be warlike and treacherous, but not suspecting the buccaneers, who kept themselves in the wood, ready to swoop down upon their prey, like the kite upon the dovecote.

Already well acquainted with the paths and foot-tracks, Alexandre's men crept quietly through the trees, which grew thick and dark, and, defiling by secret avenues, surrounded the principal approach by which the Spaniards had already entered, in good order and on the alert, but with apprehensions already subsiding. The adventurers being very inferior in number and scantily armed, kept themselves hidden, waiting for chance to give them some momentary advantage. When the enemy was well encircled in the defile, mistaking perhaps the lighted matches for fire-flies among the branches, the French suddenly opened a murderous fire upon the soldiers, who found themselves girt by a belt of flame, coming from they knew not where. A pilgrim seeing a volcano opening at his feet could not be more astonished. The Spaniards, seeing no enemies to aim at, withheld their fire, thinking that the Indians were burning the forest. The absence of arrows, and the report of muskets, convinced them more deadly enemies awaited them, and that Europeans and not Indians were the preparers of the ambush. With much promptitude, instead of flying in a foolish headlong rout, they threw themselves upon their faces; and the captain gave the word of command not to fire till the enemy came in sight, being ignorant yet of their number and their nation.

The adventurers looked through the loopholes which they had cut in the thick underwood for the passage of their firearms, to see what effect their volley had produced, the smoke now clearing away and permitting them to see more clearly. To their astonishment they could see no one; the enemy had vanished, as if blown to pieces by the fire. They began to think that they had retreated, although they had heard no sound of their retreat; they could scarcely believe that they were all dead.

Alexandre's impatience soon decided the question; determined to conquer, he chafed at the delay and mystery. His resolution was soon made. He left his ambush and broke out from the wood into the open. The mystery was quickly solved, for he was instantly attacked by the Spaniards, who, when they saw him break cover, sprang up to their feet, with a shout, as swift as the foes of Cadmus. Alexandre, retreating for a moment to make his spring the surer, leaped upon the hostile captain and aimed a blow at his head with his sabre, which was warded off by a large scull-cap, from which the steel glanced. Bras-de-Fer was about to repeat his blow with better effect, when his foot caught in a root and he fell. Closely pressed by his antagonist, and requiring all his skill to save his life, rising up, with his left hand and with his strong right arm, he struck the uplifted sabre from the hand of his enemy. This lucky blow of a defenceless man gave Alexandre time to leap up and call the adventurers, who had not then left the ambush, and were now pouring out on every side, pressing the enemy in the rear and on the flank. Having made a great carnage among the Spaniards, the *flibustiers*, at a signal from Alexandre, closed in, and, bearing down upon the craven and terrified foe sword in hand, slew them to a man, taking special care that not a single one should escape, for fear of spreading an alarm.

The Spanish crew remaining to keep guard in the vessel, had heard the sound of musketry, and at once supposed that their people had fallen in with some hostile Indians, but knowing that their troops were brave and numerous, and believing they could easily cut a few savages to pieces, they sent no reinforcement, but contented themselves by discharging a noisy broadside to turn the scale of the supposed battle, and increase the terror of the fugitives. On the other hand, the victorious adventurers lost no time in following up their ambush by an ingenious stratagem. They stripped the dead, and arrayed themselves in their dress and arms. They then collected a quantity of their own Indian arrows, which they had previously taken from savages which they had killed. Then pulling their broad-brimmed Panama hats over their eyes (even the captain's, with a red gash through it), and shouldering their arms, imitating the Spanish march, and uttering shouts of "victory, victory," proceeded to the shore at the point nearest the vessel. The guards on board, seeing their supposed companions returned so soon, victorious, laden with spoil, and each one carrying a sheaf of arrows, received them with open arms as they clambered up by the main-chains. Before they could recover from their astonishment, the buccaneers were masters of the vessel. There was scarcely any struggle, for only the sailors and a few marines had been left on board. The surprise was complete and sudden, and the most watchful might be pardoned for being deluded by such an artifice. The adventurers found the vessel laden with costly merchandise, and soon started with it upon a trip of a very different nature from that for which it had been first intended.

Oexmelin laments that in many other adventures which Alexandre told him, he found that he passed too lightly over his own exploits, and attributed all the glory to the courage of his companions. But when his *comerades* related the story, they were not so generous to him as he had been to them, and, either from envy or shame, suppressed many of his noblest actions. He concludes his sketch of the two Alexanders with incomparable *naïveté* in the following manner:

> *Au reste, je ne prétends pas que la comparaison soit toute-à-fait juste, car s'il y a quelque rapport, il y a encore plus de différence. En effet il étoit aussi brave que téméraire, et lui étoit brave que prudent. Alexandre aymoit le vin, et lui l'eau-de-vie. Aussi Alexandre fuyoit les femmes par grandeur d'âme, et luy les cherchoit par tendresse de coeur; et pour preuve de ce que je dis il s'en trouve une assez belle dans le vaisseau dont j'ay parlé, qu'il préféra à tout l'avantage du butin.*

To conclude: if I have compared him to the Great Alexander, I do not pretend that the comparison is altogether just; for, if there are some points of resemblance, there are many more of difference. Of a truth, the one Alexander was as brave as he was headstrong, the other as brave as he was prudent; the one loved wine, and the other brandy; the one fled from women through real greatness of heart, the other sought them from a natural tenderness of soul; and, as a proof of what I say, he met a beautiful woman in the vessel of which I have spoken, whom he valued more than all the other spoil.

Providence, a French moral philosopher ventures to suggest, raised up the buccaneers to revenge on the Spaniards all the sufferings and injustices of the Indians. The Spaniard was the scourge of the Indian, and the buccaneer the scourge of the Spaniard.

Lolonnois and Montbars are always considered as equal claimants for the hateful pre-eminence of being the most ferocious of the whole buccaneer brotherhood, considering them from their origin to their extinction. But the sovereignty of blood must be at once awarded to Lolonnois. Montbars seldom killed a Spaniard who begged for mercy, while Lolonnois delighted to spurn them from his feet, and slew all he could without pity, or even regard for ransom. It was from the very lips of Lolonnois that Oexmelin was informed that Montbars was sprung from one of the best families in Languedoc. He was well educated, but soon disregarded every other study to practise martial exercise, and particularly shooting. These warlike sports he pursued with a concentrated, unremitting eagerness, approaching insanity. Even as a boy, when firing with his cross-bow, he said he only wished to shoot well that he might know how to kill a Spaniard. His mind had already become filled with a generous but cruel determination, which grew rapidly into monomania. The animal force of a strong but ill-balanced mind all grew to this point, and his thoughts by day, and his dreams by night, became but a reiteration and reblending of the one master passion. No one ever became his confidant, but the following is the general explanation given of the deeds of his after life. It is said that, in his early childhood, Montbars had read of the almost incredible cruelties practised by the Spaniards during the conquest of America. In the Antilles, they had exhibited the horrors of the Inquisition in broad daylight. Fanaticism, avarice, and ambition had ruled like a trinity of devils over the beautiful regions, desolated and plague-smitten; whole nations had become extinct, and the name of Christ was polluted into the mere cypher of an armed and aggressive commerce. These books had impressed the gloomy boy with a deep, absorbing, fanatical hatred of the conquerors, and a fierce pity for the conquered. He believed himself marked out by God as the Gideon sent to their relief. Dreams of riches and gratified ambition spurred him unconsciously to the task. He thought and dreamed of nothing but the murdered Indians. He inquired eagerly from travellers for news from America, and testified prodigious and ungovernable joy when he heard that the Spaniards had been defeated by the Caribs or the Bravos.

He indeed knew by heart every deed of atrocity that history recorded of his enemies, and would dilate on each one with a rude and impatient eloquence. The following story he was frequently accustomed to relate, and to gloat over with a look that indicated a mind capable of even greater cruelty, if once led away by a fanatic spirit of retaliation. A Spaniard, the story ran, was once upon a time appointed governor of an Indian province, which was inhabited by a fierce and warlike race of savages. He proved a cruel governor, unforgiving in his resentments, and insatiable in his avarice. The Indians, unable any longer to endure either his barbarities or his exactions, seized him, and, showing him gold, told him that they had at last been able, by great good luck, to find enough to satisfy his demands. They then held him firm, and melting the ore, poured it down his throat till he expired in torments under their hands.

On one occasion, Montbars openly showed that his reason was somewhat disturbed, and that, on the one subject of his thoughts, he had ceased to be able to reflect calmly. While a boy, he had to take part in a comedy which was to be acted by himself and the fellow-students of the college, for his friends either ignored or disregarded his dreams and fancies. Amongst other scenes was a prologue, in the shape of a dialogue between a Spaniard and a Frenchman. Montbars was to represent the Frenchman, and his companion the Spaniard. The Spaniard, appearing first upon the stage, began to utter a thousand invectives against France, mingled with much ribald *rhodomontade*, and Montbars became excited, and could not contain his impatience. To his heated mind the mimic scene became a reality. He broke in upon the stage, furiously interrupted his *comerade* in the middle of his speech, and, loading him with blows, would certainly have put him to death on the spot, as "a Spanish liar and murderer," had the combatants not been separated by the terrified bystanders.

His father, rich, and loving his son much, perhaps all the better for these wayward eccentricities, which, he believed, contact of the world and the pleasures of youth would soon drive from his memory, desired to enrol him in the army, or induce him to enter some profession. But to all his questions and entreaties the boy only replied, that all he wanted was "to fight against the Spaniards." Seeing that his friends would oppose his project, he ran away from his father's house, and took refuge at Havre with an uncle who commanded one of the French king's ships. He was about to start on a cruise against Spain, with whom France was then at war, and, pleased at the boy's avowed attachment to a maritime life, wrote to his father, approving of the boy's resolution. The father reluctantly gave what could be construed into a consent, and in a few days the vessel sailed.

During the voyage out, the young fanatic evinced the greatest eagerness for an engagement, and directly a vessel appeared in sight ran to arm himself, hoping it might be a Spaniard. At length, one did in reality appear, and he had an opportunity of distinguishing himself against his declared enemies. They gave chase to the Spanish vessel, and received her broadside. The elder Montbars, seeing his nephew intoxicated with joy, and, disregarding all risk of exposure, determining to throw away his life, clapped him under hatches, as a reckless boy, and only let him rush out when the boarding commenced, and the enemy's vessel was evidently their own. The liberated youth led the boarders with all the calmness of a veteran man-of-war's-man. Leaping, sabre in hand, upon the foe, he fought with them pell-mell, broke through their thickest ranks, and, followed by a few whom his courage animated to rival his own rashness, rushed twice from end to end of the Spanish vessel, mowing down all he met to the right and left. The Spaniards were refused quarter, those who escaped the sword perished in the sea, and Montbars, to whom the honour of the victory was unanimously awarded, refused quarter to a single one. The prize was found full of spoil, the hold crammed with riches, containing 30,000 bales of cotton, 2000 bales of silk, besides Indian stuffs, 2000 packets of incense, and 1000 of cloves, which made up the treasure. In addition to all this, they found a small casket of diamonds, the case clasped with iron, and fastened with four locks, which alone outvalued all the bulkier merchandise. While his uncle and the sailors exulted over these treasures, Montbars was counting the dead Spaniards, and gloating over the first victims of the hecatomb he still hoped to slay. Blood, and not booty, was his object.

In spite of the young victor, a few Spanish sailors and officers had been spared in the general carnage. From these survivors they learnt that two other vessels had been parted from them in a storm, near where they then were (St. Domingo), and that their rendezvous had been fixed at Port Margot. Captain Montbars determined to wait for them there, and to capture them by the stratagem of sending the captured vessel with its Spanish colours out to meet them, as a decoy. While the French vessel and its prize lay waiting at the rendezvous, some huntsmen's boats came off to sea, bringing *boucaned* meat to barter for brandy. The buccaneers apologised for bringing so little meat, saying, "that a band of Spanish *fifties* had lately ravaged their district, burnt their hides, stolen their dried meat, and burnt their *boucans*."

"And why do you suffer it?" said Montbars, impetuously, for he had been listening eagerly all this time, to the recital of a new proof of Spanish perfidy.

"We do not suffer it," answered the huntsmen, roughly. "The Spaniards know well what sort of people we are, and they chose a time when we were all away cow-killing; but our day is coming. We are now collecting our companions, who have suffered worse than we have; we have given notice far and wide, and if the fifty grow to 1000, we shall soon bring them to bay."

"If you are willing," says Montbars, "I will march at your head. I do not want to command you, but to expose myself first, to show you what I am ready to do against these accursed Spaniards."

The old hunters, astonished at the daring of a mere youth, and glad of another musket, accepted his proposal. His uncle, unable to rein him in, and already weary of so hot-brained a volunteer, yielded to his entreaties. He permitted him to go, giving him a party of seamen to guard him, and supplied him with but few provisions, in hopes of bringing him quickly back. He threatened, on parting, to leave him behind if he was not on board to the very hour, then calling him a foolish madcap, and cursing him for a hair-brain, he dismissed him with his blessing, swearing the next minute there wasn't a braver lad at that moment treading a plank.

Montbars departed with some uneasiness, not caring about his uncle's advice or the scantiness of provisions, but only afraid that he might miss the Spaniards on land, and be absent also when the Spanish vessels were attacked. He wanted no greater inducement to hurry his return than the prospect of a naval engagement. He had scarcely landed with his men, when the hunters brought them into a small savannah surrounded by hills and woods. They had not taken many steps across this broad hunting-ground before they saw some mounted Spaniards appear in the distance—these men were part of a troop that had collected, hearing that the buccaneers were assembling to attack them.

Montbars, transported with rage at the sight of a Spaniard, would have rushed at once upon them, single-handed, but an old experienced buccaneer caught him by the arm: "Stop," said he, "there is plenty of time, and, if you do what I tell you, not one of these fellows shall escape." These words, "not one," would at any time have arrested Montbars, and they did so then. The old buccaneer, crying a halt, bade the men turn their backs on the Spaniards, as if they had not seen them. He next unrolled the linen tent, which he carried in the usual fashion of his craft, and began to pitch it, followed by all his companions, who did the same, imitating their fugleman, without inquiry, trusting to the address that had often before delivered them out of danger. They then drew out their brandy flasks and affected to prepare for a revel, intending to deceive the Spaniards, who, they knew, would give them time to drink, in hopes of surprising them, an easy prey, when asleep. The empty horns were passed round with jokes, and songs, and shouts, and the corked flasks circulated as merrily as if the feast had been a real one. Without appearing to observe, they could see the Spanish patrols disappear over the ridge of the hill, to warn their men in the valley to prepare for a night surprise. The buccaneer leader, passing the signal from hand to hand, sent an *engagé* into the woods to quickly rouse all the "brothers" in the neighbourhood, to bid them come and help them, and to prepare an ambush in the opposite forest. In the mean time, other scouts were sent to watch the motions of the enemy, to be sure that they were coming, and were not making any flank movement.

At dusk the buccaneers slipped quietly from beneath their tents, and crept into the adjacent woods. Here they found their companions and their *engagés* already assembled and eager for the attack. Montbars, weary of all preparations, was now burning to see the Spaniards, declared they never would come, and that they had better go out and surprise them while night lasted; but the Spaniards were purposely delaying, knowing that the longer they delayed the deeper would be the sleep of the revellers. At daybreak, they could see a dark troop beginning to move forward over the ridge, and soon to descend the hill into the plain in good order, a small detachment marching before them as a forlorn hope. The buccaneers, well posted and unobserved, waited for them, sure of their prey, for the tents being pitched at some distance one from the other, they could see every movement of the Spaniards. As they drew nearer, the *fifties* broke into small troops, and each encircled a tent. To their astonishment, at that moment the wood grew a flame, and a hot rolling fire led on the advancing buccaneers, who, breaking out with yell and shout, very terrible in the silence of the dawning, overthrew horse and rider. Montbars, inspired by the fever of the onslaught, which always seemed for a moment to restore the balance of his mind, leaped on a horse, whose rider he had killed, and headed the attack. Wherever resistance was made, he rode in, charging every knot of troopers as they attempted to rally. Hurrying on too far beyond his companions, while breaking into the heart of the squadron, he was surrounded, and would have been quickly overpowered had he not been rescued by a determined rush of his men. More furious at this escape, he pursued the scattered enemy right and left, with increased fury, inflicting blows as dreadful as they were unusual. One of the buccaneers, seeing many of his men suffering from the Indian arrows, cried out to the Indians, in Spanish, pointing to Montbars, "Do you not see that God has sent you a liberator, who fights for you, to deliver you from the Spaniards, and yet you still fight for your tyrants?"

Hearing these words, and astonished at Montbars' contempt for death, the archers changed sides and turned their arrows against the Spaniards, who fled, overwhelmed by this new misfortune, and perhaps impelled by an undefinable and superstitious terror.

Montbars looked upon this day as the happiest in his life. He had seen the Indians he had so pitied fighting by his side, and regarding him as their protector. Cleaving down a wounded Spaniard, who clung to his knees and begged for mercy, he cried, "I would it were the last of this accursed race."

An eye witness of the battle describes the carnage as horrible—the living trampling on the living, and stumbling over the dying and the dead.

The buccaneers and the Indians, rejoicing in their liberty and their revenge, entreated Montbars to follow up his successes, and wanted at once to ravage the Spanish plantations, and extirpate the survivors, while they were still discouraged. Montbars gladly consented to the proposal, and was about to march exultingly at their head, when the boom of a cannon was heard. It was the report of a gun from his uncle's vessel, and he could not resist obeying a signal that might be the signal of an approaching battle. He instantly hurried back, but found, to his annoyance, that the signal had been only fired as a warning to announce the hour of instant sailing.

The hunters, already attached to their young leader, refused to leave him, and the Indians were afraid to abide the vengeance of the Spaniards. They were all therefore at once placed on board the prize, and supplied with muskets and sabres. The delighted uncle appointed Montbars as captain, with an old officer, under the name of lieutenant, to act as his guardian.

After eight days' sail, Montbars was attacked, at the mouth of a large key, by four Spanish vessels, each one larger than his own. They surrounded him so suddenly that he had no time to escape, and he lay amongst them like a wolf at bay. They formed, in fact, the van of the great Indian plate fleet, which was, every year, as eagerly expected by the king of Spain as it was by all the marauders of the Spanish main. The elder Montbars, bold and hardy, unhesitatingly attacked two of the vessels, and several times drove back their boarders. Although gouty himself and unable to move, the staunch old Gascon shouted his orders from his elbow chair; and, cursing alternately the enemy and the disease, defended his ship to the last extremity. Having fought for more than three hours with ferocious obstinacy, and seeing his young hero terribly pressed by his two adversaries, he resolved upon a final effort, the last struggle of a wild beast that feels the knife is at his throat. Firing a tremendous broadside, he attacked both his enemies with such fury that he sank them and himself, and died "laughing" in all the exultation of that revenge which is the only victory of despair.

Montbars the younger made great exertions to save himself and to avenge his uncle. The old lion was dead, but the cub had much life in him yet. He sank one of his antagonists with a crashing shot and boarded the other. His Indians, seeing their leader enter the Spanish vessel at one end, threw themselves into the water and clambered promptly up the other. Their war-cries and arrows produced a powerful diversion, and took the Spaniards by surprise. Throwing many into the sea, they killed others, while Montbars put all that resisted to the sword. In a short time he was master of a vessel larger even than those that had been sunk. The friendly Indians, who now looked upon him as an invincible demigod, he employed in a fruitless search for his uncle's body. Conquerors and conquered were destined to remain locked in each other's arms, and piled over with bloody trophies of burnt wreck until the day that the sea should give up her dead.

The hunters renewed their proposal of a descent upon the mainland, and Montbars agreed to any scheme which would enable him to avenge his uncle and his friends. He had formerly lived to avenge the wrongs of others, to these were now added his own. The governor of the province, hearing of the contemplated attack, prepared an ambuscade of negroes and militiamen. Putting himself at the head of 800 men, divided into three battalions, his wings strengthened with cavalry and his van guarded with cannon, he prepared to prevent the landing of the "Exterminator."

These preparations only increased the ardour of Montbars. It seemed cowardly to ravage an unprotected country: its devastation, after defeating its defenders, was a reward of conquest. Montbars was the first to leap from the canoes, and the first to rush upon the Spanish pikes. The front battalion was soon repulsed, and some Indians taking the reserve force in the flank, they were driven back in great disorder. Montbars, hotly pursuing, made a prodigious carnage of the enemy, and carried fire and sword far into the interior.

One day, while at sea, the young captain, already a veteran in experience, was obliged to put into a bay to careen. To his great surprise, although the place was a mere track of sand, he saw some Spaniards on a distant plain, marching in good order and well-armed. Fearing that if they saw his men they would take to flight, he sent a few of his favourite Indians to decoy them towards him. Then falling upon them with fury as they cried out for quarter Montbars shouted, in Spanish, that they had nothing to hope for till they had killed himself and all his men. These dreadful words, together with his revengeful looks, drove them to take up their arms and fight with dogged and brutal despair, till they were slain almost to a man. Advancing into the country in search of more human prey, Montbars carried off the arms of the Spaniards and a great quantity of fruits and provisions.

It appeared, from a survivor, that the Spaniards had arrived in that country in a singular manner. They had formed the crew in guard of a vessel full of negro slaves who had conspired together to drive the ship on shore. They had secretly bored holes in the ship's hold, in which they had placed pluggets, which they drew out, and replaced, unseen, and in a moment. While the Spaniards were seated together, talking with their usual stately, stolid phlegm, this unaccountable leak would break out and fill the cabin, or drench them in their hammocks. The slaves never seemed alarmed, but always astonished, and filled the air with interjections, in the Congo language. The water rushing in pell-mell, even the ship's carpenter did not know from where, drove all hands, at great danger to the ship, almost to leave the helm to save the cargo, which was already damaged. The negroes, quiet and orderly, would generally succeed, after a time, in stopping the leak, and excited general admiration by their promptitude and naval skill. All then went on well for a time; but with the least wind or storm the leak recommenced, till the very captain began reluctantly to confess, with tears in his eyes, that they were all as good as lost, for the vessel was dangerous, and not seaworthy. In the middle of the night, or at meal time, this supernatural leak would recommence, till the pumps were all but worn out, and the men faint with want of sleep.

One day, when the vessel was skirting a reef, the negroes watched the opportunity, and the leak commenced with redoubled fury, the slaves howling as if from the very disquietness of their hearts. The Spaniards, thinking all hope lost, and the vessel, as they declared, already beginning to settle down, abandoned the ship, and threw themselves on that very tongue of land where Montbars afterwards surprised them. The trick had been cleverly planned and cleverly executed, but a hitch in the machinery had nearly ruined all. One of the blacks, more timid or less sagacious than the rest, seeing the water pour in with more than usual impetuosity, and on all sides, lost his presence of mind. Not able at once, in his panic, to find the hole which he had to stop, he believed that his companions had also failed, and that all was indeed lost, and, throwing himself overboard without inquiring, he joined the Spaniards, who were thanking God (prematurely) for their deliverance.

Looking back for his companions, to his horror he saw a dozen of them tugging at the helm, and putting out wildly to sea. The truth flashed upon him, and he knew in a moment that his safety was a loss. Giving way to uncontrollable despair, he tore his wool, and stamped his feet, and cursed his fetish, and stretched out his hands, as if to stay the parting vessel. The Spaniards, astonished at this apparently passionate desire to be drowned, began slowly to discover the successful stratagem. They looked: *"Demonio, St. Antonio!"*—the vessel did not sink, but glided swiftly out to sea. They could see the blacks laughing, pulling at the ropes, and grinning from the port-holes. They turned with fury on the unhappy survivor, and put him to the torture till he confessed the truth.

And this story completes all that history has preserved of one of the strangest combinations of fanatic and soldier that has ever appeared since the days of Loyola. In another age, and under other circumstances, he might have become a second Mohammed. Equally remorseless, his ambition, though narrower, seems to have been no less fervid. If he was cruel, we must allow him to have been sincere even in his fanaticism. Daring, untiring, of unequalled courage, and unmatched resolution, the cruelty of the Spaniards he put down by greater cruelty. He passes from us into unknown seas, and we hear of him no more. He died probably unconscious of crime, unpitying and unpitied.

Oexmelin, who saw Montbars at Honduras, describes him as active, vivacious, and full of fire, like all the Gascons. He was of tall stature, erect and firm, his air grand, noble, and martial. His complexion was sun-burnt, and the colour of his eyes could not be discerned under the deep, arched vaulting of his bushy eyebrows. His very glance in battle was said to intimidate the Spaniards, and to drive them to despair.

In 1659, Santiago was pillaged by the *flibustiers*, in revenge for the murder of twelve Frenchmen, who had been shot by a Spanish captain, who took them from a Flemish vessel, sparing only a woman, and a child who hid itself under the robe of a monk.

Determined on retaliation, the people of the coast assembled to the number of 500. Obtaining an English commission, they embarked on board a frigate from Nantes, and a number of small craft—De L'Isle being their commander, and Adam, Lormel, and Anne le Roux their lieutenants. They landed at Puerto de Plata, "*le Dimanche des Rameaux*," and marched upon St. Jago at daybreak. Passing over the bodies of the guards, they rushed to the governor's house, and surprised him in bed. He, knowing French, threw himself on his knees, and told them that peace was about to be declared between the two nations. They replied, that they carried an English commission, and, reproaching him for his cruelties, bade him either prepare for death, or pay down 60,000 crowns. Part of this ransom he instantly paid in hides. The pillage of the town lasted twenty-four hours, and nothing was spared; the very bells were carried from the churches, and the altars stripped of their plate. No violence, however, we are glad to record, was offered to the women, the Brotherhood having agreed, that any such offender should lose his share of the spoil.

CHAPTER 7
Sir Henry Morgan

Morgan's campaigns furnish one of the amplest chapters of buccaneer history. Equally daring, but less cruel than Lolonnois, less fanatical than Montbars, and less generous and honest than De Lussan or Sharp, he appears to have been the only freebooting leader who obtained any formal recognition from the English government. From an old pamphlet, we find, that the expedition to Panama was undertaken under the commission and with the full approbation of the English governor of Jamaica.

Sir Henry Morgan was the son of a Welsh farmer, of easy circumstances, "as most who bear that name in Wales are known to be," says Esquemeling, his Dutch historian. Taking an early dislike to the monotonous, unadventurous life of his father's house, he ran away from home, and, coming to the coast, turned sailor, and went to sea.

Embarking on board a vessel bound for Barbadoes, that lay with several others in the port, he engaged himself in the usual way to a planter's agent, who resold him for three years immediately on his arrival in the West Indies. Having served his time and obtained his hard-earned liberty, he repaired to Jamaica, a place of which wild stories were told all over the Main. He resolved to seek his fortune at that El Dorado, and arriving there, saw two buccaneer vessels just fitting out for an expedition. Being now in search of employment, and finding this suit his daring and restless spirit, he determined to embrace the life of a *flibustier*. The gentlemen of fortune were successful, and had not been long at sea before they took a valuable prize.

This early success was as fatal to Morgan as good luck is to a young gambler on his first visit to a hell. It roused his ambition, heightened his hope, and encouraged him to continue a career so auspiciously begun. He followed the buccaneer chiefs, and learnt their manners of living. In the course of only three or four voyages, he signalized himself so much as to acquire the reputation of a good soldier, remarkable for his valour and success. He was a good shot, and renowned for his intrepidity, coolness, and determination. He seemed to foresee all contingencies, and set about his schemes with a firm confidence that insured their success.

Having already laid by much money, and being fortunate both in his voyages and in gambling, Morgan agreed with a few rich *comerades* to join stock, and to buy a vessel, of which he was unanimously appointed commander. Such was the usual beginning of an adventurer's career. Setting out from Jamaica, he soon became remarkable for the number of prizes which he took, his well known stations being round the coast of Campeachy. With these prizes he returned triumphantly to Jamaica, his name established as a terror to the Spaniard, and a war-cry to the English. Finding Mansvelt, an old buccaneer, lying in harbour, about to start on a grand expedition to the mainland, he joined him, and was at once elected as vice-admiral of a small fleet of fifteen vessels and 600 men, part English and part French.

They sailed first to the island of St. Catherine, near the continent of Costa Rica, and distant about thirty-five degrees from the river of Chagres. Here they made their first descent, and found the Spaniards well entrenched in forts, strongly built of hewn stone, but landing most of their men they soon forced the garrisons to surrender. Morgan distinguished himself remarkably in this expedition, forcing even his very enemies to laud his skill and valour. He now proceeded to demolish all the castles but one, in which he placed 100 men, and the slaves and prisoners, and proceeded to attack a small neighbouring island. In a few days they threw over a bridge to join it to St. Catherine's, and conveyed over it all the larger ordnance which they had taken, laying waste their first conquest with fire and sword. They then set sail again, having first set their prisoners ashore near Portobello, intending to cruise along Costa Rica, as far as the river Colla, and burn and pillage all the towns up to Nata. They had, in fact, only taken the island in order to procure a guide who could lead them on their way to Nata, knowing that the Spaniards used St. Catherine's as a depot for their prisoners of all nations. The first step towards a buccaneer expedition was to procure a guide. They found, to their delight, a mulatto who knew Nata, and who undertook to lead them to the destruction of a people whom he hated. It is probable, too, that Mansvelt had already projected founding a colony at St. Catherine's, which might be neither dependent on the French nor the English. But their schemes were frustrated, for the governor of Panama, hearing of their approach, and of their past success, advanced to meet them with a body of men, and compelled them to retreat suddenly, for the whole country was now alarmed and their plans all known.

Morgan, however, seeing St. Catherine's to be a well-fortified island, easily defended, and important as to situation, because its harbour was good and near the Spanish settlements, resolved to hold it, appointing as governor Le Sieur Simon, a Frenchman, whom he left behind, with a garrison of 100 men. St. Simon had behaved well in his absence, and put the island in a good posture of defence, had strengthened the four large forts, and turned the smaller island into a citadel, guarding carefully the three accessible spots, planting vegetables and clearing plantations in the smaller island, where abundance of fresh water could be procured, providing victual enough for the fleet for two voyages.

The two commanders now determined to return to Jamaica, promising to send recruits to Simon, for fear of an invasion, and themselves to bring speedy succours, intending to make the island a sanctuary and refuge for the brotherhood of both nations. The governor of Jamaica refused to accede to Mansvelt's requests for soldiers, afraid to weaken the forces of the island without permission from England. Mansvelt, worn out with delay, hastened to Tortuga, and died while collecting volunteers, his plans being still in embryo. Had his scheme succeeded, and been pushed with energy, the buccaneers might have founded a republic, and have eventually driven the Spaniards out of the Indies.

While Simon was impatiently expecting succour from Jamaica, and astonished at Mansvelt's really unavoidable silence, the Spaniards were preparing to smoke out the wasps' nest that lay so dangerously near their orchard. A new governor of Costa Rica threw unusual decision into their plans. Fearing they should lose the Indies piecemeal, they resolved to crush the evil ere it grew indestructible. Don Juan Perez de Guzman equipped a fleet of four vessels with fifty or sixty men each, commanded by Don Joseph Sancho Ximenes, major-general of the garrison of Porto Bello. Don Juan, in a letter to Simon, promised him a reward if he would surrender the island to his Catholic Majesty, and threatened him with punishment if he resisted. Simon, seeing the impossibility and uselessness of resistance, surrendered it after a few shots, on the same condition with which Morgan had obtained it from the enemy.

The Spaniards made much of their victory, publishing...

> ...a true relation and particular account of the victory obtained by the arms of his Catholic Majesty, against the English pirates, by the direction and valour of Don Juan Perez de Guzman, knight of the order of St. James, governor and captain-general of Terra Firma, and the province of Veraguas.

The account goes on to describe the arrival of fourteen English vessels on the coast, 1665, their arrival at Puerto de Naos, and the capture of St. Catherine's from the governor, Don Estevan del Campo, the enemy landing unperceived. Upon this the valorous Don Juan called a council of war, wherein he declared the great progress the said pirates had made in the dominions of his Catholic Majesty, and propounded:

> ...that it was absolutely necessary to send some forces to the isle of St. Catherine, sufficient to retake it from the pirates, the honour and interest of his Majesty of Spain being very narrowly concerned herein, otherwise the pirates, by such conquests, might *easily*, in course of time, possess themselves of 'all the countries thereabout.'

The less vapouring, or more pacific, ingeniously proposed to leave the pirates alone till they perished for want of provisions, but Don Juan, overruling their timidity, sent stores to the militia of Porto Bello, and conveyed himself there, with no small danger of his life. At this port he found the *St. Vincent*, a good ship, belonging to the Negro Company, which he equipped with a crew of 270 soldiers, thirty-seven prisoners, thirty-two of the Spanish garrison, twenty-nine mulattos of Panama, twelve Indian archers, seven gunners, two lieutenants, two pilots, a surgeon, and a Franciscan chaplain. Before they set sail, Don Juan (*who did not go with them*) encouraged them to fight against the enemies of their country and their religion, "those inhuman pirates who had committed so many horrid cruelties upon the subjects of his Catholic Majesty," promising liberal rewards to all who behaved themselves well in the service of their king and country. At Carthagena, they received a reinforcement of one frigate, one galleon, a boat, and 127 men.

On arriving at the island, the pirates discharged three guns, refused to surrender, and declared they preferred to lose their lives. The next day three negro deserters, swimming to the admiral, told him there were only seventy-two men on the island, and two days after the day of the Assumption the Spaniards landed and commenced the affray. The *St. Vincent* attacked the Conception battery, the *St. Peter* the St. James's forts, the pirates driving off many of the enemy by loading their guns with part of the pipes of a church organ, threescore pipes at a time. The pirates lost six men before surrendering, the Spaniards one. They found in the island 800 lbs. of powder, and 250 lbs. of bullets. Two Spanish deserters, discovered amongst the prisoners, were "shot to death" the next day. The prisoners were transported to Puerto Velo, all but three, who, by order of the governor, were kept as a trophy, like chained Samsons, to work in the castle of St. Jerome at Panama, a fortress building by the governor at his own expense.

A day or two after this unavoidable surrender, a vessel arrived at St. Catherine, bringing reinforcements and provisions from the governor of Jamaica, who had repented of his rejection of Mansvelt's proposal, but had not even yet the courage to be boldly dishonest. The Spaniards, hoisting an English flag, persuaded Simon to welcome it, and betray it into their hands. There were fourteen men on board and two women, all of whom were made prisoners.

On the death of Mansvelt, Morgan became without opposition the leader of all the adventurers of Jamaica. He at once published far and wide his intention of setting out on a grand expedition, and named Cuba as a rendezvous, St. Catherine's not being far distant. Morgan had been no less anxious than Mansvelt to make this island a fortress and a storehouse. He had written to the merchants of Virginia and New England, to contract with them for ammunition and provisions; but this hope being ended by the Spanish conquest, he felt himself free to embark on a wider and more ambitious field. His plans were for a moment defeated, but his courage and ambition were not a whit humbled.

Two months spent in the southern ports of Cuba sufficed him to collect a fleet of twelve sail, with 700 fighting men, part English, part French, resolved to follow him to the death. To prevent the disunion so frequent between the two nations, Morgan had a clause inserted in the charter-party, empowering him to condemn to instant death any adventurer who killed or wounded another. A council was then called to decide on what place they should first fall. Some proposed Santiago, which had been before sacked, others a swoop on the tobacco of the Havannah, or the dye-woods of Campeachy. Many voices were strong for a night assault on the Havannah, which, they said, could be taken before the castle could be ready to defend itself. The very ransom of the clergy they might carry off, would be worth more than the pillage of a smaller town. But some buccaneers, who had been prisoners there, said nothing could be done with less than 1500 men, and the proposal was abandoned, when they proved that they must first go to the island de los Pinos, and land in small boats at Matamana, fourteen leagues from the city.

At last some one proposed a visit to Port-au-Prince, a town of Cuba, very rich from its traffic in hides, and which, being far inland and built on a plain, could be very easily surprised. The speaker knew the city well, and was sure that it never had been sacked. Despairing of collecting forces enough to attempt the Havannah, they pursued the Spaniard's plan. Morgan at once acceded to this scheme, and, giving the captain the signal of weighing anchor, steered for Port St. Mary, the nearest harbour to Port-au-Prince. The night of their arrival in the bay a Spanish prisoner threw himself into the sea, and swimming on shore went to inform the governor of the buccaneers' plans, having, with a scanty knowledge of English, gathered a full insight, deeper than history tells us, of Morgan's intentions.

The governor instantly sent to the neighbouring town for succour, and collected, in a few hours, a force of 800 armed freemen and slaves, occupying a pass which the buccaneers must traverse.

He cut down the trees, barricaded the approaches, and planned eight ambuscades, strengthened by cannon to play upon them on their march. He then marched out into a savannah, where he might see the buccaneers at a long distance.

The townsmen, in the meanwhile, prepared for the worst with the usual timidity of the rich, hiding their riches and carrying away their movables. The adventurers, on entering the place, found the paths almost impassable with trees, but, supposing themselves discovered, took to the woods, and thus fortunately escaped the ambuscade.

The governor, seeing the enemy, to his astonishment, emerge from the trees into the plain, instantly ordered his cavalry to surround them as he would have done a troop of wolves, intending to disperse them first with his horse and then pursue them with his main body. The buccaneers, nothing daunted by the flashing of the spears or the tramp of the horsemen, advanced boldly, with drums beating and colours displayed. They drew up in a semicircle to receive the charge, and advanced swiftly towards the enemy, not waiting to be attacked. The Spaniards charged them hotly for a while, but, finding their enemies dexterous at their arms, moving their feet forward rather than backward, and seeing their governor and many of their companions dead at their feet, fled headlong to the town; those who escaped towards the wood were killed before they could reach it. The buccaneers with few men either killed or wounded, advancing still in their phalanx, killed without mercy all they met, for the space of the four hours that the fight lasted. The fugitives of the town barred themselves in their houses and kept up a fire from the windows and loopholes. The shots from the roofs and balconies still continuing, though the town was taken, the buccaneers threatened, if the firing did not cease, to set the town in a flame, and cut the women and children in pieces before the eyes of the survivors.

Having thus silenced all resistance, Morgan drove all his prisoners, men, women, children, and slaves, into the cathedral, where he placed a guard. He then gave the town over to pillage, for the benefit of his joint-stock company, finding much that was valuable, but little money, so skilful had the Spaniards grown in hiding. Parties were next sent out, as usual, to plunder the suburbs, and bring in provisions and prisoners for the torture.

The revelry then began, while the prisoners were allowed to starve in the churches; old women and children were daily tortured to make them disclose where their money was hidden.

The monks had been the first to fly from the English heretics, but bands of them were frequently captured in the woods, and thrown, half dead with fear, to confess the dying in the prisons. When pillage and provisions grew scanty, and they themselves began to feel the privations they had inflicted on others, the buccaneers resolved to depart, after fifteen days' residence, a favourite time with the brotherhood.

They now demanded a double ransom of their chief prisoners; first, for themselves, under pain of being transported to Jamaica; and secondly, for the town, or it would be burned to the ground. Four merchants were chosen to collect the contributions, and some Spaniards were first tortured in their presence, to increase the zeal of their applications. After a few days, they returned empty-handed, and demanded a respite of fifteen days, which Morgan granted. They had searched all the woods, they said, and found none of their countrymen. Delay now grew dangerous—a party of foragers had captured a negro, with letters from the governor of Santiago, telling the citizens not to make too much haste to pay the ransom, but to put off the pirates with excuses till he could come to their aid. Enraged at what he deemed treachery, Morgan swore he would have no more delay, and would burn the town the next day if the ransom was not paid down, but not alluding to the detected letter, and betraying no apprehension. Still unable to obtain money, Morgan consented to take 500 oxen, which he insisted on the Spaniards placing on board his ships at Port-au-Prince, together with salt enough to "powder" them, needing the flesh to re-victual for a fresh and more profitable expedition.

The same day Morgan left the city, taking with him six of the principal citizens as hostages. The next day came the cattle, but he now required the Spaniards to assist him in killing and salting them. This was done in a great hurry, Morgan expecting every moment the Santiago vessels would appear in sight. As soon as the butchering was completed he released his hostages and set sail, unwilling to fight when nothing could be gained by victory.

At this juncture, the smouldering jealousy of the two nations that formed his crews broke into a flame. The grudges of the last voyage had been perpetuated, and had grown into a deep and lasting feud, producing ultimately a disunion fatal to all increase of the power of the brotherhood of the coast.

While the prisoners were toiling at salting the beeves, the sailors employed themselves in drinking and rejoicing at their success, cooking the richest morsels while they were still fresh, and all hands intent on securing the hot marrow bones, the favourite delicacy of the hunters of Hispaniola. A Frenchman, employed as one of the butchers, had drawn out the dainty and placed it by his side, as a *bonne bouche* when his work was over. An English buccaneer, more hungry than polite, passing by, and knowing no reservation of property in such a republic, snatched up the reeking bone and carried it off. The Frenchman, pursuing him with angry vociferations, challenged him to fight for it, but before they could reach the place of combat, the aggressor stabbed his adversary in the back, and laid him dead on the spot. The Frenchmen, rising in arms, made it a national quarrel, and demanded redress. Morgan, just and impartial by nature and from policy, arrested the murderer and condemned him to be instantly shot, declaring that he had a right to challenge his adversary, but not to stab him treacherously. Oexmelin says, the man was sent in chains to Jamaica (and there tried and hung), Morgan promising to see justice done upon him. The French, however, remained discontented, lamented the fate of their comrade, and vowed revenge.

Morgan, not waiting for the governor of Jamaica to share his spoil, sailed to a small island, at some distance, to make the dividend. To the general grief and disgust, they found the whole amounted to only 60,000 crowns, not enough to pay their debts at Jamaica: this did not include the silk stuffs and other merchandise, which gave a poor pittance of 80 crowns to each man, as the return for so much danger and privation.

Morgan, as unwilling as the rest to revisit Port Royal empty-handed, proposed a new expedition, in search of a greater prize. But the French, not able to agree with the English, left the fleet, in spite of all their commander's persuasions, but still with every external mark of friendship, entreating to the last to have justice done to the "*infame.*"

Morgan, who had always placed great reliance on the courage of the French adventurers, was not going to relinquish his new expedition on account of their desertion. He had inspired his men with courage and the hope of acquiring riches, and they all resolved to follow him to the attack of the place, whose name he would not yet disclose, exciting them by a mystery, which prevented the possibility of treachery.

He put forth to sea with eight small vessels, but was soon joined by an adventurer of Jamaica, just returning from Campeachy; with this new ally, he had now a force of nine vessels and 470 men, many French being still among them, and arrived at Costa Rica with all his fleet safe.

As soon as they sighted land, he disclosed his design to his captains, and soon after to all his seamen. He intended to storm Porto Bello by night, and to put the whole city to the sack: he was confident of success, because no one knew of his secret; although some of his men thought their force too small for such an enterprise. To these Morgan replied, that if their number was small, their courage was great, and the fewer they were the more booty for each, with the greater prospect of union and secrecy; and upon this, all agreed unanimously to the design.

By good fortune, or by preconcerted arrangement, one of Morgan's crew turned out to be an Englishman who, only a short time before, had been a prisoner at Porto Bello, and his past sufferings now proved to have been the foundation of his future good fortune. Having escaped from that place, he knew every inch of the coast, which had been so painfully impressed on his mind, and Morgan submitted, with perfect confidence, to his guidance. By his advice, they steered straight for the bay of Santa Maria, arriving there purposely about dusk, and reached a spot about twelve leagues from the city, without meeting any vessel. They then sailed up the river to Puerto Pontin, four leagues distant, taking advantage of the land wind that sprang up, cool and fresh, at night.

They here anchored, and embarked in boats, leaving a few men to bring on the ships. Rowing softly, they reached about midnight a place called Estera de Longa lemos, where they all landed, and marched upon the outposts of the city.

Michael Scott describes Porto Bello as built in a miserable, dirty, damp hole, surrounded by high forest-clad hills, wreathed in mist, and reeking with dirt and fever. Everlasting vapours obscure the sun, and mingle with the exhalation of the steaming marshes of the lead-coloured, land-locked cove that forms the harbour.

They were now within reach of the strongest city in the Spanish West Indies, except Havannah and Carthagena, the port of Panama, and the great mart for silver and negroes. Leaving as usual a party to guard the boats, and preceded by their guide, they began halfway to the town to prepare their arms. Upon approaching the first sentinel, Morgan sent forward the guide and three or four others to surprise him. They did it cunningly, before he could fire his musket, and brought him with his hands bound to Morgan, who, threatening him with death, asked him how things in the city went, and what forces they had, making a "thousand menaces to kill him if he did not speak the truth." The terrified Spaniard informed them that the town was well garrisoned, but that there were very few inhabitants; the merchants only residing in the town while the galleons are loading, and that he would be able to take the place in spite of all the fortresses and the 300 soldiers. Morgan then pushed on to the fort, carrying the man bound before them, and after a quarter of a league reached the castle, where the man's company was stationed, closely surrounding it, so that no one could get in or go out. The prisoner had in vain attempted to avoid this redoubt, to which he had served as picket, encouraged by Morgan's promises of reward, and avowal that he would not give him up to his countrymen.

The Spaniards, finding the sentinel gone, had already spread the alarm of the buccaneers' approach. From beneath the walls Morgan commanded the sentinel to summon the garrison to surrender at once to his discretion, or they should be cut in pieces without quarter. Not regarding these threats, the Spaniards began instantly to discharge their guns and muskets to alarm the town and obtain succour. But though they made a good resistance they were soon overpowered, and the buccaneers, driving them into one room, set fire to the powder which lay about on the floor, and blew the tower and its defenders together into the air; all the survivors they put to the sword, in order to strike terror in the city.

At daybreak they fell upon the city, and found the inhabitants, some still asleep and others scared and alarmed; many had thought of nothing but hiding their treasure, and only the professional soldier prepared for resistance. The governor, unable to rally the citizens, fled into the citadel, and fired upon the town as well as the enemy. The frightened herd, stupid with fear, were throwing their money and jewels into wells and cisterns, or burying their treasure in their courtyards, cellars, gardens, and chapels. The adventurers, abstaining from pillage, sent a chosen party to the convents to make prisoners of the religious, male and female; while another division prepared ladders to escalade the fort, not relaxing for a moment either in attack or defence. They attempted in vain to burn down a castle-gate which proved to be of iron, and baffled their efforts, and kept up a warm fire at the embrasures, aiming with such dexterity at the mouths of the guns as to kill a gunner or two every time the pieces were either run out or loaded.

The firing continued from daybreak till noon, and even then the result seemed doubtful, for when the adventurers approached the walls with their grenades to burn the doors the defenders threw down upon them earthen pots full of powder, and lighted by a fusee, together with showers of stones and other missiles. Morgan himself began to despair of success, and did not know how to escape from that strait, when the English flag arose above the smaller fort, and a troop of men ran forth to proclaim victory with shouts of joy. The remaining castle, however, was the *pièce de resistance*, being the storehouse of the church plate, and the wealth of the richer citizens now with the garrison. A stratagem was suggested, appealing strongly to Spanish superstition, and, as it happened, successfully. Ten or twelve ladders were made so broad and strong that three or four men might mount them abreast. To all threats the governor replied he would never surrender alive, although the religious should themselves plant the ladders. The monks and nuns were then dragged to the heads of the companies, and forced to plant the ladders, in spite of the hot rain of fire and shot; the governor...

> ... using his utmost endeavours to destroy all who came near the walls, firing on the servants of God, although his kinsmen, and prisoners, and forced to the service. Delicate women and aged men were goaded at the sword's point to this hateful labour, derided by the English, and unpitied by their countrymen.

All this time the buccaneers maintained an unceasing fire along the whole line of grey battlements at every aperture where a pike head glittered or a lighted match smouldered; suffering much in return, unarmed as they were, guarded neither by steel-cap nor cuirass, and unsheltered by palisade or earthwork. In spite of the cries of the religious as they reared the ladders, their prayers to the saints, and their entreaties to the garrison to remember their common blood and nation, many of the priests were shot before the walls could be scaled. The more superstitious of the Spaniards were unnerved at hearing the dying curse of the consecrated servants of God, rising shrill above the roar of the battle. The ladders were at last planted, amid a shower of fire-pots that killed almost as many of the Spaniards as the English, and the buccaneers sprang up with all the agility of sailors and the determination of Berserkers; their best marksmen shooting down the few Spaniards who awaited their arrival at the summit. Their falling bodies struck a few buccaneers from their ladders. Every man that went up carried hand grenades, pistols, and sabre, but the musket was now laid aside, for it had done its work, and was a mere encumbrance in the grapple of closer combat. The English swarmed up in great numbers, and reaching the top kindled their fusees and threw down their fire-pots upon the crowded ranks of the enemy, with destructive effect. Before they could recover their dismay, sabre in hand, as if they were boarding, they leaped down upon the garrison, who drove them off with pikes and clubbed muskets, and, closing with them, hurled many from the ramparts, or, stabbing them, fell clenched with the foe in their despair. When their cannon was taken, the Spaniards threw down their arms and begged for quarter, except the governor and a few officers, who determined to die fighting against the robbers and heretics, the enemies of God and Spain.

The buccaneers, seeing the red flag flying from the first fort, which was the strongest, and built on an eminence which commanded the towers below, advanced with confidence to the attack of the remaining one, hitherto thought impregnable, which defended the port, and prevented the entrance of their vessels, which they wished to secure safe in the harbour, as the number of their wounded would require their long stay in the place they had captured. The governor, proud and brave, still refused to surrender, and fired upon them with his cannon, which were soon silenced by the superior fire of the newly-taken fort, which flanked his position. Out of this last stronghold, the weary and despairing defenders were quickly driven.

Major Castellon, the stout-hearted governor, disdaining to ask quarter of a pack of heretic seamen, killed several of his own men who would not stand to their arms and called on him to save their lives, and struck down many of the hunters who tried to take him alive, not from a generous compassion, for pity seldom entered a buccaneer's heart, but in order to obtain his ransom. A still more cruel trial of his courage, and duty to his king, awaited him: his wife and children fell at his knees, and, with cries and tears, begged him to lay down his arms and save both their lives. But he obstinately and sternly refused, replying, "Better this than a scaffold," preferring to die as a valiant soldier at his post, than to be hanged as a coward for deserting it. He died the death of a brave man, fighting desperately, and was found buried under the bodies of his dead enemies. If unpitied by his ferocious foes, he has left a name to be honoured by all brave men, as one worthy of a more chivalrous age, and a better cause.

It now being nearly sunset, and the city their own, the adventurers enclosed all their prisoners in the citadel, separating the wounded, and, although heedless of their sufferings, employing the female slaves to wait upon them. It now being nearly night, they gave way to all the excesses of soldiers in a town taken by storm, exasperated by the recollection of past danger, and the death of friends, and maddened by both the certainty of present pleasure and the power of indulging in every success. Oexmelin says, fifty brave Spaniards might have put all the revellers to death, and recovered the place. We do not, however, hear that a single Spanish *Jael* was found to revenge herself on these modern *Siseras*.

The following morning Morgan summoned his vessels into the harbour, and collecting all the loose wealth of the town, had it brought into the fort. Directing the repairs of the ramparts, scorched and shattered, he remounted the guns, in order to be ready to repel any attack from Panama. He collected a few of the prisoners who had been persuaded to say they were the richest merchants in Porto Bello, and put all who would not confess to the torture. He maimed some and killed others, who remained silent because they were in reality poor, and had concealed no treasure. Having spent fifteen days in these alternate cruelties and debaucheries, Morgan resolved to retreat. No buccaneer general had ever taken a city which could not be stripped clean in fourteen days. Famine and disease began ungratefully to take the part of the Spaniard against the nation that had fed them with so many victims. Wild waste compelled them already to devour their mules and horses, rather than die of hunger, or turn cannibals. Parties of hunters were sent into the suburbs to hunt the cattle, whose flesh they then devoured, saving the mules for the prisoners, who, between their wounds and their hunger, were reduced to dreadful extremities.

A death more terrible than that of a blow in battle now appeared in their midst. Many had already died victims of excess, and even the most prudent perished. The bad food, the sudden transition from excess to want, and the impurity of the tainted air, produced a pestilence. The climate of Porto Bello, always unhealthy, as Hosier's squadron afterwards experienced, was poisoned by the putrefaction of the dead bodies, hastily buried, and scarcely covered by earth. The wounded nearly all sickened, and the intemperate were the first to die.

The prisoners, crowded together, and already weakened mentally by despondency, and physically by famine, soon caught the fever, and died with dreadful rapidity. Rich merchants, accustomed to every luxury, and to the most varied and seasoned food, pined under a diet of half-putrid mule's flesh, and bad, unfiltered water. Everything warned Morgan that it was time to weigh anchor, for the president of Panama was already on his march towards the city at the head of 1500 men. Informed of their approach from a slave captured by a hunting party, Morgan held a council, at which it was agreed not to retreat until they had obtained a ransom for the town greater than the spoil at present collected; and, in order to prevent a surprise, he placed a body of 100 well-armed men in a narrow defile, where but a few men could go abreast, and through which the president must pass. They found that that general had fewer troops with him than was reported, and these took flight at the first encounter, and did not attempt again to force a passage, but waited for reinforcements. The president, with the usual gasconade of a Spaniard, sent word to Morgan, that if he did not at once leave Porto Bello he should receive no quarter when he should take him and his companions, as he hoped soon to do.

To this, Morgan, knowing he had a sure means of escape, said he should not leave till he had received 180,000 pieces of eight as a ransom for the city, and if he could not get this he should kill all his prisoners, blow up the castle, and burn the town, and two men were sent by him to the president to procure the money.

The president, seeing that nothing could either deceive or intimidate Morgan, gave up Porto Bello to its fate, not caring to erect a silver bridge for a flying enemy. In vain he sent to Carthagena for a fleet to block up the ships in the river; in vain he kept the citizens in suspense as to the money, in hopes of gaining time. He was deaf and obdurate to all the entreaties of the citizens, who sent to inform him that the pirates were not men but devils, and that they fought with such fury that the Spanish officers had stabbed themselves, in very despair, at seeing a supposed impregnable fortress taken by a handful of people, when it should have held out against twice the number.

Don Juan Perez de Guzman, the president, a man of "great parts," and who had attained high rank in the war in Flanders, expressed himself, with candour, as astonished at the exploits of 400 men (not regular soldiers) who, with no other arms but their muskets, had taken a city which any general in Europe would have found necessary to have blockaded in due form. He gave the people of Porto Bello, at the same time, leave to compound for their safety, but offered them no aid to insure it.

To Morgan himself he could not refrain from expressing astonishment. He admired his success, with no ordnance for batteries, and against the citizens of a place who bore the reputation of being good soldiers, never wanting courage in their own defence. He begged, at the same time, that he would send him some small pattern of the arms wherewith he had, with such vigour, taken so great a city. Morgan received the messenger with great kindness and civility, flattered by the compliment from an enemy, and glad of an opportunity of expressing contempt of any assailants. He took a hunter's musket from one of his men, and sent it, together with a handful of buccaneer bullets, to the president, begging him to accept it as a small pattern of the arms wherewith he had taken Porto Bello, hoping he would keep it a twelvemonth or two, at which time he hoped to visit Panama and fetch it away. The Spaniard, astonished at the wit and civility of the captain, whom he had deemed a mere brutal sea thief, sent a messenger to return the present, as he did not need the loan of weapons, but thanking Morgan and praising his courage, remarking at the same time that it was a pity that such a man should not be employed in a just war, and in the service of a great and good prince, and hoping, in conclusion, that he would not give himself the trouble of coming to see him at Panama, as he would not fare there so well as he had done at Porto Bello. Having delivered this message, so chivalrous in its tone, the messenger presented Morgan with a beautiful gold ring, set with a costly emerald, as a remembrance of his master Don Guzman, who had already supplied the English chief with fresh provisions.

Having now provided himself with all necessaries, and stripped the unfortunate city of almost everything but its tiles and its paving stones, carried off half of the castle guns and spiked the rest, he then set sail, taking on board the ransom, which was punctually paid in the shape of silver bars. Corn seldom grew where his foot had once been, and he left behind him famine, pestilence, poverty, and death. Orphans and widows, mutilated men and violated women leaped for joy as his fleet melted into the distance.

Setting sail, with great speed, he arrived in eight days at Cuba, where the spoil was divided.

They found that they had in gold and silver, whether in coin or bar, and in jewels, which from haste and ignorance were seldom estimated at one-fourth part of their value, to the value of 260,000 pieces of eight. This did not include the silks and merchandise, of which they paid little heed, only valuing coin or bullion, and regarding the richest prize without coin as scarce worth the taking. This division accomplished, to the general satisfaction of all but the people of Porto Bello, who were now poor enough to defy all thieves, they returned at once to Jamaica, where they were magnificently received, Oexmelin says, "*surtout des cabaretiers.*" Every door was open to them, and for a whole week all loudly praised their generosity and their courage; at the end of a month, every door was shut in their faces, all but one—the prison for debts, and that closed behind their backs. "They spent in a short time," says one of their historians, "with boundless prodigality, what they had gained with boundless danger and unremitting toil." The people of Tortuga considered them as mere slaves, who dived to get their pearls, and cared not whether they perished by the wave or by the shark, so the pearls which they had gathered could be first secured.

"Not long after their arrival in Jamaica," says Esquemeling, "being that short time needed to lavish away all their riches, they concluded on another enterprise to seek new fortunes:" a sailor spends his money quickly, and so does a highwayman—in them both trades were combined. Morgan remained at rest as long as most buccaneers did, that is to say, till he had drunk out half his money, strung the jewels of Spanish matrons around the necks of the fairest courtesans in Jamaica, and stripped himself at the gambling-table today in the hope of recovering the losses of yesterday. As his purse grew thin his heart grew stout, as his hunger grew greater his thirst for blood began also to increase. At last he looked seaward, turned his back on the lotus-land and the sirens, and prepared for sea.

His rendezvous this time was fixed in a small island on the south side of Hispaniola, in order to invite both the French hunters and the sailors of Tortuga. By this sign of confidence Morgan hoped to remove all rankling prejudice between the French and English adventurers, and to obtain recruits from both nations. He resolved this time upon an expedition which would enable him and his men to retire from the sea life for ever, or at least to hold a longer revel.

The buccaneers of the coast seeing him always successful, and never returning without booty, less cruel and less rash than Lolonnois, and not only very brave but very fortunate, flocked to his flag almost without a summons. Every one furbished up his musket, cast bullets, bought powder, or fitted up a canoe. Parties were at once despatched to hunt in the savannahs, and to prepare salted meat sufficient for the voyage. Great numbers of French and English crowded to Cow Island.

A powerful ally appeared at this crisis, in the shape of a French vessel, *Le Cerf Volant*, of St. Malo, which had come out to the Indies, virtuously intending to trade with the Spaniards, but, finding this difficult or unprofitable, had less virtuously determined to live by plundering them, and was now manned by French adventurers from Tortuga, no friends to Morgan, but anxious to share his booty. The vessel, which had also a long-boat towing at its stern, had a short time before attacked a Genoese ship, trading with negroes, but which, mounting forty-eight cannon, had driven it off, and compelled the captain to return home and refit. The crew seemed unwilling to trust the English, and would not listen to any terms. Morgan, who had just been joined by a ship from New England with thirty-six cannon, longed to add the twenty-four iron guns and the twelve brass ones of *Le Cerf Volant* to his collection. In spite of his wish to unite the two nations, and close the green and still rankling wound, the temptation was rather too strong for him. His guardian angel slept for a moment, and when she awoke the English flag floated at the Frenchman's peak.

The change happened thus: the French captain having refused to join Morgan's expedition, unless he drew up a peculiar charter party opposed to all buccaneer law, and quarrelling about this, he swore *ventre St. Gris*, he would return to Tortuga, reload his cargo, and return to France.

The blow was to be struck now or never. The English part of the St. Malo crew had already deserted to Morgan. Some of these men furnished him with an opportunity of revenge. The merchant captain, unaccustomed to the looseness of buccaneer discipline, had treated them as sailors, and not as *matelots* and brothers. They told Morgan, that being short of victual, he had lately stopped an English vessel, and taken provisions by force, paying the commander only with bills of exchange, cashable at Jamaica, and that he carried secretly a Spanish commission, empowering him to plunder the English. These charges, though full of malice, had a specious appearance of truth. The captain had indeed stopped an English vessel, but had paid for all he had taken with honest bills. He did also carry a Spanish commission, having been driven to anchor at the port of Baracoa, on the north-east side of Cuba, where he had obtained letters of marque from the governor, in order to conceal his real errand. Morgan considered this a sufficient pretext, and sounded his crew to ascertain how far they would help him at the moment of need. It was at this very moment of indecision that the New England vessel joined the fleet, and enabled him to bear down any opposition. This ship, which Oexmelin calls the *Haktswort* (*Oxford?*) carried a crew of 300 men. It was said to belong to the king of England (Charles II.), and to have been lent by him to the present captain.

A strange, improbable story, unless the English government had really determined to encourage the buccaneer movement. The *Haktswort* was really sent by the governor of Jamaica to join the expedition.

With this timely succour Morgan's mind was instantly made up. He asked the St. Malo captain and all his officers to dinner, on board the newly-arrived vessel, and there made them prisoners, without any resistance, away from their crew, and with their ship exposed to an overwhelming fire. He then affected the anger of indignant justice, declared they were robbers, who plundered the English under a commission from the enemy, and came there as mere spies and traitors. Fortunately for him, the English vessel that had been stopped by the St. Malo crew arrived at the very moment to repeat and exaggerate the charge. The ship was now his own, and only God could take it from him. And "God did so," says Esquemeling, who sees a judgment in all misfortunes that befall an enemy, but none in those that befall his friends.

Morgan, victorious and exulting, called a council of war, and summoned all his captains to attend him on board his large prize. They praised the vessel, laughed at the tricked Frenchmen, and discussed their plans. They calculated what provisions they had in store, and of what their force was capable. The island of Savona was agreed upon as a rendezvous, as at that east corner of Hispaniola they might lurk and cut off stragglers from the armed Spanish *flota*, now daily expected. Having completed their arrangements they gave way to pleasure, the real occupation and business of a buccaneer's life, his toil being only expended to procure the means for pleasure, and time to enjoy it. They began to feast and drink healths, the officers below and the sailors on deck. Prayers for a successful voyage were blended with drunken songs, and unintelligible blasphemies. The captain and the cook were both drunk, the very gunners who discharged a broadside when the toasts were drained, fell senseless beside their smoking guns. Those who could not move slept, those who could walk drank on. By some accident, a spark from a smoking match caught the powder, and in an instant the vessel blew up. In perfect equality all ranks were lifted up towards heaven, in a column of flame, only to fall back again to perish, burnt and helpless, in the sea. More than 350 of the 400 men that formed the crew were drowned. By a singular coincidence, the officers nearly all escaped. The English having their powder stored in the fore part of the vessel, and not in the stern like the French, the sailors only perished; the officers and the St. Malo prisoners who were drinking with them were merely blown, much bruised, into the water. The English adventurers, declaring that the French had set fire to the powder, would have killed them on the spot, but Morgan, not apparently the least chapfallen by the disappointment, sent them all as prisoners to Jamaica. The thirty men, seated in the great cabin at some distance from the main force of the powder, escaped, and many more would have been saved had they been sober.

The French prisoners in vain endeavoured to obtain justice in Jamaica, were long detained in confinement, and threatened with death when they demanded a trial. Had Morgan returned unsuccessful they might have perhaps been listened to.

Eight days after this loss Morgan commanded his men to collect the floating bodies now putrifying, not to give them Christian burial, but to save the clothes, and to remove the heavy gold rings which the English buccaneers wore upon their forefingers, abandoning their unsaleable bodies to the birds and to the sharks.

Undaunted by this accident, Morgan found he had still a force of fifteen vessels, and 860 men, but his gun ship, the largest of all, only carried fourteen small guns. They now made way to Savona, where all were to repair and careen, and the swift to wait for the slow. Letters were soon placed in bottles, and buried at a spot indicated by a mark agreed on. Coasting Hispaniola, they were detained by contrary winds, and attempted for three weeks in vain to double Cape Lobos. Their provisions ran short, but they were relieved by an English vessel, bound to Jamaica, which had a superfluity for sale.

Always seeking for pleasure, though in emergencies capable of the severest self-denials, six or seven of the fleet remained clustering round this vessel to purchase brandy, as eager and thoughtless as stragglers round a *vivandière*. The more thoughtful and earnest pressed on with Morgan, and, reaching the bay of Ocoa, waited for them there, the men spending their time usefully, as they had agreed before, in hunting, and foraging for water and provisions, killing some oxen and a few horses. Detained here by continued bad weather, Morgan maintained strict discipline, compelling every captain to send, daily, on shore eight men from each ship, making a total force of sixty-four. He also instituted a convoy, or a body of armed men, who attended the hunters as a guard, for they were now near St. Domingo, which was full of Greek soldiers and Spanish matadors. The Spaniards, few in number, did not attack them, but, adopting a Fabian policy, which suited their pride and phlegm, sent for 300 or 400 men to kill all the cattle round the bay. Another party drove all the herds far into the interior, wishing to starve the foe out of the island, knowing that a buccaneer, pressed by hunger, did not care whether he ate horse, mule, or ass, falling back upon monkeys and parrots, and resorting to sharks' flesh or his own shoes as a last resource. But when the buccaneers spread further inland, a body of soldiers was despatched to the coast, to practise a stratagem, and to form an ambuscade.

The following was their plan, which completely succeeded, but nevertheless ended in the Spaniards' total rout. A band of fifty buccaneers having resolved to venture further than usual into the woods, a party of Spanish muleteers were ordered to drive the bait, a small herd of cattle, past the shore, where they had landed, pretending to fly when they caught sight of their enemies. When they approached the ambuscade two Spaniards were sent out, carrying a white flag of truce. The buccaneers, ceasing the pursuit, pushed forward two men to parley.

The treacherous Spaniards beseeched them plaintively not to kill their cows, offering to sell them cattle, or furnish them with food. The buccaneers, with all the good faith of seamen, replied that they would give a crown and a-half for each ox, and that the seller could make his own profit besides on the hide and the tallow. During this time, which was planned to give time for the operation, the Spanish troops were turning the flank of the enemy, and had now surrounded the small band on all sides. They interrupted the conversation by breaking out of the wood, with shots and cries of "*Mata, mata*"—"kill, kill," imagining they could cut to pieces so small a force without a struggle. The buccaneers, differing from them in opinion, faced about with good heart, threw themselves into a square, and beat a slow retreat to the forest, keeping up a rolling fire from all four sides of their brave phalanx.

The Spaniards, considering the retreat a sure proof of despair and fear, attacked them with great courage, but great loss. The buccaneers losing no men, while the Spaniards fell thick and fast, cried out, in imprudent bravado, that they were only trying to frighten them, and put no balls in their muskets. This jest cost them dear, for the Spaniards had been only aiming high, wishing to kill them on the spot and to make no prisoners. They now tried to maim as well as kill, and soon wounded so many in the legs that the buccaneers were obliged to retreat to a clump of trees, where they stood at bay, and from whence the Spaniards did not dare to beat them. They then began to prepare to carry off their dead and wounded to the vessels, but seeing a small party of Spaniards piercing one of the bodies with their swords, they fired upon them, charged them, and drove them off, tracking their way by their dead, and then retreated, killing the cattle and bearing them off in sorrowful triumph to their vessels. The very next day, at the first light, Morgan, furious to revenge this treachery of the Spaniards, landed himself at the head of 200 men, and entered the woods, visiting the scene of the last night's skirmish. But the Spaniards had long since fled, discovering that in driving cattle towards the shore as a lure for the buccaneer, they only brought destruction upon themselves, and a dangerous enemy nearer to their homes and treasures. Morgan, finding his search useless, returned to his ship, having first burned down all the deserted huts he could find: "Returning," says Esquemeling, "somewhat more satisfied in his mind for having done considerable damage to the enemy, which was always his ardent desire."

The day after, deciding not to venture an attack upon Bourg d'Asso, Morgan, impatient at the delay of his vessels, resolved to sail without them, and visit Savona, hoping there to meet his lingering companions. Alarming the people of St. Domingo, he coasted round Hispaniola. He determined to wait eight days at Savona, and, weary of rest, still wanting provisions, he sent some boats and 150 men to plunder the towns round St. Domingo, but they, finding the Spaniards vigilant and desperate, gave up the enterprise as hopeless, and returned empty-handed to endure the curses and sneers of their commander. Morgan now held a council of war, for provisions were very scanty and time was going. The eight ships did not arrive, and all agreed, with their seven small vessels and their 300 men, some place of importance might still be taken. Morgan had hitherto resolved to cruise about the Caraccas and plunder the towns and villages, mere hen-roost robbing and footpad work, compared with the enterprise proposed by one of his French captains amid great applause.

This captain was Pierre le Picard, the *matelot* of the famous Lolonnois when he took Maracaibo: he it was who had steered the vessels over the bar, and had served both as pilot at sea and guide on land; he reefed and fought, and could handle a rope as well as a musket. He now proposed a second attack upon the same place, and, with all the rude eloquence of sincerity, proved the facility of the attempt, and the riches that lay within their reach. As he spoke good English that could be understood by all, and was, moreover, much esteemed by Morgan, the scheme for a new campaign was at once rapturously approved. He disclosed in the council all the entries, passages, forces, and means. A charter-party was drawn up, containing a clause, that if the rest of the fleet joined them before they had taken a fortress, they should be allowed to share like the rest.

Having left a letter at Savona, buried in the usual way, the buccaneers set sail for Curaçoa, stopping after some days' sail at the island of Omba, to take in water and provisions. This place was distant some twelve leagues from Maracaibo. Here they stayed twenty-four hours, buying goats of the natives for hanks of thread and linen. Sheep, lambs, and kids were the only products of the island, which abounded with spiders whose bite produced madness, unless the sufferer was tied hands and feet, and left without food for a night and a day. The fleet set sail in the night, to prevent the islanders discovering the object of their voyage.

The next morning they sighted the small islands that lie at the entrance of the lake of Maracaibo, anchoring out of sight of the *Vigilia*, in hopes to escape notice, but were observed by the sentries, whose signal gave the Spaniards ample time for defence. The fleet remained becalmed, unable to reach the bar till four o'clock in the afternoon. The canoes were instantly manned, in order to take the Bar Fort, rebuilt since Picard's last visit. Its guns played upon the boats as they pulled to land. Morgan exhorted his men to be brave and not to give way—for he expected the Spaniards would defend themselves desperately, seeing their fire was so rolling and incessant that the fort seemed like the crater of a small volcano, and they could now see that the huts round the wall had been burnt and removed, to leave them no protection or shelter.

The dispute continued very hot, being managed with great courage from morning till dark night.

That latterly the fighting died away to occasional shots is evident, for, at six o'clock when it grew dusk, Morgan reconnoitred the fort, and found it deserted. The cessation of the fire had already roused their suspicions. Suspecting treachery, Morgan searched the place to see if any lighted fuses had been placed near the powder, and a division was employed to enter the place before the main body. There was no lack of volunteers for this experimental and cat's-paw work. Morgan himself clambered up first. As they expected, they found a lighted match, and a dark train of powder communicating with the magazine. A little later and the whole band had perished together. Morgan himself snatched up the match. This fort was a redoubt of five *toises* high, six long, and three round. In the magazine they found 3,000 pounds of gunpowder that would have been wasted had the place been blown up; fourteen pieces of cannon, of eight, twelve, and fourteen pounds calibre, and abundance of fire-pots, hand-grenades, and carcases; twenty-four muskets and thirty pikes and bandoliers had been left by the runaways. The fort was only accessible by an iron ladder, which could be drawn up into the guard-room. But courage requires no ladder, and, like love, can always find out a way. When they had once examined the place, the buccaneers broke down the parapet, spiked the cannon, threw them over the walls, and burnt the gun-carriages.

The Spaniards waited in vain for the roar of their bursting mine. Their own city was rocking beneath their feet; a more dreadful visitation than the earthquake or the hurricane was at their doors. At daybreak the fleet sailed up the lake, the ruined fort smoking behind them. Making great haste, they arrived at Maracaibo the next day, having first divided among themselves the arms and ammunition of the fort. The water being very low and the shoals numerous, they disembarked into their boats, with a few small cannon. From some cavaliers whom they could see on the walls they believed that the Spaniards were fortifying themselves. The buccaneers therefore landed at some distance from the town, anchoring and disembarking amid discharges of their own cannon, intending to clear the thickets on the shore. Their men they divided into two divisions, in order to embarrass the enemy by a double attack.

But these precautions were useless. The timid people had already fled into the woods; only the beggars, who feared no plunderers, and the sick, who were praying for death, remained in Maracaibo. The brave fled with the coward, the monk with the sinner, the thief from the thieves, the soldiers from the seamen, the Catholic from the dreaded Protestant, and the Spaniard from the enemies of his name and race. The sick were expecting death, and cared not if it came by the hand of the doctor or the buccaneer; the beggar hoped to benefit by those who could not covet, and might pity, their rags. "A few miserable folk, who had nothing to lose," says Esquemeling, "alone remained." Crippled slaves, not worth removing, lay in the streets; the dying groaned untended in the hospital. Children fled from parents, and parents from children; rich old age was left to die in spite of all the inducements of avarice. The prostitute fled to escape dishonour, and the murderer to avoid bloodshed.

The houses were empty, the doors open, the chambers stripped of every movable, costly or precious. The first care of the invaders was to search every corner for prisoners, the next to secure, each party as they arrived, the richest palaces for their barracks. The palaces were their dens, the churches their prisons; everything they defiled and polluted, the loathsome things they made still more horrible, the holy they in some degree contaminated. At sea they were brave, obedient, self-denying, religious in formula (half the world goes no further), determined, and irresistible; on land cruel, bloody, rebellious, and ferocious. At sea they exceeded most men in the practice of the sterner virtues, on land they were demons of wrath, devils of drunkenness and lust, mercenaries and outlaws in their bearing and their actions. The three former days of terror had sapped the courage of the bravest, and alarm and fear had, by a common panic, induced the inhabitants to hide the merchandise in the woods. The men who fled had had fathers and children killed and tortured in the first expedition. Friends, still maimed by the rack, increased their fears by their narrations. The buccaneers seemed a judgment from God, irresistible and unavertable. The desire to defend riches seems to be a weaker principle in the human mind than the desire to obtain them. Great conquerors have generally been poorer than the nations they have conquered.

Scarcely any provisions remained in the town. There was no vessel or boat in the port, all had been removed into the wide lake beyond. The small *demilune* fort, with its four cannon, that was intended to guard the harbour, was also deserted. The richer the man, the further he had escaped inland; the needy were in the woods, the drunken beggars revelled alone in the town, rejoicing in an event that at least made them rich: "It is an ill wind that blows nobody good."

The very same day the buccaneers despatched a body of 100 men to search the woods for refugees, any attempt to secrete treasure being a heavy offence in the eyes of Morgan. These men returned the next evening with thirty prisoners, fifty mules, and several horses laden with baggage and rich merchandise. Both the male and female prisoners seemed poor and worthless. They were immediately tortured, in order to induce them to disclose where their richer and more virtuous fellow citizens were hidden. Morgan, finding none to resist him, quartered his men in the richest houses, selecting the church as their central guard-house and rallying point, their store-room for plunder, their court of justice (blind and with false weights), and their torture-chamber.

Some of the prisoners offered to act as guides to places where they knew money and jewels were hidden. As several places were named, two parties went out the same night upon this exciting search. The one party returned on the morrow with much booty, the other did not wander in for two days, having been misled by a prisoner, who, in the hopes of finding means to escape through his knowledge of the country, had led them into such dangerous and uninhabited places that they had had a thousand difficulties in avoiding. Furious at finding themselves mocked by their guide, they hung him on a tree without any parley. In returning they came, however, suddenly upon some slaves who were seeking for food by night, having been hiding in the woods all day. Torture was at once resorted to, to find out where the masters lay, for slaves could not be there alone. The braver of the two suffered the most horrible pain without disclosing a syllable, and was eventually cut to pieces without confessing; the weaker, and perhaps younger negro, endured his sufferings at first with equal fortitude, although he was offered liberty and reward if he would speak. But when the seamen drew their sabres, still red with the blood of his companion, and began to hew and gash his brother's limbs that still lay palpitating on the ground, his courage fell, and he offered to lead them to his master. The Spaniard was soon taken with 30,000 crowns' worth of plate.

For eight days the men practised unheard-of cruelties upon the wretched townsmen, already starved and beggared, wretches whose only crime had been their yielding to the natural impulse of self-preservation. They hung them up by their beards and by the hair of their heads, by an arm or a leg; they stretched their limbs tight with cords, and then beat with rattans upon the rigid flesh; they placed burning matches between their fingers; they twisted cords about their heads, tightening the strain by the leverage of their pistol stocks, till the eyes sprang from the sockets. The deathblow was never given from pity, but as the climax and consummation of suffering, and when the executioners were weary of their cruelty. In vain the tortured Spaniards screamed that the treasure was all removed to Gibraltar, and that they were not the rich citizens but very poor men, monks and servants of Jesus, God help them! Many died before the rack could be loosened.

Captain Picard, exulting in the success of his expedition, was now very urgent in pressing Morgan to advance on Gibraltar before succours could arrive there from Merida, believing that it would surrender as it had done to Lolonnois. Morgan having in his custody about 100 of the chief families of Maracaibo, and all the accessible booty, embarked eight days after his landing, and proceeded to Gibraltar, hoping to rival Lolonnois in every virtue. His prisoners and plunder went with him, and he determined to hazard a battle. Expecting an obstinate defence, every buccaneer made his will, consoling himself by the thought of revelry at Jamaica if he was one of those lucky enough to escape. "Death," says Oexmelin, "was never much mixed up in their thoughts, especially when there was booty in view, for if there were only some hopes of plunder they would fight like lions." Before the fleet started, two prisoners had been sent to Gibraltar to warn the governor that Captain Morgan would give him no quarter if he did not surrender.

Picard, who remembered the former dangerous spots, made his men land about a quarter of a league from the town, and march through the woods in hopes of taking the Spaniards in the rear, in case they should be again entrenched. The enemy received them with quick discharges of cannon, but the men cheered each other, saying, "We must make a breakfast of these bitter things ere we sup on the sweetmeats of Gibraltar."

They landed early in the morning, and found no more difficulty than at Maracaibo. The Spaniards, deceived by a stratagem, had expected their approach by the road, and not by the woods. They had no time to throw up entrenchments, and only a few barricades, planted with cannon, protected their flight. They remembered Lolonnois; their hearts became as water, and they fled as the buccaneers took peaceable possession of the town. The Spaniards took with them their riches, and all their ammunition, to use at some more convenient period. Morgan, rejoicing in the easy victory, posted his men at the strong points of the town, while 100 men, under Picard, went out to pursue and bring in prisoners. They found the guns spiked, and every house sacked by its owner, much spoiled, much carried off, and the heavy and the worthless alone left.

The only inhabitant remaining in the town was a poor half-witted Spaniard, who had not clearly ascertained what he ought to do. He was so well dressed that they at first took him, much to his delight, for a man of rank, and asked him what had become of all the people of Gibraltar. He replied, "they had been gone a day, but he did not know where; he had not asked, but he dare say they would soon be back, and for his part he, Pepé, did not care." When they inquired where the sugar-mills were, he replied that he had never seen any in his life. The church money, he knew, was hid in the sacristy of the great church. Taking them there he showed them a large coffer, where he pretended to have seen it hid. They opened it and found it empty. To all other inquiries he now answered, "I know nothing, I know nothing."

Some of the buccaneers, angry at the disappointment, and vexed at the subtlety of the Spaniards, declared the fellow was more knave than fool, and dragged him to torture. They gave him first the *strapado*, till he began to wish the people were returned; they then hung him up for two hours with heavy stones tied to his feet, till his arms were dislocated. At last he cried out, "Do not plague me any more, but come with me and I will show you my goods and my riches." He then led them to a miserable hovel, containing only a few earthen pots and three pieces of eight, wrapped in faded finery, buried under the hearth. He then said his name was Don Sebastian Sanchez, brother of the governor of Maracaibo, that he was worth more than 50,000 crowns, and that he would write for it and give it up if they would cease to hang and plague him so. They then tortured him again, thinking he was a *grandee* in disguise, till he offered, if he was released, to show them a refinery. They had not got a musket-shot from the hut before he fell on his knees and gave himself up as a criminal. "*Jesu Maria!*" he cried, "what will you do with me, Englishmen? I am a poor man who live on alms, and sleep in the hospital." They then lit palm-leaves and scorched him, and would have burnt off all his clothes had he not been released by one of the buccaneers who now saw he was an idiot. The poor fellow died in great torment in about half-an-hour, and before he grew cold was dragged into the woods and buried.

The following day Picard brought in an old peasant and his two daughters; the old man, his crippled limbs having been tortured, offered to serve as guide, and lead them to some houses in the suburbs. Half blind and frightened, he mistook his way, and the buccaneers, thinking the error intentional, made a slave, who declared he had intentionally misled them, hang him on a tree by the road side.

Slavery here brought its own retribution, for this same slave, burning to avenge some ill treatment he had received, offered, on being made free, to lead them to many of the Spanish places of refuge. Before evening ten or twelve families, with all their wealth, were brought into Gibraltar. It had now become difficult to track the fugitives, as fathers refused even to trust their children; no one slept twice in the same spot, for fear that some one who knew of the retreat would be captured, and then, under torture, betray the spot, generally huts in the darkest recesses of the woods, where their goods were stored from the weather. These exiles were, however, obliged to steal at night to their country houses to obtain food, and then they were intercepted. From some of these merchants Morgan heard that a vessel of 100 tons, and three barges laden with silver and merchandise belonging to Maracaibo, now lay in the river; about six leagues distant, and 100 men were despatched to secure the prize.

In scouring the woods again with a body of 200 human bloodhounds, Morgan surprised a large body of Spaniards. Some of these he forced the negro guide to kill before the eyes of the others, in order to implicate him in the eyes of the survivors. After eight days' search the band returned with 250 prisoners, and a long train of baggage mules, bound for Merida. The prisoners were each separately examined as to where the treasure was hid. Those who would not confess, and even those who had nothing to confess, were tortured to death—burnt, maimed, or had their life slowly crushed out of them.

Amongst the greatest sufferers in this purgatory on earth was an old Portuguese of venerable appearance, perhaps either a miser or purposely disguised. This man the blood-thirsty negro, now high in favour with the buccaneers, and trying to rival them in cruelty, declared was very rich. The poor old man, tearing his thin grey hair, swore by the Virgin and all the saints that he had but 100 pieces of eight in the whole world, and these had been stolen from him a few days before, during the general chaos, by a runaway slave. This he vowed on his knees with tears and prayers, doubly vehement when coming from one already on the grave's brink. The cruel slave still looked sneeringly on, and swore he was known to be the richest merchant in all Gibraltar. The buccaneers then stretched the Portuguese with cords till both his arms broke at the shoulder, and then bound him by the hands and feet to the four corners of a room, placing upon his loins a stone, weighing five cwt., while four men, laughing at his cries, kept the cords that tied him in perpetual motion. This inhuman punishment they called "swimming on land." As he still refused to speak, they held fire under him as he swung groaning, burnt off his beard and moustaches, and then left him hanging while they *strapadoed* another. The next man they threw into a ditch, after having pierced him with many sword thrusts, for they seem to have been as insatiable for variety of cruelty as they were for cruelty itself. They left him for dead, but he crawled home, and eventually recovered, although several sword blades had passed completely through his body.

As for the old Portuguese, his sufferings were far from ended; putting him on a mule they brought him into Gibraltar, and imprisoned him in the church, binding him to a pillar apart from the rest, supplying him with food barely sufficient to enable him to endure his tortures. Four or five days having passed, he entreated that a certain fellow prisoner, whom he named, might be brought to him. This request being complied with, as the first step to obtaining a ransom while he still remained alive, he offered them, through this agent, a sum of 500 pieces of eight. But the buccaneers laughed at so small a sum, and fell upon him with clubs, crying "500,000, old *hunx*, and not 500, or you shall not live."

After several more days of continued suffering, during which he incessantly protested that he was a poor man and kept a small tavern, the miser confessed that he had a store of 2,000 pieces of eight, buried in an earthen jar, and all these, bruised and mutilated as he was and much as he loved money, he gave for his liberty, and a few days more of life.

Upon the other prisoners, without regard to age, sex, or rank, they inflicted tortures too disgusting and shocking to mention. Fear, hatred, and avarice generated crimes, till the prisoners grew as vile as their persecutors.

A slave, who had been cruelly treated by his master, persuaded the buccaneers to torture him on the plea that he was very rich, although he was in reality a man of no wealth. The other prisoners, roused from the selfishness of self-preservation by a thrill of involuntary compassion, told Morgan that the Spaniard was a poor man, and that the slave had perjured himself to obtain revenge. Morgan released the Spaniard directly, but he had been already tortured.

The slave was given up to his master to be punished by any sort of death he chose to inflict. Handed over to the buccaneers, he was chopped to pieces in his master's presence, still exulting in his revenge. This, says Oexmelin with a cold *naïveté*:

> ... satisfait l'Espagnol, quoyqu'il fust fort mal traité, et en danger d'estre estropié

> ...satisfied the Spaniard, though he had been very badly treated, and almost lamed for life.

Some of the prisoners were crucified, others were burnt with matches tied between their toes or fingers, many had their feet forced into the fires till they dropped from the leg black and charred. All that the Indians had suffered was now retaliated on the Spaniards. The buccaneers themselves considered the punishment a vengeance of Providence. The only mercy ever shown to a Spaniard was to end his sufferings by death. The *coup de grace* was a kindness when it ended the misery of a groaning wretch, bruised and burnt, lying in the hot sun, half mortified, or with his body already paralyzed four or five days since.

The masters being all tortured, the slaves next received the *strapado*. These men, weaker in their moral nature and with no motive for concealment but fear, told everything. Many of the hiding-places were, however, not known to them. One of them, during the fever of his wound, declared he knew where the governor of the town was secreted, with many of the ladies of Gibraltar, and a large portion of the treasure. Threats of death revealed the rest, and he confessed that a ship and four boats, laden with Maracaibo wealth, lay in a river of the lake. The buccaneers were instantly on their feet. Morgan, with 200 men and the slave guide, set out to capture the governor; and 100 others, in two large *settees* (boats), sallied out to capture the treasure and the ships. The governor was not easily caught, for it needed a battalion of balloons to surprise him. His first retreat was a fort thrown up in the centre of a small island in the river, two days' march distant. Hearing that Morgan was coming in force, he retreated to the top of an adjoining mountain, into which there was but one ascent, so straight, narrow, and perilous, that it could only be mounted in single file.

The expedition altogether broke down, the rock proved inaccessible to any but eagles; a "huge rain" wetted their baggage and ammunition; in fording a river swollen by this "huge rain," many of their female prisoners were lost, and, what they valued more, several mules laden with plate were whirled down the torrents. Many of the women and children sank under the fatigue, and some escaped. Involved in a marshy country, up to their middles in water, the buccaneers had to toil on for miles. A few lost their lives, others their arms (the means of preserving them). A body of fifty determined men, the buccaneer historian himself says, could have destroyed the whole body. But the Spaniards were already so paralyzed by fear that they fled at the very rustle of a leaf. Twelve days were spent in this dangerous and useless expedition. Two days after them arrived their comrades, who had been somewhat more successful. The Spaniards had unloaded the vessels, and were beginning to burn them when they arrived, but many bales were left in the haste of flight, and the boats, full of plunder, were brought away in tow.

Morgan had now been lord in Gibraltar for five whole weeks, practising all insolences that a conqueror ever inflicts on the conquered; revenging on them the sufferings of the conquest, and trampling them under foot for the very pleasure of destruction. Provisions now failing, he resolved to depart; the provisions of Gibraltar, except the fruits, coming entirely from Maracaibo, were delayed and intercepted. He first sent some prisoners into the woods to collect a ransom from the fugitives, under pain of again burning down their newly rebuilt city. He demanded 5,000 pieces of eight. They promised to pay it in eight days, and gave four of their richest citizens as hostages. The governor, safe from all danger himself, had, however, forbidden them to pay any ransom, and they prayed Morgan to have patience.

Setting sail with his hostages he arrived in three days at Maracaibo, afraid that, during his long absence, the Spaniards had fortified themselves, and he should have to fight his way through the passes. Before his departure he released all his prisoners who had paid ransom, but detained the slaves. He refused particularly to give up the treacherous negro, because he knew they would burn him alive.

The only inmate of all the rich palaces and wide squares of Maracaibo, was a poor sick man, who informed him (Morgan), to his astonishment, that three Spanish men-of-war had arrived at the bar, and had repaired and garrisoned the fort. Their commander was Don Alonso del Campo d'Espinosa, the vice-admiral of the Indian fleet, who had been despatched to those seas to protect the Spanish colonists, and put to the sword every adventurer he could meet. This news did not alarm those who every day "set their lives upon the hazard of a die," but it enraged men who thought themselves secure of their plunder, and which they now might have to throw off to lighten them in their retreat. Morgan instantly despatched his swiftest vessel to reconnoitre the bar. The men returned next day, assuring him that the story was too true, and they were in very imminent danger. They had approached so near as to be in peril of the shot, the biggest ship mounted forty guns, the next thirty, and the smallest twenty, while Morgan's flag-ship had only fourteen. They had seen the flag of Castile waving on the redoubt. There was no means of escape by sea or land, and all were in despair at such enemies so placed.

Morgan, undaunted and roused to new courage by the extremity, grew more full of audacity than ever. He at once sent a flag of truce to the *Magdalene*, the Spanish admiral's vessel, demanding 20,000 pieces of eight, or he should set Maracaibo in flames. The admiral, amused and astonished at such temerity, wrote back to say, that hearing that they had committed hostilities in the dominions of his Catholic Majesty, his sovereign lord and master, he had come to dispute their passage out of the lake, from that castle, which they had taken out of the hands of a parcel of cowards, and he intended to follow and pursue them everywhere, as was his duty. The letter continued:

> Notwithstanding if you be contented to surrender with humility all you have taken, together with the slaves and other prisoners, I will let you pass freely without trouble or molestation, on condition that you retire home presently to your own country. But if you make any resistance or opposition to what I offer you, I assure you I will command boats to come from the Caraccas, wherein I will put my troops, and, coming to Maracaibo, will put you every man to the sword. This is my last and absolute resolution; be prudent, therefore,

and do not abuse my bounty with ingratitude. I have with me very good soldiers, who desire nothing more ardently than to revenge on you and your people all the cruelties and base infamous actions you have committed upon the Spanish nation in America.

This vapouring letter Morgan read aloud to his men in the broad market-place at Maracaibo, first in French and then in English, begging their advice on the whole matter—asking them whether they would surrender everything for liberty, or fight for both liberty and hard-won treasure. They all answered unanimously, they did not care for the Spanish brag, and they would rather fight to the last drop of their blood than surrender booty got with such peril. One of the men, stepping forward, cried, "You take care of the rest, I'll build a *brûlot*, and with twelve men will burn the biggest of the three Spaniards."

The scheme was adopted, but resolved once more to try negotiation, now that he was prepared for the worst, Morgan wrote again to Don Alonso, offering to leave Maracaibo uninjured, surrender all the prisoners, half the slaves, and to give up the hostages. The Don, trusting in his superior strength, and believing Morgan fairly intimidated or at least entirely in his mercy, refused to listen to any terms but those he had proposed, adding, that in two days he should come and force him to yield. Morgan resolved upon this to fight his way out and surrender nothing, his men, though discouraged, being still brave and desperate. All things were put in order to fight.

The Englishman of Morgan's crew proceeded as fast as possible with his *brûlot*, or fire-ship. He took the small vessel captured in the Rivière des Espines, and filled it full of palm-leaves dipped in tar, and a mixture of brimstone and gunpowder. He put several pounds of powder under each of the ten sham guns, which were formed of negro drums. The partitions of the cabins were then broken down, so that the flame might spread unimpeded. The crew were wooden posts, dressed up with swords, muskets, *bandoliers*, and hats or *montero* caps. This fire-ship bore the English colours, so that it might pass for Morgan's vessel; and in eight days, by all hands working upon it, it was ready. During the preparation an extra guard was kept upon the prisoners, for one escaping would have destroyed all their hopes of safety. The male prisoners were kept in one boat, and the females, slaves, plate, and jewels in another. In others, guarded by twelve men each, came the merchandise. The *brûlot* was to go first and grapple with the admiral's ship.

All things being now completed, Morgan, with a heart as gay as if he fought for God and the right, made his men take the usual buccaneer oath, employed on all occasions of pressing danger, when mutual confidence was peculiarly necessary. They vowed to fight till death, and neither to give nor take quarter. He promised a reward to all who distinguished themselves, exciting all the strongest feelings of their nature—revenge, avarice, and self-preservation.

With these desperate resolves, full of hope, for they were accustomed to consider his promises of victory as certain prophecies, they set sail on the 30th day of April, 1669, to seek the Spaniards.

They found the Spanish fleet riding at anchor in the middle of the entry of the lake, like gaolers of their spacious prison. It being late and almost dark, Morgan gave orders to anchor within range of the enemy, determined to resist if attacked, but to wait for light. They kept a strict watch, and at daybreak lifted anchor and set sail, bearing down straight upon the Spaniards, who, seeing them move, advanced to meet them.

Poor fishing boats the buccaneers' barks seemed beneath those proud floating castles; "but the race is not always to the swift, nor the battle to the strong." The *brûlot* sailed first, pushing on to the admiral's vessel, which lay stately between its two companions, and was suffered to approach within cannon shot. The Spaniards believing that it was Morgan's vessel, and intended to board them, waited till it came closer to crush it with a broadside. They little thought that they were fighting with the elements. The fire-ship fell upon the Spaniard and clung to its sides, like a wild cat on an elephant. Too late the Spaniard attempted to push her off, but the flames had already leaped from their lurking places; first the sails were swathed in fire, then the tackling shrivelled up, and soon the solid timbers burst into a blaze. The stern was first consumed, and the fore part sank hissing into the sea. The wretched crew, flying from one element to the other, perished, some by fire, some by water; the half-drowning clung to the burning planks and withered in the glare; the burning sailors were sucked down by the vortex of the sinking wreck. Don Alonso, seeing the danger, called out to them in vain to cut down the masts, and, throwing himself with difficulty into his sloop, escaped to land. The sailors, refusing quarter, were allowed to perish by the buccaneers' boats' crews, who at first offered to save them. Perhaps the recollection of their oath lessened their exertions.

The boats were pulling round the burning vessel in hopes of saving plunder, and not of saving lives. The second vessel was boarded by the buccaneers and taken, in the confusion, almost without resistance. The third ship, cutting its cables, drifted towards the fort, and there ran ashore, the crew setting fire to her to prevent capture. The buccaneers, proud of their victory, determined to push it to extremities by landing and attempting to storm the fort at the bar, without ladders, and relying only on their hand grenades, but their artillery was too small to make any practicable breach. The fort they found well supplied with men, cannon, and ammunition. The garrison had not suffered personally by the loss of a fleet manned by strangers, and they repulsed all attacks. Unwilling to retire, Morgan spent the whole of the day till dusk in firing muskets at any defenders who showed themselves above the walls, and at dusk lit them up with a shower of fireballs, but the Spaniards desperately resisted, and shot so furiously at them as to drive them back to the ships, with the loss of thirty killed and as many wounded—more loss than they had suffered in the capture of Maracaibo and Gibraltar, while the fleet had been destroyed without the loss of a single man. The garrison, expecting a fresh attack at daybreak, laboured all night to strengthen their works, levelling the ground towards the sea, and throwing up entrenchments from spots that commanded the castle.

The next day Morgan, not intending to renew the attack, employed himself in saving the Spanish sailors who were still floating on charred pieces of the wreck; not rescuing them from mercy, but in order to make them help in recovering part of the sunk treasure. They acknowledged that Don Alonso had compelled them before the engagement, after they had confessed to the chaplain, to come and take an oath to give the enemy no quarter, which was the reason many had refused to be saved. The admiral's vessel, the *Magdalene*, had carried thirty-eight guns and twelve small brass pieces, and was manned by 350 sailors; the second, the *St. Louis*, had thirty-four guns and 200 men; and the third, the *Marquise*, twenty-two guns and 150 men. The *Marquise* derived its name from the Marquis de Coquin, who had fitted it out as a privateer. The *Concepcion* and *Nostra Signora de la Soledad*, two larger vessels, had been sent back to Spain from Carthagena; a fourth, *Nostra Signora del Carmen* (for the Spaniards generally drew the names of their war vessels from the lady of love and peace), had sunk near Campeachy.

The pilot of the smaller vessel being saved, and promised his life, disclosed all Don Alonso's plans. He had been sent, upon the tidings of the loss of Porto Bello, by direction of the supreme council of state, with orders to root out the English pirates in those parts, and to destroy as many as he could, for dismal lamentations had been made to the court of Spain, to the Catholic king, to whom belonged the care and preservation of the New World, of the damages and hostilities committed by the English, and he had resolved to punish these proceedings and avenge his subjects. The king of England being complained to, constantly replied that he never gave any letters-patent to such men or such ships. Sending home his more cumbrous ships, the Don had heard at St. Domingo of the fleet sailing from Jamaica, and a prisoner, taken at Alta Grecia, disclosed Morgan's plan on the Caraccas. On arriving there the wild fire had already broken out at Maracaibo a second time, and hither he came to extinguish it. A negro slave had indeed informed the admiral of the fire-ship, but with short-sighted pride he derided the idea, saying that the English had had neither wit, tools, nor time to build it.

The pilot who made these disclosures was rewarded by Morgan, and, yielding to his promises, entered into his service. He informed him, with the usual zeal of a deserter, that there was plate to the value of 40,000 pieces of eight in the sunken ship, for he had seen it brought on board in boats. The divers eventually recovered 2000 pounds' worth of it, some "in plate" and others in *piastres*, that had melted into large lumps, together with many silver hilts of swords and other valuables.

Leaving a vessel to superintend this profitable fishery, Morgan hurried back to Maracaibo, and, fitting up his largest prize for himself, gave his own ship to a companion. He also sent to the governor, now somewhat crest-fallen, to re-demand the ransom, threatening more violently than before to burn down the city in eight days if it was not brought in. He also demanded, in addition, 500 cows as victual for his fleet. These were brought in in the short space of two days, with part of the money, and eleven more days were spent in salting the meat and preparing for sea. Then returning to the mouth of the lake, he sent to Don Alonso to demand a free passage, offering to send all the prisoners on shore as soon as he had once passed out, but otherwise to tie the prisoners to the rigging, exposing them to the shot of the fort, and then to kill and throw overboard those who were not struck. The prisoners also sent a petition, praying the governor to spare their lives. But the Don, quite undaunted, sternly answered to the hostages, who besought him on their knees to save them from the sword and rope, "If you had been as loyal to your king in hindering the entry of these pirates as I shall be in hindering their going out, you had never caused these troubles, either to yourselves or to our whole nation, which hath suffered so much through your pusillanimity. I shall not grant your request, but shall endeavour to maintain that respect which is due to my king, according to my duty."

When the terrified messengers returned and told Morgan, he replied, "If Alonso will not let me pass, I will find out a way without him," resolving to use either force or stratagem, and perhaps both.

Fearing that a storm might separate his fleet, or that some might not succeed in escaping, Morgan divided the booty before he attempted to pass the bar. Having all taken the usual oath, he found they had collected 250,000 pieces of eight, including money and jewels, and in addition a vast bulk of merchandise and many slaves. Eight days were spent in this division, which took place within sight of the exasperated garrison in the fort.

The following stratagem was then resorted to. Knowing that the Spaniards were expecting a final and desperate attack on the day before their departure, the buccaneers made great show of preparing to land and attack the fort. Part of each ship's crew embarked with their colours in their canoes, which were instantly rowed to shore. Here the men, concealed by the boughs on the banks, lay down flat in their boats, and were rowed back again to their vessels by only two or three sailors. This feigned landing they repeated several times in the day. The Spaniards, certain of an escalade, at night brought down the great eighteen pound ship guns of the fort to the side of the island looking towards the land, and left the sea-shore almost defenceless. When night came Morgan weighed anchor, and, by moonlight setting sail, at the commencement of the ebb tide, dropped gently down the river, till the vessels were almost alongside of the castle. Then spreading sails, quick as magic, he drove past, firmly but warily. Every precaution was taken. The crew were couched flat on the poop, and some placed below to plug the shot-holes as they came. The Spaniards, astonished at their daring, and enraged at their escape, ran with all speed and shifted their battery, firing hastily, furiously, and with little certainty; but by this time, a favourable wind springing up, the buccaneers were almost out of reach, few men were killed, and little damage done.

In this manner escaped Morgan from the clutches of Don Alonso, who had thought himself sure of his prey. The baffled rage of the Spaniards and the wild joy of the buccaneers, their clamorous approval of Morgan's skill, the exultation of their triumph, and the prisoners' dismay, may be easily imagined. Generous in success, Morgan, once out of range of the guns that thundered in pursuit, sent a canoe on shore with his prisoners from Maracaibo, but those of Gibraltar he carried off, as they had not yet paid their ransom. The joy of one and the grief of the other, their parting and the tears, were painful to witness. As he set sail, and the fort was still looming to the right, Morgan discharged a farewell salute of eight guns, to which the chapfallen Spaniards had not the heart to return even a single musket shot.

But out of Scylla into Charybdis was a buccaneer's fate: one danger was succeeded by another, hope by hope, despair by despair. The very day of their escape the judgment of Heaven seemed to overtake the sea rovers, as if to warn them that no stratagems could defeat God. The fleet was surprised by such a tempest that they were compelled to anchor in five or six fathom water. The storm increased, they were obliged to weigh again, and at any risk keep off the land. Their only choice seemed to be death by the Spaniard, the Indian, or the wave—all equally hostile and deaf to mercy.

Oexmelin says he was on board the least seaworthy vessel of the whole fleet, that, having lost anchors and mainsail, they had great difficulty in keeping afloat, and were obliged to bale as well as work night and day at the pumps, amid deafening thunder and mountainous seas that threatened to drown them even while the vessel still floated. The ship, but for the ropes that held it together, would have instantly sunk. The lightning and the wave disputed for their prey, but the rude arbiter, the wind, came in and snatched them from these destroyers.

> Indeed, though worn out with fatigue and toil, we could not make up our minds to close our eyes on that blessed light which we might so soon lose sight of for ever, for no hope of safety now remained. The storm had lasted four days, and there was no probability of its termination. On one side we saw rocks on which our vessel threatened every instant to drive, on the other were Indians who would no more have spared us than the Spaniards who were behind us; and by some evil fortune the wind drove us ceaselessly towards the rocks and the Indians, and away from the place whither we desired to go.

In the midst of these distresses, six armed vessels gave them chase through the storm when they were near the bay of Venezuela. They turned out to be vessels of the Count d'Estreés, the French admiral, who generously rendered them aid, and the wind abating enabled them to reach the shore. Morgan and some others made for Jamaica, and the French for St. Domingo,—the Spaniards at the fort probably believing they had perished in the gale.

The laggers of Morgan's fleet, who had never joined him, were less fortunate than the admiral they deserted. 400 in number, they landed at Savona, but could not find the buried letter. They determined to attack the town of Comana, on the Caraccas, choosing Captain Hansel, who had distinguished himself at Porto Bello, as their commander. This town was distant sixty leagues from Trinidad. On landing they killed a few Indians who awaited them on the beach, but the Spaniards, disputing briskly the entry of the town, drove them back at last to their ships with great loss and confusion. On returning to

Jamaica they were jeered at by Morgan's men, who used to say, "Let us see what sort of money you brought from Comana, and if it be as good as that which we won at Maracaibo."

Morgan, encouraged by success, soon determined on fresh enterprises. On arriving at Jamaica...

> ...he found many of his officers and soldiers already reduced to their former indigency by their vices and debaucheries. Hence they perpetually importuned him for new exploits, thereby to get something to expend still in wine and strumpets, as they had already done what they got before. Captain Morgan, willing to follow fortune's call, stopped the mouths of many inhabitants of Jamaica who were creditors to his men for large sums, with the hopes and promises of greater achievements than ever in a new expedition. This done, he could easily levy men for any enterprise, his name being so famous through all these islands, as that alone would readily bring him in more men than he could well employ.

Affecting a mystery, attractive in itself, and necessary where Spanish spies might be present, Morgan appointed a rendezvous at Port Couillon, on the south side of Hispaniola, and made known his intentions to the English and French adventurers, whether in Tortuga or St. Domingo. He wrote letters to all the planters and old buccaneers in Hispaniola, and desired their attendance at a common council. At many a hunting fire this announcement was read, and many an *engagé*'s heart beat high at the news, for Morgan was now the champion and hero of the buccaneers of America. Great numbers flocked to the port in ships and canoes, others traversed the woods and arrived there by land, through a thousand dangers. Such crowds came that it soon became difficult to obtain a place in the crews. Vessels and provisions were now all that was wanted. Plunder was certain, and they had but to choose on what rich coast they should land. The French adventurers, ever gay and ready, were first in the field. Morgan himself, punctual and prompt, followed in the *Flying Stag*, the St. Malo vessel we have before mentioned, carrying forty-two guns. The vessel had been lately confiscated and sold by the governor of Jamaica, the unfortunate captain escaping with his life, happy in being free although penniless.

At the rendezvous on the 24th day of October, 1670, 1600 men were present, and twenty-four vessels assembled at the muster, amid shouting, gun firing, flag waving, and great joy and hope. Morgan's proposition was to attack some rich place which was well defended—the more danger the more booty, for it was only rich places that the Spaniards cared to defend. Several previous expeditions had failed from want of provisions, and the necessity of attacking small places to obtain food gave the alarm to the Spaniards and frustrated their plans. They therefore resolved to visit La Rancheria, a small place on the banks of the River de la Hache, on the mainland, with four vessels and 400 men. This was a place where corn and maize were brought by the farmers for the supply of the neighbouring city of Carthagena, and they hoped to capture in the port some pearl vessels from that place.

In the meanwhile, Morgan, not caring for lesser prey, employed his men in careening, cleaning, rigging, and pitching their vessels ready for sea, that all might be ready to weigh anchor the moment the expedition of foragers returned. It augured terribly to the Spaniard that it was necessary to sack a town or two before the buccaneer fleet could even set sail.

Part of the men were in the woods boar-hunting, and others salting the flesh for the voyage. Each crew had a certain part of the woods allotted it for its own district, so perfect was Morgan's discipline. Each party prepared the salt pork for its own use, while the cauldrons of pitch were smoking on the beach, and the clank of the shipwrights' hammers could be heard all night by the hunters. The English, who were not so expert in hunting as their Gallic brethren (so says a French writer), generally took a French hunter with them, to whom they gave 150 or 200 *piastres*. Some of these men had trained packs of dogs that would kill enough boars in a day to load twenty or thirty men.

The Rancheria expedition arrived in six days within sight of the river, and was unfortunately becalmed for some time within a gunshot of land. This gave the Spaniards time to prepare for their defence, and either to bury their goods or throw up entrenchments, for these repeated visits of the buccaneers had rendered them quick on such occasions. A land-wind at last springing up, gave a corn vessel from Carthagena, lying in the river, an opportunity to sally out and attempt its escape, but being a bad sailor it was soon captured, much to the Englishmen's delight, for corn was the object of their visit. By a singular coincidence, it turned out to be that very cocoa vessel which Lolonnois sold to the governor of Tortuga, who, on its return from France, had sold it to Captain Champaigne, a French adventurer, who in his turn sold it to the same merchant captain who then commanded it. He told the buccaneers that it made the twelfth vessel taken from him by the brotherhood of the coast in five years only, and yet that with all these losses he had contrived to make a fortune of 500,000 crowns. *"On peut juger par là,"* says Oexmelin, with a shrug, *"s'il y a des gens riches dans l'Amérique."*

Landing at daybreak, in spite of the mowing fire from a battery, and under protection of their own cannon, they drove the Spaniards back to their strongly fortified village, which they at once attacked. Here the enemy rallied and fought desperately, hand-to-hand, sword blow and push of pike, from ten in the morning till night, when they fled, having suffered great loss, into secret places in the woods. The buccaneers, who had suffered scarcely less loss, pushed on at once headlong to the town, which they found deserted; and next day pursuing the Spaniards took many prisoners, and proceeded to torture them, inflicting on fear and innocence all the horrors of the Madrid inquisition. In fifteen days they captured many prisoners and much booty, and with the usual threats of destroying the town, they obtained 4,000 *hanegs*, or bushels of maize, sufficient for the whole of the fleet. They preferred this to money, and in three days, the whole quantity being brought in by the people, eager for their departure, they at once sailed.

Morgan, alarmed at their five weeks' absence, had begun to despair of their return, thinking Rancheria must have been relieved from Carthagena or Santa Maria. He also thought that they might have had good fortune, and deserted him to return to Jamaica. His joy was great to see them arrive laden with corn, and more in number than when they departed. A council of war was actually holding to plan a new expedition, when Captain Bradley and his six vessels hove in sight. The maize was divided among the fleet, but the plunder was awarded to the captain who had risked his life for the general good.

The captured ship arrived very opportunely, and it was instantly awarded by general consent to Le Gascon, a French adventurer who had lately lost his vessel. Morgan having divided the meat and corn, and personally inspected every bark, set sail for Cape Tiburon, at the west end of Hispaniola, a spot convenient for laying in stores of wood and water. Here he was joined by several ships from New England, refitted at Jamaica. Morgan now found himself suzerain of a fleet of thirty-seven vessels, large and small, carrying sixteen, fourteen, twelve, ten, even down to four pound guns. To man these there were 2200 sailors, well armed and ready for flight and plunder. The fleet was divided into two squadrons, under his vice-admiral and subordinate officers. To the captains he gave letters-patent, guaranteeing them from all the effects of Spanish hostility, from "the open and declared enemies of the King his master," (Charles II.)

The charter-party which we give elsewhere was then signed, the rewards were higher than usual, and many modifications introduced. In the private council three places were proposed as rich and accessible—Panama, Carthagena, and Vera Cruz. In these consultations the only thing considered was whether a town was rich or poor, not whether it was well or ill defended.

"The lot fell" on Panama, as the richest of the three, though the least known to them, being further from the North Pacific than any buccaneer had yet gone. Panama was the galleon-port and the El Dorado of the adventurer's yarns. Being so unknown a place they determined to first recapture St. Catherine's, where in the prisons they might obtain many guides, who had seen both the North and South Pacifics, for outlaws made, they found, the best guides for outlaws; and they agreed before sailing that, if they took a Spanish vessel, the first captain who boarded it should have for his reward a tenth part of her cargo.

They had begun by sacking a town to victual their fleet, they now proposed to storm a fort to obtain a guide—St. Catherine's batteries, if resolutely manned, being able to beat off three such fleets.

The admiral, it was agreed, should have a share for every hundred men, and every captain eight shares if the vessel they took was large. The crews then one by one took the oath of fidelity. On the 18th December, 1670, the fleet set sail for St. Catherine's, whose prisoners would rejoice at their arrival.

The one squadron carried the royal English and the other a white flag. The admiral's division bore a red banner with a white cross, "*le pavillon du parlement*," and at the bow-sprit one of three colours, blue, white, and red. Those of the other divisions carried a white and red flag. Morgan also appointed peculiar signals for all emergencies.

On their way to St. Catherine's they chased two Dutch vessels from Cuba, which escaped by aid of contrary winds that baffled their pursuers. In four days the fleet arrived at St. Catherine's, and Morgan despatched two small vessels to guard the port.

This island was renowned for its vast flocks of migratory pigeons, and is watered by four streams, two of which are dry in summer. The land, though fertile, was not cultivated.

The next day, before sunrise, they anchored in the bay of Aguada Grande, where the Spaniards had erected a four-gun battery. Morgan, at the head of 100 men, landed and made his way through the woods, having no guides but some old buccaneers who had been there before with Mansvelt. On arriving that night at the governor's house and the Platform Battery they found the Spaniards had retreated by a bridge into the smaller and almost impregnable island, which they had made strong enough to beat off 10,000 men. Being driven back at first by a tremendous fire, Morgan was obliged to encamp that night in the woods or open country—no hardship to hunters or sailors in fine weather. There still remained a whole league of dense brush between them and their enemies, at once their protection and destruction. A chilling torrent of rain began to beat upon them, and instead of ceasing, as they had hoped, lasted till noon of the next day. They pulled down two or three thatched huts, and made small damp fires, that scorched a few but warmed none. They could not shelter themselves, and, what was worse, could not keep their arms and powder dry. But more than this, they suffered from hunger, having had no food for a whole day. The men for the greater part being dressed with no clothes but a seaman's shirt and trousers, and without shoes or stockings, suffered dreadfully after the burning of a tropic noon from this freezing cold and rain. One hundred men, says Esquemeling, even indifferently well armed, might have cut them all to pieces. At daybreak they were roused from their shivering sleep by the Spanish drums beating the *Diane*, or *reveillé*. The rain had now ceased, and their courage rose as high as ever. But they could not answer this challenge, for their own drums were loose and soaked with wet, and they had now to employ themselves in quickly drying their arms. Scarcely had they done this, when it began to cloud over and rain with increased fury, as if the "sky were melting into waters," which blinded them and prevented them again from advancing to the attack. Many of them grew faint-hearted, and talked of returning. The men were now feeble for want of sleep, and faint with cold and hunger. The eager foragers found in a field "an old horse, lean, and full of scabs and blotches, with galled back and sides." This was instantly killed and flayed, and divided in small pieces among as many as could get any, and eagerly eaten without salt or bread by the few lucky epicures—"eaten," says the historian, "more like ravenous wolves eat than men."

The rain still gushing down, and the men, worn out in mind and body, growing angry, discontented, and clamorous, it became necessary for Morgan to act with promptitude. About noon, to his great joy, the rain ceased and the sun broke out. Taking advantage of this lull—for the rain had barred even their retreat—Morgan ordered a canoe to be rigged out in great haste, and dispatched four men with a white flag to the Spanish governor, declaring that if they did not all surrender he would put them to the sword without quarter. His audacity was luckily crowned with success. Opposed armies are often men mutually afraid, trying to frighten each other. The governor was intimidated. He demanded two hours to confer with his officers. At the end of this time, on Morgan giving hostages, two soldiers with white flags were sent to arrange terms. The governor had decided in full conference that he could not defend the island against such an armada, but he proposed a certain (Dalgetty-like) stratagem of war to save his own head, and preserve the reputation of his officers at home and abroad.

Morgan was to come at night and assault the fort of St. Jerome, which stood near the bridge that joined the two islands, and at the same moment his fleet was to attack the castle of Santa Teresa by sea, and land troops near the battery of St. Matthew. These men were to intercept and take prisoner the governor as he made his way to the St. Jerome batteries. He would then at once lead them to the castle, as if they were his own men. On both sides there was to be continual firing, but only with powder, and no bullets. The forts thus taken, the island would of course surrender.

This well-arranged performance took place with great *éclat*. Morgan, in acceding to the terms, had insisted on their strict performance of every item, and gave notice, for fear of ambush, that every straggling Spaniard would be shot. Afraid of a stratagem, some buccaneers loaded their muskets with ball, and held themselves ready for any danger. With much smoke and great consumption of powder, the unsuspecting Spaniards were driven like sheep into the church, the island surrendered, and by this bloodless artifice Spanish pride remained unhurt.

But a cruel massacre now commenced. The buccaneers had eaten nothing for nearly two days. They made war upon all the poultry and cattle—the oldest cow was slain, the toughest rooster strangled. For several days the island was lit up with huge fires, round which the men roasted their meat, and revelled and caroused. When wood grew scarce they pulled down cottages to light their fires, and having no wine very wisely made use of water.

The day after the surrender they numbered their prisoners, and found they had collected 450 souls—seventy of the garrison, forty-three children, and thirty-one slaves. The men were all carefully disarmed, and sent to the plantations to bring in provisions; the women were left in the church to pray and weep. They next inspected all the ten batteries, wondering in their strength and exulting in their victory. The fort St. Jerome contained eight great guns and sixty muskets; the St. Matthew three guns; the Santa Teresa twenty guns and 120 muskets. The castle was very strong, and moated; impregnable on the sea side, and on the land side ascended by a narrow mountain path, while the guns on its summit commanded the port. The St. Augustine fort mounted three guns; the Platform two; the St. Salvador and another also two; the Santa Cruz three; and the St. Joseph six and twelve muskets. In the magazine they found 30,000 pounds of powder, which they at once shipped, with all the other ammunition. In the St. Jerome battery Morgan left a guard, but in all the other forts the guns were spiked and the gun-carriages burnt.

The object of his visit was still to seek. Examining the prisoners, who were now crowded in with merchants and grandees, he inquired for banditti from Panama, and three slaves stepped forward who knew every path and avenue to the city. These men he chose as guides, promising them a full buccaneer's share of the spoil if they brought him by a secure way to the city, and, in addition, their liberty when they reached Jamaica. These volunteers consisted of two Indians and a mulatto. The former denied all knowledge of the place; the latter—a "rogue, thief, and assassin, who had deserved breaking on the wheel rather than mere garrison service"—readily accepted Morgan's propositions, and promised to serve him faithfully. He had a great ascendancy over the two Indians, and domineered over them as he pleased, without their daring to disobey a half-blood already on the point of preferment.

The next step to Panama was to capture Chagres and its castle, and Morgan at once dispatched five vessels, well equipped, with 400 men on board, to undertake this expedition, remaining himself at St. Catherine's, lest the people of Panama should be alarmed. He was to follow his van-guard in eight days, guided by the Indians, who knew Chagres. This time he and his men prudently spent in pulling manioc roots for cassava, and digging potatoes for the voyage.

The Chagres expedition was led by the same Captain Bradley who commanded at Rancheria. He had been with Mansvelt formerly, and had rendered himself famous by his exploits both among the buccaneers and the Spaniards. He arrived in three days at Chagres, opposite Fort St. Lawrence, which was built on a mountain commanding the entrance of the river. As soon as the Spaniards saw the red flag spreading from his vessels, they displayed the royal colours of Spain, and saluted him with a volley too hasty and angry to be very destructive. The buccaneers, according to their usual stratagem, landed at Narangui, a place a quarter of a league distant from the castle, their guide leading them through thick woods, through which they had to cut a path with their sabres. It was early morning when they landed, and requiring half a day to perform the short distance, they did not reach a hill commanding the castle till two o'clock. The mire and dirt of the road combined, with the darkness of the way, to lengthen their march. The guides served them well, but brought them at one spot so near to the castle, and in so open and bare a place, that they lost many men by the shot. In other parts the wood was so thick that they could only tell that they were near the castle by the discharge of the cannon. The hill they had now reached was not within musket range, and they were thus deprived of the use of their favourite weapon. Could they have dragged cannon so far they might have taken the place without losing a man.

The castle of Chagres was built on a high mountain at the entry of a river, and surrounded by strong wooden *palisadoes* banked with earth. The top of the mountain was divided into two parts, between which ran a ditch thirty feet deep; the tower had but one entrance by a drawbridge, towards the land it had four bastions, and towards the sea two more. The south wall was inaccessible crag, the north was moated by the broad river. At the foot of the hill lay a strong fort with eight guns, which commanded the river's mouth; a little lower down were two other batteries, each of six guns, all pointing the same way. At another side were two great store-houses, full of goods, brought from the inland, and near these a flight of steps, cut in the rock, led to the castle of the summit. On the west side was a small port not more than seven or eight fathoms deep, with good anchorage for small vessels, and before the hill a great rock rose from the waves, which almost covered it at low water.

The place appeared such a perfect volcano of fire, and so threatening and dangerous, that the buccaneers, but for fear of Morgan's rage and contempt, would have at once turned back. After many disputes and much doubt and perplexity, they resolved to hazard the assault and risk their lives. When they descended from their hill into the plain, they had to throw themselves on their faces to escape the desolating shower of balls; but their marksmen, quite uncovered and without defence, shot at the Spanish gunners through the loops of the palisading, and killed all who showed themselves. This skirmishing continued till the evening, when the buccaneers, who had lost many men, their commander having his leg broken with a cannon shot, began to waver and to think of retiring, having in vain tried to burn down the place with their fireballs, and charged up to the very walls, which they tried in vain to climb, sword in hand. When the Spaniards saw them drawing back through the dusk, in some disorder, carrying their wounded men and gnashing their teeth in rage at the dark lines of defence, they shouted out "Come on, you dogs of heretics; come on, you English devils: you shan't get to Panama this bout, for we'll serve your *comerades* as we have served you." The buccaneers, astonished at their cries, now for the first time learnt that Morgan's expedition had been heard of at Panama.

Night had already begun, and the rain of bullets, shot, and Indian arrows (more deadly almost than the bullets), harassing and well-aimed, continued as grievous as by day. Taking advantage of the gloom, another party advanced to the *palisadoes*; the light of their burning fuses directed the aim of the Spaniards.

A singular accident of war gave the place, so briskly defended, into the hands of the assailants. A party of the French musketeers were talking together, devising a plan of advance, when a swift Indian arrow fell among them and pierced one of the speakers in the shoulder Esquemeling says in the back and right through the body, another writer says in the eye. A thought struck the wounded man, for the wound had spurred his imagination: coolly drawing the point from his shoulder, he said to those near him, *"Attendez, mes frères, je m'en vais faire périr tous les Espagnols—tous—avec cette sacré flèche"* (wait a bit, my mates, I'll kill all the Spaniards—all—with this d—— arrow); so saying he drew from his pocket a handful of wild cotton, which the buccaneers kept as lint to staunch their wounds, and wound it round the dart; then putting it in his loaded musket, from which he extracted the ball, he fired it back at the castle roof. It alighted on some dry thatch, which in a moment began to smoke, and in another second broke into a bright flame, more visible for the darkness. The buccaneers shouted and pushed on to the attack, and the wounded men forgot their wounds. Some of the men, seeing the result of the experiment, gathered up the Indian arrows that lay thick around them, and fired them at the roofs. Many houses were soon in flames. The Spaniards, busy with the defence, did not see the fire until it had gained some head, and reaching a parcel of powder blown it up and caused ruin and consternation within the fort. If they left the walls the buccaneers gained ground, if they left the fire the flames spread more terribly than before; the want of sufficient water increased the confusion, and while they tried to quench the conflagration, the buccaneers set fire to the *palisadoes*.

Oexmelin, who was present as a surgeon at this attack of Chagres, relates an anecdote of courage which he himself witnessed, to show the indomitable fury of the assailants. One of his own friends was pierced in the eye by an Indian arrow, and came to him to beg him to pull it out, the pain was so intense and unbearable. Although a surgeon, Oexmelin had not the nerve to inflict such torture, however momentary, on a friend, and turned away in pity, upon which the hardy seaman tore out the arrow with a curse, and, binding up the wound, rushed forward to the wall. The few buccaneers who had retreated, seeing the flames, now hurried back to the attack. The Spaniards could no longer see the enemy at whom they fired, the night was so dark and starless, while the buccaneers shot down with the unerring aim of hunters the Spaniards, whose bodies stood out dark and well-defined against the bright background of flame. All this time, before the fire of the roofs could be extinguished, the buccaneers had swarmed through the fosse, and, mounting upon each other's shoulders, burnt down part of the *palisadoes*, as we have before described, in spite of the hand grenades that were thrown from above, and which burst among them. The fire ran along the wall, leaping like a winged thing, and devoured wherever it clung, spreading with dreadful rapidity.

The fight continued all night, and when the calm daylight broke on the worn soldiers, the buccaneers saw with sparkling eyes that the gabions had smouldered through, and that the earth had fallen down in large heaps into the fosse. The breaches in many places were practicable. The armour had fallen piece-meal from their giant adversary, and he now stood before them bare, wounded, and defenceless. The buccaneers, creeping within musket shot of the walls, shot down the gunners in the breaches to which the cannon had been dragged by the governor's orders during the night. Divided into two bands, one party kept up a constant fire on the guns, and the other watched the motions of the enemy. About noon they advanced to a spot which the governor himself defended, belted round with twenty-five brave Spaniards, armed with pikes, halberds, swords, and muskets. They advanced under a dreadful hail of fire and lead, the defenders casting down flaming pots full of combustible matter and *"odious smells,"* which destroyed many of the English. But we do not know how smells could drive back men who would have marched through hell if it had been the shortest way to Panama.

Nothing could equal the unflinching courage of the Spaniards—they disputed every inch of ground—they yielded slowly like wounded lions when the hunters narrow their circles. They showered stones and all available missiles on their assailants, only wishing to kill a buccaneer, but feeling that resistance was hopeless; some, rather than yield, threw themselves from the cliffs into the sea, and few survived the fall. As the buccaneers won their way to the castle the Spaniards retreated to the *garde du corps*, where they entrenched themselves with two cannon; to the last the governor refused quarter, and at last fell shot through the brain. The few who remained surrendered when the guns were taken and would have been turned against them.

Only fourteen men were found unhurt in the fort and about nine or ten wounded, who had hid themselves among the dead. They told Morgan that they were all that were left of a garrison of 314 soldiers. The governor, seeing that he was lost, had despatched the survivors to Panama to alarm the city, and remained behind to die. No officer was left alive; they had been the first to set their men the example of a glorious death. It appeared that a buccaneer deserter, an Irishman, whom Morgan had not even informed of his design, had come to the port, and assured them of the attack on La Rancheria, and the contemplated movement on Panama. The governor of that place had instantly sent to Chagres a reinforcement of 164 men, with ammunition and provisions, and had placed ambuscades along the river. He was at that very moment, they said, awaiting them in the savannah with 3600 men: of these 2000 were infantry, 400 cavalry, and 600 Indians. He had also employed 200 muleteers and hunters to collect a drove of 1000 wild cattle to drive down upon the invaders. Says Esquemeling:

> The taking of this castle cost the pirates excessively dear, in comparison to what they were wont to lose, and their toil and labour was greater than at the conquest of the Isle of St. Catherine.
>
> On numbering their thinned ranks, many voices were silent at the roll call. More than 100 men were found to be dead,

and more than seventy grievously wounded. There were sixty who could not rise, and many in the ranks wore on their arms strips of the Spanish colours, or had their heads bound round with bloody cloths. The prisoners they compelled to drag their own dead to the edge of the cliffs and cast them among the shattered bodies on the beach, and then to bury them where the sea could not wash them out of their graves, or the birds devour them. The castle chapel they turned into an hospital for the wounded, and the female slaves were employed to tend them, for the surgeons in the heat of battle had only had time to amputate a limb or bind an artery.

CHAPTER 8

Conquest of Panama

The bodies of their *comerades*, who had died that they who survived might conquer, were buried, not without some tears even from these rude men, in large (plague pit) graves, dug by the prisoners. The women were violated in the first fury of the sack. During their plunder they found a great quantity of provisions and ammunitions stored up for the use of the fleet. Their next act was to repair the fort and render it tenable.

Morgan, instantly informed of the fall of Chagres, did not remain long behind. Having first collected all the Indian wheat and cassava he could carry, he embarked his prisoners and provisions, taking with him Don Joseph Ramirez de Leiba, the governor, and the chief officers. The cannon he spiked or threw into the sea, in places where he might recover them, intending to return and fortify the place, as a stronghold if his design on Panama failed. The forts, and church, and house he fired, with the exception of the castle of Santa Teresa.

In sailing to Chagres a storm arose and dispersed his vessels, keeping them many days at sea. The admiral, always watchful in danger, suffered himself for a moment to sleep in the hour of prosperity. When he approached the river mouth and saw the English flag floating from the blackened walls, he could not restrain the heedless joy of his crew—not waiting for the pilot canoe that was putting out to warn them of their danger, he drove on the sunken rock at the foot of the castle hill. His own and three other vessels sank, yet the crews and cargoes were all saved, and but for a strong "norther" the ships themselves would have been preserved.

Brought into the castle with acclamations and hearty congratulations at his escape, Morgan employed the Spanish prisoners from St. Catherine's in repairing the palisading of the fort, carefully destroying all thatched sheds for fear of fire. He then chose a garrison by lot, and divided the stores. He heard with delight the details of the victory, and lamented the absent dead and the many brave men that had shared so often his own hopes and fears. His next movement was to seize some *chatten*, or small Spanish vessels that were still in the river. They were small craft that went to and fro between Chagres and Porto Bello, or Nicaragua, or plied with merchandise up and down the river. They mounted six guns, two iron, and four small brass, and were navigated by six men. He also took four small frigates of fourteen and eight guns, and all the canoes he could lay hands on, requiring them for the expedition. He left behind him 100 men, under command of Captain Le Maurice, and 150 men to guard the ships.

For Panama, Morgan took with him 1300 of the best armed and the most robust of his band, five boats with artillery, and thirty-two canoes. He imprudently carried little provisions, expecting to obtain plenty from the Spaniards they should kill in the ambuscades. In spite of the recent victory, and of Morgan's certainty of conquest, many of the buccaneers were less sanguine than on former expeditions. The Spanish prisoners had succeeded in alarming them by rumours of the dangers and intricacy of the road, and the ambuscades that had been two months in preparation. Some, more superstitious than the rest, thought the wreck of Morgan's ship, and the severe loss at Chagres, bad omens for their success at Panama. But these were mocked at by the rest, as white-livered, and Morgan having divided the provisions between the garrison and the St. Catherine prisoners, reviewed his men, and examined himself their arms and ammunition. He quieted their fears and spoke of victory as already obtained. He exhorted them to show more than usual courage, in order to return as soon as possible rich and glorious to Jamaica. With a shout of "Long live the King of England, and long live Henry Morgan," they began their march towards the doomed city on the 18th of January, 1670.

The first day they advanced only six leagues to Rio de los Braços, where they got out of their canoes to sleep on shore, being crippled with overcrowding in the boats. They could have brought no provisions, for few had any food that day, but a pipe of tobacco "to stop the orifice of the stomach." They could find nothing in the deserted plantations, where even the unripe fruits had been plucked and the roots pulled up before their arrival. The men longed to fight, in order that they might eat. By noon of the next day they reached Cruz de Juan Gallego, where they were obliged to leave their canoes; the river was very dry and shallow from want of rain, and much impeded with fallen trees, but their hopes were excited by the guide's intelligence, that about two leagues further the roads grew better. Here they left their boats with 160 men to guard them, as a resource in case of defeat, giving them strict injunctions not to land for fear of ambuscades in the neighbouring woods, which were so thick as to seem impenetrable. Finding the forest almost impassable, Morgan ordered a few of the canoes to be rowed, though with immense labour, to a place called Cedro Bueno, further up the river, taking half the men at a time and returning for the rest, so by nightfall all the men were once more united. From discovering no ambuscades, in spite of all the wishes of these hungry soldiers, it was supposed that the Spanish spies, willing to avoid a fight, had frightened their officers by exaggerating the number of the adventurers. On the third day Morgan sent forward some guides, who could find no road, the country being flat, inundated, and marshy. The men, who had scarcely eaten anything since their departure, grew faint and hungry, and a few of them gathered the leaves from the forest trees. It being night before they could pass the river, they slept on the bank, exposed, half-clothed as they were, to the tropical damps and cold.

The fourth day's march they advanced in divisions; the largest went by land, the smaller in canoes. The guides were always kept two musket shots in advance, to give notice of ambuscades, and in hopes of capturing stragglers who might furnish intelligence. But the Spaniards had also scouts, very wary, and very "dexterous" in giving notice of all accidents, frequently bringing the Panama men intelligence of the buccaneers' approach six hours before the enemy arrived. About noon the army reached a post named Torna Cavallos, so called probably from the roughness of the road, and at this spot the guide of the canoes cried out that he saw an ambuscade. With infinite joy, the hungry men, thirsting for blood, flew to arms, knowing that the Spaniards always went luxuriously provided with food, and knowing that a dead Spaniard could want no more provender. As soon as they came within sight of the entrenchment, which was shaped like a half-moon, and the palisading formed of entire trees, they uttered a dreadful shout, and, driven on by rage and hunger, began to race like starved wolves, seeing which could first cross swords with the enemy, whom they believed to be about 400 strong. But their hearts fell within them when they found the place a mere deserted rampart, and all the provisions, but a few crumbs which lay scattered about, either burnt or carried off. Some leather bags lay here and there, as if left in a hasty retreat. Enraged at this, they at once pulled down the Spanish huts, and cutting the leather bags, tore them up for food. Quarrels then arose for the largest messes, but before they could well finish this unsavoury banquet, the drum sounded for the march. About 500 Spaniards seem to have held these entrenchments, and many of the men threatened to devour the first fugitive they could meet with. About night they reached another deserted ambuscade, called Torna Munni, equally bare of food, and the remainder of the bags were now devoured. Those fortunate enough to obtain a strip first soaked slices of it in water, next beat it between two stones, then scraped off the hair with their hunters' knives, and, roasting it in the fire, ate it leisurely in small pieces. "I can assure the reader," says Oexmelin, "that a man can live on this fare, but he can hardly get *very fat.*" Frequent draughts of water (which, by good fortune, they had at hand) seasoned this not very palatable food of men accustomed to revel on venison and brandy. Says Esquemeling:

> Some who were never out of their mothers' kitchens may ask how these pirates could eat and digest those pieces of leather, so hard and dry, whom I answer, that could they once experience what hunger, or rather famine, is, they would find the way as the pirates did.

The fifth day at noon they arrived at a place called Barbacoa, where there were more deserted barricades, and the adjacent plantations were equally bare of either man, animal, or plant. Searching with all the zeal and perseverance of hungry men, they found at last, buried in the floor of a cave lately hewn out of the rock, two sacks of flour, two jars of wine, and some plantains, and Morgan generously divided these among the most exhausted of his troops, some being now nearly dead with famine. The flour they mixed with water, and, wrapping the dough in banana leaves, baked it in the fire. Somewhat refreshed, they renewed their march with increased skill and vigour. The lagging men they placed in the canoes, till they reached at night some deserted plantations known as the Tabernillas, where they slept.

On the sixth day they marched slowly, after resting a time from real weakness, some of the strongest being sent into the woods to pluck berries and pull roots, many even eating leaves and grass. The same day at noon they arrived at a plantation. Eagerly foraging here, but not expecting to find anything, they turned a little from the road, and came upon a barn full of maize in the husk. Beating down the door, they fell upon it and devoured it as rapaciously as a herd of swine, till they fell off satiated. A distribution was then made of it to each man, for hunger does not care for cooking. Loaded with this grain they continued their march in high spirits for about two hours, when they came suddenly on about 200 Indians, and soon after passed a deserted ambuscade. Those who had maize still left threw it away, thinking that the Spaniards and better food were at hand. These archers were on the opposite side of the river. The buccaneers, firing, killed a few, and pursued the others as far as Santa Cruz. The nimblest escaped by swimming, and two or three adventurers, who waded after them, were pierced with arrows at the ford. The Indians, as they fled, hooted—"*Ah perros Ingleses, à la savanah, à la savanah.*" "*English dogs, English dogs, come to the savannah.*"

Passing the river they were now compelled to begin their march on the opposite side. There was little sleep that night, but great dejection, and murmurs arose against Captain Morgan and his conduct. He was blamed for not having brought provisions, and for not having yet met the Spaniards; condemned for irreconcilable errors, and reviled for even his past successes. Some declared they would return home, others would willingly have done so, yet were afraid to retreat; but a large party declared they would rather die than go back a step. One of the guides, perhaps bribed by Morgan, promised that it should not be long before they met with people from whom they should derive no small advantage, and this comforted them. A tinge of superstition would have soon converted this into one of those prophecies by which Cromwell and Cortes both consoled their desponding troopers.

On the seventh morning, expecting enemies, the men all cleaned their arms, and every one discharged his musket and pistols without ball to let the Spaniards hear they were coming, and that their ammunition was not damaged. Leaving Santa Cruz, where they had rested, they crossed the river in their canoes, and arrived at the town of Cruz.

At some distance from Cruz they had beheld to their great joy a great smoke rising above the roofs, which they thought arose from kitchen chimneys, and quickening their pace they began to laugh, and shout, and leap,—joking at the Spanish waste of fuel, and saying, "the Spanish cooks are roasting meat for our dinner when we have mastered their masters;" but as the smoke grew thicker, they began to think that the enemy were burning some houses that interfered with the fire of the entrenchments.

Two hours after, on arriving panting and hot at Cruz, they found the place deserted and stripped, and no meat, but many fires, for every Spaniard had burnt his own house, and only the royal storehouse and stables were left standing. A few crackling ruins were all that remained of the great halfway house between Chagres and Panama, for here the Chagres merchandise was always landed and transported to Panama on the backs of mules, being distant only twenty-six Spanish leagues from the river of Chagres, and eight from Panama. The disappointed buccaneers spent the remainder of the day at Cruz in seeking food and resting. Every cat and dog was soon killed and eaten, for the cattle had been all driven off. Morgan, growing now more strict in discipline, gave orders that no party of less than 100 men should leave the town. Five or six Englishmen who disobeyed the order were killed by the Indians. In the king's stables fifteen or sixteen jars of Peruvian wine were found, and a leather sack full of biscuit. Morgan, afraid that his men would fall into excesses, spread a report that the Spaniards had poisoned the wine—a report confirmed by the violent sickness of all who drank of it; although half-starved men, fed for a week on vegetable refuse, would have been injured by any excess. It was, however, eagerly drunk, and would have been had there been death in every cup. This sickness detained them a day at Cruz. The canoes, being now useless, were sent back, guarded by sixty men, to join the other boats, one alone being hid in a thicket for fear of any emergency or any necessity arising, and to transmit intelligence to the vessels. He feared that, if left at Cruz, they might be captured, and would at least require an extra guard.

On the eighth day at morning Morgan reviewed his troop, and found he had 1100 able and resolute men still at his back. He persuaded them that their *comerade* who was carried off by the Indians had returned, having only lost his way in the woods, fearing they might be discouraged at his disappearance. He then chose a band of the best marksmen as a forlorn hope, and a "hundred of these men," says Oexmelin, "are worth six hundred of any other nation." He divided the remainder into a van and wings, knowing that he should have to pass many places where not more than two men could pass abreast.

After ten hours' march they arrived at a place called *Quebrada Obscura*, a dark wooded gorge where the sunlight rarely entered. Here, on a sudden, a shower of 300 or 400 arrows poured down upon them, killing eight or nine men, and wounding ten. These arrows came from an Indian ambuscade hid on a wooded and rocky mountain, perforated by a natural arch, through which only one laden beast could pass. The buccaneers, though they could see nothing but rocks and trees, instantly returned the fire, and two Indians rolled down into the path. One of these, who appeared to be a chief, for he wore a coronet of variegated feathers, attempted to stab an English adventurer with his javelin, but a companion, parrying the thrust with his sabre, slew the Indian. This brave man was, it is supposed, the leader of the ambuscade, for the savages seeing him fall took at once to flight, and never discharged another shaft. As they entered a wood the rest of the Indians fled to seize the next height, from whence they might observe them and harass their march. The buccaneers found them too swift to capture, and pursued them in vain: but two or three of the wounded fugitives were found dead in the road. A few armed and disciplined men could have made this pass good against a hundred, but these Indians were now scattered and without a leader, and they had only fired at random, and in haste, through trees and thickets that intercepted their arrows. On leaving this defile the buccaneers entered a broad prairie, where they rested while the wounded were tended. At a long distance before them they could see the Indians on a rocky eminence, commanding the road where they must pass. Fifty active men were dispatched to take them in the rear in the hopes of obtaining some prisoners, but all in vain, for the Indians were not only more agile but knew all the passes. Two hours after they were seen at about two gunshots' distance, on the same eminence from which they had been just driven, while the buccaneers were now on an opposite height, and between them lay a wood. The buccaneers supposed that a Spanish ambuscade was hid here, for whenever they came near enough the Indians cried out "*À la savanah, à la savanah, cornudos perros Ingleses:*" "*To the savannah, to the savannah, you cuckold English dogs.*" Morgan sent 100 men to search this wood, and upon this the Spaniards and Indians came down from the mountain as if to attack them, but appeared no more.

About night, a great rain falling, the buccaneers marched faster, in order to prevent their arms getting wet, but they could find no houses to barrack in, for the Indians had burnt them all and driven away the cattle, hoping to starve out the men whom they could not drive out. They left the main road after diligent search, and found a few shepherds' huts, but too few to shelter all their company; they therefore piled their arms, and chose a small number from each company to guard them. Those who slept in the open air endured much hardship, the rain not ceasing all night. They made temporary sheds, which they covered with boughs, in order to sleep under a shelter, however imperfect; and sentinels were placed, Morgan being afraid of the Indians, who chose wet nights for their onslaughts, when fire-arms were often useless.

Next morning very early, being the ninth of their tedious journey, they recommenced their march, Morgan bidding them all discharge their guns and then reload them, for fear of the wet having damped the powder. The fresh air of the morning, clear after the storm, was still about them, and the clouds had not yet yielded to the tropical sun as they pushed on over a path more difficult than before. In about two hours' time a band of twenty Spaniards began to appear in the distance, and the Indians were also visible, but Morgan could obtain no prisoners, though he offered a reward of 300 crowns for every Spaniard brought in. When pursued the enemy hid themselves in caves and eluded all search.

At last, toiling slowly up a high mountain, the adventurers unexpectedly beheld from the top the South Sea glittering in the distance. This caused them as great joy as the sight of "Thalatta" did to the soldiers of Xenophon. They thought their expedition now completed, for to them victory was a certainty. They could discern upon the sea, never before beheld, a large ship and six small boats setting forth from Panama to the islands of Tavoga and Tavogilla, which were only six leagues distant. Fortune smiled upon them today, for, descending this mountain, they came into a grassy prairie valley, full of all sorts of cattle, which were being pursued by mounted Spaniards, who fled at the sight of the buccaneers. Upon these animals Morgan's men rushed with the avidity of half-starved hunters, the eagerness of sailors to obtain fresh meat, and all the haste that brave men exhibit to get at an enemy. One shot a horse, another felled a cow, but the greater part slaughtered the mules, which were the most numerous. Some kindled fires, others collected wood, and the strongest hunted the cattle, while the invalids slew, and skinned, and flayed. The whole plain was soon alight with a hundred fires. The hungry men cut off lumps of flesh, carbonadoed them in the flame, and ate them half raw with incredible haste and ferocity. "They resembled," Esquemeling says, "rather cannibals than Christians, the blood running down their beards to the middle of their bodies." But no hunger, no fear, no passion threw Morgan off his guard. Hungry and weary himself, and sympathising with his men's hunger, he saw the danger of this reckless gluttony, which produced a reaction of inertness as dangerous as intoxication. Dreading surprise, for he was surrounded by enemies, he beat a false alarm, and seizing their arms, his men, ashamed of their excess, renewed their march. The remainder of the meat, half-roasted or quite raw, they strung to their bandoliers. "The very look of these men," says Esquemeling, "was enough to have terrified the boldest, for we know that in love as well as war, the eyes are the soonest conquered." Morgan, anxious at not having yet obtained a prisoner as guide, again despatched a vanguard of fifty men, who about evening saw in the distance 500 Spaniards, who shouted to them they knew not what.

Soon after, almost at dusk, mounting a small eminence, they saw a better sight than even the South Sea—the highest steeples of Panama, bright in the sunset; upon this, like the German soldiers at the sight of the Rhine, the buccaneers gave three cheers, to show their extreme joy, leaping and shouting, and throwing their hats into the air as if they had already won the victory. At the same time the drums beat stormily and proudly, and each man shot off his piece, while the red flag was displayed and waved in defiance of the Spaniard, and high above all the trumpet sounded.

The camp was pitched for the night by the men, who waited impatiently for the morning when the battle should join; with equal pride and courage 200 mounted Spaniards shouted in return as they dashed up within musket shot, "Tomorrow, tomorrow, ye dogs, we shall meet in the savannah;" and as they ended, their trumpet sounded clearer than even that of Morgan's. These horsemen were soon joined by several companies of infantry and several squadrons of cavalry, who wheeled round them within cannon shot. These troops had been despatched when the sounds of the buccaneers' approach reached the gates of the city. There were still two hours of light, but Morgan determined not to fight till early in the morning, when he might be able to move freely in the unknown country, and when there would be a whole clear, bright day for the battle. As night drew on all the Spaniards retired to the city, excepting seven or eight troopers, who hovered about to watch the enemy's motions and give the alarm, if a night attack was contemplated. On his side Morgan placed double sentinels, and every now and then ordered false alarms to be beat to keep his men on the alert. Those who had any meat left ate it raw, as they had often done when hunters. No fires were allowed to be kindled, and the men lying, ready armed, on the grass, waited eagerly for the daylight. 120 cavaliers again joined the Spanish scouts, and affected to maintain a strict blockade, and the city all night played with its biggest guns upon the camp, but being at so great a distance did little harm to the buccaneers.

At daybreak of the tenth day of their march the Spaniards beat the *Diane*, and Morgan, replying heartily, began with great eagerness to push forward to the city, the Spaniards wheeling cautiously around his wings. One of the guides warned Morgan against the high road, which he knew would be blocked up and crowded with ambuscades, and the army defiled into a wood to the right, where the passage was so difficult that none but buccaneers could have forced a way, "very irksome indeed," says Esquemeling. The Spaniards, completely baffled and astonished by this diversion, left their batteries in a hurry, and, without any distinct plan of attack, crowded out into the plain. After two hours' march the buccaneers reached the top of a small hill. From this eminence they could now see their goal, and Panama, with all the roofs that hid its treasure, lay before them. Below, on the plain, they might also discern the Spanish army drawn up in *battalia*, awaiting their descent. Even Esquemeling admits that the forces seemed numerous.

> There were two squadrons of cavalry, four regiments of foot, and a still more terrible enemy, a huge number of wild bulls, roaring and tossing their horns, driven by a great number of Indians, and a few negroes and mounted matadors.

> The historian, more truthful in his confession than his boasts, says:

> They were surprised with fear, much doubting the fortune of the day; yea, few or none there were but wished themselves at home, or at least free from the obligation of that engagement, it so nearly concerning their lives. Having been for some time wavering in their minds, they at last reflected on the strait they had brought themselves into, and that now they must either fight resolutely or die, for no quarter could be expected from an enemy on whom they had committed so many cruelties. Hereupon they encouraged one another, resolving to conquer or spend the last drop of their blood.

They then divided themselves into three battalions, sending before 200 buccaneers, very dexterous at their guns, who descended the hill, marching directly upon the Spaniards, and the battle closed. The Spanish cavalry uttered cries of joy, as if they were going to a bull-fight. The infantry shouted *"Viva el rey!"* and the vari-coloured silks of their doublets glistened in the sun. The buccaneers, giving three cheers, charged upon the enemy. The forlorn hope Morgan despatched against the cavalry and the bulls. The cavalry galloped forward to meet them, but, the ground being marshy, they could not advance with speed, and sank one by one before the unceasing dropping fire of 200 buccaneers, who fell on one knee and poured in a full volley of shot, the foot and horse in vain trying to break through this hot line of flame and death. The bulls proved as fatal to those who employed them, as the elephants to Porus. Driven on the rear of the buccaneers, they took fright at the noise of the battle, a few only broke through the English companies, and trampled the red colours under foot, but these were soon shot by the old hunters; a few fled to the savannah, and the rest tore back and carried havoc through the Spanish ranks.

The firing lasted for two hours; at the end of that time the cavalry and infantry had separated, and the troopers had fled, only about fifty of their number succeeding in escaping. The infantry, discouraged at their defeat, and despairing of success, fired off one more volley, and then threw down their arms; the victory was won. Morgan, having no cavalry, could not pursue, and a mountain soon hid the fugitives from the buccaneers' sight, who would not follow, expecting the flight was a mere decoy to lure them into an ambuscade. The buccaneers, weary and faint, threw themselves down to rest. A few Spaniards, found hiding in the bushes by the seashore, were at once slain, and several *cordeliers* belonging to the army, being dragged before Morgan, were pistolled in spite of all their cries and entreaties. A Spanish captain of cavalry was taken prisoner by the English musketeers, who had hitherto given no quarter, and confessed that the governor of Panama had led out that morning 2000 men, 200 bulls, 1450 horse, and twenty-four companies of foot, 100 men in each, sixty Indians, and some negroes. In the city, he said, were many trenches and batteries, and at the entrance a fort with fifty men and eight brass guns. The women and wealth had all been sent to Tavoga, and 600 men with twenty-eight pieces of cannon were inside the town, defended by ramparts of flour sacks. The ambuscade had been waiting fifteen days in the savannah, expecting Morgan.

On reviewing their men, the English found a much greater number of killed and wounded than they had expected, so Esquemeling confesses, but does not give the number. Oexmelin puts the loss at only two killed and two wounded, an incredible statement, trustworthy as he generally is. The Spaniards lost 600 men.

> The pirates, nothing discouraged seeing their number so diminished, but rather filled with greater pride, perceiving what huge advantage they had obtained against their enemies, having rested some time, prepared to march courageously towards the city, plighting their oaths one to another, that they would fight till not a man was left alive. With this courage they recommenced their march, either to conquer or be conquered, carrying with them all the prisoners.

They avoided the high road from Vera Cruz, on which the Spaniards had placed a battery of eight pieces of cannon, and selecting that from Porto Bello, they advanced to the town before the people could rally, and while the exaggerated rumours of the defeat were still uncontradicted. Trembling fugitives filled the streets, and terror was in every face.

The Spaniards fought desperately, but without hope. In spite of Morgan's endeavour to maintain strict discipline, his men began to undervalue the enemy, and to advance straggling and reckless. The Spaniards, observing this, fired a broadside, killing twenty-five or thirty of the vanguard at the first discharge, and wounding nearly as many, but before they could reload were overpowered and slain at their guns, the buccaneers stabbing all whom they met.

Of this attack, Esquemeling gives the following graphic but rambling account:

> They found much difficulty in their approach to the city, for within the town the Spaniards had placed many great guns at several quarters, some charged with small pieces of iron, and others with musket bullets. With all these they saluted the pirates at their approaching, and gave them full and frequent broadsides, firing at them incessantly, so that unavoidably they shot at every step great numbers of men. But neither these manifest dangers of their lives, nor the sight of so

many as dropped continually at their sides, could deter them from advancing, and gaining ground every moment on the enemy; and though the Spaniards never ceased to fire and act the best they could for their defence, yet they were forced to yield after three hours' combat, and the pirates having possessed themselves, killed and destroyed all that attempted in the least to oppose them.

Morgan was now master of Panama, as he had been of St. Catherine's, la Rancheria, Maracaibo, and Gibraltar, but his vigilance did not yet relax. As soon as the first fury of their entrance was over, he assembled his men, and commanded them, under great penalties, not to drink or taste any wine, as he had been informed by a prisoner that it had been poisoned by the Spaniards. Though much wealth had been hidden, great warehouses of merchandise, they rejoiced to find, were still well stocked with silks, cloths, and linens. Morgan's only fear now was, that with so small a body of men as remained to him, the Spaniards might rally, or his men, grown intoxicated by success and intent on plunder, be cut off without resistance. Having placed guards at all the important points of defence within and without the city, he ordered twenty-five men to seize a boat laden with merchandise, that owing to the low water in the harbour could not put out to sea. The command of this vessel he gave to an English captain. The houses of Panama were built chiefly of cedar, and a few of stone.

Fortunately, Michael Scott sketches for us nearly the whole scenery of Morgan's march. One side of the harbour of Chagres is formed, he says, by a small promontory that runs 500 yards into the sea. This bright little bay looks upon an opposite shore, long and muddy, and covered with mangroves to the water's brink. On the uttermost bluff is a narrow hill, with a fort erected on its apex. The rock is precipitous on three sides. The river of Chagres is about 100 yards across, and very deep. It rolls sluggishly along, through a low, swampy country. It is covered down to the water with thick sedges and underwood, and where the water is stagnating, generates mosquitoes and fevers. The gigantic trees grow close to the water, and are laced together by black, snake-like withes. Here and there, black, slimy banks of mud slope out near the shore, and on these, monstrous alligators roll or sleep, like logs of rotting driftwood. For some miles below Cruz, where the river ceases to be navigable by canoes, oars are laid aside, and long poles used to propel the boats, like punts, over the shoals. Panama is distant about seven leagues from Cruz. The roads are only passable for mules: in some places it has been hewn out of the rock, and zigzags along the face of hills, in parts scarcely passable for two persons meeting.

> The scenery on each side is very beautiful, as the road winds for the most part amongst steeps, overshadowed by magnificent trees, among which birds of all sizes, and of the most gorgeous plumage, are perpetually glancing, while a monkey every here and there sits grimacing and chattering overhead. The small, open savannahs gradually grow larger, and the clear spaces widen, until the forest you have been travelling under breaks into beautiful clumps of trees, like those of a gentleman's park, and every here and there are placed clear pieces of water, spreading out full of pond-turtle, and short grass, that sparkles in the dew.

As you approach the town, the open spaces become more frequent, until at length you gain a rising ground, about three miles from Panama, where the view is enchanting. Below lies the city, and the broad Pacific, dotted with ships, lies broad and glassy beyond.

Basil Hall, an accurate but less poetical observer, sketches the bay of Panama, its beach fringed with plantations shaded by groves of oranges, figs, and limes, the tamarinds surmounting all but the feathery tops of the cocoa-nut trees; the ground hidden with foliage, among which peep cane-built huts and canoes pulling to shore. Tavoga he describes as a tangle of trees and flowers. "The houses of the city, very curious and magnificent," says Esquemeling, "and richly adorned with paintings and hangings, of which a part only had been removed." The buildings were all stately, and the streets broad and well arranged. There were within the walls eight monasteries, a cathedral, and an hospital, attended by the religious. The churches and monasteries were richly adorned with paintings, and in the subsequent fire may have perished some of the masterpieces of Titian, Murillo, or Velasquez. The gold plate and fittings of these buildings the priests had concealed. The number of rich houses was computed at 2000, and the smaller shops, &c., at 5000 additional. The grandest buildings in the town were the Genoese warehouses connected with the slave trade; there were also long rows of stables, where the horses and mules were kept that were used to convey the royal plate from the South to the North Pacific Ocean. Before the city, like offerings spread before a throne, lay rich plantations and pleasant gardens.

Panama was the city to which all the treasures of Peru were annually brought. The plate fleet, laden with bars of gold and silver, arrived here at certain periods brimming with the crown wealth, as well as that of private merchants. It returned laden with the merchandise of Panama and the Spanish main, to be sold in Peru and Chili, and still oftener with droves of negro slaves that the Genoese imported from the coast of Guinea to toil and die in the Peruvian mines. So wealthy was this golden city that more than 2,000 mules were employed in the transport of the gold and silver from thence to Porto Bello, where the galleons were loaded. The merchants of Panama were proverbially the richest in the whole Spanish West Indies. The Governor of Panama was the suzerain of Porto Bello, of Nata, Cruz, Veragua, &c., and the Bishop of Panama was primate of the Terra Firma, and suffragan to the Archbishop of Peru. The district of Panama was the most fertile and healthy of all the Spanish colonies, rich in mines, and so well wooded that its ship-timber peopled with vessels both the northern and the southern seas; its land yielded full crops, and its broad savannahs pastured innumerable herds of wild cattle.

The buccaneers found the booty in the half-devastated town ample beyond their expectations, in spite of all that had been destroyed, buried, or removed. The stores were still full of wealth, which not even a month of alarm had given the merchants time to remove to their overcharged vessels. Some rooms were choked with corn, and others piled high with iron, tools, plough-shares, &c., for Peru. In many was found "metal more attractive," in the shape of wine, olive oil, and spices, while silks, cloths, and linen lay around in costly heaps.

Morgan, still afraid of surprise, resorted to a reckless scheme to avert the danger. The very night he entered Panama he set fire to a few of the chief buildings, and before morning the greater part of the city was in a flame, although the first blaze had been detected in the suburbs. No one knew his motive, and few that the enemy had not done it. He carefully spread a report, both among the prisoners and his own people, that the Spaniards themselves were the authors of the fire. The citizens and even the English strove to extinguish the flames, by blowing up some houses with gunpowder and pulling down others, but being of wood, the fire spread rapidly from roof to roof. In less than half an hour a whole street was consumed. The Genoese warehouses and many of the slaves were burnt, and only one church was left standing; 200 store buildings were destroyed. Oexmelin seems to lament chiefly the slaves and merchandise, and scarcely even affects a regret for the stately city. The ruins continued to smoke and smoulder for a month, and at daybreak of the morning after their arrival, little of the great city they had lately seen glorious in the sunset remained but the president's house, where Morgan and his staff lodged, a small clump of muleteers' cottages, and two convents, that of St. Joseph and that of the Brothers of the Redemption. Still fearful of surprise, the adventurers encamped outside the walls in the fields, from a wish to avoid the confusion, and in order to keep together in case of an attack by a superior force. The wounded were put into the only church that had escaped the fire.

The next day Morgan despatched 160 men to Chagres to announce his victory, and to see that his garrison wanted for nothing. They met whole troops of Spaniards running to and fro in the savannah, but, in spite of their expectations, they never rallied. In the afternoon the buccaneers re-entered the city, and selected houses of the few left to barrack in. They then dragged all the available cannon they could find and placed them round the church of the Fathers of the Trinity, which they entrenched. In this they placed in separate places the wounded and the prisoners. The evening they spent in searching the ruins for gold, melted or hidden, and found much spoil, especially in wells and cisterns.

A few hours after, Morgan's vessels returned with three prizes, laden with plate and other booty, taken in the South Sea. The day they sailed, arriving at one of the small islands of refuge near Panama, they took a sloop with its crew of seven men, belonging to a royal Spanish vessel of 400 tons, laden with church plate and jewels, removed by the richest merchants in Panama; there were also on board all the religious women of the nunnery, with the valuable ornaments of their church, and she was so deeply laden as not to require ballast. It carried only seven guns and a dozen muskets, had no more sails than the "uppermost of the mizen," was short of ammunition and food, and even of water. The buccaneers received this intelligence from some Indians who had spoken to the seamen of the galleon when they came ashore in a cock-boat for water. Had they given chase they might have easily captured it, but Captain Clark let the golden opportunity slip through his hands. Thinking himself sure of his prize as he had got her sloop, his men spent the night in drinking the rich wines they found in the sloop, and reposing in the arms of their Spanish mistresses, the more beautiful for their tears and despair. During these debaucheries the galleon slipped by and was no more seen, and so they lost a prize of greater value than all the treasure found in Panama. In the morning, weary of the revel, they crowded all sail and despatched a well-armed boat to pursue the cripple, ascertaining that the Spanish ship was in bad sailing order and incapable of making any resistance. In the islands of Tavoga and Tavogilla they captured several boats laden with merchandise. Informed by a prisoner of the probable moorings of the galleon, Morgan, enraged at her escape, sent every boat in Panama in pursuit of her, bidding them seek till they found her. They were eight days cruising from port to creek. Returning to the isles, they found here a large ship newly come from Payta, laden with cloth, soap, sugar, biscuit, and 20,000 pieces of eight; another small boat near was also taken and laden with the divided merchandise. With these glimpses of wealth the boats returned to Panama somewhat consoled for the loss of their larger prize. The buccaneers' vessels now began to excite the astonishment of the Spaniards, they being the first Englishmen, since Drake, who had appeared as enemies on those seas.

During this expedition Morgan had employed the rest of his men in scouring the country in daily companies of 200, one party relieving another, and perpetually bringing in flocks of pale and bleeding prisoners, or mules laden with treasure. Some tortured the captives, others explored the mines, and the rest burnt glittering heaps of gold and silver stuffs, merely to obtain the metal, expecting to have to fight their way back to their ships at Chagres, and not wishing to be encumbered with unwieldy bundles on that toilsome and dangerous march. Morgan, complaining much of the fruitless labours of his foragers, at last placed himself at the head of 350 men, and sallied into the country to torture every wealthy Spaniard he could meet.

The following anecdote presents us with such a complete picture of the demoralisation of a panic, that it reminds us of Thucydides' description of Athens during the plague, or Boccaccio's of Florence during the raging of the pest. On one occasion Morgan's men met with a poor Spaniard, who, during the general confusion, had strolled into a rich man's house and dressed himself in the costume of a merchant of rank. He had just stripped off his rags, and, first luxuriating in a change of costly Dutch linen, had slipped on a pair of breeches of fine red taffety, and picking up the silver key of some coffer, had tied it to one of his points. Esquemeling represents the man as a poor retainer of the house. He was still wondering childishly at his unwonted finery, when the buccaneers broke into the house and seized him as a prize. Finding him richly dressed and in a fine house, they believed him at once to be the master. His story they treated as a subtle invention. In vain he pointed to the black rags he had thrown off—in vain he protested, by all the saints, that he lived on charity, and had wandered in there and put on the clothes by the merest chance, and without a motive but of venial theft. Spying the little key at his girdle they became sure that he lied, and they demanded where he had hid his cabinet. They had at first laughed at his ingenious story—they now grew angry at his denials of wealth. They stretched him on the rack and disjointed his arms, they twisted a cord round his wrinkled forehead "till his eyes appeared as big as eggs, and were ready to fall out," and as he still refused to answer, they hung him up and loaded him with stripes. They then cut off his nose and ears, singing his face with burning straw till he could not even groan or scream, and at last, despairing of obtaining a confession, gave him over to their attendant band of negroes to put him to death with their lances. "The common sport and recreation of the pirates," says Esquemeling, "being such cruelties."

They spared no sex, age, or condition; priest or nun, peasant or noble, old man, maiden, and child were all stretched on the same bed of torture. They granted no quarter to any who could not pay a ransom, or who would not pay it speedily. The most beautiful of the prisoners became their mistresses, and the virtuous were treated with rigour and cruelty. Captain Morgan himself seduced the fairest by alternate presents and threats. There were women found base enough to forsake their religion and their homes to become the harlots of a pirate and a murderer. But to his iron heart love found a way, and enervated the mind of the man whom nothing before could soften.

After ten days spent in the country beyond the walls, Morgan returned to Panama, and found a shipload of Spanish prisoners newly arrived. Amongst these was a woman of exquisite beauty, the wife of a Spanish merchant, then absent on business in Peru. He had left her in the care of some relations, with whom she was captured. Esquemeling says:

> Her years were few, and her beauty so great, as, peradventure, I may doubt whether in all Christendom any could be found to surpass her perfections, either of comeliness or honesty.

Oexmelin, a more skilful observer, and who saw her, being a sharer in the expedition, describes her hair as ink black, and her complexion of dazzling purity. Her eyes were piercing, and the Spanish pride, usually so cold and repulsive, served in her only as a foil to her surpassing beauty, and to attract respect. The roughest sailors and rudest hunters grew eloquent when they praised her. The common men would willingly have drawn swords for such a prize. But their commander was already the slave of her whom he had captured. His demeanour changed: he was no longer brutal and truculent: he became sociable in manner, and more attentive to the richness of his dress, for lovers grow either more careless or more regardful of their attire.

The buccaneer's aspect was changed. He separated the lady from the other prisoners, and treated her with marked respect. An old negress, who waited on her, served at once as an attendant and a spy. She was told to assure her mistress, that the buccaneers were gentlemen and no thieves, and men who knew what politeness and gallantry were as well as any. The lady wept and entreated to be placed with the other prisoners, for she had heard that her relations were afraid of some plot against her good fame.

The lady, like other Spanish women, had been told by their priests and husbands, that the buccaneers had the shape of beasts and not of men. The more intelligent reported they were robbers, murderers, and heretics; men who forswore the Holy Trinity, and did not believe in Jesus Christ. "The *oaths* of *Morgan*," says Esquemeling, with most commendable gravity, "*soon convinced her that he had heard of a God.*" It was said, that a woman of Panama who had long desired to see a pirate, on their first entrance into the city cried out, "*Jesu Maria*, the thieves are men, like the Spaniards, after all;" and some volunteers, when they went out to meet Morgan's army, had promised to bring home a pirate's head as a curiosity.

Morgan, refusing to restore the beauty to her friends, treated her with more flattering care than before. Tapestries, robes, jewels, and perfumes, lay at her disposal. Such kindness, after all, was cheap generosity, and part of this treasure may even have been her husband's. In her innocence, she began to think better of the buccaneers. They might be thieves, but they were not, she found, atheists, nor very cruel, for Captain Morgan sent her dishes from his own table. She at first received his visits with gratitude and pleasure, surprised at the rough, frank kindness of the seaman, and loudly denounced his slanderers, that had so cruelly attempted to poison her mind against him, her guardian and protector. The snares were well set, and the bird was fluttering in. But Heaven preserved her, and she passed through the furnace unhurt.

Morgan soon threw off his disguise, and offered her all the treasures of the Indies if she would become his mistress. She refused his presents of gold and pearl, and resisted all his artifices. In vain he tried alternately kindness and severity. He threatened her with a thousand cruelties, and she replied, that her life was in his hands, but that her body should remain pure, though her soul was torn from it. On his advancing nearer, and threatening violence, she drew out a poignard, and would have slain him or herself, had he not left her uninjured. Enraged at her pride, as he miscalled her virtue, he determined to break her spirit by suffering. She was stripped of her richest apparel, and thrown into a dark cellar, with scarcely enough food allowed her to support life, and the chief demanded 30,000 *piastres* as her ransom, to prevent her being sold as a slave in Jamaica.

Under this hardship the lady prayed like a second Una daily to God, for constancy and patience. Morgan, now convinced of her purity, and afraid of his men, who already began to express openly their sympathy with her sufferings, to account for his cruelty, accused her to his council of having abused his kindness by corresponding with the Spaniards, and declared that he had intercepted a letter written in her own hand. Says Esquemeling:

> I myself was an eyewitness of the lady's sufferings, and could never have judged such constancy and chastity to be found in the world, if my own eyes and ears had not assured me thereof.

Amid the blood, and dust, and vapour of smoke, the virtue of this incomparable lady shines out like a pale evening star, visible above all the murky crimson of an autumn sunset.

A new danger now arose to Morgan from this adventure, for the seamen began to murmur, saying that the love of this beautiful Spaniard kept them lingering at Panama, and gave the Spaniards time to collect their forces, and surprise them on their return. But Morgan, having now stayed three weeks, and nothing more being left to plunder, gave orders to collect enough mules to carry the spoil to Cruz, where it could be shipped for Chagres, and so sent homeward.

There can be no doubt that various causes had for some time been undermining the long subsisting attachment between Morgan and his men. He had shown himself a slave to the passions which enchained their own minds, and their riches perhaps made them independent, and therefore mutinous. It was while the mules were collecting that he became aware of the loaded mine over which he stood. A plot was discovered, in which there were 100 conspirators. They had resolved to seize the two vessels they had captured in the South Sea, and with these to take possession of an island, which they could fortify for a stronghold. They would then fit out the first large Spanish vessel they could obtain, and with a good pilot and a bold captain start privateering on their own account, and work home by the straits of Magellan. As the spoil had not yet been divided, it is probable that all these men had broken the buccaneer oath, and had secreted part of the plunder. They had already hidden in private places, cannons, muskets, provisions, and ammunition. They were on the very point of raising the anchor, when one of them betrayed the scheme, and Morgan at once ordered the vessel to be dismasted and the rigging burnt. The vessels he would also have destroyed, but these he spared at the intercession of the friend he had appointed their captain. From this time all confidence seems to have ceased between Morgan and his men. Many a king has been made a tyrant by the detection of a conspiracy. The men dreaded his vengeance, and he their treachery. From this hour he appears to have resolved to enrich himself and his immediate friends at any risk, leaving the French to shift for themselves. It is not improbable but that the old French and English feud may have had something to do with this quarrel. In war it ceased, but rankled out again in peace. The French seem to have been his greatest enemies, and the English friendly or indifferent. This distinction is visible even in the historians, for Esquemeling speaks of him with mere distrust, and Oexmelin with bitter hatred.

In a few days the mules were ready, and the gold packed in convenient bales, for Spanish or English gold it was all one to the mules. The costly church plate was beaten up into heavy shapeless lumps, and the heavier spoil was left behind or destroyed. Better burn it, they thought, than leave it to the accursed Spaniard, for we always hate those whom we have injured. The artillery of the town being carefully spiked, and all ready to depart, Morgan informed his prisoners that he was about to march, and that he should take with him all those who were either unable or unwilling at once to bring in their ransom. The sight was heart-rending, and the panic general. At his words, says the historian, there was not one but trembled, not one but hurried to write to his father, his brother, or his friends, praying for instant deliverance or it would be too late. The slaves were also priced, and hostages were sent to collect the money. While this was taking place, a party of 150 men were sent to Chagres to bring up the boats and to look out for ambuscades, it being reported that Don Juan Perez de Guzman, the fugitive president of Panama, had entrenched himself strongly at Cruz, and intended to dispute the passage. Some prisoners confessed that the president had indeed so intended, but could get no soldiers willing to fight, though he had sent for men as far as Carthagena; for the scattered troopers fled at the sight of even their own friends in the distance.

Having waited four days impatiently for the ransom, Morgan at last set out on his return on the 24th of February, 1671. He took with him a large amount of baggage, 175 beasts of burden laden with gold, silver, and jewels, and about 600 prisoners, men, women, children, and slaves, having first spiked all the cannon and burnt the gun-carriages. He marched in good order for fear of attack, with a van and rear-guard, and the prisoners guarded between the two divisions.

The departure was an affecting sight, as even the two historians, who were buccaneers themselves and eyewitnesses, admit. Lamentations, cries, shrieks, and doleful sighs of women and children filled the air. The men wept silently, or muttered threats between their teeth, to avoid the blows of their unpitying drivers. Thirst and hunger added to their sufferings. Many of the women threw themselves on their knees at Morgan's feet and begged that he would permit them to return to Panama, there to live with their dear husbands and children in huts till the city could be rebuilt. But his fierce answer was, that he did not come there to hear lamentations, but to seek money, and that if that was not found, wherever it was hid, they should assuredly follow him to Jamaica. All the selfishness and all the goodness of each nature now came to the surface. The selfish fell into torpid and isolated despair—the good forgot their own sufferings in trying to relieve those of others.

Some gazed at each other silently and hopelessly; others wailed and wept, a few cursed and raged. Here stood one mourning for a brother—there another lamenting a wife. Many believed that they should never see each other again; but would be sold as slaves in Jamaica. The first evening the army encamped in the middle of a green savannah on the banks of a cool and pleasant river. This was a great relief to the wretched prisoners, who had been dragged all day through the heat of a South American noon by men themselves insensible to climate—urged forward by the barrels of muskets and blows from the butts of pikes. Some of the women were here seen begging the buccaneers, with tears in their eyes, for a drop of water, that they might moisten a little flour for their children, who hung crying at their parched and dried-up breasts. The next day, when they resumed the march, the shrieks and lamentations were more terrible than before. "They would have caused compassion in the hardest heart," says Esquemeling; "but Captain Morgan, as a man little given to mercy, was not moved in the least." The lagging Spaniards were driven on faster with blows, till some of the women swooned with the intense heat, and were left as dead by the roadside. Those who had husbands gave them the children to carry.

The young and the beautiful fared best. The fair Spaniard was led between two buccaneers, still apart from the rest. She wept as she walked along, crying that she had entrusted two priests in whom she relied to procure her ransom money, 30,000 *piastres*, from a certain hidden place, and that they had employed it in ransoming their friends. A slave had brought a letter to the lady and disclosed the treachery. Her complaint being told to Morgan he inquired into it, and found it to be true. The religious men confessed their crime, but declared they had only borrowed the money, intending to repay it in a week or so. He therefore at once released the lady, and detained the monks in her place, taking them on to Chagres and despatching two men to obtain their ransom.

On arriving at Cruz the mules were unloaded, preparatory to embarkation. The buccaneers encamped round the king's warehouse, where it was stored. Three days were given to collect the ransom. The Spaniards, tardy or unwilling in the collection, brought in the money the day after. Vast quantities of corn, rice, and maize were collected here for victualling the ships. Morgan embarked 150 slaves, and a few poor and obstinate Spaniards who had not yet paid their ransom. The monks were redeemed, and escaped happy enough. A part of the buccaneers marched by land. Many tears of joy and sorrow were shed when the prisoners and those who were liberated took farewell.

On reaching Barbacoa the division of the spoil began. Mustering his men, Morgan compelled them all to swear they had concealed nothing, even of the smallest value, and, what was more unusual, he ordered them all to be individually searched from top to toe, down even to the very soles of their shoes. This search was suspicious and insulting. The Frenchmen, hot-blooded and mutinous, would have openly resisted had they not been in the minority. Morgan allowed himself to be first searched to lessen the general discontent, and one man in every company was employed as searcher. No precautions were neglected that could be suggested by long experience of plundering.

This unusual vigilance was a mere cloak for Morgan's own dishonesty. Every man was now compelled to discharge his musket before the searchers, that they might be sure no precious stones were hidden in the barrel. These searchers were generally the lieutenants of each crew, and had all taken an additional oath to perform their duty with fidelity. The murmurs against Morgan had now reached such a height, and were so hourly increasing, that many Frenchmen threatened to take his life before they reached Jamaica. The more temperate controlled the younger and the more impetuous, and the band reached Chagres without any revolt. They found the garrison short of provisions and glad to be relieved, but the wounded had nearly all died of their wounds.

From Chagres Morgan sent a great boat to Porto Bello with all the St. Catherine's prisoners, and demanded a ransom for sparing the castle of Chagres. The people of Porto Bello replied they would not give one farthing, and he might burn it as he chose.

The day after their arrival, Morgan divided the booty. It amounted to only 443,000 pounds, estimating at ten *piastres* the pound. The jewels were sold unfairly, the admiral and his cabal buying the greater part very cheap, having already, it was believed, retained all the best of the spoil. Every one had expected at least 1000 pieces each, and was disappointed and indignant at receiving only about 200. There was an end now to all cooperation between English and French adventurers, and the hopes of a buccaneer republic were at an end for ever. The murmurs again rose uncontrollably high, and some proposed to seize Morgan and force him to a fair division.

The suspected admiral, trying in vain to pacify them, and finding he could obtain no price for Chagres, divided the provisions of the fort among the vessels, removed the cannon and ammunition, then demolished the fortifications, and burnt the buildings. Suddenly taking alarm, or more probably following a preconcerted plan, Morgan sailed out of the harbour without any signal or notice, and hurried to Jamaica, followed by four English vessels, whose captains had been his confidants.

In the first paroxysm of their rage, the French adventurers would have pursued Morgan, and attacked his vessel, but he escaped while they were still hesitating. We shall find him finally settled in Jamaica, and married to the daughter of the chief person of the island, a sure proof, says the indignant and philosophical Oexmelin, that any one is esteemed in this world provided he has money.

The same vivacious writer gives a lively picture of the rage of the crews at the treacherous flight of Morgan. They shouted, swore, stamped, clenched their fists, gnashed their teeth, and tore their hair, fired off their pistols in the air, and brandished their arms, with imprecations loud and deep. They longed for the plunder they had lost, and longed still more eagerly for revenge. They never now mentioned the Welsh name but with an execration. Strange anomaly of the human mind, that men who lived by robbery, should be astonished at a small theft committed by a comrade! In the first bitterness of their vexation, they drew their sabres, and hewed and thrust at their imaginary enemy. They bared their arms, and pointed out to each other the cicatrices of their half-healed wounds.

Confirmations of the admiral's treachery reached them from every side. They remembered that Morgan had been latterly unusually reserved and unsociable, closeting himself with a few English confidants, to whom he had been seen whispering even during public conferences. He had, it was now recollected, grown silent during all discussions, and more particularly when the booty was mentioned.

Oexmelin (a surgeon) also mentions, that on one occasion, as he was visiting a wounded buccaneer, Morgan came up to the hammock, and said in English, thinking he could not be overheard, "Courage, get soon well, you have helped me to conquer, and you must help me to profit by the conquest." Another day, as Oexmelin was searching by the river for a medical herb, he turned round suddenly, and saw Morgan secreting something in the corner of a canoe, and looking frequently over his shoulder to see if he was observed. When he observed Oexmelin, he looked troubled, and, coming up, asked him what he was doing there, to which the surgeon made no answer, but, stooping down, picked the plant he was in search of, and began to tell him its properties. Morgan turned off the subject, beginning to converse on indifferent topics, and, although the proudest of men, insisted on accompanying him home. Oexmelin took care to find an opportunity afterwards to rummage the canoe, but found nothing; but this same canoe he always observed Morgan took great care of, and never permitted to row out of his sight. But these stories none had dared to utter, for since the victory of Panama, the admiral, always proud, sensual, and cruel, had grown every day more stern, and had rendered himself dreaded by his severities.

The adventurers sought for a long time some means of avenging themselves on Morgan for his successful treachery. They at last heard that he had resolved to take possession of St. Catherine's island, being apprehensive of the governor of Jamaica. In this spot he had determined to fortify himself, renew his Buccaneering, and defy both open enemies and treacherous friends. The buccaneers agreed to waylay him on his passage, and carry him off, with his wife, children, and ill-gotten treasure. They then planned either to kill him, or compel him to render an account of the spoil of Panama. But an unexpected accident saved Morgan, and defeated their scheme of vengeance. At the very crisis, a new governor, Lord G. Vaughan, arrived at Port Royal, and brought a royal order for Morgan to be sent to England to answer the complaints of the King of Spain and his subjects. Of his trial we hear nothing, but we soon after see the culprit knighted by Charles II., and appointed Commissioner of Admiralty for Jamaica. The king, who frolicked with Rochester, and smiled at the daring villainy of Blood, had no scruples in disgracing knighthood by such an addition.

In the autumn of 1680, the Earl of Carlisle, then governor of Jamaica, finding his constitution undermined by the climate, returned to England, leaving Morgan as his deputy.

His opportunity of revenge had now come, and he remembered his old dangers of ruin and assassination. Many of the buccaneers were hung by his authority, and some of them were delivered up to the governor of Carthagena. A new governor arrived, and terminated his cruelties, and the justice inspired by a personal hatred. He still remained commissioner. In the next reign he was thrown into prison, where he remained three years. Of his final fate we know nothing certain.

Chapter 9

The Companions & Successors of Morgan

On the departure of Morgan, the buccaneers, without food, and without leaders, underwent many sufferings, and remained uncertain what to do.

Oexmelin and a few of his French friends being informed by a female slave that an old buccaneer lived in the neighbourhood, determined to go to him and barter goods, as they were told that, although a Spaniard, such was his custom. Following the slave with great expectation, they reached the veteran's fort after about six hours' march. The buccaneers' "peel" towers were scattered all over the West Indies, and Waterton mentions seeing the ruins of one near Demerara. This fort was defended by a fosse of immense depth, and by massy walls of an extraordinary thickness, flanked at each corner by a bastion well supplied with cannon. The Frenchmen displayed their colours and beat their drums as a greeting, yet no one appeared, and no one answered; but, at the end of a quarter of an hour, they saw a light in one of the bastions, and perceived a man about to discharge a cannon. Throwing themselves on their faces with professional dexterity, the shot flew over their heads, and they then rose and retreated out of range. Believing at once that they had been betrayed, for many dangers had made them suspicious, they were about to cut their guide to pieces, when, running from them, she cried to the gunner, "Why is your master false to his word? did he not promise to receive these gentlemen?"

"It is true," cried the soldier, "but he has changed his mind; and if you and your people do not go off, I will blow out your brains."

The buccaneers, enraged at the insolence of this threat, and the capricious change of intention, were about to attempt to storm the place, when four Spaniards advanced and demanded a truce, in the name of their master.

"We had," they explained, "been alarmed at your numbers, and feared foul play or treachery."

The old adventurer was now willing to receive them, if they would send four of their band as ambassadors and hostages. Oexmelin was one of the four chosen. They found the old man, grey and venerable, seated between two others. He was so old and feeble that he could not speak audibly, but he smiled and moved his lips, and stroked his long white beard, as they entered, and they could observe that he was pleased to see once more the well-remembered dress of the buccaneer seamen. His majestic bearing was impressive. Though he could not rise to welcome them, he bent his head in answer to their greetings, and beckoned to one of his attendants to speak for him. By his orders they were at once taken to his storerooms, where they bartered their goods, and obtained all that they required. They first eagerly selected some brandy, and Oexmelin is never tired of repeating *"ses gens l'aiment avec passion."* On their way back to the ships with the guide, delighted at their success, the Spaniards who carried the goods they had bought told them their master's history. He was, it appeared, properly speaking, neither an adventurer nor a Castilian, but a Portuguese, who had lived long both with adventurers and with Spaniards. A Spanish ship had picked him up in a drifted canoe when quite a boy, and he had been employed among the slaves in a cocoa plantation, where he soon became a successful steward, and much beloved by his master. His patron sent every year a vessel to his plantation to be loaded with cocoa. One day, as the steward was on board superintending the lading, a sudden squall came on, snapped the cable, and drove them out to sea. He being a good pilot, and accustomed to navigation, attempted to put back to land as soon as the storm abated, but the slaves, with one voice, declared that they would not return, and that he should not take them, for they knew that their master would suspect, and would cruelly punish them. At that time the slightest offence of a slave was punished with death. The steward remonstrated with them; but the slaves resolved to be free, although they knew not where to steer. At this crisis the bark was pursued by a buccaneer vessel, from which a storm for a short time released them, but they were eventually overtaken and captured.

The buccaneer captain brought these prisoners to the fortress they had just visited. Here he became again a faithful steward, and finally inherited the place at his master's death, and continued to trade with the buccaneers, as his predecessor had done. The fortress had been originally built to repel the Spaniards, who had been several times beaten off with loss.

It is very seldom that we can follow the buccaneer to the last scene of all: he flashes across our scene from darkness to darkness, and we hear of him no more. In the present instance, Oexmelin enables us to fill up the vacuum and tell out the tale. In a subsequent voyage he returned to the old spot, the scene of an oft told story. Devastation had fallen upon the devastator, the fortress was completely demolished and no dwelling remained. He ascertained from the Spaniards that the old man had died and left his riches to his two sons, who, impatient of a slothful wealth, and with imaginations excited from their youth by the recital of buccaneer adventures, had at last turned *flibustiers*. Before their father's death they had often expressed a wish to conquer the country of the ferocious Bravo Indians, but he had always discouraged them from the dangerous and unprofitable expedition, being afraid of attacks from the Spaniards in their absence. They were never heard of again, but report was current that, having been shipwrecked, the two buccaneers had been taken by the Indians, and killed and eaten.

Leaving the Boca del Toro, about thirty leagues distant from Chagres, Oexmelin and his companions arrived at the country of the very dreaded Bravo Indians. These people were known to be warlike cannibals, cruel and very treacherous. They were expert archers, and could discharge their arrows, like the Parthians, even when in full retreat. They had axes and spears, and wore metal ornaments, the clash of which animated them to the charge. They carried tortoise-shells for shields, which covered their whole bodies, and were most to be dreaded when few in number and quite overpowered, for they would then throw themselves like wild-cats on the foe, and think only of destroying their enemy's life, regardless of their own. Morgan, who seems to have made every preparation for an extensive buccaneer empire, had often sworn to totally destroy this nation which had slain so many shipwrecked men, and so frequently frustrated his plans. No buccaneer historian ever seems to have reflected that these savages, rude as they were, fought as patriots defending their country. We sing of Tell and rave of Wallace, but we have no interest in a hero without breeches!

These Indians had at first been friendly to the buccaneers, who had sold them iron in exchange for food, but on one fatal occasion, at a buccaneer debauch, a quarrel had arisen, and some Indians had been killed and their wives carried off. From this time irreconcilable hatred existed between the two people, and to be wrecked on the Bravo shore was equivalent to certain death. On reaching Cape Diego (so called, like many other points of land, from an old adventurer), Oexmelin was compelled by hunger to feed on crocodile eggs, which were found buried in the sand. Meeting here with some French adventurers, they all removed to an adjacent spot, where they caught turtle and salted it for the voyage.

Ascending a river to obtain provisions, they surprised and killed two Indians, of whom one had a beard-case of tortoise-shell and another of beaten gold: the latter they took for a chief. Putting off from here, and meeting with contrary winds that drove them from Jamaica, they returned again to Chagres, and were pursued by a ship of Spanish build, which they feared had been sent from Carthagena to rebuild the fort.

They attempted in vain to escape, and were clearing the decks, preparing to fight to the last, when the enemy hoisted the red flag, and proved to be one of their companions' vessels driven back by the *bise*, or north-east wind. They lost two days' sail by this accident, more than they could regain in a fortnight, and returned to the Boca del Toro to get provisions and kill sea-cows, and then passed on to the Boca del Drago. The islands here they knew to be inhabited, for the fragrance of the fruits was wafted on the sea wind. One day a fishing party gave chase to two Indians in a canoe, which they instantly drew ashore and carried with them into the woods. This boat, weighing above 2,000 lbs. and requiring 11 men afterwards to launch it, was made of wild cedar, roughly hewn; being nimble the savages both escaped the buccaneers. A pilot who had been often in those parts, told them that a few years before, a buccaneer squadron arriving in that place, the men went in canoes to catch the humming birds that swarmed round the flowering trees of the coast. They were observed by some Indians who had hid themselves in the trees, who, leaping down into the sea, carried off the boats and men before their companions could arrive to their aid. The admiral instantly landed 800 men to rescue the prisoners, but so many Indians collected that they found it necessary to retreat in haste to their ships.

The next day the buccaneers arrived at Rio de Zuera, but the Spaniards were all fled, leaving no provisions; they therefore filled their boats with plantains, coasting for a fortnight along the shore to find a convenient place to careen, for the vessel had now grown so leaky that slaves and men were obliged to work night and day at the pumps. Arriving at a port, called the Bay of Blevelt, from a buccaneer who used to resort there, half the crew were employed to unload and careen the bark on the shore, and half to hunt in the woods—still much afraid of the Indians, though they had as yet seen none.

The huntsmen shot several porcupines of great size, and many monkeys and pheasants. The men took great pleasure in the midst of their danger in this pursuit. They laughed to see the females carrying their little ones on their backs, just like the negro women, and they admired the love and fidelity which some showed when their friends were wounded, and were delighted when they pelted their pursuers with fruit and dead boughs. The men were obliged to shoot fifteen or sixteen to secure three or four, as even when dead they remained clinging to the trees, and remained so for several days, hanging by their fore-paws or their tails. When one was wounded the rest came chattering round him, and would lay their paws on the wound to stop the flow of blood, and others would gather moss from the tress to bandage the place, or, gathering certain healing herbs, chew them and apply them as a poultice. If a mother was killed the young ones would not leave the body till they were torn away.

But these amusements were soon to come to an end. The Indians were upon their track. They had been now eight days hunting. It was the daybreak of the ninth day, and the fishermen and hunters were preparing their nets and guns to start for the sea and for the woods. The slaves were on the beach burning shells to make lime, which served instead of pitch for the vessels, and the women were drawing water at the wells which had been dug in the shore. A few of them were washing dishes, and others sewing, for they had risen earlier than usual. While the rest went to the wells, one of them lingered behind to pick some fruit that grew near the beach. Seeing suddenly some Indians running from the spot where she had left her companions, she ran to the tents, crying, "Indians, Indians, Christians, the Indians are come." The buccaneers, running to arms, discovered that three of their female slaves were lying dead in the wood, pierced with fourteen or fifteen flint-headed arrows. These darts were about eight feet long, and as thick as a man's thumb; at one end was a wooden hook, tied on with a string, at the other, a case containing a few small stones. Searching the woods, no traces of Indians, or any canoes, were to be found, and the buccaneers, fearing they should be surrounded and overpowered, re-embarked all their goods, and sailed in great haste and fear.

They soon arrived at Cape Gracias à Dios, and rejoiced to find themselves once more among friendly Indians; and at a port where buccaneer vessels often resorted, the rudest sailors giving thanks to God for having delivered them out of so many dangers, and brought them to a place of refuge. The Indians provided them with every necessary, and treated them with friendship. For an old knife or hatchet the men each bought an Indian woman, who supplied them with food. These people often went to sea with the buccaneers, and, remaining several years, returned home with a good knowledge of French and English. They were used as fishermen, and for striking tortoises and manitees, one Indian being able to victual a vessel of 100 men. Oexmelin's crew having on board two sailors who could speak the Indian tongue, they were unusually well received.

This nation was not more than 1700 in number, including a few negro slaves, who had swum ashore from a wreck, having murdered the Spanish crew, and, in their ignorance of navigation, stranded the vessel. Some of them cultivated the ground, and others wandered about hunting and fishing. They wore little clothes but a palm leaf hat, and a short apron, made of the bark of some tree. Their arms were spears, pointed with crocodile's teeth. They believed in a Supreme Being, and, as Esquemeling quaintly says, "believe not in nor serve the devil, as many other nations of America do, and hereby they are not so much tormented by him as other nations are." Their food was chiefly fruit and fish. They prepared pleasant and intoxicating liquors from the plantain, and from the seed of the palm, and at their banquets every guest was expected to empty a four-quart calabash full of *achioc*, as the palm drink was called, merely a whet to the feast to follow. Their *achioc* was as thick as gruel. When they were in love, they pierced themselves with arrows to prove their sincerity. When a youth wished to marry a maiden, the first question of the bride's father to the lover was, whether he could make arrows, or spin the thread with which they bound them. If he answered in the affirmative, the father called for a calabash of *achioc*, and he himself, the bride, and the bridegroom, all tasted of the beverage. When one of these hardy women was delivered, she rose, went to the nearest brook, washed and swathed the child, and went about her ordinary labour. When a husband died, the wife buried him, with all his spears, aprons, and ear jewels, and for fifteen moons after (a year) brought meat and drink daily to the grave. Some writers contend that the devil visited the graves, and carried away these offerings to the manes; but Esquemeling says, he knows to the contrary, having often taken away the food, which was always of the choicest and best sort. At the end of the year, an extraordinary custom prevailed. The widow had then to open the grave, and take out all the bones; she scraped, washed, and dried them in the sun; then placed them in a satchel, and for a whole year was obliged to carry them upon her back by day, and sleep upon them by night. At the end of the year, she hung up the bag at her door-post, or, if she was not mistress of her house, at the door of her nearest relation. A widow could not marry again till this painful ceremony was completed, and if an Indian woman married a pirate, the same custom prevailed. The negroes maintained the habits of their own countries.

After refreshing themselves in this friendly region, the buccaneers steered for the island de los Pinos, and, arriving in fifteen days, refitted their vessel, now become dangerously leaky. Half the crew were employed in careening, and half in fishing, and by the help of some of the Cape Gracias Indians who accompanied them they killed and salted a sufficient number of wild cattle and turtle to revictual the ship. In six hours they could capture fish sufficient for a thousand persons. "This abundance of provision," says Esquemeling, "made us forget the miseries we had lately endured, and we began to call one another again by the name of *brother*, which was customary among us, but had been disused in our miseries." They feasted here plentifully, and without fear of enemies, for the few Spaniards who were on the island were friendly, and past dangers grew mere dreams in the distance. Their only anxiety now was about the crocodiles, which swarmed in the island, and, when hungry, would devour men.

On one occasion a buccaneer and his negro slave, while hunting in the wood, were attacked by one of these monsters. With incredible agility it fastened upon the Englishman's leg, and brought him to the ground. The negro fled. The hunter, a robust and courageous man, drawing his knife, stabbed the crocodile to the heart, after a desperate fight, and then, tired with the combat and weak with loss of blood, fell senseless by its side. The negro, returning, from curiosity rather than compassion, to see how the duel had ended, lifted his master on his back and brought him to the sea-shore, a whole league distant, where he placed him in a canoe and rowed him aboard. After this, no buccaneer dared to go into the woods alone, but the next day, sallying out in troops, they killed all the monsters they could meet. These animals would come every night to the sides of the vessel and attempt to climb up, attracted probably by the smell of food. One of these, when seized with an iron hook, instead of diving or swimming, began to mount the ladder of the ship, till they killed him with blows of pikes and axes. After remaining some time here they sailed for Jamaica, and arrived there in a few days after a prosperous voyage, being the first adventurers who had arrived there from Panama since Morgan.

In 1673, when the war between the French and Hollanders (Dutch) was still raging, the inhabitants of the French West Indian colonies equipped a fleet to attack the Dutch settlements at Curaçoa, engaging all the buccaneers that could be induced to join the white flag, either from hopes of plunder or from hatred to the Dutch. M. D'Ogeron, the Governor of Tortuga, the planner of this invasion, headed the fleet in a large vessel named after himself, built by himself, and manned by 500 picked adventurers. His unlucky star led them to misfortune. The new frigate ran upon the rocks near the Guadanillas Islands, and broke into a thousand pieces, during a storm near Porto Rico. Being at the time very near to land, the governor and all his men swam safe to shore. The next day, discovered by the Spaniards, they were attacked by a large force, who supposed they had come purposely to plunder the islands as the buccaneers had done before. The whole country, alarmed, rose in arms. The shipwrecked men were surrounded by an overpowering army, who, finding them almost without arms, refused to give them quarter, slew the greater part without mercy, and made the remainder prisoners. Binding them with cords, two by two, they drove them through the woods into the open champaign. To all inquiries as to the fate of their commander, whom they could not distinguish from the rest, they replied that he had sunk with the wreck. D'Ogeron, following up this deception with French sagacity, behaved himself as a mere half-witted suttler, diverting the Spanish soldiers by his tricks and mimicry, and was the only buccaneer whom they allowed to go at liberty. The troopers at their camp fires gave him scraps from their meals and rewarded him with more food than his companions.

Among the prisoners there was also a French surgeon who had on former occasions done some service to the Spaniards, and him they also allowed to go at large. D'Ogeron agreed with him to attempt an escape at all risks, and after mature deliberation, they both agreed upon a plan, and succeeded in escaping safely into the woods, and in making their way to the sea-side. They determined to attempt to build a canoe, although unsupplied with any tool except a hatchet. By the evening they reached the sea-shore, to their great joy, and caught some shell fish on the beach from a shoal that ran in upon the sands in pursuit of their prey. Fire to roast them they obtained by rubbing two sticks together in the Indian fashion. The next morning early they began to cut down and prepare timber to build the canoe in which to escape to Vera Cruz. While they were toiling at their work they observed in the distance a large boat, which they supposed to contain an enemy, steering directly towards them. Retreating to the woods, they discovered as soon as it touched land that it held only two poor fishermen. These unsuspecting men they determined if possible to overpower, and to capture the boat. As the mulatto came on shore alone, with a string of calabashes on his back to draw water, they killed him with a blow of their axe, and then slew the Spaniard, who, alarmed at the sound of voices, was attempting in vain to push from the shore. Having filled the dead man's calabashes they set sail, using the precaution of taking the dead bodies with them out into the deep sea, in order to conceal their death from the Spaniards.

They steered at once for Porto Rico, and passed on to Hispaniola. A fair wind soon brought them to Samana, where they found a party of their people. Leaving the surgeon to collect men at Samana, D'Ogeron sailed to Tortuga to collect vessels and crews to return and deliver his companions, and revenge his late disaster. He sailed eventually with 300 men, and took great precautions to prevent the Spaniards being aware of his coming, using only his lower sails in order that his masts should not rise above the horizon. In spite of this the Spaniards, informed of his approach, had placed troops of horse upon the shore at various assailable points.

D'Ogeron landed his men under favour of a discharge from his great guns, which drove the horsemen into the woods, where, as he little suspected, the infantry lay in ambush. Eagerly pursuing, his men, who thought the victory their own, found themselves hemmed in on every side. Few escaped even to the ships. The Spaniards, cruel from the reaction of fear, cut off the limbs of the dead and carried them home as trophies. They lighted bonfires on the shore as tokens of defiance to the retreating fleet.

The first prisoners were now treated worse than ever. Some of them were sent to Havannah and employed on the fortifications all day, and chained up like wild beasts at night to prevent their desperate attempts at escape. Many were sent to Cadiz, and from thence escaped over the Pyrenees into France, and, assembling together, like sworn members of a common brotherhood, returned by the first ship to Tortuga.

These very men some time after equipped a small fleet, under command of Le Sieur Maubenon, which sacked Trinidad, and put the island to a ransom of 10,000 pieces of eight, and from thence proceeded to the Caraccas.

The buccaneers fought against the Dutch, in 1676, and helped the French to recover Cayenne, that had been taken by Vice-Admiral Binkes. After this conquest, M. D'Estrees attacked Tobago, but was repulsed with the loss of 150 killed, and 200 wounded. His ship, the *Glorieux*, of seventy guns, was blown up, and two others stranded; several of the Dutch vessels were, however, burnt.

D'Estrees, returning to Brest, was ordered back to Tobago, with twenty sail of vessels of war, besides a great number of small craft. 1500 men were landed, and, approaching a fortified place called Le Cort, summoned Heer Binkes to surrender. The French began their attack by throwing fire-balls into the castle; the third grenade fell upon some loose powder in the path leading to the magazine, and blew it up. Heer Binkes and all his officers but one were killed. 500 French instantly stormed the works, killing all but 300 men, who were sent prisoners to France. D'Estrees then destroyed every fort and house in the island, and sailed away.

It was in 1678 that the same Comte D'Estrees collected 1200 buccaneers from Hispaniola, and twenty vessels of war, besides fire-ships, to capture Curaçoa, which could have been taken with 300 buccaneers and three vessels. This fleet was, however, lost on the Isles d'Aves, as we shall describe in Dampier's voyage.

In the year 1678, Captain Cook loaded his vessel with logwood, at Campeachy, and, while anchoring at the island of Rubia, on his way to Tobago, was captured by three Spanish men-of-war, who left his crew upon the shore, and carried off his ship and cargo. They had not lain there long before a Spanish sloop of sixteen men arrived, laden with cocoa and plate, and gave them opportunity for escape and for revenge. Borrowing muskets of the Dutch governor, they employed six of their men in seizing the sloop's boat as it came to land, and then embarked and took the larger vessel, leaving their prisoners bound upon the beach, to watch the combat that would decide their fate. Two men navigated, two more loaded the guns, and two others fired into the enemy as fast as they could pour their shot into the stern-ports. The Spaniards resisted stoutly for some time, but, seeing their priest and captain shot dead, threw their arms overboard, and cried for quarter. The buccaneers gave the Dutch governor a handsome reward, with a recompense for the arms, and divided among themselves about £4,000 worth of plate. On arriving at Jamaica they burnt the prize, and embarked their goods for England.

In the year of our Lord 1679, a buccaneer fleet of five sail, commanded by Captains Coxen, Essex, Alliston, Rose, and Sharp, set sail from Port-Royal, and steered for the island of Pines, losing two vessels in their passage, at the Zamballos islands. They met a French ship, whose commission was only for three months, and showed its captain, with great exultation, their forged commission for three years, purchased for only ten pieces of eight.

Chapter 10

The Cruises of Sawkins & Sharp

The cruises of Sawkins and Sharp are recorded in the travels of Ringrose, who was present at all their exploits. At this time the buccaneers widened their field of operations, and passed from the South into the North Pacific. The whole coast of South America, on either side, met the fate of the West Indian islands. The gold mines of Peru were the next object of their speculation.

A fleet which took Porto Bello a second time rendezvoused at Boca del Toro. A new expedition was then formed to follow Captain Bournano, a French commander, who had lately attacked Chepo, to Tocamora, a great and very rich place, whither the Darien Indians had offered to conduct him, in spite of a late treaty with the Spaniards.

The vessels first dispersed into coves and creeks to careen and salt turtle, and then reunited at the Water key. The fleet consisted of nine vessels, with a total of 22 guns and 458 men, in the following order:—Captain Coxen, a ship of 80 tons, with 8 guns, and 197 men; Captain Harris, 150 tons, 5 guns, and 107 men; Captain Bournano, 90 tons, 6 guns, and 86 men; Captain Sawkins, 16 tons, 1 gun, and 35 men; Captain Sharp, 25 tons, 2 guns, and 40 men; Captain Cook, 35 tons, and 43 men; Captain Alleston, 18 tons, and 24 men; Captain Row, 20 tons, and 25 men; Captain Macket, 14 tons, and 20 men.

The expedition sailed March 26, 1679. The first place to touch at was the Zemblas Islands, where they traded with the friendly Indians, who brought fruits and venison in exchange for beads, needles, knives, and hatchets. These Indians were quite naked, but richly decorated with gold and silver plates of a crescent form, and gold rings worn in the nose, which they had to lift up when they drank. They were generally painted with streaks of black and red, but were a handsome race, and frequently as fair as Europeans. The sailors believed that they could see better by night than by day.

The Indians dissuaded the captains from the march upon Tocamora, and agreed to guide them to the vicinity of Panama. The way to Tocamora, they declared, was mountainous and uninhabited, and ran through wild places, where no provisions could be obtained. In this change of plan, Row and Bournano, whose crews were all French, separated, being unwilling to risk a long march by land, and remained at the Zemblas, while Andreas, an Indian chief, guided the remaining vessels to the Golden Island, a little to the westward of the mouth of the great river of Darien. There the seven remaining vessels rendezvoused April 3, 1680.

They here agreed to follow the Indians' advice, and attack the town of Santa Maria, situated on the river of the same name, which runs into the South Sea by the gulf of St. Miguel. It was garrisoned by 400 soldiers, and from hence the gold gathered in the neighbouring mountains was carried to Panama, on which they could march if they could not find enough at Santa Maria.

On the 5th of April they landed 331 men, leaving Captains Alleston and Macket to guard the ships in their absence. Each man carried with him three or four "dough-boys" (cakes), trusting to the rivers for drink. Captain Sharp, who went at their head, was still faint from a late sickness. His company carried a red flag and a bunch of white and green ribbons. The second division, led by Captain Richard Sawkins, had a red flag, striped with yellow. Captain Peter Harris, with the third and fourth divisions, had two green flags; Captain John Coxen, two red flags; while Captain Edmund Cook bore red colours, striped with yellow, with a hand and sword for the device. All the men carried fusees, pistols, and hangers.

The Indian guides led them through a wood and over a bay two leagues up a woody valley, along a good path, with here and there old plantations. At a river, then nearly dry, they built huts to rest in. Another Indian chief, a man "of great parts," and called Captain Antonio, now promised to be their leader, as soon as his child, who was then sick, had died, which he expected would be next day. This Indian warned them against lying in the grass, which was full of large snakes.

The men, breaking some of the stones washed down from the mountains, found them glitter like gold; but, in spite of this, several grew tired and returned to the ships, leaving only 327 sailors and six Indian guides.

The next day they ascended a very steep hill, and found at the foot of it a river, on which Andreas told them Santa Maria was built. About noon they ascended another and higher mountain, by so perpendicular and narrow a path that only one man could pass at a time. Having marched eighteen miles, they halted that night on the banks of the same river, much rain falling during both nights. The next day they crossed the river, after wading sometimes up to the knee, sometimes to the middle, in a steep current. At noon they reached the Indian village, near which the king of Darien resided. The houses were neatly built of cabbage-tree, with the roofs of wild canes, thatched with *palmito royal*, and were surrounded by plantain walks; they had no upper storeys. The king, queen, and family, came to visit them in royal robes. Like most savages, he was all ornament and nakedness, gold and dirt. His crown was made with woven white reeds, lined with red silk. In the middle was a thin plate of gold, some beads, and several ostrich feathers; in each ear a gold ring; and in his nose a half-moon of the same metal. His robe was of thin white cotton, and in his hand he held a long bright lance, sharp as a knife. The queen wore several red blankets, and her two marriageable daughters and young child were loaded with coloured beads, and covered with strips of rag. The women seemed "free, easy, and brisk," but modest and afraid of their husbands. The king gave the sailors each three plantains and some sugar-canes to suck, but, after that regal munificence, did not disdain to sell his stores like his subjects, who proved very cunning dealers in their purchases of knives, pins, and needles. Resting here a day, Captain Sawkins was appointed to lead the forlorn hope of eighty men. Their march still lay along the river, and here and there they found a house. The Indians, standing at the doors, would present each with a ripe plantain or cassave root, or count them by dropping a grain of millet for each one that passed. They rested at night at some native houses.

The next day Sharp, Coxen, and Cook, and ninety men, embarked in fourteen canoes to try how far the stream was navigable, Captain Andreas being with them, and two Indians in each canoe serving as guides. But the water proved more tedious than the land; for at the distance of every stone's-cast, they were constrained to get out of the boats and haul them over sands, rocks, or fallen trees, and sometimes over spits of land. That night they built huts on the bank, being worn out with fatigue.

The next day proved a repetition of the past; at night a tiger came near them, but they dared not fire for fear of alarming the Spaniards. The following day was worse than before, and their men grew mutinous and suspicious of the Indians, who, they thought, had divided the troop in order to betray them. The fourth day, resting on "a beachy point of land," where another arm joined the river, they were joined by their companions, whom they had sent their Indians to seek, and who had grown alarmed at their continued absence. That night they prepared their arms for action. On the morrow they re-embarked, in all sixty-eight canoes and 327 Englishmen, with fifty Indian guides. They made themselves paddles, threw away the Indian poles, and rowed with all speed, meeting several boats laden with plantains. About midnight they arrived within half-a-mile of Santa Maria, and landed. The mud was so deep that they had to lay down their paddles and lift themselves up by the boughs of the trees; then cutting a way through the woods, they took up their lodging there for the night, hoping to surprise the Spaniards.

At daybreak, to their disappointment, they were awoke by the discharge of a musket and the beating of a drum. The Spaniards had already prepared some lead for their reception, and had sent away their gold to Panama. Directly they emerged into the plain, the enemy ran into a large palisaded fort, twelve feet high, and began to fire quick and close. The vanguard, running up, pulled down part of the stockade and broke in and took them prisoners, the whole 280 men. A few English were wounded, not one being killed of the fifty men who led the attack. 200 other Spaniards were in the mines conveying away the gold, the mines there being the richest of the western world. Twenty-six Spaniards were killed in the fort and sixteen wounded, but the governor, priest, and chief men all escaped by flight. The town proved to be merely a few cane houses, built to check the Indians, who frequently rebelled. Some days before, three cwt. of gold had been sent in a bark to Panama, the same quantity being despatched twice or thrice a-year.

During the fight the Indians, frightened at the whistling of the bullets, had hid themselves in a hollow; when all was over they entered the place, with great courage stabbing the prisoners with their lances, and putting about twenty to death in the woods, till the buccaneers interfered. In the town the Indians found the eldest daughter of the Darien king, whom one of the garrison had carried off, and who was then with child by him. Rather than be left to the mercy of the Indians, this man offered to lead them to Panama, where they hoped to capture all the riches of Potosi and Peru. Sawkins in a canoe attempted in vain to overtake the governor and his officers, and rather than return empty-handed, resolved to go to Panama, to satisfy what Ringrose calls "their hungry appetite of gold and riches."

Captain Coxen was chosen commander, and the booty and prisoners sent back to the ships under a guard of twelve men. The Indians, being rewarded with presents of needles and beads, also returned, all but the king. Captain Andreas, Captain Antonio, and the king's son, King Golden Cap (*bonete d'oro*), as the Spaniards called him, resolved to go on, desiring to see Panama sacked, and offering to aid them with a large body of men. The Spanish guide declared he would not only lead them into the town, but even to the very door of the governor of Panama's bed-chamber, and that they should take him by the hand, and seize him and the whole city, before they should be discovered by the Spaniards.

After remaining two days at Santa Maria, they departed April 17th, 1680, for Panama.

They embarked in thirty-five canoes and a *piragua* which they had found lying at anchor, rowing down the river to the gulf of Belona, where they would enter the South Sea and work round to Panama. At the request of the Indian king the fort, church, and town were all burnt. The Spanish prisoners, afraid of being put to death by the savages if left behind, collected some bark logs and leaky canoes, although the buccaneers could scarcely find boats for themselves, and went with them.

Ringrose and four other men were put in the heaviest and slowest canoe, and, getting entangled between a shoal two miles long, and obliged to wait for high water, the boat being too heavy to row against tide, were soon left behind. At night, it being again low water, they stuck up an oar in the river, and, in spite of a weltering rain, slept all night by turns in the canoe. The next morning, rowing two leagues, they overtook their companions filling water at an Indian hut, there being no more for six days' journey. Hurrying to a pond a quarter of a mile distant with their calabashes, they returned to their boats and found the rest again gone and out of sight. Ringrose moralises:

> Such is the procedure of these wild men, that they care not in the least whom they lose of their company or leave behind. We were now more troubled in our minds than before, fearing lest we should fall into the same misfortune we had so lately overcome.

They rowed after them as fast as possible, but in vain, and lost their way among the innumerable islands of the river's mouth; but at last, with much trouble and toil, hit the Bocca Chica, the desired passage. But though they saw the door, they could not pass through, the "young flood" running violently against them—although it was only a stone's-cast off, and not a league broad. Here, then, in despair they put ashore, fastening the rope to a tree, almost covered by a tide that flowed four fathoms deep.

As soon as the tide turned, they rowed to an island about a league-and-a-half from the river's mouth, in the gulf of St. Miguel, in much danger from the waves, their boat being twenty feet long, but not quite a foot-and-a-half broad. Here they rested for the night, wet through with the continual and impetuous rain, without water to drink, and unable to light a fire, "for the loss of our company, and the dangers we were in," says Ringrose, "made it the sorrowfullest night that, until then, I ever experimented."

None slept that tedious night, for a vast sea surrounded them on one side, and the mighty power of the Spaniards on the other. They were all without shoes, and their clothes were drenched through. They could see nothing but sea, mountain, and rock.

At break of day they rowed past several islands to the Point St.

Laurence, one man incessantly employed in baling. As they passed one of these islands, a huge sea overturned their boat, but they gained the beach, swimming for life, and the canoe came tumbling beside them. The arms fast lashed at the bottom of the boat, the locks cased and waxed down like the cartouche boxes, and powder horns, escaped uninjured, but the bread and fresh water were either spoiled or lost. While carefully wiping and cleaning their arms, for a buccaneer's musket was as his wife and child to him, they saw another canoe tossed to shore, a little to leeward. This proved to be six of the Spanish prisoners, who had escaped in an old *piragua* which was split to pieces, the English boat, formed of wood, six inches thick, having escaped unhurt. A common misfortune makes all men friends, and the English and Spaniards sat down together and broiled their meat amicably at the same fire. They then held a council, discussing for two or three hours what course to take, and all the men but Ringrose were for returning and living with the Indians, if they could not reach the ships lying in the northern sea.

With much ado, Ringrose prevailed on them to persist for one day longer, and, just as they were concluding their debate, the man on the look-out cried that he saw Indians. Pursued into the woods by two buccaneers, they found that he was one of the expedition, and had arrived with seven others in a great canoe. They were glad to see them, and declared, to their joy, that, all in one canoe, they could overtake the boats in the course of a day. On seeing the Spaniards (wankers they called them), they would have put them to death but for Ringrose's interposition, for his men stood by indifferent.

They then insisted on keeping one as a slave. Ringrose, still fearing for their lives, gave the five Spaniards his own canoe, and bade them shift for their lives. Now in a large canoe, with a good sail, and a fresh and strong gale, they made brave way, with infinite joy and comfort of heart, the smooth and easy passage, and the pleasant, fresh ripple of the sea, filling them with hope and gladness; but that very evening it grew very dark, and rained heavily. Suddenly two fires were seen to blaze up from the opposite shore of the continent, and the Indians, thinking they must indicate the encampment of their people, shouted, "Captain Antonio, Captain

Andreas," and made for the shore as fast as they could pull. The canoe, however, had hardly got amongst the breakers, before sixty Spaniards, armed with clubs, leaped from the woods; and, drawing the boat on land, made all the crew their prisoners.

Ringrose seized his gun, and prepared for resistance, but was pulled down by four or five of the enemy. The Indians, leaping overboard, escaped nimbly into the woods. Ringrose spoke to his captors in French and English, without obtaining any answer. On addressing the strangers in Latin, he discovered that they were the Spanish prisoners from Santa Maria, who had been liberated, for fear they might escape when nearer Panama, and inform the city of the buccaneers' approach. The Englishmen were presently taken with shouts of joy into a hut made of boughs, and examined by the Spanish captain, who meditated retaliating upon them the injuries inflicted on the town. At this critical juncture, the Spaniards whom Ringrose had liberated came in, and explained how they had been delivered from the Indians. On hearing this, the Spanish captain rose, and, embracing Ringrose, said, "The English were good people, and very friendly enemies, but the Indians very rogues, and a treacherous nation."

He then made him sit down and eat with him, and consented, for the kindness he had shown his countrymen, to give him and all his men, and even the Indians, if they could find them, their lives and liberties, which otherwise would have been forfeited. Finally, giving them a canoe, the noble-hearted enemy bade them go in God's name, praying that they might be as fortunate as they had been generous. All that night they skirted a dangerous and iron coast, without daring to land.

The next morning, after sailing, paddling, and rowing for a few hours, they saw a canoe suddenly making towards them. It was one of the English boats, which had mistaken them for a Spanish *piragua*. They at once conducted them to a deep bay, sheltered by rocks, where the rest lay at anchor. They were all delighted to see Ringrose and his men, having given them up as lost. They then made their way with all speed to a hilly island, about seven leagues distant, and surprised an old man, who was stationed there to watch. The road up to the hut was very steep, and the buccaneers surrounded the old man, who did not see them till they had already entered his plantain walk. They were much encouraged by his declaration, that no tidings of their arrival had yet reached Panama.

About dusk, two of their boats surprised a small bark that came and anchored outside the island. The crew had been absent eight days from the city, landing soldiers on the adjacent shore, to curb and drive back the Indians. The crews of the smaller canoes now crowded into this vessel to the number of 137 men, together with Captain Cook and Captain Sharp, the latter of whom Ringrose calls "a sea artist, and valiant commander."

Next morning, rowing all day over shallow water, they chased a bark, which Captain Harris took after a sharp dispute, putting on board a prize crew of thirty men. During this pursuit the vessels scattered, and did not reunite till next day at the island of Chepillo, a preconcerted rendezvous. They again chased a bark, but with less success, and Captain Coxen's canoe missed the prize, owing to a breeze springing up, having one man killed and another wounded, and, what was worst of all, the vessel not only escaped, but spread the alarm at Panama. At Chepillo they took fourteen negro and mulatto prisoners, and secured two fat hogs, plenty of plantains, and some good water. Believing it useless now to attack Panama, the buccaneers resolved to hurry on to the town to at least surprise some of the shipping. Their boats had the addition of another *piragua*, which they found lying at Chepillo. Before starting, the captains cruelly decided, for reasons which Ringrose could not fathom, to allow the Indians to murder all the Spanish prisoners before their eyes, the savages having long thirsted for their blood. But by a singular coincidence the prisoners, though without arms, forced their way by a sudden rush through all the Indian spears and arrows, and escaped unhurt into the woods, to the chagrin of both white and black savages.

Staying only a few hours at Chepillo, the boats started at four o'clock in the evening, intending to reach Panama, which was only seven leagues distant, before the next morning. The next day (St. George's day), before sunrise they arrived at Panama, "a city," says Ringrose, "which has a very pleasant prospect seaward." They could see all the ships of the city lying at anchor at the island of Perico, two leagues distant, where storehouses had been built. There now rode at anchor five great ships and three smaller *armadillas*, (little men-of-war). This fleet, which had been hastily manned to defend the city, as soon as they saw the buccaneers, weighed anchor, got under sail, and bore down at once upon them, directly before the wind, and with such velocity as to threaten to run them down. The Spanish admiral's vessel was manned by ninety Biscayans, agile seamen and stout soldiers. They were all volunteers, and had come out to show their valour under the command of Don Jacinto de Barahona, high-admiral of those seas. In the second were seventy-seven negroes, led by a brave old Andalusian, Don Francisco de Peralta. In the third, making 228 men in all, were sixty-five mulattoes, under Don Diego de Carabaxal. The Spaniards had strict orders given them to grant no quarter.

To add to the disparity of numbers, only a few of the buccaneers' boats were able to arrive in time. The first five canoes that came up, leaving the heavy *piraguas* still lagging behind, contained only thirty-seven men, and these were tired with rowing in the wind's eye, and trying to get close to the windward of the enemy. The lesser *piragua* coming up with thirty-two more men, made a total force of sixty buccaneers, including the king of Darien, engaged in this daring resistance to an overwhelming force.

Carabaxal's vessel, passing between Sawkins's and Ringrose's canoes, fired at both, wounding four men in the former and one in the latter, but being slow in tacking, the Spaniard paid dear for his passage, the first return volley killing several men upon his decks. Almost before they had time to reload, the admiral passed, but the buccaneers' second volley quite disabled their giant antagonist, killing the man at the helm; and the ship ran into the wind and her sails lay aback. She fell now like a lamed elephant at the mercy of the hunters; the canoes, pulling under her stern, fired continually upon the deck, killing all who dared to touch the helm, and cutting asunder the mainsheet and mainbrace. Sawkins, whose canoe was disabled, went next into the *piragua* to meet Peralta, leaving the four canoes to harass the admiral. Between Sawkins and Peralta, lying alongside of each other, the fight was desperate, each crew trying to board, and firing as quick as they could load. In the mean time the first vessel tacked about and came to relieve the admiral, but the canoes, seeing the danger of being beaten from the admiral's stern and allowing him to rally, sent two of their number (Springer and Ringrose) to meet Peralta. The admiral stood upon his quarter-deck, waving his handkerchief as a signal for his captains to come at once to his help. The canoes pursued Peralta, and would have boarded him had he not given them the helm and made away.

Giving a loud shout, the remaining boats wedged up the admiral's rudder and poured in a blinding volley, that killed the admiral and chief pilot. Two-thirds of the Spaniards being now killed, many wounded, and all disheartened at the bloody massacre of the buccaneers' shot, cried for quarter, which they had been already several times offered, and at once surrendered. Captain Coxen then boarded the prize, taking with him Captain Harris, who had been shot through both legs as he was heading a boarding party. They put all their other wounded men on board, and, manning two canoes, hurried off to aid Sawkins, who had already been three times beaten off by Peralta.

Coming close under his side and giving him a full volley, they were expecting a return, when suddenly a volcano of fire spouted up from the deck, and all the Spaniards abaft the mast were blown into the air or sea. While the brave captain, leaping overboard, was helping the drowning men in spite of the rain of shot and the pain of his own burns, another jar of powder blew up in the forecastle. Under cover of the smoke and confusion, Sawkins boarded and took the ship, or at least all that was left of it. Ringrose says it was a miserable sight, not a man but was either killed or desperately wounded, blind, or horribly burnt with the powder. In some cases the white wounds where the flesh had peeled to the bone, showed through the blackening of the powder. The admiral had but twenty-five men left out of eighty-six, and of these twenty-five only eight were now able to bear arms.

The blood ran down the deck in streams, and every rope and plank was smeared with gore.

Peralta, as prudent as he was brave, attempted by every possible argument, forgetful of his own wounds and the death of his men, to induce the buccaneers not to attack the remaining vessels in the harbour. In the biggest alone he said there were 350 men, and the rest were well defended. But a dying sailor, lifting up his head from the deck, contradicted him, and said that they had not a man on board, all their crews being placed in the *armadillas*. Trusting to dying treason rather than living fidelity, the buccaneers instantly proceeded to the island, and found the ships deserted. The largest, *La Santissima Trinidada*, had been set on fire, the crew, loosing her foresail, having pierced her bottom. The captains soon quenched the fire, and stopping the leak turned their prize into a floating hospital-ship. They found they had eighteen men killed and twenty-two wounded (only two of whom died) in this desperate sea battle, which began an hour after sunrise and ended at noon. The third vessel, it appeared, while running away had met with two others, but even with this reinforcement refused to fight.

Their brave prisoner, Peralta, now that all was over, broke out into repeated praises of their courage, which was so congenial to his own. He said: "You Englishmen are the valiantest men in the whole world, always desiring to fight open, while all other nations invent all the ways imaginable to barricade themselves, and fight as close as possible."

"Notwithstanding all this," adds Ringrose, "we killed more of our enemies than they of us."

Two days after the battle the buccaneers buried Captain Harris, a brave Englishman of the county of Kent, whose death was much lamented by the fleet.

The new city of Panama, built four miles more easterly than that which Morgan burnt, had been three times destroyed by fire since that event. A few people still lived round the cathedral in the old town. The new city was bigger than the old one, and built chiefly of brick and stone, and was defended by a garrison of 300 soldiers and 1,000 militiamen. They afterwards learnt that the troops were then absent, and that if they had landed instead of attacking the fleet, they might have taken the place, all the best shots being on board the admiral's vessel.

In the five vessels taken at Perico there was much spoil. The *Trinidada* (400 tons) was laden with wine, sugar, sweetmeats, skins, and soap. The second, of 300 tons, partly laden with bars of iron, one of the richest commodities brought into the South Sea, was burnt by the buccaneers, because the Spaniards would not redeem it. The third, of 180 tons, laden with sugar, was given to Captain Cook; the fourth, an old vessel (60 tons), laden with meal, was burnt as useless, with all her cargo. The fifth, of 50 tons, with a *piragua*, fell to the lot of Captain Coxen. The two *armadillas*, the rigging and sails being saved, and a bark laden with poultry, were also burnt.

Captain Coxen, indignant at charges made against him of cowardice in the late action, determined to rejoin the ships in the northern seas, together with seventy men who had assisted in his election. The Indian king, Don Andreas, and Don Antonio, returned with him. The king left his son and nephew in the care of Captain Sawkins, who was now commander-in-chief, and desired him not to spare the Spaniards. A few days after Captain Sharp returned from the King's islands, having taken a Spanish vessel and burnt his own. Captain Harris's crew had also taken a vessel, and, dismasting their own, turned their prisoners adrift in the hulk, and soon after taking a poultry vessel, the meanest of the Spaniards were treated in the same way.

Having remained now ten days at Panama, the fleet steered to the island of Tavoga, where they found a village of 100 houses quite deserted, and many of these were burnt by the carelessness of a drunken sailor. The Panama merchants came here to sell the buccaneers commodities and to purchase the plunder from their own vessels, giving 200 pieces of eight for every negro. Staying eight days, they captured a vessel from Truxillo laden with money to pay the garrison of Panama, while in the hold were 2,000 jars of wine and fifty jars of gunpowder. A flour vessel from the same place informed them that a ship was coming in a few days laden with 100,000 more pieces of eight.

To a message from the president, who sent by some merchants to ask why they came into those parts, Captain Sawkins replied, that he came to assist the King of Darien, the true lord of the country, and he required a ransom of 500 pieces of eight for each sailor, and 1,000 for the commander. He must also promise not to molest the Indians, who were the natural owners of the soil. Hearing from the messengers that a certain priest, now bishop of Panama, formerly of Santa Martha, lay in the city, Sawkins, remembering that he had been his prisoner when he took that city five years before, sent him two loaves of sugar as a present. The next day the bishop replied by forwarding him a gold ring. The president, at the same time, sent another letter, desiring to see his commission, that he might know to what power to complain. Sawkins replied, that as yet all his men were not come together, but when they had met, they would come up to Panama, and bring their commissions on the muzzles of their guns, at which time he should read them as plain as the flame of gunpowder would let him.

The men growing now mutinous for fresh meat, Sawkins was compelled to give up his hopes of capturing the rich vessel from Peru, and to sail to the island of Otoque, to buy fowls and hogs, losing two barks, one with seven, and the other with fifteen men. While lying off the pearl fishery of Cayboa, Sawkins and Sharp made an unfortunate attack with sixty men on the town of Puebla Nueva. They were piloted up the river in canoes by a negro prisoner. A mile below the town, great trees had been laid to block up the stream, and before the town three strong breastworks were thrown up. Sawkins, running furiously up the sloping ramparts, was shot dead, and his men driven back to their boats, two men being killed, and three wounded, in the retreat, which was made in pretty good order.

They soon after, however, captured a vessel laden with indigo, and burnt two others. This Captain Sawkins, Ringrose says, was as valiant and courageous as any, and, next to Captain Sharp, the best beloved. His death was much lamented, and occasioned another overland expedition. Sharp, surrendering his last prize to Captain Cook, took his vessel and gave it to the sixty-three men who wished to return home. They led with them all the Indians to serve as guides overland.

Before they started, Sharp, in full council on board the *Trinidada*, offered to insure to all who would carry out Sawkins's scheme, and go home by the Straits of Magellan, a £1000 profit, but none would stay. Ringrose himself acknowledges he should have left with them, but was afraid of the Indians, and the long and dangerous journey in the rainy season.

At Cayboa, the men took in water and cut wood, killing alligators, and salting deer and turtle. Here two "remarkable events" happened to Ringrose. In the first place, he ate an oyster so large that he found it necessary to cut it into four large mouthfuls: secondly, as he was washing himself in a pond, some drops fell on him from a *mançanilla* tree, and these drops broke out into a red eruption that lasted a week. Here Sharp burnt one of his prizes for the sake of the iron work, and received Captain Cook, whose men had revolted, on board his own ship, making John Cox, a New Englander, commander in his stead.

Sharp now determined to careen at the island of Gorgona, and then to proceed to Guayaquil, where Captain Juan, the captain of the Tavoga money ship, assured them they might throw away their silver and lade with gold. They selected Gorgona, because, on account of the perpetual rain, the Spaniards seldom touched there. The sailors, who had lost their money at gambling, were impatient of these delays, and declared that the Spaniards would now gain time, and the whole coast be alarmed, and on the defensive. But the richer men, wanting rest, decided for Gorgona.

In this island, they fished their mainmast, shot at whales, killed monkeys, snakes, and turtle for food, being short of provision, caught a large sloth, and killed a serpent, fourteen inches thick, and twelve feet long. While moored here, Joseph Gabriel, the Chilian, who stole the Indian king's daughter, died of a malignant calenture. He had been very faithful, and discovered many plots and conspiracies among the prisoners of intended escapes and murders.

Sharp now abandoned the design on Guayaquil, and resolved to attack Arica, the depot of all the Potosi plate. An old man who had served much with the Spaniards, promised them £2000 a-man.

After a fortnight's sail they arrived at the island of Plate, so called from Drake dividing his plunder there among his men. The Spaniards had a tradition, that he took twelve score tons of plate in the galleon armada, and that each of his forty-five men had sixteen bowls full of coined money—his ships being so full that they were obliged to throw much of it overboard. In the adjoining bay of Manta, in Cromwell's time, a Lima vessel, laden with thirty millions of dollars, on its way as a present to Charles I., was lost by keeping too near the shore. While catching goats on this island, on which the cross of the first Spanish discoverer still stood, they were joined by Captain Cox, whom they had lost a fortnight before, as they feared, irrecoverably. They killed and salted on this island 100 goats in a day, and one man alone, in a few hours, in one small bay turned seventeen turtle. Peralta congratulated them on getting as far to windward in two weeks as the Spanish captains did in three months, from their keeping boldly so far from the shore.

While passing Guayaquil, they espied a Spanish vessel and gave chase. Being hailed in Spanish by an Indian prisoner, to lower their topsails, the enemy replied they would pull down the Englishman's first, and answered with their arquebuses to the buccaneers' muskets, till, one bullet killing the man at the helm and another cutting their maintop halliards, they cried out for quarter. There were thirty-five men on board, including twenty-four Spaniards and several persons of quality. The captain's brother, since the death of Don Jacinto de Barahona at Panama, was admiral of the armada. The buccaneers' rigging was much cut during the fight, and two men were wounded, besides a sailor who was shot by an accident. The captain, it appears, had in a bravado sworn to attack their fleet if he could meet it. The Spaniard, a very "civil and meek gentleman," informed them that the governor of Lima, hearing of their visit to Panama, had collected five ships and 750 sailors; while two other vessels and 400 soldiers, furnished by the viceroy, were preparing to start. A *patache* with twenty-four guns was also lying at Callao, ready to remove the king's plate from Arica. At Guayaquil they had built two forts, and mustered 850 men of all colours. The same day the English unrigged their new prize and sank her.

Reckoning up the pillage, they found they had now 3,276 pieces of eight, which were at once divided. The same day they punished a Spanish friar, who was chaplain in the last prize, and, shooting him on the deck, flung him overboard before he was dead. says Ringrose:

> Such cruelties, though I abhorred very much in my heart, yet here I was forced to hold my tongue and not contradict them, as having no authority to oversway them.

The prisoners now confessed they had killed a boat full of the buccaneers' men, lost near Cayboa, and had discovered from the only survivor the plan on Guayaquil.

Captain Cox's vessel being so slow as to require towing, they sank it, so there were now 140 men and boys and fifty-five prisoners in one and the same bottom. While to the leeward of Tumbes,

Peralta told them a legend of a priest having once landed there in the face of 10,000 Indians, who stared at his uplifted cross. As he stepped out of his boat on the shore, before the water could efface his footprints, two lions and two tigers came out of the woods to meet him, but when he gently laid the cross on their backs, they fell down and worshipped it, upon which all the Indians came forward and were baptised.

The night they passed Paita they espied a sail and gave chase, following it by the lights which it showed through negligence. Scantiness of provisions made them more eager in the pursuit, and coming up the Spaniard instantly lowered all her sails and surrendered. The buccaneers casting dice as to who should first board, the lot fell to the larboard watch. The vessel contained fifty packs of cocoa, and a great deal of raw silk and India cloth, besides many bales of thread stockings. The prize being plundered and dismasted, the prisoners were turned adrift in it, supplied with only a foresail, some water, and a little flour. The chief prisoners, as Don Thomas de Argandona, commander of the Guayaquil vessel, and his friends Don Christoval and Don Baltazar, gentlemen of quality, Captain Peralta, Moreno, a pilot, and twelve slaves, to do the drudgery, were still kept. The next day the sailor wounded in taking the Guayaquil vessel, died, and was buried with ceremony, three French volleys being fired as the body was let down into the deep.

Their next expedition was to attack Arica with 112 men, first sending five boats to capture some fishermen at the river of Juan Diaz, whom they might employ as spies.

To their great chagrin they found the landing impracticable, and the whole coast in arms. Troops of horse covered the low hills round the bay, and close beneath six ships rode at anchor. Abandoning this project, these indefatigable marauders (more pirates than real buccaneers) despatched four canoes and fifty men, to plunder the town of Hillo. On the shore the English were met by some horsemen, who fled after a few volleys. Marching to the town, they forced their way through a small breastwork of clay and sandbags, and took the town. Keeping good watch for fear of surprise, a dying Indian, wounded in the skirmish, told them that the townspeople had heard from Lima nine days before, and expected their coming. In the town they found pitch, wine, oil, and flour, and sixty of the ablest men were sent up the adjoining valley to reconnoitre. They found it beautifully planted with fig, lemon, lime, olive, and orange trees, and four miles up came to a sugar-mill, the greater part of the sugar having been removed. The Spaniards, watching them from the hills, rolled stones upon them, but hid themselves when a musket-shot was fired in retaliation. Captain Cox and a Dutch interpreter being despatched with a flag of truce to the Spaniards, they agreed to give eighty beeves as a ransom for the mill, and a message was despatched to Captain Sharp not to injure the drivers of the oxen when they came. Hearing that sixteen beeves had already arrived at the port, the men, contrary to Ringrose's opinion, returned to the ships laden with sugar, and found the whole story of the oxen's arrival a mere *ruse de guerre*. The Spaniards being appealed to promised the cattle should arrive that night, but at last declared the wind was so high they could not drive the herds. Enraged at this delay, the buccaneers, who had now taken in water, marched 100 men up the valley, and burned the house, the mill, and the canes, carried off the sugar, broke the oil jars, and cracked the copper wheels. Near the shore they were charged by a body of 300 horsemen, who took them by surprise, but not before they had thrown down the sugar and taken up their arms.

Ringrose shall tell the rest:

> We being in good rank and order fairly proffered them battle upon the bay; but as we advanced to meet them, they retired and rid towards the mountains, to surround us, and take the rocks from us, if possibly they could. Hereupon, perceiving their intentions, we returned back and possessed ourselves of the said rocks, and also of the lower town, as the Spaniards themselves did of the upper town (at the distance of half-a-mile from the lower), the hills and the woods adjoining thereunto. The horsemen being now in possession of those quarters, we could perceive as far as we could see, more and more men resort unto them, so that their forces increased hourly to considerable numbers. We fired at one another as long as we could see, and the day would permit. But in the mean time we observed that several of them rid to the watch hill and looked out often to the seaward. This gave us occa-

sion to fear that they had more strength and forces coming that way, which they expected every minute. Hereupon, lest we should speed worse than we had done before, we resolved to embark silently in the dark of the night.

They carried off a great chest of sugar (seven pounds and a-half to each man), thirty jars of oil, and much fruit, wild and cultivated. From appearances next morning they believed the enemy had also fled in the night, as only fifty men could be seen. The prisoners, seeing a comet at dusk, told the Englishmen that many such appearances had preceded the arrival of the buccaneers in the South Sea. Their brave prisoner, Captain Peralta, began at this time to show signs of insanity, his mind being shaken by continued hardship and despair at his long imprisonment.

The buccaneers next landed 100 men, hoping to take by surprise the city of La Serena. Here, too, they found the Spaniards vigilant, and had to break through 100 horsemen to reach the town, killing three officers and wounding four men. The town contained seven great churches and many rich merchants' houses surrounded by gardens. The inhabitants had fled, and either carried away or buried all their treasures, and a Chilian prisoner said the Spaniards had killed most of their negro and even their Chilian slaves, for fear of their revolting and joining the buccaneers. A party of forty men, with a Chilian guide, searched the woods in vain to secure prisoners for guides. The Spaniards, sending a flag of truce, agreed to pay 95,000 pieces of eight as ransom for the town; but, not bringing it in, the place was set on fire. Taking advantage of an earthquake, the Spaniards opened the sluices and inundated the streets. Every house, Ringrose says, was separately fired to render the conflagration complete. Two parties were then despatched laden with booty to the ships, who on their way beat up an ambuscade of 250 Spanish horse. During their absence, a daring attempt was made to burn their ship. The enemy hired a man who floated under the stern of the ship on a horse's hide, blown out like a bladder. He then stuffed oakum and brimstone between the keel and the stern-post, and set the rudder on fire. The men, alarmed at the smoke, ran up and down, not knowing where the fire could be, and believing the prisoners had done it in order to escape. The source of the evil was at last discovered, and the flames extinguished. The buccaneers, before sailing, released all their prisoners, not knowing what to do with them, and fearing that they would revolt or perhaps try to burn the ship.

On reaching the island of Juan Fernandez, they solemnized the festival of Christmas by discharging three volleys of shot, and killing sixty goats in one day. The shore was covered so thick with seals that they were obliged to shoot a few in order to land. They then filled 200 water-jars, and were nearly lost in a place called "False Wild Harbour," where they killed several sea-lions. Their beds they made of fern. It was on this island, their pilot told them, a deserted sailor (Alexander Selkirk) had lived five years.

The men now in the midst of storms and dangers, were all in a mutiny. Some were for going back to England or the plantations, and returning by the straits of Magellan; others for continuing longer in those seas. All agreed to depose Captain Sharp and elect John Watling, an old privateer, "and a stout seaman." The next Sunday was the first, says Ringrose, that had been kept by common consent since the death of Sawkins, who would throw the dice overboard if he found any in use on that day.

Juan Fernandez abounded in cabbage palms and building timber. The fish swarmed in such quantities that they could be caught with the bare hook, one sailor in a few hours capturing enough for the whole crew. Shoals a mile long were seen in the bay. While busily employed in catching fish, shooting goats, and cutting timber, the hunters suddenly gave the alarm of three Spanish men-of-war approaching the island, and, slipping their cables, the buccaneers put out hurriedly to sea. In the confusion, William, a Mosquito Indian, who could not be found at the time, was left behind to endure the hardships that a few days before he may have heard the pilot relate as experienced by the celebrated Alexander Selkirk (the prototype of Robinson Crusoe).

The three Spanish vessels proved to be the *El Santo Christo*, of 800 tons, carrying twelve guns; the *San Francisco*, of 600 tons, with ten guns; and a third of 350 tons. As soon as they came in sight, they hung out "bloody flags;" and the buccaneers, nothing daunted, did the same. The English, keeping close under the wind, were very unwilling to fight, as the Spaniards held together, and their new commander, Watling, showed a faint heart. The trio eventually sheered off, glad to escape uninjured.

Determining to pay a second visit to Arica, twenty-five men and two canoes were despatched to obtain guides from the island of Yqueque. On the shore of the mainland they found a hut built of whales' bones, a cross, and some broken jars.

They brought away from the island, which they could not at first discover, two old white men and two Indians. The people of Arica, they found, came to this place to buy clay, and the natives were obliged to fetch all the water they used from the mainland. The Indians wore no clothes, and chewed leaves which dyed their teeth green. One of the old prisoners being examined was shot to death by order of the commander, who believed him to be lying, although, as it afterwards appeared, he told nothing but the truth. Sharp was troubled and dissatisfied at this cruel and rash order, and, taking water and washing his hands, he said, "Gentlemen, I am clear of the blood of this old man, and will warrant you a hot day for this piece of cruelty whenever we come to fight at Arica."

The other prisoner said that he was the superintendent of fifty slaves belonging to the governor of the town. These slaves caught fish and sold them when dried in the inland towns. There were then three Chilian ships and a bark in the harbour, and a fortification of twelve guns in the town. The people had already, he said, heard from Coquimbo of their arrival, and removed and buried their treasure. There were also, they heard, breast-works round the town, and barricades in every street.

Disregarding these warnings, the buccaneers embarked next day in a launch and four canoes, rowing and sailing all night, in hopes of surprising Arica. At daybreak they hid themselves under the cliffs for fear of being seen, and at night began again to row. On Sunday (Jan. 30), 1680—"sacred to the memory of King Charles the Martyr"—they landed among some rocks four miles to the south of the town, ninety-two men going on shore, the rest staying to defend the boats. The signal agreed on was, that at one smoke, they should come up to the harbour in one canoe; but if there were two smokes, they should "bring all away, leaving only fifteen men with the boats." Mounting a steep hill, they could see no Spaniards, and hoped that the surprise was complete; but as they were descending the other side, three horsemen on the look-out hill rode down at full speed and alarmed the city. The forty men who attacked the fort with hand grenades, seeing their companions overpowered, ran down into the valley to join them.

> Here the battle was very desperate, and they killed and wounded two more of our men from their outworks before we could gain upon them. But our rage increasing with our wounds, we still advanced, and at last beat the enemy out of all, and filled every street in the city with dead bodies. The enemy made several retreats from one breast-work to another, but, we had not a sufficient number of men to man all places taken. Insomuch, that we had no sooner beat them out of one place but they came another way, and manned it again with new forces and fresh men.

So says Ringrose.

Imprudently overburdening themselves with prisoners, they found there were in the place 400 soldiers from Lima, 200 armed townsmen, and 300 men garrisoning the fort. Being now nearly masters of the place, the English sent to demand the surrender of the fort, and, receiving no answer, advanced to the attack. Several times repulsed, the buccaneers at last mounted the top of a neighbouring house and fired down into the castle; but, being again surrounded by the enemy, they were obliged to desist. The number and vigour of the enemy increased hourly, and, almost overpowered, the English were compelled to retreat to the hospital where the surgeons were tending the wounded. Captain Watling and both quartermasters were killed, and many were disabled. We will let Ringrose tell the rest:

> So that now, the enemy rallying against us, and beating us from place to place, we were in a very distracted condition, and in more likelihood to perish, every man, than escape the bloodshed of that day. Now we found the words of Captain Sharp true, being all very sensible that we had a day too hot for us, after that cruel heat in killing and murdering in cold blood the old Mestizo Indian.
>
> Being surrounded with difficulties on all sides, and in

great disorder, having nobody to give orders, what was to be done? We were glad to have our eyes upon our good old commander, Captain Bartholomew Sharp, and beg of him very earnestly to commiserate our condition, and carry us off. It was a great while before he would take any notice of our request, so much was he displeased with the former mutiny of our people against him, all which had been occasioned by the instigation of Mr. Cook.

But Mr. Sharp is a man of an undaunted courage, and excellent conduct, not fearing in the least to look an insulting enemy in the face, and a person that knows both the theory and practice of navigation as well as most do. Hereupon, at our earnest request and petition, he took upon him the command in chief again, and began to distribute his orders for our safety. He would have brought off our surgeons, but they, having been drinking while we assaulted the fort, would not come with us when they were called. They killed and took of our number twenty-eight men, besides eighteen that we brought off, who were desperately wounded. At that time we were all extremely faint for want of water and victuals, whereof we had none all that day. We were likewise almost choked with the dust of the town, being so much raised by the work that their guns had made, that we could scarce see each other. They beat us out of the town, then followed us into the savannahs, still charging as fast as they could. But when they saw that we rallied, again resolving to die one by another, they ran from us into the town, and sheltered themselves under their breast-works. Thus we retreated in as good order as we possibly could observe in that confusion. But their horsemen followed us as we retired, and fired at us all the way, though they would not come within reach of our guns, for theirs reached further than ours, and outshot us above one-third. We took the sea-side for our greater security, which when the enemy saw, they betook themselves to the hills, rolling down great stones and whole rocks to destroy us. Meanwhile, those of the town examined our surgeons, and other men whom they had made prisoners. These gave them our signs that we had left to our boats that were behind us, so that they immediately blew up two fires, which were perceived by the canoes. This was the greatest of our dangers; for had we not come at that instant that we did to the sea-side, our boats had been gone, they being already under sail, and we had inevitably perished every man. Thus we put off from the shore, and got on board about ten at night, having been involved in a bloody fight with the enemy all the day.

The buccaneers, thus cruelly baffled, plied for some time outside the port, hoping to be revenged on the three ships, but they did not venture out. Arica Ringrose describes as a square place, with the castle at one corner. The houses were only eleven feet high, and built of earth. It was the place of embarkation for all minerals sent to Lima. Of the English prisoners, only ten survived. The Spaniards lost more than seventy men, three times as many being wounded, and of forty-five allies from Hillo only two returned alive.

On dividing the plate, they found only thirty-seven pieces of eight fell to each man. Landing at Guasco, they took in 500 jars of water, and carried off 120 sheep, 80 goats, and 200 bushels of flour. At Hillo they surprised the townsmen asleep, and heard a false report that 5000 Englishmen had taken Panama. They carried off eighteen jars of wine and some new figs, and, ascending to the sugar-work they had before visited, laded seven mules with molasses and sugar. The townsmen told them, that the owner of the mill had brought an action against them for having done him more injury than the buccaneers.

A few days after this another mutiny broke out, and forty-seven men, refusing to serve any longer under Captain Sharp, landed near the island of Plate, with five Indian slaves to serve as guides. Near the island of Chica they captured two Spanish vessels, one of them the very ship they had captured before at Panama. They heard here that some of their overland parties had taken a good ship at Porto Bello. Capturing some Spanish shipwrights at this place, they employed them for a fortnight in altering their vessel, and then set them at liberty, with some others of their prisoners, giving them one of their prizes, and manning the other with six men and two slaves.

They now agreed in council to bear up for Golfo Dolce, there to careen their vessels, and then to cruise about under the equinoctial. They landed in Golfo Dolce, and, treating kindly some Indians whom they took prisoners, bought honey and plantains off them. Here they learned that the Spaniards, having treacherously captured forty Darien chiefs, had forced the natives into a peace. Having careened here, they soon after captured a rich prize, the *San Pedro*, bound from Truxillo to Panama, deeply laden with 37,000 pieces of eight, in chest and bags, besides plate. This was the same vessel they had taken the year before, and it was now their prize a second time in fourteen months. The crew consisted of forty men, besides friars and merchants. Taking out part of her lading of cocoa, they cut down her masts and turned her adrift with all the old slaves, as "*a reward for good service*," taking new ones from the prize. Francisco, a negro, who had attempted to escape by swimming on shore in the Golfo Dolce, they retained as a prisoner, as a punishment for his insubordination. From this prize each buccaneer received 234 pieces of eight, much being left for a future division. They learnt from this vessel that a new Viceroy of Peru, arrived at Panama, had not dared to venture to Lima in his ship of twenty-five guns, but had waited for the armada as a convoy. A few days later, they captured the packet that ran between Lima and Panama. A friar and five negroes escaped on shore, but two white women were captured. Rummaging the boat, they found nothing of value but a letter announcing the departure of the viceroy with four ships. The prisoners and the boat were then released. "That week," says Ringrose, "we stood out to sea all night long, most of our men being fuddled."

The next day they captured a Spanish vessel that had at first frightened them by its size. The volleys of the buccaneers soon drove the Spaniards into the hold and made them cry for quarter, having killed the captain at the first fire, and wounded the boatswain. Captain Sharp and twelve others were the first to board. She proved to be *El Santo Rosario*, commanded by Don Diego Lopez, bound from Callao to Panama. The crew were forty in number. She was deeply laden with plate and coined money, and carried 620 jars of wine and brandy. At Cape Passao Sharp sank the bark taken at Nicoya, preserving her rigging, and disabling the last prize set the prisoners adrift in it, keeping only the one man, named Francisco, who had described himself as the best pilot in those seas. They then divided the booty, which came to ninety-four pieces of eight a man. From these prisoners they learned that their men taken at Arica had been kindly treated at Callao. Of the last party that one had been captured, and the rest had had to fight their way overland through Indians and Spaniards. Ten buccaneers were also announced as about to enter the South Sea. In August they landed again to kill goats on the island of Plate, where Ringrose and James Chappel, a quartermaster, fought a duel on shore, with what result we do not know. The same evening a conspiracy of the slaves was detected, in which they had plotted to slay all their masters when in drink, not sparing any. The ringleader, San Jago, a prisoner from Yqueque, leaped overboard when the plot was discovered, and was shot by the captain. The rest, being terrified at his death, were forgiven, and the same night the usual debauch took place in spite of the danger. From their pilot they heard that a Lima vessel bound for Guayaquil had run ashore lately on Santa Clara, losing 100,000 pieces of eight, that would have been their prize. They heard also that the Viceroy of Peru had beheaded the great Admiral Ponce for not destroying the buccaneer fleet while at Gorgona.

They next made a descent on Paita, but found the place garrisoned by three companies horse and foot, well armed, from Puira, twelve leagues up the country. 150 musketeers and 400 lancers occupied a hill and a breast-work, and fired upon the canoes. Had they suffered them to land they might have killed them to a man. Finding the whole coast now alarmed, they bore at once away for the Straits of Magellan. Touching at some unknown islands, they were almost inclined to winter there. Here they shot geese, made broth of limpets, and one of the boats captured an Indian and shot another dead. The prisoner was clad in a seal's skin, and carried a net to catch penguins. He was so strong as to be able to open mussels with his fingers, and they kept him as a slave, and called him Orson. They then proceeded to divide eight chests of money still unallotted, and each man received 322 pieces of eight. On December 7th Captain Sharp received intelligence of a conspiracy to shoot him during the ensuing festivities of Christmas-day. The only precaution he took was at once to divide all the wine in store, believing that no sober man would attempt so dastardly an act. Each mess received three jars. The cold grew now so intense that several of the negro slaves had their feet mortify, and some died.

Christmas-day was celebrated by killing a fat sow, this being the first flesh the men had eaten since they left the island of Plata. By January 16th the days grew very hot again, and the nights cool and dewy. The men, weary of the voyage, offered a piece of eight "each man" to him who first discovered land. The sight of birds soon indicated this, and January 28th the look-out spied Barbadoes; but hearing of peace they dared not put in for fear of being seized, and therefore steered for Antigua, much afraid of frigates, and shunning even a Bristol interloper that lay in the offing. Ringrose says:

> Here I cannot easily express the infinite joy we were possessed with all this day, to see our own countrymen again.

They then freed a negro shoemaker, whom they had kept as a prisoner, and who had been very serviceable during the voyage. To Captain Sharp the men gave a mulatto boy as slave, for a token of the respect of his whole company to him for having led them safely through so many dangerous adventures. They then divided the last parcels of money, and received twenty-four pieces of eight a man. A little Spanish shock dog, taken from a prize, was also sold at the mast by public outcry, for forty pieces of eight, the owner promising all he gained should be devoted to a general feast. Captain Sharp bought the dog, saying he would eat it if they did not soon get leave to land. 100 pieces of eight was also added to the store, the boatswain, carpenter, and quartermaster having quarrelled about the last dividend.

On reaching Antigua Sharp sent a canoe ashore to buy tobacco and other necessaries, and to ask leave of the governor to land. The conclusion of Ringrose's book tells the rest:

> The gentry of the place and common people were very willing and desirous to receive us, but on Wednesday, February 1st, the governor flatly refused us entry, at which all the gentry were much troubled, showing themselves very kind to us; hereupon we agreed among ourselves to give the ship to those of our company who had no money left them of all

their purchase in this voyage, having lost it at play, and then put ourselves on board two ships bound for England. So I myself and thirteen more of our company went on board Captain Robert Porteen's ship called the *Lisbon Merchant*, set sail from La Antigua February 11th, and landed in England March 26th, *anno* 1682.

On his arrival in England Captain Sharp was tried for piracy and acquitted. He at once resolved to return to the West Indies, but all the merchant ships refused to carry him, afraid he would tempt their men to revolt against their master, and run away with the ship for a privateer, as he had done before. No promises or entreaties could avail, and he seemed doomed to remain a prisoner in an island for which he entertained no filial affection.

He therefore hit upon a desperate scheme, worthy of such a man. Collecting a little money he bought an old, half-rotten boat, lying near London-bridge, for £20, and embarked with sixteen desperadoes equally fearless as himself, carrying a supply of butter and cheese, and two dozen pieces of salt beef. He sailed down the river and reached the Downs, and there he boarded and captured a French vessel and sank his boat. By a foray on Romney Marsh he supplied himself with cattle, and sailed away like a bold buccaneer as he was, to die no one knows where.

CHAPTER 11

Dampier's Voyages

Dampier, one of the wisest and best of English travellers, was himself a buccaneer. Son of a Somersetshire farmer, he went early to sea, and became a freebooter without much compunction, just at the time when the brothers of the coast were sinking into mere pirates. "No peace beyond the line" was their early motto; "Friends to God and enemies to all mankind," was the later. The flag, once reddened by the Spaniards' blood, grew now black with the shadows of death and of the grave.

Dampier was among those who left Captain Sharp after the dreadful repulse from Arica. His party consisted of forty-four Englishmen and two Mosquito Indians, who determined to re-cross the Isthmus of Darien, and return to the North Pacific Ocean. They carried with them a large quantity of flour and chocolate mixed with sugar, and took a mutual and terrible oath, that if any of their number sank from fatigue, he should be shot by his comrades, rather than allow him to fall into the hands of the Spaniards, who would not only torture him horribly, but compel him to betray his companions.

In a fortnight after leaving the vessels they landed at the mouth of a river in the Bay of St. Michael, where unloading their provisions and arms they sank their boats; and while preparing for the inland journey, the Indians caught fish, and built huts for them to sleep in. The next day they struck into an Indian path and reached a village, but found, to their alarm, that the Spaniards had placed armed ships at the mouths of all the navigable rivers to intercept them on their return. Hiring an Indian guide, they reached the day after a native house, but the savage would neither give them food nor information. At any other time the buccaneers would have at once put him on the rack, or hung him at his own door, but they felt this was no place to be angry, for their lives lay in the enemy's hands. Neither dollars, hatchets, nor knives, would move this stubborn man, till a sailor pulled a sky blue petticoat from his bag and threw it over the head of the Indian's wife. Delighted with the gift, she coaxed her husband till he gave them information and found a guide. It had rained hard for two days, the country was difficult and fatiguing, and there was no path that even an Indian eye could discover. They guided themselves by day by the rivers, and at night by the stars. They had frequently to ford the rivers twenty or thirty times in twelve hours. Rain, cold, fatigue, and hunger made them forget even the Spaniards.

In a few days they reached the house of a young Spanish Indian, who had lived with the bishop of Panama, and who received them kindly. Here, while resting to dry their arms and powder, their surgeon, Mr. Wafer, had his knee burnt by an accidental explosion. After dragging himself along with pain for another day, he determined to remain behind with two or three more. He stayed five months with the Indians, and the published account of his experiences still exists.

The rainy season that frightened Mr. Ringrose had now set in, and the thunder and lightning was frequent and violent. The valleys and river banks were overflowed, and the buccaneers had to sleep in trees or under their shade, instead of building warm and sheltering huts. In the very height of their misery, the slaves fled and carried away all they could. Dampier, whose only anxiety was to preserve his journal, placed it in a bamboo, closed at both ends with wax. In fording one of the rivers, a buccaneer, who carried 300 dollars on his back, was swept down the stream and drowned, but the survivors were too hopeless and weary to look for either body or gold.

In eighteen days the English reached the river Concepcion, and, obtaining Indian canoes, rowed to Le Sound's Key, one of the Samballas islands, where buccaneers rendezvoused. Here they embarked on board a French privateer, commanded by Captain Tristian, dismissing their Indian guides with presents of money, beads, and hatchets. At Springer's Key, Tristian joined them with other vessels, and would have attacked Panama had not Dampier and his men deterred them. For a week the council deliberated about the available towns worth plundering from Trinidad to Vera Cruz. The French and English could not agree, but at last all sailed for Carpenter's River, touching at the isle of St. Andreas. The ships separated in a gale; and Dampier taking a dislike to his French commander, induced Captain Wright, an Englishman, to fit out a small vessel and cruise for provisions along the coast. While the sailors shot pecary, deer, parrots, pigeons, monkeys, and cuvassow birds, their Mosquito Indians struck turtle for their use.

On returning to Le Sound's Key they were joined by Mr. Wafer, who had escaped from the Darien Indians, but he was so painted and bedizened that it was some time before they could recognize him. An Indian chief had offered him his daughter in marriage, and he had only got away by pretending to go in search of English dogs for hunting. Passing Carthagena, they cast wistful eyes at the convent dedicated to the Virgin, situated on a steep hill behind the town. There was immense wealth hoarded in this place, rich offerings being frequently made to it, and many miracles worked by our Lady. Any misfortune that befell the buccaneer was attributed to this Lady's doing, and the Spaniards reported that she was abroad that night the Oxford man-of-war blew up at the isle of Vaca, and that she came home all wet, and with clothes soiled and torn.

Captain Wright's company pillaged several small places about the Rio de la Hache and the Rancherias pearl fisheries, and captured, after a smart engagement, an armed ship of twelve guns and forty men, laden with sugar, tobacco, and marmalade, bound to Carthagena from Santiago, in Cuba. The Dutch governor of Curaçoa, having much trade with the Spaniards, would not openly buy the cargo, but offered, if it was sent among the Danes of St. Thomas, to purchase it through his agents. The rovers, declining this, sold it at another Dutch colony, and then sailed for the isle of Aves, so called from the quantity of boobies and men-of-war birds. On a coral reef, near this island, Count d'Estrees had shortly before lost the whole French fleet. He himself had first run ashore, and firing guns to warn the rest of the danger, they hurried on to the same shoal, thinking, in the darkness, that he had been attacked by the enemy. The ships held together till the next day, and many men were saved. The ordinary seamen died of hunger and fatigue, but the buccaneers, hardier, and accustomed to frequent wrecks, made the escape an excuse for revel and debauchery. As Dampier says:

> ... they, being used to such accidents, lived merrily, and if they had gone to Jamaica with £30 in their pockets, could not have enjoyed themselves more; for they kept a gang by themselves and watched when the ships broke up, to get the goods that came out of them, and, though much was staved against the rocks, yet abundance of wine and brandy floated over the reef where they waited to take it up... There were about forty Frenchmen on board one of the ships, in which was good store of liquor, till the after part of her broke, and floated over the reef and was carried away to sea, with all the men drinking and singing, who, being in drink, did not mind the danger, but were never heard of afterwards.

This wreck having left the Bird Island a storehouse of masts and spars, the buccaneer vessels had begun to repair thither to careen and refit. Among others, a Captain Pan, a Frenchman, had been there. A Dutch vessel of twenty guns, despatched from Curaçoa to fish up the sunken cannon, observing the privateer, resolved to capture him before he began his diving. Pan, afraid of the Dutchman's superior force, abandoned his vessel, and, landing his guns, prepared to throw up a redoubt. While thus engaged, a Dutch sloop entered the road, and at night anchored at the opposite end of the island. In the night, Pan, with two canoes, boarded the ship, and made off, leaving his empty hulk for the Dutch man-of-war.

At this island, Dampier's men careened their largest vessel, scrubbed the sugar prize, and recovered two guns from the wreck. At the island of Rocas, a Knight of Malta, captain of a French thirty-six gun ship, bought ten tons of their sugar. Failing to sell any more sugar at Petit Guaves, they sailed for Blanco, an uninhabited island, full of lignum-vitae trees, and teeming with iguanas, that were to be found in the swamps, among the bushes, or in the trees. Their eggs were eaten by the buccaneers, who made soup of the flesh for their sick.

While cruising on the Caraccas coast, they landed in some of the bays, and took seven or eight tons of cocoa, and three barks laden with hides, brandy, earthenware, and European goods. Returning to the Rocas, they divided the spoil, and Dampier and nineteen others embarking in one of the prizes, reached Virginia July 1682.

Dampier's next voyage was with a Creole, named Cook, who arrived at Virginia with a French vessel he had captured by a trick at Petit Guaves. He had been quartermaster, or second in command, under a French *flibustier* named Gandy. By the usual buccaneer law, he had been made captain of a large Spanish prize. The French commanders in the same fleet, jealous of this promotion, seized the ship, plundered the English prize crew, and sent them ashore. Tristan, another French captain, took ten of them with him to Petit Guaves. Cook and his nine companions, taking advantage of a day when Tristan and many of his men were absent, overpowered the rest of the crew, sent them ashore, and sailed to the Isle à la Vache. Here he picked up a crew of English buccaneers, and steered for Virginia, taking two prizes by the way, one of which was a French vessel, laden with wines. He then sold his wine and two of the ships, and equipped the largest, the *Revenge*, with eighteen guns. Amongst the crew were Dampier, Wafer and Cowley, all of whom have written narratives of their voyages. They sailed from the Chesapeake on the 23rd of August 1683, and captured a Dutch vessel, laden with wine and provisions. At the Cape de Verd islands they encountered a dreadful storm, that lasted a week. While the ship scudded before wind and sea under bare poles, she was suddenly broached to by order of the master, and would have foundered but for Dampier and another man who, going aloft and spreading out the flaps of their coats, righted the ship. At the isle of Sal, the sailors feasted on flamingo tongues. These birds stood in ranks round the feeding ponds, so as to resemble a new brick wall. They purchased here some ambergris, which Dampier says he had in a lump of 100 lbs. weight. Its origin was at that time unknown; it is now believed to be a secretion of the whale. The governor and his court at this island rejoiced in rags, their revenues being small, and drawn principally from the salt ponds, from which the island derives its name. Having dug wells, watered, and careened, they went to Mayo to obtain provisions, but were not allowed to land, as only about a week before Captain Bond, a pirate of Bristol, had carried off the governor and some of his people.

Steering to the Straits of Magellan, they were driven to the Guinea coast, and there captured a Danish ship by a stratagem. Captain Cook, concealing his men under deck, approached the Dane like a weak, unarmed merchant vessel. When quite close, he commanded in a loud voice the helm to be put one way, while by a preconcerted plan the steersman shifted into another, and fell on board the Dane, which was captured with the loss of only five men. She was double their size, carried thirty-six guns, and was equipped and victualled for a long voyage.

This vessel they called *The Bachelor's Delight*, and they at once burned the *Revenge*, that she might "tell no tales."

During frequent tornadoes near the straits, being short of fresh meat, the sailors caught sharks during the calms, and boiling their flesh, stewed it with pepper and vinegar. When they reached the Falkland, or Sebald de Weist islands, as they were then called, Dampier proposed to the captain to reach Juan Fernandez by Cape Horn, avoiding the straits. Their men being privateers, wilful, and not much in command, he feared would not give sufficient attention in a passage so difficult, and, though he owns they were more than usually obedient, he says he could not expect to find them at an instant's call in critical moments. At these islands they found the sea for a mile round red with shoals of small, scarlet-shelled lobsters. Dampier's advice was not taken, but on entering the South Sea they met the *Nicholas*, of London, a vessel fitted out ostensibly as a trader, but being in reality a buccaneer. The captain came on board, related his adventures, and gave them a supply of bread and beef. They reached Juan Fernandez together, and heard from the *Nicholas* of a vessel from London, called the *Cygnet*, commanded by Captain Swan, which was sailing in those latitudes. It was a trader, holding a licence from the Duke of York, then High Admiral of England.

The crews discovered on the island the Mosquito Indian left behind by Captain Watling, in Lussan's expedition, because he was hunting goats when the vessel sailed. He was warmly greeted by Dampier, a fellow-countryman named Robin, and some old messmates. Robin, running up to him, fell flat on his face at his feet, and then rose and embraced him. They found he had killed three goats, and prepared some cabbage palms, to feast his visitors. The interview, writes Dampier, was tender, solemn, and affecting. When abandoned, William had nothing with him but his gun and a knife, some powder, and some shot. By notching his knife into a saw, he cut his gun barrel into pieces. These he hammered in the fire, and ground them into lances, harpoons, hooks, and knives. He hunted goats, fished, and killed seals. His clothes he made of skins, and with these also he had lined his hut; and he had contrived to elude the search of the Spaniards. Wild goats, originally brought by the Spaniard, abounded on the hills and in the grassy valleys. There was abundance of water and good timber, and the bays abounded with seals and sea-lions, that covered the sea for a mile.

Remaining here sixteen days, for the sake of the sick and those ill with the scurvy, and getting in water and provision, Cook then steered for the American coast, standing out fourteen or fifteen leagues to escape the notice of the Spaniard. The ridges were blue and mountainous. They soon captured a timber ship from Guayaquil laden with timber for Lima, from whose crew they heard that their arrival was known. They anchored next at the sandy islet of Lobos de la Mar, and scrubbed their ships. Captain Eaton, of the *Nicholas*, proposing to march with them in their descents, and the two vessels mustering 108 able men, Cook soon took another prize, and Eaton two more, which he pursued. They were laden with flour from Lima for Panama, and in one of them was eight tons of quince marmalade. The prisoners informed them that, on the rumour of their approach, 800,000 pieces of eight had been landed at an intermediate port. They sailed next to the Galapagos islands, abandoning a design on Truxillo, which they heard had been lately fortified. On these rocky, barren shores they feasted on turtle, pigeons, fish, and the leaves of the *mammee* tree. Off Cape Blanco, Captain Cook died, and was buried on land.

Capturing some Spanish Indians who had been sent as spies by the Governor of Panama, they used them as guides, and landed on the coast in search of cattle. Here a few of the men were surprised by fifty armed Spaniards, and their boat burned. The sailors thus imperilled waded out neck deep to an insulated rock near the shore, and remained there for seven hours exposed to the Spanish bullets, till they were taken off by a boat from their ship just as the tide was rising to devour them. The Spanish, lurking in ambush, made no attempt to resist the rescue.

The quartermaster, Edward Davis, was now elected commander; and after cutting lancewood for the handles of their oars, they bore away for Ria Lexa, steering for a high volcano that rises above the town and the island that forms the harbour. But here, too, the Spaniards had thrown up breast-works and placed sentinels, and the buccaneers sailed for the Gulf of Ampalla and the island of Mangera. Davis captured the padre of a village and two Indian boys, and, proceeding to Ampalla, informed the people that he commanded a Biscay ship, sent by the King of Spain to clear those seas of pirates, and that he had come there to careen. The sailors were well received, and entertained with feasts and music, and they all repaired together to celebrate a festival by torchlight in the church. Here Davis hoped to cage them till he could dictate a ransom, but the impatience of one of his men frustrated the plan. Pushing in a lingering Indian, the man spread an alarm, the people all fled, and the buccaneers, firing, killed one of their chiefs. They remained, however, good friends, and these very Indians soon after helped to store the ship with cattle belonging to a nunnery, situated on an island in the gulf. On leaving, Davis gave them one of his prize ships, and a quantity of flour, and released the priest who had helped him in his first stratagem.

The crews now quarrelled, and Davis, who claimed the largest share of the common plunder, left them, taking Dampier with him. Eaton touched at Cocos Island, purchased a store of flour, and took in water and cocoa nuts. Davis landed at Manta, a village near Cape St. Lorenzo, and captured two old women, in order to obtain information. They learnt that many buccaneers had lately crossed the isthmus, and were coming along the coast in canoes and *piraguas*. The viceroy had left no means untried to check them; the goats on the uninhabited islands had been destroyed, provisions were removed from the shore, and ships even burnt to save them from the enemy. At La Plata, Davis was joined by Captain Swan in the *Cygnet*, who had turned freebooter in self-defence. He had been joined by Peter Harris, who commanded a small bark, and was nephew of the buccaneer commander killed in a sea-fight at Panama three years before. They now sent for Eaton, but found from a letter at the rendezvous at Lobos, that he had already sailed for the East Indies. While the ships were refitting at La Plata, a small bark taken by Davis, after the Spaniards had set it on fire, captured a Spaniard of 400 tons, laden with timber, and brought word that the viceroy was fitting out ten frigates to sweep them from the seas. Captain Swan, at this crisis, turned wholly freebooter, and cleared his ship of goods by selling them to every buccaneer on credit. The bulky bales he threw overboard, the silks and muslins he kept, and retained the iron bars for ballast. In compensation for these sacrifices, the buccaneers agreed to set aside ten shares of all booty for Captain Swan's owners.

Having cleaned the vessels and fitted up a fire-ship, the squadron landed at Paita, but found it deserted. Anchoring off the place, they demanded as ransom 300 pecks of flour, 3000 pounds of sugar, twenty-five jars of wine, and 1000 of water, and having coasted six days and obtained nothing, they burnt the town in revenge, and sailed away. They found afterwards that Eaton had been there not long before, landed his prisoners, and burnt a ship in the road. Burning Harris's vessel, which proved unseaworthy, the squadron steered for the island of Lobos del Tierra, and, being short of food, took in a supply of seals, penguins, and boobies, their Mosquito men supplying them with turtle, while the ships were cleaned and provided with firewood, preparatory to a descent upon Guayaquil. Embarking in their canoes, they captured in the bay a small ship laden with Quito cloth and two vessels full of negroes. One of these they dismasted, and a few only of the slaves they took with them. From disagreement between the two crews, the expedition failed. Having lain in the woods all night, and cut a road with great difficulty, they abandoned the scheme without firing a shot, when almost within a mile of the town, which they believed was alarmed, and on the watch.

Dampier now proposed a scheme as feasible and grand as any of Raleigh's. He declared that they never had a greater opportunity of enriching themselves. His bold plan was, with the 1000 negroes lying in the three prizes, to go and work the gold mines of St. Martha. The Indians would at once join them from their hatred of the Spaniards. For provision they had 200 tons of flour laid up in the Galapagos islands; the North Sea would be open to them; thousands of buccaneers would join them from all parts of the West Indies; united they would be a match for all the forces of Peru, and might be at once masters of the west coast as high as Quito. This golden cloud melted into mere fog. The buccaneers returned to La Plata, divided the Quito cloth, and turned the Guayaquil vessel into a tender for the *Swan*. The old buccaneers of Davis now quarrelled with the new recruits in the *Swan*, accused them of cowardice and of having baulked the attempt on Guayaquil, and complained of having to supply them with flour and turtle, for they had neither provisions nor Indian fishermen. Unable to divorce, the ill-assorted pair proceeded to attack together Lavelia, in the Bay of Panama. From charts found in the prizes they checked the deceptions and errors of the Spanish and Indian prisoners whom they employed as pilots. Their object was now to search for canoes in rivers unvisited by the Spaniards, where their schemes might remain still undiscovered.

Such rivers abounded from the equinoctial line to the Gulf of St. Michael. When five days out from La Plata they made a sudden swoop on the village of Tomaco, and captured a vessel laden with timber, with a Spanish knight, eight sailors, and a canoe containing twelve jars of old wine. A boat party that rowed up the St. Jago river visited a house belonging to a lady of Lima, whose servants traded with the Indians for gold, several ounces of which were found left by them in their calabashes when they fled.

The twin vessels next sailed for the island of Gallo, capturing by the way a packet boat from Lima, fishing up the letters, which the Spaniards had thrown overboard attached to a buoy. From these they learnt that the governor of Panama was hastening the departure of the triennial plate fleet from Callo to Panama, where it would be carried on mules across the isthmus. To intercept this fleet and to grow millionaires in a day was now their only dream. They proceeded at once to careen their ships at the Pearl islands in the bay of Panama. Their force consisted of two ships, three barks, a fire-ship, and two small tenders. Near the uninhabited island of Gorgona they captured a flour ship, and landing most of their prisoners at Gorgona, they proceeded to the bay, captured a small provision boat, and continued their watch, cruising round the city.

Having cut off all communication between Panama and the islands in the bay, Davis proposed an exchange of prisoners, surrendering forty monks, whom he was glad to get rid of, for one of Harris's band and a sailor who had been surprised while hunting on an island. The Lima fleet still delaying, the buccaneers anchored at Tavoga, an island abounding in cocoa and *mammee* trees, and beautiful water. About this time they were nearly ensnared by a Spanish ship, sent to the island at midnight under pretence of clandestine traffic. This scheme originated in Captain Bond, an English pirate who had deserted to the enemy. The squadron, which had scattered in alarm, to avoid the fire-ship, were just re-uniting and looking for their abandoned anchors, when a cry rose that a fleet of armed canoes were steering direct towards them through the island channel. This was the French *flibustiers* of which we have given an account in the adventures of Ravenau de Lussan. After joining in the sea-fight off Panama, and the descent upon Leon and Ria Lexa, the buccaneers again split into small parties. Dampier joined Swan and Townley, who determined to cruise along the shores of the mine country of Mexico, and then, sailing as high as the southwest point of California, cross the Pacific, and return to England by India. At Guatalico, famous for its blowing rock, they landed their sick for a few days, and obtained provisions, and, in a descent near Acapulco, stopped a string of sixty laden mules and killed eighteen beeves, carrying off all the cattle safely to their ships.

To obtain provisions, Swan sacked the town of St. Pecaque, on the coast of New Gallicia, where large stores were kept for the use of the slaves of the neighbouring mines. A great many of these he carried off the first day on horseback and on the shoulders of his men. These visits were repeated—a party of buccaneers keeping the town till the Spaniards had collected a force. Of this Captain Swan gave his men due warning, exhorting them, on their way to their canoes with the burdens of maize, to keep together in a compact body, but they chose to follow their own course, every man straggling singly while leading his horse, or carrying a load on his shoulder. They accordingly fell into the ambush the Spaniards had laid for them, and to the amount of fifty were surprised and mercilessly butchered. The Spaniards, seizing their arms and loaded horses, fled, before Swan, who heard the distant firing, could come to the assistance of his men. Fifty-four Englishmen and nine blacks fell in this affair, which was the most severe the buccaneers had encountered in the South Sea. Dampier relates that Captain Swan had been warned of this disaster by an astrologer he had consulted before he sailed from England. Many of the men, too, had foreboded the misfortune; and the previous night, while lying in the church of St. Pecaque, had been disturbed by frequent groanings which kept them from sleeping.

This disaster drove Swan from the coast to careen at Cape St. Lucas, the south point of California—in revenge for his loss leaving his pilot and prisoners on an uninhabited island. While lying here, Dampier was cured of dropsy by being buried all but his head in hot sand. The whole 150 men were now living on short allowances of maize, and the fish the Indians struck salted for store. One meal a-day was now the rule, and the victuals were served out by the quartermaster with the exactness of gold. Yet, even in this distress, two dogs and two cats received their daily shares. They now started for their cruise among the Philippines. In a long run of 7,302 miles they saw no living thing—neither bird, fish, nor insect, except one solitary flight of boobies. At the end of the voyage the men were almost in mutiny at the want of food, and had secretly resolved to kill and eat their captain (Swan), and afterwards, in regular order, all who had promoted the voyage. At the island of Gualan, where there was a Spanish fort and a garrison of thirty men, the buccaneers traded with the natives, who took them for Spaniards from Acapulco.

Captain Eaton, who had visited the island before them on his way to India, had, at the instigation of the Spaniards, plundered and killed many of the natives, and driven the rest to emigration. While trading here the Acapulco vessel arrived, and, being signalled by the governor, took to flight; but in her hurry to escape ran upon a shoal, from which she was with difficulty extricated. Swan, who now grew anxious for quiet commerce, discouraged the pursuit, and proceeded quietly on his voyage. At Mindanao, Captain Swan and thirty-six men were left behind by his crew, who were only anxious for plunder, and soon after captured a Spanish vessel bound for Manilla. Captain Swan was eventually drowned while attempting to escape to a Dutch vessel lying in the river. Weary of the mean robberies of the crew, who now turned mere pirates, Dampier left them at the Nicobar islands, and, embarking in canoes, reached Sumatra, and eventually sailed for England.

The buccaneers left behind in the South Sea prospered, and made many successful descents. At Lavelia Townley captured the treasure and merchandise landed from the Lima ship in the former year, for which Swan had watched so long in vain, and for which the buccaneers had fought in the Bay of Panama. Townley died of his wounds. Harris followed Swan across the Pacific; and Knight, another English buccaneer, satiated with plunder, returned home laden with Spanish gold; and off Cape Corrientes they lay in wait in vain for the Manilla ship, the great prize aimed at by all adventurers. Soon after, a malignant fever breaking out among the crews, many left the squadron and returned towards Panama, carrying back the Darien Indians, but leaving the Mosquito Indians in the *Cygnet*.

Davis sailed from Guayaquil to careen at the Galapagos islands, which were in the South Pacific what Tortuga was in the North, the harbour and sanctuary of the buccaneers. In returning by Cape Horn, Davis discovered Easter island, and left five of his men and five negro slaves on Juan Fernandez. These men had been stripped at the gambling-table, and were unwilling to return empty-handed. *The Bachelor's Delight* eventually doubled Cape Horn, and he reached the West Indies just in time to avail himself of a pardon offered by royal proclamation.

Dampier reached England in 1691, and having published his travels, was sent out in 1691 by William III. on a voyage of discovery to New Holland, and was wrecked near Ascension. In Queen Anne's reign, during the war of the succession, he commanded two privateers, and cruised against the Spaniards in the South Sea. His objects were to capture the Spanish plate vessels sailing from Buenos Ayres, to lie in wait for the gold ship from Boldivia to Lima, and to seize the Manilla galleon. Off Juan Fernandez he fought a French buccaneer vessel for seven hours, but parted without effecting a capture. So strong were his old *flibustier* habits upon him, that he confesses it with reluctance he attacked any vessel not a Spaniard. Before they reached the proper latitude the Boldivia vessel had sailed.

Captain Stradling, the commander of his companion ship, parted company. A surprise of Santa Maria, in the bay of Panama, failed, but Dampier made a few small prizes. While lying in the gulf of Nicoya, his chief mate, John Clipperton, mutinied, and, seizing his tender, with its ammunition and stores, put out to sea. A worse disappointment awaited the commander—off the Fort de Narida he came suddenly upon the Manilla galleon, and gave her several broadsides before she could clear for action. But even at this disadvantage the Spaniards' twenty-four pounders soon silenced Dampier's five pounders, drove in the rotten planks of his vessel, the *St. George*, and compelled him to sheer off—the galleon's crew quadrupling that of the English.

The men growing despondent and weary of the voyage, Dampier put thirty-four of them into a prize brigantine of seventy tons, and appointed one named Funnel as their commander. Allowing them to sail for India, he with twenty-nine men returned to Peru and plundered the town of Puna. The vessel being no longer fit for sea, they abandoned her at Lobos de la Mar, and embarking in a Spanish brigantine crossed the Pacific. In India, Dampier, having had his commission stolen by some of his deserters, was imprisoned by the Dutch. When he reached England at last, he found that Funnel had returned and published his voyage to the West Indies. A few of his men who had lost their money in gambling remained in *The Bachelor's Delight* with Davis.

It is supposed he now fell into very extreme poverty, for in 1708 we find him acting as pilot to the two Bristol privateers that circumnavigated the globe, and were as successful as he had been unfortunate. At Juan Fernandez the commander, Woodes Rogers, brought off the celebrated Alexander Selkirk, who had been abandoned here four years before, by Dampier's mutinous consort, Captain Stradling, and, by the traveller's advice, the poor outcast was made second mate of the *Duke*. At Guayaquil, where Dampier commanded the artillery, they obtained plunder to the value of £21,000, besides 27,000 dollars, as ransom for the town. Off Cape Lucas they captured a rich Manilla ship, laden with merchandise, and containing £12,000 in gold and silver. They also encountered the great Manilla galleon, but were beaten off after a severe engagement with a loss of twenty-five men. After a run of two months they reached Gualan, and obtained provisions by anchoring under Spanish colours. Visiting Batavia, they waited a long time at the Cape for a home-bound fleet, and in July, 1711, entered the Texel five-and-twenty sail, Dutch and English; and in October sailed up the Thames with booty valued at £150,000. Of the great Dampier we hear no more, and his very burial place is unknown.

Van Horn was originally a common Dutch sailor, who, having, by dint of the prudence of his nation, saved 200 dollars, entered into partnership with a messmate who had laid by the same sum, and, going to France, obtained a privateer's commission, and fitted up a fishing-boat with a crew of thirty men. Cruising first as Dutch, he then purchased a large vessel at Ostend, and, hoisting the French flag, made war on all nations. The French court ordered M. d'Estrees to detain this Flying Dutchman, whose commission had now expired, and a ship was sent for the purpose; but as the commander had no orders to proceed to extremities, and Van Horn was determined not to go alive, he was suffered to escape. Quite undaunted he proceeded to Puerto Rico, entered the bay, sounding his trumpets, and, sending on shore, told the governor that he had come to offer his services to escort the galleons which were then ready to sail. The governor accepted the offer, and Van Horn sailed off with them; but being soon joined by some buccaneer companions, he turned on the prey, seized the richest, sank some others, and pursued the rest. Such was the commencement of this adventurer's career. His after life was worthy of such a beginning.

Van Horn was immensely rich. He usually wore a string of pearls of extraordinary size, and a large ruby of great beauty. His widow lived afterwards at Ostend.

In 1683, Van Horn, who had all his life fought under French colours, though not very scrupulous about what nation a vessel was, so it were rich, having gone to St. Domingo to sell negroes, had his ship confiscated by the Spanish governor. The buccaneer's ungovernable passions could no more brook such an insult than a knight would have borne a blow. buccaneer pride desired revenge; buccaneer cupidity desired redress. Resolved on vengeance, the angry Dutchman hastened to Petit Guaves, and took out a commission from the governor of Tortuga, and at once enrolled 300 of the bravest buccaneers, with a determination of attacking

Vera Cruz. Among his crew were enrolled several of the leading buccaneer chiefs. Grammont, who had lately lost his ship at the Isles des Aves, lately a commander, was now a mere volunteer. Such were the vicissitudes of buccaneer life. Laurence de Graff was also there. He was a Dutchman like Van Horn, but one came from Ostend and the other from Dort. Among the less celebrated were Godefroy and Jonqué. Their numbers soon swelled to 1,200 picked men, in six vessels, under the command of Van Horn and De Graff, who had each a frigate of fifty guns, while the rest had simple barks. Their common aim was Vera Cruz, the emporium of all the riches of New Spain, and they needed no other incitement to urge them to speed and unity.

From some Spanish prisoners they heard that two large vessels laden with cocoa were hourly expected at Vera Cruz from the Caraccas. The buccaneer leaders instantly fitted up two of their largest ships in the Spanish fashion, and, hoisting the Spanish flag, sent them boldly into the harbour, as if just returning as peaceful but armed traders from a long and successful voyage. It was the eve of the Assumption, crowds of sailors and townsmen lined the quays, and the expectant populace cheered the rich merchantmen as they steered with a stately sweep into the haven. The keener eyes, however, soon observed that the Caraccas vessels advanced very slowly, although the wind was good, and their suspicions became excited almost before the buccaneers could work into port. Some even ran to tell the governor that all was not right, but Don Luis de Cordova told them that their fears were foolish, the two vessels he knew by unmistakable signs to be the two vessels he expected; and he returned the same answer to the commander of the fort at St. Jean d'Ulloa, who also sent to bid him be upon his guard.

About midnight the French, under cover of the dark, landed at the old town, about three leagues to the west of the more modern city. They obtained easy access to the place, and surprised the governor in his bed. The drowsy sentinels once overpowered, the small fortress with its twelve guns was in the possession of their men. At every corner pickets were placed. The surprise was so complete, that when the tocsin rang at daybreak, the watchmen being alarmed at some musket shots they heard, they found the town already bound hand and foot. At the first clang of the bell, the garrison rushed out of their barracks, and ranged themselves under their colours, but saw the French already in arms at the head of all the principal streets. They were surrounded and helpless. When the day broke, nobody dare show themselves, for all those who ran out armed were instantly struck down. Sentinels were placed at every door in the principal streets, a barrel of powder with the lid off by their sides, ready to fire the train that connected one with the other at the least signal of danger. We believe it was on this occasion that Van Horn forced a monk into the cathedral, who preached to the people on the vanity of worldly riches, and the necessity of abandoning them to the spoiler. The buccaneers then drove all the Spaniards into their houses, and forced the women and children into the churches. Here they remained, crowded together, weeping and hungry, for three days, while their enemies collected the booty. The buccaneers, now safe, abandoned themselves, as usual, to debauchery and gluttony—some dying from immoderate gluttony. Fortunately for this wretched people, the bishop of the town, happening to be near Vera Cruz at the time, began to treat for their ransom. It was fixed at two million *piastres*, of which a part was paid the very same day—the buccaneers only dispensing with the remaining million, as the Vice-Royal was already approaching the town at the head of a large force. Dangers were now hemming in the Dutchman and his band. About eleven o'clock in the morning, the look-out on the tower of St. Catherine's reported that a fleet of fourteen sail was approaching the city.

The buccaneers, alarmed, sprang to arms. Aghast at this intelligence, the French, dreading to be shut in between two fires, decided upon an immediate retreat. The townspeople, terrified at the prospect of being massacred by their infuriated and despairing enemies, were as apprehensive of danger as the buccaneers themselves. Van Horn embarked with speed all the plate and cochineal, and the more valuable and portable of the spoil, and waited eagerly for the ransom which was now almost in sight. It, however, never arrived, for the drivers of the mules, hearing the firing, halted till the fleet came within sight. The buccaneers had no time to lose, and compensated themselves by carrying off

1,500 slaves to their vessels, which lay moored at some leagues' distance, at Grijaluc, a place of safety.

They spent the night in great disorder, in continual apprehension of being attacked by the Spanish fleet, which was, at the same time, congratulating itself on reaching Vera Cruz unharmed. The danger of the buccaneers was indeed not yet removed, for they had neither water nor sufficient provisions, and some 1,500 prisoners were on board. About these hostages the leaders differed in opinion, and words ran high. The two chiefs fought, and Van Horn received a sword thrust in the arm from De Graff. The several crews took up their captains' quarrels, and would have come to blows, had not De Graff divided the prey, and at once set sail. Van Horn followed, but died on the passage, a gangrene having formed upon a wound at first very slight. He was devotedly beloved by his men, says Charlevoix, though he was in the habit of cutting down any sailor whom he saw flinch at his guns. He left his frigate with his dying breath to Grammont, who reached St. Domingo, after dreadful sufferings, having lost three-fourths of his prisoners by famine—his *patache* being cast away and taken by the Spaniards. De Graff's vessel was also wrecked, but the crew made their way one by one to St. Domingo, where, in spite of the ill reception of the governor, they were welcomed by the hospitality of the inhabitants, who longed to share the treasure of Vera Cruz. The governor, M. de Franquesnoy, without fortress or garrison, and exposed to the inroads of the Spaniards, could make no resistance to these wild refugees, who, on one occasion, hearing that he intended to seize upon part of the Vera Cruz booty, surrounded his house to the number of 120 men, and threatened his life. At this time, a general outbreak of the French was expected.

It was in the very next year that the governor of Carthagena, hearing that Michael le Basque and Jonqué were cruising near his port, sent two vessels against them, one of 48 guns and 300 men, and the other of 40 guns and 250 men, with a small bark as a decoy. The buccaneer chiefs each commanded a vessel of 30 guns and 200 men. They both grappled the Spaniards, held them for an hour and a-half, swept their decks with musketry, tortured them with hand grenades and missiles, and eventually bore them off in triumph. All the Spaniards who were not killed were put on shore with a note to the governor, thanking him for having sent them two such good vessels, as their own had long been unfit for service. They, moreover, promised to wait fifteen days off Carthagena for any other vessel he might wish to get rid of, provided he would send money in them, of which they were in great need.

Chapter 12
Ravenau de Lussan

For the cruises of Grogniet we are indebted to the pages of Ravenau de Lussan, a young soldier, as brave and as sagacious as Xenophon.

On the 22nd of November, 1684, Ravenau de Lussan departed from Petit Guaves with a crew of 120 adventurers, on board of a prize lately taken near Carthagena by Captain Laurence de Graff. Their intention was to join themselves to a buccaneer fleet then cruising near Havannah. They had hitherto acted as convoy to the Lieutenant-General and the intendant of the French colonies, who were afraid of being attacked by the Spanish *piraguas*. Soon after descrying the mainland, they were hailed by a French *tartane*, who, not believing that they were of his own nation, or had a commission from the Count of Tholouse, the Lord High Admiral of France, gave them two guns and commanded them to strike. The buccaneers, thinking they had met a Spaniard, knocked out the head of two barrels of powder, intending to burn themselves and blow up the vessel, rather than be cruelly tortured and hung at the yard-arm with their commissions round their necks. A signal, however, discovered the mistake, and they were soon after joined by the vessels they sought. One of these was the *Mutinous*, formerly the *Peace*, commanded by Captain Michael Landresson, and carried fifty guns. The other was the *Neptune*, formerly the *St. Francis*, and carried forty-four guns. They had both been Spanish *armadillas*, had sallied out of Carthagena to take Captain De Graff, Michael, Quet, and Le Sage, and were themselves captured before the very walls. The four other boats belonged to Rose Vigneron, La Garde, and an "English traitor from Jamaica." They were then watching for the *patache* of Margarita, and a squadron of Spanish ships.

At Curaçoa they sent a boat ashore to ask leave to land and remast Laurence de Graff's vessel that had suffered in a hurricane, but were refused, although they showed their commission, and the men who landed were required to leave their swords at the gate. At Santa Cruz they saluted the fort, and the governor, finding 200 of them roaming about the town, commanded them by drum-beat to return to their ships, offering them two *shallops* for two pieces of eight a man to take them to their ships, but refusing to let them walk through the island. They found the reason of this was that Michael and Laurence's ships had lately taken 200,000 pieces of eight in two Dutch ships near the Havannah. This the freebooters did not touch, being at peace with Holland, but the sailors had stolen it and laid it to the French.

Arriving at Cape La Vella, they placed fifteen sentinels to watch for the *patache*, and sent a boat to the La Hache river to obtain prisoners, but, in spite of various stratagems, failed in the attempt. A dispute now arose among the crews, who were weary of waiting for the *patache*, such disputes invariably breaking out in all seasons of misfortune, when union was more than usually necessary.

Laurence de Graff, whom they accused of fraud, sailed at once for St. Domingo, followed by eighty-seven men in the prize, and Ravenau accompanied Captain Rose and Captain Michael to Carthagena, where they captured seven *piraguas* laden with maize. From the prisoners they heard that two galleons lay in the port, that the fleet was at Porto Bello, and that some ships were about to set out. Soon after this, finding themselves separated from Captain Rose and Michael, Ravenau determined to cross over the continent and get into the South Sea, as he heard a previous expedition some months before had done.

Near Cape Matance a remarkable adventure happened. A Spanish soldier, belonging to the galleons, who had been taken in one of the maize vessels, although treated with every kindness, attempted to drown himself by throwing himself into the sea; his body, however, floated on its back, although he did all he could to drown, till at last, refusing the tackle thrown him from very compassion, he turned himself upon his face, and sank to the bottom. On landing at Golden Island and fixing a flag to warn the Indians, they saw a pennon hoisted upon the shore, and discovered it to belong to three of Captain Grogniet's men, who had refused to follow the expedition, which had just started for the South Sea. Some Indians soon after brought them letters left for the first freebooters who should land, announcing that Grogniet and 170 men had gone into the South Sea, and that 115 Englishmen had preceded them. Soon after Michael and Rose, pursuing a Spanish vessel from Santiago to Carthagena, came in to water, and many of the crew resolved to join their march. 118 men left Michael, and the whole sixty-four of Rose's crew, reimbursing the owners, burnt their vessel and joined them. Ravenau's ship was left in the care of Captain Michael, and the united 264 men now encamped on shore.

On Sunday, March 1st, 1685, after recommending themselves to the Almighty's protection, the expedition set out under the command of Captains Rose, Picard, and Desmarais, with two Indian guides and forty Indian porters.

The country proved so rugged that they could only travel three leagues a day; it was full of mountains, precipices, and impenetrable forests. Great rains fell, and increased the hardship of the journey, and the weight of their arms and ammunition clogged them in ascending the precipices. On descending into the plain, which, though pathless, appeared smooth and level, they found they had to cross the same river forty-four times in the space of only two leagues, and this upon dangerous and slippery rocks. Arriving next day at an Indian *caravansery*, they remained some time shooting deer, monkeys, and wild hogs, flame-coloured birds, wild pheasants, and partridges that abounded in the woods. At length, after six days of painful and wearisome travel, the buccaneers reached the Bocca del Chica river, that empties itself in the South Sea. Here, guided by the Indians, they fell to work making canoes, and bartered knives, needles, and hatchets, with the savages, for maize, potatoes, and bananas. Though well assured that their march had been impossible but for the friendliness of these savages, they still kept on their guard, fearing treachery. "They had," says Ravenau, with a pious sigh of pity, "no sign of religion or of the knowledge of God amongst them, holding that they have communion with the devil," and, indeed, as he declares, after spending solitary nights in the woods, often foretelling events to the Frenchmen, that came true to the minutest detail.

Just as they had finished making their canoes, Lussan heard that the English expedition, under Captain Townley, had captured two provision vessels from Lima, and soon after one of Grogniet's men, who had been lost while hunting, joined them. Hearing that Grogniet awaited them at King's Islands, before he attacked the Peru fleet, they started on the 1st of April in fourteen canoes, with twenty oars a piece, and with a score of Indian guides, who were sanguine of plunder. On the fourth they halted for stragglers, and mended their canoes, much injured by the rocks and flats of the river. In some places they were even forced to carry their boats, or to drag them over fallen trees that blocked the deeper parts by the flood. Several men died, and many were seized with painful diseases, produced by hard food and immersion in the water. They were now reduced to a handful of raw maize a day.

From some Indians sent forward to meet them, they heard that provisions awaited them at some distance, and that 1000 Spaniards had prepared an ambuscade on the river's banks. This, however, they avoided, by stirring only at dark, and then without noise. Surprised one night by the tide, the canoes were driven swiftly down the river, and some of them upset against a snag; the men were saved, but the arms and ammunition were lost. On approaching the Indian ambuscade at Lestocada, they placed their canoes one in the other, and telling the sentinels that they were Indian boats, bringing salt into the South Sea, escaped unhurt. On the 12th it grew so dark that the rowers could hardly see each other, and the heavy rain filled the boat so dangerously as to require two men to bale perpetually. At midnight they entered shouting into the South Sea, and found the provisions awaiting them at Bocca Chica, together with two barks to bring them to the fleet. Resting for a day or two, they repaired to the King's Islands to await the ships. These mountainous islands were the stronghold of Maroon negroes.

On the 22nd, Easter Day, the fleet arrived. It consisted of ten vessels, Captain David's frigate of thirty-six guns, Captain Samms, vice-admiral, with sixteen guns, Captain Townley, with two ships; Captain Grogniet, Captain Brandy, and Captain Peter Henry had also each a vessel, and the two small barks were commanded by quartermasters. Except Grogniet, who was a Frenchman, and David, who was a Fleming, the rest were all Englishmen. Their total force amounted to the number of 1100.

Of the different vessels, Ravenau gives the following laudatory account. The admiral's belonged to the English, who, at St. Domingo, had surprised a long bark, commanded by Captain Tristan, a Frenchman, while waiting for a wind. They took next a Dutch ship, and, changing vessels, went and made several prizes on the coast of Guinea, and, at Castres capturing a vessel from Hamburg, joined this expedition. They were, Ravenau declared, little better than pirates, attacking even, their own countrymen, which no true buccaneer ever did. They had, a short time before, been chastised by a frigate, who, giving them a broadside and a volley of small shot, killed their captain and twenty men.

The vice-admiral's was a vessel they had forced to join them, and had lately taken a ship called the *Sainte Rose*, laden with corn and wine, bound from Truxillo to Panama, and this vessel Davis gave to the French. The others were all prizes captured in the South seas.

The holy alliance soon after took an advice boat that was carrying letters from Madrid to Panama, and despatches from the viceroy of Peru; but both the captain and pilot were bound by an oath rather to die than deliver up their packets or divulge any secret, and had thrown overboard the rolls as well as a casket of jewels. On the same evening 500 men, in twenty-two canoes, embarked to take La Seppa, a small town seven leagues to windward, of Panama. The next day, early in the morning, two armed *piraguas*, manned with Spanish mercenaries, seeing some of the buccaneer canoes and forty-six men approaching them, ran ashore on an island in the bay and prepared to defend themselves. These troops were composed of all nations, and had been sent to defend this coast. One of the "Greek" boats split on the beach. The other the buccaneers took, but the fugitives, planting their flag of defiance on a rising ground, fought desperately, and compelled the freebooters to land on another part of the island and take them in the rear. After an hour's conflict they fled into the woods, leaving thirty-five men dead round their colours and two prisoners.

The attack upon La Seppa proved a failure, for the Sea Rovers had to row two leagues up a river, where they were soon discovered by the sentinels. Yet for all this they fell furiously on, and took it with the loss of only one man; but the booty proved inconsiderable.

The fleet now anchored at the beautiful islands called the Gardens of Panama. All the rich merchants of the city had pleasure-houses here surrounded by rich orchards and arbours of jessamine, and watered by rills and streams. The hungry sailors revelled in the fruits, and reaped plentiful harvests of maize and rice, which Ravenau says "the Spaniards, I believe, did not sow with an intention they should enjoy."

On the 8th of May they passed the old and new towns of Panama in bravado with colours and streamers flying, anchored at Tavoga, another island of pleasure. Having caulked their ships, they sent out a long bark as a scout, and arranged a plan of attacking the Spanish fleet. Davis and Grogniet were to board the admiral; Samms and Brandy the vice-admiral; and Henry and Townley the *patache*; while the armed *piraguas* would hover about and keep off the enemy's fire-ships. The next day they put ashore forty prisoners at Tavoga; and the same day, the sound of cannon, which they could not account for, announced the unobserved arrival of the Spanish fleet at Panama. The whole buccaneer squadron, expecting a battle soon, took the usual oath that they would not wrong one another to the value of a piece of eight, if God was pleased to give them the victory over the Spaniard.

They had scarcely discovered from a Spanish prisoner that the fleet had actually arrived, and was careening and remanning before they ventured out, when Captain Grogniet, raising his flag seven times, gave notice to make quickly ready. The buccaneers doubled the point of the island where they had anchored, and saw seven great vessels bearing down upon them with a bloody flag to the stern and a royal one at their masts. The Frenchmen, mad with joy at the prospect of such prizes, and thinking them already their own, threw their hats into the sea for joy. It was now noon. The rest of the day was spent by both fleets in trying to obtain the weather-gauge, and at sunset they exchanged a broadside. In the night a floating lanthorn deceived the buccaneers, and in the morning they found themselves all still to leeward, with the exception of two vessels which had no guns. Although terribly mauled by the Spanish shot, the English admiral and vice-admiral resolved to die fighting rather than let one vessel be taken, although both being good sailors they might have at once saved themselves. The Spaniards, refusing to board, battered them safely at a distance, and prevented Grogniet from joining them, while Peter Henry's ship, having received more than 120 cannon shot, sheered off and was taken by two *piraguas*.

The long bark, sorely handled, was deserted by her crew, who threw their guns overboard and left the Spanish prisoners to shift for themselves. These wretches attempted to rejoin their countrymen; but the Spanish admiral, mistaking them for enemies, sank them with his cannon.

Peter Henry's vessel reached the isle of St. John de Cueblo, twenty-four leagues from Panama, with five feet of water in the hold, and having repaired, rejoined his fleet in about a fortnight. They found that Captain Davis had been hard plied, having received two shots in his rudder, and six of his men were wounded, but only one killed. Captain Samms had been no less put to it. His poop was half swept off, and he had received several shots between wind and water. He had had three men wounded, and his mate had had his head carried off by a cannon ball. The smaller vessels had lost no men, but had a few wounded. The Spanish admiral, they found, had carried 56 guns, the vice-admiral 40, the *patache* 28, and the conserve 18. The fire-ships had also been mounted with cannon to conceal their real purpose. On considering the disparity of force, and the little loss his companions received, Ravenau seems to have no doubt that if they could have intercepted the Spaniards before they entered Panama, and could have got the weather-gauge of them, he should have returned through the straits with wealth enough to have lived all his life at ease, and have escaped three more years of danger and fatigue.

Not the least discouraged by this repulse, the freebooters landed 300 men, from five canoes, to surprise the town of Puebla Nueva. Rowing two leagues up a very fine river, they captured one sentinel, but another escaped and gave the alarm. They found the place deserted, but took a ship on their way back.

A quarrel broke out here between the French and the English. The latter, superior in numbers, would have taken Grogniet's ship away, and given it to Townley, had not the Frenchmen put on a determined front. Refusing to acknowledge this assumption of dominion, 130 of them banded themselves apart, and Grogniet's crew made them altogether 330 in number. Says Lussan:

> Besides national animosity, one of the chief reasons that made us disagree was their impiety against our religion, for they made no scruple when they got into a church to cut down the arms of a crucifix with their sabres, or to shoot them down with their fusils and pistols, bruising and maiming the images of the saints with the same weapons, in derision to the adoration we Frenchmen paid unto them. And it was chiefly from these horrid disorders that the Spaniards equally hated us all, as we came to understand by divers of their letters that fell into our hands.

We have no doubt at all that, but for these "horrible disorders," the Spaniards would have considered the death of their children and the loss of their money as real compliments.

Returning to the isle of St. John, both nations in separate encampments began to cut down acajou trees to hollow into canoes in place of those they had lost in the fight.

These trees were so large that one trunk would hold eighty men. Afraid of the English, the Frenchmen placed a sentinel in a high tree on the sea-shore, to watch both the camps, and also to give the signal if any Spanish vessel approached. A buccaneer ship putting into the harbour, they discovered it to be commanded by Captain Willnett. Forty of his crew left him, and joined the English, but eleven Frenchmen remained with Grogniet. This vessel had just captured a corn ship near Sansonnat, and hearing of other brothers being on the south coast, had set out in search of them. The Frenchmen were now very short of food, having little powder, and not daring to waste it upon deer and monkeys when Spaniards were at hand, for in fifteen days the Englishmen had eaten or driven away all the turtle. They were reduced to an allowance of two turtle for 330 men in forty-eight hours. Many of the men wandering into the woods ate poisonous fruits. Others were bitten by serpents, and died enduring terrible pains, ignorant of the fruit which is an antidote to such wounds. Several were devoured by crocodiles.

While in this strait, the English sent a quartermaster to ask the French to join in an expedition against the town of Leon, being too weak by themselves. The wounded vanity of the French contended with their hunger. They knew that the English had plenty of provisions, brought in Willnett's ship, and thirty men, weary of fasting, left Grogniet and joined Davis. But Ravenau's party having but one ship asked for another, in order that they might keep together, and this being refused, broke off the treaty.

As soon as the Leon party had embarked, the French, commanded by Captain Grogniet, also started with 120 men in five canoes, leaving 200 in the island to build more canoes, and join them on the continent. Coming on the mainland to a cattle station, and afterwards to a sugar plantation, they took several prisoners whom they found ignorant of the disjunction of the French and English. Sending back a canoe with provisions to the island, they landed again about forty leagues to leeward of Panama, and at cock-crowing surprised a Spanish *estantia*, and took fifty prisoners, including a young man and woman of rank who promised ransom. These they carried to the island Ignuana, and received the money after a fortnight's delay.

On their return to St. John's they found that 100 men had been to Puebla Nueva, and taken the place, although discovered by the sentinels, and had remained there two days in spite of continual attacks. The commander of the place had come with a trumpet to speak to them, and inquired why, being English, they fought under French colours. But they, not satisfying his curiosity, fiercely told him to be gone from whence he came. Eight of them, having strayed from the main body, had been bravely set on by 150 Spaniards, who killed two of them, but, with all the advantage they had of numbers, could not hinder the other six from recovering the main guard, who fought and retreated with extraordinary vigour.

Once more reunited, these restless Norsemen started to the mainland in six canoes, 140 in number, to visit the sugar plantation near St. Jago, where they had been before. Two men were sent to the cattle station to obtain the ransom of the master, whom they kept prisoner, and others visited the sugar works in search of some cauldrons, which they needed; and, fired at hearing the governor of St. Jago, with 800 men, had visited the place since their departure, they sent to dare him to meet them.

Careening their ships and taking in water and wood, they would at once have sailed away, but were detained by eighteen days' rain, during which time the sun did not once appear. This part of the South Sea was proverbial for continual rains, and was called by the Spaniards "The Droppings." Ravenau says:

> These rains not only rotted their sails, but produced dysentery among the men, and bred worms, half a finger long and as thick as a quill, between their skin and their flesh.

Soon after leaving the island they were nearly cast away in a dreadful storm, and were compelled to repair their shattered sails with shirts and drawers, wherewith they were already very indifferently provided.

At Realegua, where there was a volcano burning, they landed 100 men in four canoes, and obtained some prisoners by surprising a *hatto*. They found the English had already taken Leon and burnt Realegua. In spite of Spanish reinforcements from eight neighbouring towns, they stayed at Leon three whole days, and challenged the Spaniards to meet them in the Race savannah. But the Spaniards replied, they were not yet all come together; "which means," says our friend Ravenau, "that they were not yet six to one." While here, one of their quartermasters, a Catalonian by birth, fled to the Spaniards, and compelled the French to abandon a design on the town of Granada. At Realegua six men tried to swim ashore to fill some water casks, in spite of the Spaniards on the beach, and one of them was drowned in the attempt. They landed at the port, and found the churches and houses and three entrenchments half burnt. Surprising the sentinels of Leon, they discovered that in spite of a garrison of 2000 men, the inhabitants, hearing the buccaneers had landed, were hiding their treasure. They soon after put to flight a detachment of horse, and took the captain prisoner.

A few days after this 150 men left the vessels to take a small town of Puebla Vieja, near Realegua, which they found still deserted. It had become the custom now among the Spaniards, when the freebooters had frequently taken the same place, for the prelate to excommunicate it, and henceforward not even to bury their dead there. Discovered by the sentinel, the buccaneers found the enemy entrenched in the church of Puebla, and about

150 horse in the market-place. A few discharges drove the horsemen away, and the defenders of the church fled through a door in the vestry. Staying a day and a-half in the captured town, the freebooters carried away all the provisions they could find on horses and on their own backs, taking with them a Spanish gentleman who promised ransom. The next day a Spanish officer brought a letter signed by the vicar-general of the province, written by order of the general of Costa Rica, declaring that France and Spain were at peace and leagued to fight the infidel, and offering them a passage to the North Sea in his Catholic Majesty's galleons. To this they returned a threatening answer, and, putting thirty prisoners ashore, proceeded to careen their ships, the Spaniards lighting fires along the coast as they departed.

An expedition, with fifty men in three canoes, against the town of Esparso failed, but the hungry men killed and ate the horses of the sentinels whom they took prisoners, for they had now tasted hardly anything for four days. At Caldaria they visited a bananery, and loaded their canoes with the fruit, and at Point Borica stored their boats with cocoa-nuts, which Ravenau takes care to describe as nuts unknown in Europe. Laden with gold, but nevertheless, like Midas, starving for want of food, they landed sixty men in three canoes and took some prisoners at a *hatto* which they surrounded, but finding they were very near Chiriquita, and a garrison of 600 men, retreated to their ships, forcing their way through 400 horse who reviled them, and challenged them to revisit the town, which they took care soon after to do.

On the 5th of January, 1686, they started 230 men in eight canoes to revisit this place, going ashore at night without a guide, and marched till daylight without being discovered. On the 7th they hid all day in a wood, and as night approached again pushed forward, the 8th they spent also hid in a covert, and then found they had gone ashore on the wrong side of the river. Fatigued as they were, they waited till night, and then, returning to their canoes, crossed the river. Surprising the watch, they found the Spaniards, even on the former alarm, had removed all their treasure. On the 9th, they reached Chiriquita two hours before day, and found the inhabitants asleep. The townsmen had been two days disputing with one another about the watches, and the buccaneers ridiculed them by telling them they had come to spare them the trouble. The soldiers they discovered playing in the court of guard, and they found a small frigate ashore at the mouth of the river.

About noon, five of the buccaneers, straggling into the suburbs to plunder a house and obtain prisoners, were set upon by an ambuscade of 120 men. Finding no hope of escape, rather than be taken alive they resolved to sell their lives dearly, and back to back fought the enemy for an hour and a-half, when only two remained capable of resistance. The main body, who thought they had been simply firing at a mark, came to their relief, upon which the enemy at once fled. Of this skirmish, at which Lussan was present, he says:

> This succour coming in so seasonably, did infallibly save our lives; for the enemy having already killed us two men and disabled another, it was impossible we should hold out against such a shower of bullets as were poured in upon us from all sides; and so I may truly say I escaped a scouring, and that without receiving as much as one wound, but by a visible hand of protection from heaven. The Spaniards left thirty men dead upon the spot; and thus we defended ourselves as desperate men, and, to say all in a word, like freebooters.

The buccaneers having burnt all the houses in the town, fearing a night attack, retreated into the great church, exchanging a shot now and then with the enemy. This town was built on the savannahs, and surrounded by *hattoes*, its chief trade being in tallow and leather. The men rested here till the tenth, rejoicing in plenty of provision after nearly four days' fast. They then removed their prisoners to an island in the river, where the Spaniards could only approach them openly in a fleet of *shallops*. The enemy, driven out of an ambuscade, sent to demand the prisoners, saying they would recover them or perish in the attempt; but grew pacified when Grogniet declared they should all be put to death if a single bullet was fired. Driving off a guard of 100 men, they also plundered the stranded vessel, and discovered by the letters that the admiral of the Peru fleet had lately been lost with his 400 men, by his vessel being struck by a thunderbolt. On the sixteenth, obtaining a ransom for their prisoners, they returned to the island of St. John.

The Spaniards, from fear of the freebooters, having put a stop to their navigation, no ships were to be captured, and having no sails, and their ship being useless without them, the French began to cut down trees and build *piraguas*. On the 27th they descried seven sail at sea, and put out five canoes to reconnoitre, suspecting it was the vanguard of the Peruvian fleet. Soon after discerning twelve *piraguas* and three long barks coasting in the distance, they retreated to their docks in the river, and ran their bark ashore to render it useless to the Spaniards, placing an ambuscade of 150 men along the banks. The enemy, suspecting a trick, disregarded the two canoes that were sent to draw them into the snare, but commenced to furiously cannonade the grounded ship, which contained nothing but a poor cat, and then, perceiving her empty, bravely boarded and burnt her for the sake of the iron work, and soon afterwards sailed away. They learnt afterwards that the Chiriquita prisoners had reported that they had fortified the island, and the fleet had been sent to land field-pieces and demolish the works. This alarm of the Spaniards had been encouraged by the buccaneers having purposely asked at Chiriquita for masons, and obliged the prisoners to give bricks as part of the ransom.

On the 14th of March, they left the island of St. John, in two barks, a half galley of forty oars, ten large *piraguas*, and ten smaller canoes, built of *mapou* wood. Taking a review of their men, fourteen of whom had died in February, they found they had lost thirty since the departure of the English. To prepare for a long-planned attack on Granada, a half galley and four canoes were despatched to get provisions at Puebla Nueva. Entering the river by moonlight, the buccaneers approached within pistol shot of a small frigate, a long bark, and a *piragua*, which they supposed to be their old English allies, but were received by a splashing volley of great and small shot that killed twenty men. The ships were, in fact, a detachment of the Spanish fleet left to guard some provision ships lading for Panama. Quickly recovering from their surprise, the adventurers, though without cannon, fought them stiffly for two hours, killing every man that appeared in the shrouds, and bringing down one by one the grenadiers from the main-top. But as soon as the moon went down, the buccaneers sheered off with four dead men and thirty-three wounded, waiting for daylight to have their revenge. In the mean time, the enemy had retired under cover of an entrenchment, to which the country people, attracted during the night by the firing, had crowded in arms; against these odds, the buccaneers were unwillingly compelled to retire, and soon rejoined their canoes at *St. Peter's*.

Landing at a town ten leagues leeward of Chiriquita, they obtained no provisions, and had, with the loss of two men, to force their way through an ambuscade of 500 Spaniards. Rejoining their barks they spent some days in hunting in the Bay of Boca del Toro, and obtaining nourishing food for the wounded men. Their next enterprise was against the town of Lesparso, which they found abandoned. While lying in the bay they were joined by Captain Townley and five canoes, who, with his 115 men, begged to be allowed to join in the expedition against Granada. Remembering the old imperious dealing of the English, the French at first, to frighten them, boarded their canoes, and offered to take them away. Says Lussan:

> Then we let the captain know we were *honester* men than he (a curious dispute), and that though we had the upper hand, yet we would not take the advantage of revenging the injuries they had done us, and that we would put him and all his men in possession of what we had taken from them four or five hours before.

The men were then assembled in a bananery island, in the bay, and an account taken of their supply of powder, for fear any should expend it in hunting. Orders were also enacted that any brother found guilty of cowardice, violence, drunkenness, disobedience, theft, or straggling from the main body, should lose his share of the booty of Granada.

On the 25th the French and English departed in *piraguas* and canoes, 345 men, and landed on a flat shore, following a good guide, who led them for two days through a wood. They were, however, seen by some fishermen, who alarmed the town, which had already received intelligence of their march from Lesparso. Great fatigue obliged them to rest on the evening of the 9th at a sugar plantation belonging to a knight of St. James, whom they were too tired to pursue.

On the 10th they saw two ships on the distant lake of Nicaragua, carrying off all the wealth of the town to a neighbouring island. From a prisoner they learnt that the inhabitants were strongly entrenched in the market-place, guarded by fourteen pieces of cannon and six *patereroes*, and that six troops of horse were waiting to attack them in the rear.

This information, which would have damped the courage of any but buccaneers, drove them only the faster to the charge. At two in the afternoon they entered the town, over the dead bodies of a party that had awaited them in ambuscade, and sent a party to reconnoitre the fort. The skirmishers, after a few shots, returned, and reported that there were three streets leading to the fort, so they all resolved to concentrate in one of these.

Lussan describes the scene, of which he was an eye-witness, too graphically to need curtailing.

> After we had exhorted one another to fall on bravely, we advanced at a good round pace towards the said fortification. As soon as the defendants saw us within a good cannon-shot of them, they fired furiously upon us; but observing that at every discharge of their great guns, we saluted them down to the ground, in order to let their shot fly over us, they bethought themselves of false priming them, to the end we might raise our bodies, after the sham was over, and so to be really surprised with their true firing. As soon as we discovered this stratagem, we ranged ourselves along the houses, and having got upon a little ascent, which was a garden plot, we fired upon them from thence so openly for an hour and a-half that they were obliged to quit their ground, which our hardy boys, who were got to the foot of their walls, contributed yet more than the other by pouring in hand-grenades incessantly upon them, so that at last they betook themselves to the great church or tower, but they wounded us some men. As soon as our people, who had got upon the said eminence, perceived that the enemy fled, they called to us to jump over the walls, which we had no sooner done than they followed us, and thus it was that we made ourselves masters of the town, from whence they fled, after having lost a great many men. We had on our side but four men killed

and eight wounded, which in truth was very cheap. When we got into the fort we found it to be a place capable of containing 6,000 fighting men; it was encompassed with a wall the same as our prisoners gave us an account of. It was pierced with many holes, to do execution upon the assailants, and was well stored with arms. That part of it which looked towards the street, through which we attacked it, was defended by two pieces of cannon and four *patereroes*, to say nothing of several other places made to open in the wall through which they thrust instruments made on purpose to break the legs of those who should be adventurous enough to come near it; but these, by the help of our grenadiers, we rendered useless to them. After we had sung *Te Deum* in the great church, and set four sentinels in the tower, we fixed our court of guard in the strong-built houses that are also enclosed within the place of arms, and there gathered all the ammunition we could get, and then we went to visit the houses, wherein we found nothing but a few goods and some provision, which we carried into our court of guard.

The next evening 150 men were despatched to a distant sugar plantation, to capture some ladies of rank and treasure; but on the next day a monk came to treat about the ransom they would require to spare the town. Unluckily the Spaniards had captured a buccaneer straggler, who told them that his companions never meant to burn the place, but intended to stop there some months, and return into the North Sea, by the lake of Nicaragua. The freebooters, being refused the ransom, set fire to the houses in revenge. Had the French indeed had but canoes to capture the two ships in the island and secure the treasure, they would undoubtedly have carried out this plan. To a handful of hungry men, without food and without ships, even the gardens of Granada appeared hateful.

On leaving the town the buccaneers took with them one piece of cannon and four *patereroes*, drawn by oxen, having to fight their way for twenty leagues to the shore over the savannah, surrounded by 2,500 Spaniards thirsting for their blood. In every place the enemy fled at the first discharge of their pieces. From a prisoner they learnt that a million and a-half pieces of eight, kept for ransom, was buried in the wall of the fort, but the men felt no disposition to return. They were soon obliged to leave their cannon behind, the oxen choked with the dust, worn out with the heat, and dying of thirst; but the *patereroes* were still dragged on by the mules. At the little village of Massaya, near the lake, they were received with open arms by the Indians, who only entreated them not to burn their huts.

All the water in the village had been tainted by the Spaniards, but the natives brought them as much as they needed. While they lay here a Spanish monk came to them to obtain the release of a priest who had been taken armed and with pockets filled with poisoned bullets. They refused to surrender him but in exchange for one of their own men. The next day, passing from the forest into a plain, they were attacked by 500 men, drawn up upon an ascent, and commanded by their Spanish deserter. Each party displayed bloody flags, but the vanguard beat them with wonderful bravery, and took fifty horses. The enemy fled, leaving their arms and the wounded, and turned out to be auxiliaries from Leon. In three days more they reached the beach, and, resting several days to salt provisions, sailed to Realegua, where they collected provisions and 100 horses. They then burnt down the borough of Ginandego, in spite of 200 soldiers and an entrenchment, because the inhabitants had defied them to come. Even here they were, however, much straitened for provision, the *corregidor* of Leon having desired all men to burn the provisions wherever the buccaneers landed.

The same day at noon the sentinels rang the alarm bell in the steeple, and gave notice that 800 men from Leon were advancing across the savannah to fight them. The men, bustling out of their houses, marched at once, 150 in number, under their red colours, and drove off the enemy after a few shots.

There now arose a dissension in the *flibustier* councils. 148 Frenchmen and all the English, headed by Captain Townley, determined to go up before Panama to see if the navigation had yet been resumed. 148 Frenchmen, under Captain Grogniet, resolved to go lower westward and winter upon an island, waiting for some abatement of the rains and southerly winds. The barks, canoes, and provisions were then divided, and the *chirurgeons* brought in the accounts of the wounded and crippled. There were found to be four men crippled and six hurt: to the latter were given 600 pieces of eight a man, and to the former 1000, being exactly all the money then in store.

Ravenau joined the Panama division, which, touching again at their old quarters on the island of St. John, took off a prisoner who had made his escape when they were last there, and proceeded to land and capture the town of Villia with 160 men. Marching with great rapidity they reached the town an hour after sunrise, and surprising the inhabitants at mass, took 300 prisoners. They then attempted to capture three barks lying in the river, but the Spanish sailors sank one and destroyed the rigging of the other two. Gathering together all the merchandise of the town left by the fleet, the invaders found it to amount to a million and a-half, valued at 15,000 pieces of eight in good silver. Much treasure was, however, buried, the Spaniards submitting to death rather than confess their hiding-places.

The next day a party of fourscore men were sent to drive the pack horses to the river side to load the booty in two Spanish canoes. They despaired of obtaining any ransom for the town, as the *alcalde* major had sent to them to say that the only ransom he should give was powder and ball, whereof he had a great deal at their service; that as to the prisoners, he should entrust them to the hands of God, and that his people were getting ready as fast as they could, to have the honour of seeing them. Upon receiving this daring answer, the buccaneers, in a rage, fired the town and marched to the river. As the Spanish ambuscades prevented the boats coming up to meet them, the adventurers put nine men on board the boats, the men marching by their side to guard them from attack. On the other side, unknown to them and hidden by the trees, marched 900 Spaniards. When they had proceeded about a league, an impassable thicket compelled them to make a diversion of some 200 paces, an accident which involved the loss of the whole plunder of Villia.

Before they left the boats, the captain ordered the crews to stop a little higher up, where the three Spanish barks lay, and endeavour to bring them away. On arriving there they were surprised by an ambuscade, and as they defended themselves against the Spaniards, the current drove them on beyond the three barks and far from the main body. Seeing them now helpless, the enemy discharged sixty musket shots at them, and killed four men and wounded one. The rest, abandoning the canoes, swam to the other side of the river, while a dozen Indians wading in brought the boat to the Spaniards; cutting off the head of a wounded man and setting it on a pole by the shore.

The buccaneers who did not hear the firing, were astonished on returning to the river to see no canoes, and while waiting for them to come up, for they supposed they were behind, the rowers, who had escaped, broke breathless through the thicket, and told their story. Luckily in their flight through the wood they had discovered the rudders and sails of the three barks, in which the buccaneers at once embarked, and sent fifty-six men on shore to recover the fittings, agreeing that each should fire three guns as a signal. Soon after they had landed, the report of about 500 guns was heard, but before they could reach the enemy the Spaniards had fled. Going ashore the next day, they found the two canoes dashed to pieces, and the bodies of the dead much mutilated—the head of one set upon a pole, and the body of another burnt in the fire. These objects so enraged the buccaneers, that they instantly cut off four of their prisoners' heads, and set them on poles in the same place. Their own dead they carried with them to bury by the sea-side—the fitting burial-place for seamen. Three times they had to land to break through ambuscades at the river's mouth, in the last attack losing three men. With a Spaniard who came on board, they agreed for a ransom of 10,000 pieces of eight, but threatened to kill all the prisoners if the money was not brought in within two days. Upon the stubborn *alcalde* seizing the hostages who were sent ashore to obtain money to release their wives, the buccaneers cut off the heads of two prisoners and sent them to the town, declaring that if no ransom was paid, they would serve the rest the same, and having put the women on an island, would come and capture the *alcalde*. The same evening came in a promise to pay all the ransoms, and to bring besides, every day while they stayed, ten oxen, twenty sheep, and 200 lbs. of meal. For a buccaneer's fire-arms which the enemy pretended to have lost (for the Spaniards were fond of French arms), they paid 400 pieces of eight. They also bought one of the captured barks for 600 pieces of eight and 100 lbs. of nails, of which the adventurers stood in great need, but her tackle and anchors were not surrendered. They obtained also a *flibustier* passport that the bark should not be retaken, although her cargo might be confiscated. Having then obtained a parting present of 100 salted beeves, from this long-suffering place the French set sail. Afraid to land on the continent, which was guarded by 4,000 men, they abstained, till, nearly dying with thirst, they made a descent with 200 sailors, driving off the Spaniards, whom they found lying on the grass about 100 paces from the sea. Lussan says they saw "we were a people who would hazard all for a small matter."

Landing at midnight at a small island near Cape Pin, they were discovered by the pearl divers, but still contrived to capture a ship at daybreak. From their prisoners they heard that the Spaniards had lately defeated a party of thirty-six, French and English, from Peru, who were attempting to pass into the North Sea by the river Bocca del Chica. Two parties of English, forty each, on their way into the South Sea, had also been massacred all but four, who were prisoners at Panama. To balance these ill omens, tidings of prizes reached the buccaneers on every hand. A bark was lying in the Bocca del Chica river, waiting for 800 lbs. of gold from the mines to bring to Panama. Two ships laden with meal and money for the garrison of Lima were also expected; and from a prisoner (a spy, it afterwards appeared), captured at the King's Islands, they learnt that two merchant barks and a *piragua* with sixty Indians lay in the river of Seppa, besides a frigate and scout galley under the guns of Panama.

Much in want of vessels, and not suspecting the prisoner, four canoes were sent at once to cut out the barks of Panama, the "Greek" soldier going with them readily as a guide. They arrived two hours before daylight, and the moon shining very bright they waited for a cloud to obscure it, seeing, as they thought, the anticipated prize lying near with her sails loose. By mere chance, the adventurers, to waste no time, pursued a vessel just leaving the port, thinking it was the scout galley, and took it without a shot. Upon examination, the captain confessed their guide was the commander of a Greek *piragua*, and had been promised a large reward by the governor of Panama to betray them into his hands. The ship they saw was a mere sham of boards and sails, built upon firm land, only a pistol shot from the port. They supposed that the buccaneers, eager to take her, would row up, and so drive their canoes far on shore, and hoped to overpower them before they got off. The Greek captain being at once identified as a spy, was, says Ringrose, "sent to that world where he had designed to send us." The fleet then proceeded to take the islands of Ottoqua and Tavoga, losing two men in the Greek's second ambuscade at Seppa, but capturing in their way a bark from Nata laden with provisions, after a few discharges of musketry, the Spanish captain swimming to shore. From Tavoga they sent a message to the governor of Panama, to say that if he did not at once surrender his five English and French captives, they would at once put to death fifty Spanish prisoners.

They then anchored again at the King's Islands, and sent a galley and four canoes up the Bocca Chica river to see if the Indians were at peace with Spain or not, and to destroy an ambuscade of 100 Spaniards, who they heard were lying in wait on the banks for thirty freebooters, on their way from the South to the North Pacific. Carried swiftly up the river by the current, the guide, compelling them to row faster just before daybreak, brought them, much to their astonishment, at a bend of the river, opposite the camp fires of the enemy. The guide being hailed, replied they were from Panama; and being asked the name of the commander, hesitated about a fitting title, and received a volley in return. The buccaneers driving off the enemy with two *patereroes*, passed them quickly, and, anchoring out of reach, waited for the ebb tide to return. Putting all their men under deck, the adventurers returned about an hour before daylight, saluting them with four *paterero* shots as they passed, and receiving no injury in return. The next day, taking a small Indian vessel, the buccaneers landed lower down the river, intending to take the Spanish entrenchment in the rear; but seeing the enemy putting out a *piragua* to attack their galley, they returned in great haste and landed opposite the Spanish court of guard, killing a great many men and driving out the rest. They also shot an Indian, who, mistaking them for Spaniards, followed them and reviled them as they were re-embarking. The prisoners told them that the neighbouring town of Terrible was prepared for their coming. A letter to the camp-master of Terrible was found in the entrenchment. It concluded thus:

I have sent you 300 men to defeat these enemies of God and goodness; be sure to keep upon your watch; be afraid of being surprised, and your men will infallibly be gainers in defeating of them.

The prisoners also put them on their guard as to many ambuscades and secret dangers. Having burnt the guard-house, and carried off the *piragua* with some pounds of gold-dust, the buccaneers departed, dismissing the Indians to propitiate the nation who had received commission from the President of Panama to arm canoes against them. While descending the river, having put some Spanish prisoners on deck to deceive the Indians, some natives came and brought gold-dust to them, taking them for friends. A few days after this, forty Spanish prisoners put ashore at the King's Islands, met accidentally with some canoes, and escaped to Panama.

The French were now again surprised as they had been before, three of the enemy's vessels approaching under cover of an island. By venturing a dangerous passage between the island of Tavaguilla and a rock the buccaneers at last obtained the weather-gauge. The fight lasted till noon, and the Spaniards were driven off in all attempts at boarding. Throwing grenades into the biggest ship, one of them set fire to some loose powder and burnt a great many men; and during this confusion, the adventurers boarded the enemy, who rallied in the stern, and made a vigorous resistance, but at last begged for quarter. The second was also at the same time carried and taken. The third, a kind of galley, pursued by three buccaneer vessels, ran ashore and staved to pieces, few of the crew escaping, not more than a dozen, Ringrose thinks. In the frigate eighty men were killed and wounded out of 120 on board. The second ship had only eighteen unhurt out of eighty. All the officers were killed and wounded, and the captain received no less than five musket shots. He was the soldier that had received five wounds resisting them at Puebla Nueva, and he had also planned the ambuscade at Villia.

While busily employed in splicing the rigging and throwing the dead overboard, two more sail were seen bearing down from Panama. The English instantly put up Spanish colours to allure them, and placed the French and English beneath them. As the foe drew near, they received a volley, and, firing hurriedly, at once fled to the frigate which they supposed still theirs. The frigate replied by some grenades, which sent one to the bottom, and the *piragua* boarded the other, and, finding four packs of halters on board, put all the crew to death in revenge. They had been directed to spare none but the buccaneer surgeons, and to send troops of horse to cut off all that escaped in canoes. On the very next day they took a *shallop* from Panama which the president had sent to pull up an anchor that the adventurers had left in the bay. Only one buccaneer was killed in the fight, but Captain Townley and twenty men were wounded, and most of these died, for the Spaniards poisoned their bullets. They now sent a prisoner to the president, demanding his five captives and medicines for the use of his own people. The messenger was also told to complain heavily of the massacre of the three parties at Darien.

To these remonstrances the officer sent the following answer:

Gentlemen, I wonder that you, who should understand how to make war, should require those men of me that are in our custody. Your rashness hath something contrary to the civility wherewith you ought to treat those people that were in your power. If you do not use them well, God will perhaps be on our side.

To this they returned a threat of beheading all their prisoners without mercy; and having done this, sailed at once to the isles of Pericòs, fearing the Spanish fire-ships. The Bishop of Panama, who, they knew, had stirred up the president to war, sent a letter, entreating them to show mercy, saying the president had the king's orders to restore no prisoners, and that the Englishmen, having turned Roman Catholics, did not wish to leave Panama.

Upon this the buccaneers sent the president twenty Spaniards' heads in a canoe, threatening to kill all the rest, if the prisoners were not restored by the next day.

Very early the next morning came the prisoners, four Englishmen and one Frenchman, with medicines for the wounded, the president leaving to their honour to give as many men as they chose in exchange. They at once sent a dozen of the most wounded on shore, accusing the president of being the murderer of the twenty they had killed, and threatening the death of the rest, unless 20,000 pieces of eight were paid for their ransom. The Spaniards at first tried to make it only 6,000; but when the buccaneers hung out their main flag, fired a gun, and prepared to enter the port, they hung out a white flag at a bastion, and promised the money shortly. The next day a Knight of Malta came in a bark with the money, and received the prisoners. While staying at Ottoqua to victual their ships, the Spaniards landed at night and murdered their Indian guides. The day after the French chased a provision vessel to the very guns of Panama, when the garrison hoisted the Burgundian flag on the bastion, and by mistake fired upon their own vessel, which the buccaneers took. Putting nineteen prisoners on shore, they again attempted to surprise Villia, but failed, finding all the people in arms, and a reinforcement of 600 men newly come from Panama. They next took the town of St. Lorenzo, and surprising it at twilight, burnt it. They learned the Spaniards had orders to drive away the cattle from the sea-shore, to lay ambuscades, and to obtain from women intelligence of the buccaneers' movements. A dreadful storm which overtook the fleet in the Bay of Bocca del Toro induced Lussan, with a naïve philanthropy, to tell his readers:

> If you would enter into it with safety, you must keep the whip of your rudder to starboard, because it is dangerous to keep to the east side.

While here the same writer gives us the following trait of *flibustier* manners:

> On the 25th, being Christmas-day, after we had, according to custom, said our prayers in the night, one of our quartermasters being gone ashore in order to take care about our eating some victuals (for our ships being careening all our provisions were then put out), one of our prisoners, who served us as cook, stabbed him with a knife in six several places, wherewith crying out, he was presently relieved, and the assassin punished with death.

On the 1st of January, 1687, leaving their ships in the bay of Caldaira, the buccaneers embarked 200 men in canoes and crossed to the island of La Cagna.

Their treacherous guide, under the pretence of hiding them in a covert, led them into a marsh, where the mud, in the soundest places, rose above their middles; five men sinking up to their chins were dragged out with ropes tied to the mangrove branches. The men, anxious for escape, lifted up their guide to the top of a tree, to discover by the moonlight where sound land commenced. But he, once at liberty, skipped like a monkey from tree to tree, railing at them and deriding their helplessness. They spent the whole night in marching a hundred paces round this marsh, and groped out at daybreak, bedaubed from head to toe, with their fire-arms loaded with mud. Says Lussan:

> When we were in a condition to reflect a little upon ourselves, and that we saw 200 men in the same habit, all so curiously equipped, there was not one of us who forgot not his toil to laugh at the posture he found both himself and the rest in.

Inveighing against their guide, they returned to their canoes, and proceeded two leagues up a river to an entrenchment, where they found the remains of two vessels the Spaniards had some time before burnt, at the approach of Betsharp, an English freebooter. Guided by the barking of dogs, they surprised the borough of Santa Catalina, and, mounting sixty men on horses, entered Nicoya and drove out the enemy, carrying off the governor's plate and movables. They found here some letters from the President of Panama, describing the doings of "these new Turks," how they had landed at places where the sea was so high that no sentinels had been placed, and passed through the woods like wild beasts. The letters stated how much the Spaniards had been astonished by the buccaneer mode of attack—"briskly falling on, singing, dancing, as if they had been going to a feast;" they were described also as "those enemies of God and His saints who profane His churches and destroy His servants." In one battle, it says, being blocked up, "they became as mad dogs. Whenever these irreligious men set their feet on land they always win the victory."

Landing at Caldaira the sentinels set fire to the savannahs, through which they marched to Lesparso, and towards Carthage, but retired, hearing of 400 men and an entrenchment. Hiding five men in the grass, they captured a Spanish trooper, who had reviled them, and putting him to the rack, laughing at his grimaces of pain, heard that Grogniet was in the neighbourhood, and soon after they heard cannons fired off, and were joined by him in three canoes.

He now told them his adventures at Napalla. Three sailors, corrupted by the Spaniards, who had taken them prisoners, persuaded him on his return to visit a gold mine, fourteen leagues from the sea-shore. They luckily got there before the ambuscade, and took some prisoners and a few pounds of gold, but 450 lbs. weight had been removed an hour before. At their return they found the traitors and prisoners all escaped. He then landed at Puebla Vieja and attacked an ambuscade and entrenchment of 300 men. Half of these fled, half were made prisoners, and their three colours taken, the freebooters losing only three men. Eighty-five of his men then determined to visit California, and he and his sixty men to return to Panama.

Grogniet now consented to join in the French expedition, and, after taking Queaquilla, to force a way to the North Sea. They landed and burnt Nicoya a third time, and Lussan treats us here with an amusing piece of buccaneer superstition. He says:

> Though we were *forced* to chastise the Spaniards in this manner, we showed ourselves very exact in the preservation of the churches, into which we carried the pictures and images of the saints which we found in particular houses, that they might not be exposed to the rage and burning of the English, who were not much pleased with these sorts of precautions; they being men that took more satisfaction and pleasure to see one church burnt than all the houses of America put together. But as it was our turn now to be the stronger party, they durst do nothing that derogated from that respect we bore to all those things.

On their return the French had to force their way through burning savannahs, but got safe to their ships, putting next day forty prisoners on shore who were too chargeable to keep.

A new division now arose between the English and French, and the former insisting on the first prize taken, the two parties again separated, Grogniet staying with the former: making in all 142 men, Ravenau's party being 162, in a frigate and long bark. Both vessels now tried to outsail each other and reach Queaquilla first, but the French, soon finding the English beat them in speed, resolved to accompany them, for they had so little food as to be obliged to eat only once in every forty-eight hours, and but for rain water would have died of thirst. Off Santa Helena, they gave chase to a ship, and found it to be a prize laden with wine and corn, lately taken by Captain David's men, for they had been making descents along the coast, at Pisca had beaten off 800 men from Lima, and had also taken a great many ships, which they pillaged and let go. Having got to the value of 5,000 pieces of eight a man, they sailed for Magellan, and on the way many of the men lost all they had by gaming. Those who had won joined Willnett, and returned to the North Sea; but the losers, sixty English and twenty French, joined David, and determined to remain and get more spoil in the South.

Henry and Samms had gone to the East Indies. The eight men of David's crew who commanded the prize joined them against Queaquilla. Furling their sails to prevent being seen, they anchored off the White Cape, and at ten in the morning embarked 260 men in their canoes. On the 15th they reached, at sunset, the rocky island of Santa Clara, and on the 16th rested all day, weak from long fasting, in the island of La Puna, escaping any detection from the forty sentinels. The 17th they spent on the same island, and arranged the attack. Captain Picard and fifty men led the forlorn hope, another captain and eighty grenadiers formed a reserve. Captain Grogniet and the main body were to make themselves masters of the town and port, and the English captain, George Hewit, with fifty men, were to attack the smaller fort; while 1000 pieces of eight were promised to the first ensign who should plant the colours on the great fort. They left their covert in the evening, and hoped to reach the town by dawn, but only having three hours of favourable tide, had to remain all day at the island, and at night rowing out, were overtaken after all by the light, when a sentinel seeing them, set a cottage on fire and alarmed his companions.

Marching across a wood to the fire, they killed two of the Spaniards and captured a boy. Remaining in covert all day, they thought themselves undiscovered, because the town had not answered the fire signal, and at night they rowed up the river, the rapid current carrying them four leagues in two hours. All the 19th they spent under cover of an island in the river, and at night went up with the current, not rowing for fear of alarming the sentinels. They attempted in vain to put in beyond the town, on the side least guarded, but the tide going out forced them to land two hours before day, within cannon shot of the town, where they could discern the lights burning, for the Spaniards burnt lamps all night. They landed in a marshy place, and had to cut a path through the bushes with their sabres. They soon met with a sentinel, and were discovered by one of the men left to guard the canoes striking a light, against orders, to light his pipe. The sentinel, knowing that this was punishable by death among his countrymen, suspected enemies and discharged a *paterero*, which the fort answered by a discharge of all their cannon.

The buccaneers, overtaken by a storm, entered a large house near to light the matches of their grenades and wait for day, the enemy firing incessantly in defiance. On the 20th, at daybreak, they marched out in order, with drums beating and colours, and found 700 men waiting for them behind a wall, four feet and a-half high, and a ditch. Killing many of the buccaneers at the onset, the enemy ventured to sally out, sword in hand, and were at once put to flight. In spite of the bridge being broken down, the pursuers crossed the ditch, and, getting to the foot of the wall, threw in grenades, and drove the enemy to their houses. Driven also from this, they fled to a redoubt in the Place d'Armes, and from thence, after an hour's fighting, to a third fort, the largest of all. Here they defended themselves a long time, firing continually at their enemies, who could not see them for the smoke. From these *palisadoes* they again sallied, and wounded several buccaneers and took one prisoner. They at last retreated with great loss.

The *flibustiers*, weary with eleven hours' fighting, and finding their powder nearly spent, grew desperate; but, redoubling their efforts, with some loss made themselves masters of the place, having nine men killed and a dozen wounded. Parties were then sent out to pursue the fugitives, and a garrison having been put in the great fort, the Roman Catholic part of the band went to sing *Te Deum* in the great church.

Basil Hall describes Guayaquil as having on the one side a great marsh, and on the other a great river, while the country, for nearly 100 miles, is a continued level swamp, thickly covered with trees. The river is broad and deep, but full of shoals and strange turnings, the woods growing close to the water's edge, stand close, dark, and still, like two vast black walls; while along the banks the land-breeze blows hot, and breathes death, decay, and putrefaction.

The town was walled, and the forts built on an eminence. The houses were built of boards and reared on piles, on account of the frequent inundations. The chief trade of the place was cocoa.

The buccaneers took 700 prisoners, including the governor and his family. He himself was wounded, as were most of his officers, who fought better than all the 5,000 men of the place. The place was stored with merchandise, precious stones, silver plate, and 70,000 pieces of eight. Upwards of three millions more had been hidden while the fort was taking. As soon as the canoes had come up, they were sent in pursuit of the treasure, but it was too late. They captured, however, 22,000 pieces of eight, and a vermilion gilt eagle, weighing 66 lbs., that had served as the tabernacle for some church. It was of rare workmanship, and the eyes were formed of two great "rocks of emeralds." There were fourteen barks in the port—the galleys they had fought at Puebla Nueva, and two royal ships unfinished on the stocks. As a ransom for all these things, the governor promised a million pieces of eight in gold, and 400 sacks of corn, requiring the vicar-general to be released to go to Quito and procure it.

The women of the town, who were very pretty, had been assured by their confessors that the buccaneers were monsters and cannibals, and had conceived a horror and aversion to them. Says Lussan:

> They could not be dispossessed thereof till they came to know us better. But then I can boldly say that they entertained quite different sentiments of our persons, and have given us frequent instances of so violent a passion as proceeded sometimes even to a degree of folly.

As a proof of the calumnies circulated against the ruthless conquerors, Lussan tells us the following:

It is not from a chance story that I came to know the impressions wrought in these women that we were men that would eat them; for the next day after the taking of the town, a young gentlewoman that waited upon the governor of the place, happened to fall into my hands. As I was carrying her away to the place where the rest of the prisoners were kept, and to that end made her walk before me, she turned back, and, with tears in her eyes, told me, in her own language—'*Senor, pur l'amor di Dios ne mi como*'—that is, 'Pray, sir, for the love of God, do not eat me;' whereupon I asked her who had told her that we were wont to eat people? She answered, 'The fathers,' who had also assured them that we had not human shape, but that we resembled monkeys.

On the 21st, part of the town was accidentally burnt down by some of the men lighting a fire in a house, and leaving it unextinguished when they returned at night to the court of guard. Afraid that it would reach the place where they had stored their powder and merchandise, the French removed all the plunder to their vessels, and carried the prisoners to the fort; but not till all this was done endeavouring to save the town, a third part of which was, by this time, destroyed. Afraid the Spaniards might now refuse to pay the ransom, they charged them with the offence, threatening to send some fifty prisoners' heads if they did not pay them what they had lost by the fire.

The enemy, surprised at this, attributed the incendiarism to traitors, and promised satisfaction. The stench of the 900 dead carcases, still lying unburied up and down the town, now producing a pestilence, the buccaneers dismounted and spiked the cannon, and carried off the 500 prisoners to their ships, anchoring at Puna. Captain Grogniet died of his wounds soon after this removal. The Spaniards obtaining four days' further respite, and then still further delaying the ransom, the adventurers made the prisoners throw dice for their lives, and cutting off the heads of four, sent them to Queaquilla, threatening further deaths. They were now joined by Captain David and a prize he had lately taken. He was planning a descent on Paita, to obtain refreshments for some men wounded in a fight with a Spanish ship, the *Catalina*, off Lima.

They fought for two days, David's men, being drunk, constantly getting to leeward, and failing twenty times in an attempt to board. The Spaniards, gaining courage from these failures, hoisted the bloody flag; but the third day, David, getting sober, got his tackle and rigging in good order, got properly to windward, and bore down with determination. The enemy in terror ran ashore, and went to pieces in two hours. Two men were saved by a canoe, and said that their captain had had his thigh shot off by a cannon ball. David's ship, wanting refitting, was employed to cruise in the bay to prevent surprises from the Spaniards. By a letter taken from a courier, they found that the people of Queaquilla were only endeavouring to obtain time.

The buccaneers spent thirty days on the island of La Puna, living on the luxurious food brought from Queaquilla, and employing the prisoners with lutes, *theorbos*, harps, and guitars, to delight them by perpetual concerts and serenades. Lussan says:

> Some of our men grew very familiar with our women prisoners, who, without offering them any violence, were not sparing of their favours, and made appear, as I have already remarked, that after they came once to know us, they did not retain all the aversion for us that had been inculcated into them when we were strangers unto them. All our people were so charmed with this way of living that they forgot their past miseries, and thought no more of danger from the Spaniards than if they had been in the middle of Paris.

Ravenau also treats us with his own personal love adventure, which we insert as a curious illustration of the vicissitudes of a South Sea adventurer's life.

> Amongst the rest myself had one pretty adventure. Among the other prisoners we had a young gentlewoman, lately become a widow of the treasurer of the town, who was slain when it was taken. Now this woman appeared so far comforted for her loss, out of an hard-heartedness they have in this country one for another, that she proposed to hide me and herself in some corner of the island till our people were gone, and that then she would bring me to Queaquilla to

marry her, that she would procure me her husband's office, and vest me in his estate, which was very great. When I had returned her thanks for such obliging offers, I gave her to understand that I was afraid her interest had not the mastery over the Spaniards' resentments; and that the wounds they had received from us were yet too fresh and green for them easily to forget them. She went about to cure me of my suspicion, by procuring secretly, from the governor and chief officers, promises under their hands how kindly I should be used by them. I confess I was not a little perplexed herewith, and such pressing testimonies of goodwill and friendship towards me brought me, after a little consultation with myself, into such a quandary, that I did not know which side to close with; nay, I felt myself, at length, much inclined to close with the offers made me, and I had two powerful reasons to induce me thereunto, one of which was the miserable and languishing life we lead in those places, where we were in perpetual hazard of losing it, which I should be freed from by an advantageous offer of a pretty woman and a considerable settlement: the other proceeded from the despair I was in of ever being able to return into my own country, for want of ships fit for that purpose. But when I began to reflect upon these things with a little more leisure and consideration, and that I resolved with myself how little trust was to be given to the promises and faith of so perfidious as well as vindictive a nation as the Spaniards, and more especially towards men in our circumstances, by whom they had been so ill-used, this second reflection carried it against the first, and even all the advantages offered me by this lady. But however the matter was, I was resolved, in spite of the grief and tears of this pretty woman, to prefer the continuance of my troubles (with a ray of hope of seeing France again), before the perpetual suspicion I should have had of some treachery designed against me. Thus I rejected her proposals, but so as to assure her I should retain, even as long as I lived, a lively remembrance of her affections and good inclinations towards me.

After some negotiation with a priest, the people of Queaquilla brought in twenty-four sacks of meal, and 20,000 pieces of eight in gold. On their refusing more than 22,000 pieces of eight more for ransom, a council was held to decide upon putting all the prisoners to death, but at last, Ravenau being in the majority, decided to spare them. They then took fifty of the richest prisoners with them to the point of St. Helena, and surrendered the rest on 22,000 more being paid.

While at La Puna, the buccaneers sallied out to attack two Spanish *armadillas*, but not having any *piraguas* to tow them to the windward, could only cannonade at a distance. The French vessels were much shattered, but no man killed. The next day they came to close fight, both sides using small arms and great guns, but no buccaneer was killed. The Spaniards lost many men, and the blood ran out of their scupper holes, but they still cried at parting, *"A la manana, la partida"*—(tomorrow, again.) The next night the buccaneers unrigged and sank one of their prizes, and fitted out another, manning her with twenty Frenchmen, who wanted to leave David. The same night four Spaniards seized one of the prizes, and escaped to Queaquilla. Being now within half cannon shot, the rival vessels pounded each other all day; the French had their tackle spoiled, and sails riven, and the frigate received five cannon-shot in the foremast, and three in the mainmast, but had not one man killed or wounded. The next day the Spaniards hoisted Burgundian colours, and poured in volleys of musket-shot, but neither party boarded. The ensuing day the buccaneer musketry was so destructive, that the Spaniards closed their port-holes and bore up to the wind. That day the French received sixty shots in their sides, two-thirds between wind and water, the rigging was torn, and Ravenau and another man were wounded. At night the Spaniards failed in an attempt to board. "We spent this night at anchor," says Lussan, "to stop our cannons' mouths, which otherwise might have sent us into the deep." To his astonishment, the next morning the *armadillas* had fled. During these successive days' fighting, the governor and officers of Queaquilla had been brought on deck to witness the defeat of their countrymen.

They then set their prisoners ashore and divided the plunder, the whole amounting to 500,000 pieces of eight, or 15,000,000 *livres*, and in shares to 400 pieces of eight a man. The uncoined gold and the precious stones being of uncertain value were sold by auction, that those who had silver and had won in gambling might buy. All who expected an overland expedition were anxious for jewels, as more portable and less heavy than silver. They sought now in their descent for nothing but gold and jewels, quite disregarding silver as a mean metal and heavy to carry. They even left many things in Queaquilla, and neglected to send a canoe for the 100 *caons* of coined silver (11,000 pieces of eight in all) which had been sent to the opposite river side.

Taking advantage of their indifference, Spanish thieves mixed with the buccaneers, and pillaged their own countrymen. They landed at Point Mangla, and surprised a watch of fifteen Spanish soldiers who had been placed to guard a river abounding in emeralds. A few days after they took a vessel from Panama going to Porto Bello to buy negroes off the point of Harina. The French fleet was next attacked by a Spanish galley and two *piraguas*. From a prisoner they heard of 300 Frenchmen, who had defeated 600 Spaniards and killed their leader in the savannahs. While careening in the bay of Mapalla they were joined by these men, who proved to be part of Grogniet's men, who had left their companions on the coast of Acapulco, refusing to go further towards California.

The adventurers next landed in the Bay of Tecoantepequa, and dispersing a body of 300 Spaniards, drawn up upon an eminence, marched inland towards the town, sleeping all night in the open air. Nothing but hunger and despair could have induced this attack. The town was intersected by a great and very rapid river, encompassed by eight suburbs, and defended by 3000 men. The buccaneers forded the river, the water up to their middles, and after an hour's fighting forced the Spaniards from their entrenchment. In two hours these men, enraged with hunger, took the place by hand-to-hand fighting, and eighty sailors then dislodged the enemy from the abbey of St. Francis, whose terraces commanded the town.

Finding the river overflowing and no ransom coming, the buccaneers departed the next day, and landing at Vatulco, took the old governor of Merida prisoner, and obtained some provisions. They also landed at Muemeluna and victualled, the Spaniards having strong entrenchments, but making little resistance. They found upon the shore the musket and dead body of a sailor of a frigate that had attempted to land a month before. The Spaniards had not seen the body, or they would have cut in pieces or burnt it, as they were in the habit of even digging up the buccaneers buried on their shores. At Sansonnat they landed in the face of 600 Spaniards to fill their water-casks, being faint from thirst. One of the men, more impatient than the rest, and goaded by four days' drought, swam ashore and was drowned, without any being able to help him.

They now held serious councils about the return by land. The prisoners declared their best way was by Segovia, where they would *only* meet 5,000 or 6,000 Spaniards, and that the way was easy for the sick and wounded. The French determined to land and obtain more certain information, and this was one of the most daring of their adventures. They landed seventy men, and marched two days without meeting anybody, upon which eighteen, less weary than the rest, tramped on and soon got into a high road. Capturing three horsemen, they learnt that they were but a quarter of a league distant from Chiloteca, a little town with about 400 white inhabitants, besides negroes, Indians, and mulattoes, who were not aware of their approach.

Afraid to waste time in running back after their companions, they entered the town, frightened the Spaniards, and took the Teniente and fifty others prisoners. Had there not been horses ready mounted, on which they made their escape, the enemy would, every man, have submitted to be bound, being overcome with a panic fear, and believing the enemy very numerous. They learned from the prisoners that the Panama galley lay waiting for them at Caldaira, and the *St. Lorenzo*, with thirty guns, at Realegua. They also said that 600 men would be in the town by the next day. The Spaniards now began to rally, and compelled the buccaneers to entrench themselves in the church. The prisoners, seeing them hurry in, and thinking them hard pressed, ran to a pile of arms and prepared to make a resistance; but the buccaneers, retreating to the doors, fired at the crowd till only four men and their wives were left alive. They then mounted horses and retreated, carrying off four prisoners of each sex, and firing at a herald who tried to parley. Joining their companions, whom they found resting at a *hatto*, they made a stand and drove back 600 Spaniards.

The statements of the prisoners increased their fears of the overland route, but determining rather to die sword in hand than to pine away with hunger, they at once resolved upon their design. Running all the vessels ashore but the galley and *piraguas*, which would take them from the island to the mainland, leaving no other means of escape to the timorous, they formed four companies of seventy men, choosing ten men from each as a forlorn hope, to be relieved every morning. Those who were lamed were to have, as formerly, 1000 pieces of eight, the horses were to be kept for the crippled and wounded. The stragglers who were wounded were to have no reward, whilst violence, cowardice, and drunkenness were to be punished.

While maturing their plans, a Spanish vessel approached, and anchoring, began to fire at the grounded vessels, and soon put them out of a condition to sail. Afraid of losing their *piraguas*, the buccaneers sent their prisoners and baggage to some flats behind the island. The next day, the Frenchmen, sheltering themselves behind the rocks that ran out to the sea, kept the vessel at a distance; but now afraid of total destruction, the buccaneers sent 100 men to the continent at night to secure horses, and wait for them at a certain port. On the next day, the Spanish ship took fire, and put out to sea to extinguish the flames. The next day the buccaneers escaped by a stratagem. Having spent the whole night in hammering the vessel, as if careening, to prevent all suspicion of their departure, they charged all their guns, grenades, and four pieces of cannon, and tied to them pieces of lighted matches of various lengths, in order to keep up an alarm throughout the night. In the twilight they departed as secretly as they could, the prisoners carrying the surgeons' medicines, the carpenters' tools, and the wounded men.

On the 1st of January, 1688, the buccaneers arrived on the continent. On the evening of the same day the men joined them with sixty-eight horses and several prisoners, all of whom dissuaded them in vain from attempting to go by Segovia, where the Spaniards were fully alarmed. The men, nothing deterred, packed up each his charge, and thrust their silver and ammunition into bags. Those who had too much to carry, gave it to those who had lost theirs by gaming, promising them half "in case it should please God to bring them safe to the North Sea." Ravenau de Lussan tells us his charge was lighter but not less valuable than the others, as he had converted 30,000 pieces of eight into pearls and precious stones. He says:

> But as the best part of this was the product of luck I had at play, some of those who had been losers, as well in playing against me as others, becoming much discontented at their losses, plotted together to the number of seventeen or eighteen, to murder those who were richest amongst us. I was so happy as to be timely advertised of it by some friends, which did not a little disquiet my mind, for it was a very difficult task for a man, during so long a journey, to be able to secure himself from being surprised by those who were continually in the same company, and with whom we must eat, drink, and sleep, and who could cut off whom they pleased of us in the conflicts they might have with the Spaniards, by shooting us in the hurry.

To frustrate this scheme, Ravenau therefore divided his treasure among several men, and by this means removed a weight both from his mind and body.

On the 2nd of January, after having said prayers and sunk their boats, the buccaneers set out, resting at noon at a *hatto*. On the 4th they lay on a mountain plateau, the Spaniards visible on their flanks and rear. On the 5th the barricades began, and on the 6th, at an *estantia*, they found the following letter lying on a bed in the hall:

> We are very glad that you have made choice of our province for your passage homewards, but are sorry you are not better laden with silver; however, if you have occasion for mules we will send them to you. We hope to have the French General Grogniet very quickly in our power, so we will leave you to judge what will become of his soldiers.

On the 7th the vanguard drove off an ambuscade, and lay that evening in a *hatto*. The Spaniards burnt all the provisions in the way, and set fire to the savannahs to windward, stifling the French horses with smoke and scaring them with the blaze. While their march was thus retarded and they waited for the fire to burn out, the enemy threw up entrenchments and erected barricades of trees. On the 8th the French set fire to a house at a sugar plantation, and, hiding till the Spaniards came to put it out, captured a prisoner, who told them that 300 auxiliaries were on the march to meet them. Says Lussan:

> These 300 men were our continual guard, for they gave us morning and evening the diversion of their trumpets, but it was like the *music of the enchanted palace of Psyche,* who heard it without seeing the musicians, for ours marched on each side of us, in places so covered with pine trees that it was impossible to perceive them.

During this march the buccaneers never encamped but upon high ground, or in the open savannah, for fear of being hemmed in.

The advanced guard was now strengthened by forty men, who discharged their muskets at the entries and avenues of woods, to dislodge the ambuscades, but they did not shoot when the plain was open and free from wood; although the Spaniards, who were lying on their bellies on each side of them, opened their fire and killed two stragglers. On the 10th they repulsed an ambuscade and captured some horses. On the 11th they dispersed another ambuscade, and entered Segovia, but all the provisions had been burnt, and the Spaniards fired upon them from among the pine trees that grew on the hills around the town. Fortunately at this spot, where the old guides grew uncertain of the way, they captured a new prisoner, who led them twenty leagues to the river they were in search of.

The road now grew wilder, and dangers thickened around them. They had to creep with great danger to the tops of great mountains, or to bury themselves in narrow and dark valleys. The cold grew intense, and the fogs lasted for some hours after daybreak. In the plains no chill was felt, but the same heat that prevailed on the mountains after noon. Says Lussan:

> But the hopes of getting once more into our native country made us endure patiently all these toils, and served as so many wings to carry us.

On the 12th, they ascended several mountains, and had incredible trouble to clear the road of the Spanish barricades, and all night long the enemy fired into their camp. On the 18th, an hour before sunrise, they ascended an eminence which seemed advantageous for an encampment, and saw on the edge of an eminence, separated from them by a narrow valley, what they believed to be cattle feeding.

Rejoiced at the prospect of food, forty men were sent to reconnoitre. They returned with the dismal intelligence that the supposed oxen were really troopers' horses ready saddled, and that the mountain on which they stood was encircled by three entrenchments, rising one above another, commanding a stream that ran through the valley. They had no other way but this to pass, and there was no possibility of avoiding it. They added, that one of the Spaniards had seen them, and shook his naked cutlass at them from a distance. Every man's heart fell at this news, and their pining appetite sickened at the loss of its expected meal. There was no time for delay, for the Spaniards from the adjacent provinces were gathering in their rear, and if any time was lost they must be surrounded and overpowered by numbers.

Ravenau de Lussan, the Xenophon of this retreat, did not attempt to conceal the extent of the danger. He confesses himself that they were hard put to it, and that escape would have seemed impossible to any other men but to those who had been hitherto successful in almost every undertaking. He addressed his companions, and artfully persuaded them to agree to his plans, by first elaborating the extent of their difficulties. He said that 10,000 men could not force their way through such entrenchments, guarded by so many men as the Spaniards had, judging from the number of their horses. Nor could they pass by the side of it, with all their horses and baggage, seeing that the path could only be entered in single file. Except the road, all was a thick, pathless forest, full of quagmires, and encumbered by fallen trees; and even if these impediments were passed, the Spaniards would have still to be fought with. The buccaneers agreed to these as truisms, but cried out that it was to no purpose to talk of difficulties so apparent, without proposing some method of surmounting them, and suggesting some means for its execution. Upon this hint De Lussan spoke. He proposed to cross those woods, precipices, mountains, and rocks, how inaccessible soever they seemed, and gaining the weather-gauge of the enemy, take them at once in the rear, suddenly and unexpectedly. The success of this plan he would answer for at the peril of his life.

The prisoners, horses, and baggage he resolved to leave guarded by eighty men, to keep off the 300 Spaniards who hovered around them at day and at night, encamped at a musket-shot distance. These eighty men could answer for four times as many Spaniards. After some deliberation, De Lussan's plan was agreed to, and the execution at once resolved upon. Examining the mountain carefully with the keen eyes of both hunters and sailors, they could see a road winding along the side of the mountain, above the highest entrenchment. This they could only trace here and there by light spots visible between the trees, but once across this they were safe.

Full of hope, and with every faculty aroused, some of the men were sent to a spot higher than the main body, to cover another party who had on previous occasions proved themselves ingenious and expert, and who were sent to pick out the safest and most direct spots by which they could get in the rear of the enemy before day broke. As soon as these scouts returned the men made ready for their departure, leaving their baggage guarded by eighty men. To prevent suspicion, the officer in command had orders to make every sentinel he set or relieved in the night-time fire his fusil and to beat his drum at the usual hour. He was told that if God gave them the victory they would send a party to bring him off, but that if an hour after all firing ceased they saw no messenger, they were to provide for their own safety.

The immediate narrative of this wonderful escape we give in De Lussan's own words:

> Things being thus disposed we said our prayers as low as we could, that the Spaniards might not hear us, from whom we were separated but by the valley. At the same time, we set forward to the number of 200 men by moonlight, it being now an hour within night; and about one more after our departure we heard the Spaniards also at their prayers, who, knowing we were encamped very near them, fired about 600 muskets in the air to frighten us. Besides, they also made a discharge at all the responses of the litany which they sang.

We still pursued our march, and spent the whole night (in going down and then getting up) to advance half a-quarter of a league, which was the distance between them and us, through a country, as I have already said, so full of rocks, mountains, woods, and frightful precipices, that our posteriors and knees were of more use to us than our legs, it being impossible for us to travel thither otherwise. On the 14th, by break of day, as we got over the most dangerous parts of this passage, and had already seized upon a considerable ascent of the mountain by clambering up in great silence, and leaving the Spaniards' retrenchments to our left, we saw their party that went the rounds, who, thanks to the fogs, did not discover us. As soon as they were gone by, we went directly to the place where we saw them, and found it to be exactly the road we were minded to seize on. When we had made a halt for about half an hour to take breath, and that we had a little daylight to facilitate our march, we followed this road by the voice of the Spaniards, who were at their morning prayers, and we were but just beginning our march, when, unfortunately, we met with two out-sentinels, on whom we were forced to fire, and this gave the Spaniards notice, who thought of nothing less than to see us come down from above them upon their entrenchments, since they expected us no other way than from below; so that those who had the guard thereof, and were in number about 500 men, finding themselves on the outside, when they thought they had been within, and consequently open without any covert, took the alarm so hot, that falling all on them at the same time, we made them quit the place in a moment, and make their escape by the favour of the fog.

The sequel is soon told. The defenders of the two first lines of wall drew up outside the lowermost, the buccaneers firing at them for an hour under cover of the first entrenchment. But finding they gave no ground, and thinking the fog interfered with the aim, the French rushed forward and fell upon them with the butt ends of their muskets, till they fled headlong down the narrow road. Here they got entangled in their own impediments, and the buccaneers, commanding the road from the redoubt, killed an enemy at every shot. Weary at last of running and killing, the French returned to the entrenchments and drove off the 500 Spaniards, who had now rallied, and were attacking the garrison. The pursuit ceased only from the fatigue of the conquerors and their weariness of slaughter. The Spaniards neither gave nor took quarter, and were saved in spite of themselves. De Lussan says, either from pride or a natural fierceness of temper, the Spanish soldiers, before an engagement, frequently took an oath to their commander neither to give nor receive quarter. The buccaneers, struck with compassion at the quantity of blood running into the rivulet, spared the survivors, and returned a second time into the entrenchment with only one man killed and two wounded. The Spaniards lost their general, a brave old Walloon officer, who had given them the plan of their entrenchment. It was only at the solicitation of another commander that the rounds had been set, and the sentinels placed at the top of the mountain. The general had consented, but said there was no danger if the French were only men. It would take them eight days to climb up, and if they were devils, no entrenchment could keep them out. In his pocket were found letters from the Governor of Costa Rica, who had intended to send him 8000 men, but the Walloon asked for only 1500. He advised him to take care of his soldiers, as no glory could be gained by such a victory. The letter concluded thus:

> Take good measures, for those devils have a cunning and subtlety that is not in use amongst us. When you find them advance within the shot of your arquebuses, let not your men fire but by twenties, to the end your firing may not be in vain; and when you find them weakened, raise a shout to frighten them, and fall on with your swords, while Don Rodrigo attacks them in the rear. I hope God will favour our designs, since they are no other than for his glory, and the destruction of these new sort of Turks. Hearten up your men, though they may have enough of that according to your example they shall be rewarded in heaven, and if they get the better, they will have gold and silver enough wherewith these thieves are laden.

Having sung a *Te Deum* of thankfulness to God, Ravenau de Lussan mounted sixty men upon horseback, as he words it, "to give notice to our other people of the success the Almighty was pleased to give us." They found them about to attack the 300 Spaniards, who seeing the night-march the main body had made, and believing them defeated at the entrenchments, had sent an officer to parley with the residue. He told them that the 1,500 Spaniards were lying ready to surround their troops, but promised them good terms if they surrendered; saying that, by the intercessions of the almoner, and for the honour of the holy sacrament and glorious Virgin, they had spared all the prisoners they had hitherto taken. The buccaneers, somewhat intimidated at these threats, took heart when they saw their companions coming, and returned the following fierce answer:

> Though you had force enough to destroy two-thirds of our number, we should not fail to fight with the remaining part; yea, though there were but one man of us left, he should fight against you all. When we put ashore and left the South Sea, we all resolved to pass through your country or die in the attempt; and though there were as many Spaniards as there are blades of grass in the savannah, we should not be afraid, but would go on and go where we will in spite of your teeth.

The officer at Ravenau's arrival was just being dismissed, and seeing the new allies were booted and mounted on Spanish horses, he shrugged up his shoulders and rode back as fast as he could to his comrades, who were not more than a musket-shot off upon a small eminence commanding the camp, to tell them the news. As soon almost as he could get to them, the buccaneers advanced with pistols and cutlasses, and without firing fell on them and cut many to pieces before they could mount, but let the rest go, detaining their horses. They then, with the loss of one killed and two maimed, rejoined the main body at the entrenchments.

The enemy now lit a fire upon the top of a neighbouring mountain to collect the scattered troops, in order to defend an entrenchment six leagues distant; but the buccaneers lying in wait cut off their passage, then hamstringing 900 horses, took 900 others to kill and salt when they arrived at the river.

On the 15th they passed the entrenchment unfinished and undefended, and on the 16th day came very joyfully to the long desired river. Immediately they entered into the woods that covered the banks, and fell to work in good earnest to cut down trees and build *piperies*, or rafts. These were made of four or five trunks of the *mahot* trees, a light buoyant wood, which they first barked and then bound together with parasite creepers, which were tough and of great length. Two men, generally standing upright, guided each of these frail barks, the decks sunk two or three feet under water. They were built purposely narrow, to be able to thread the rocky passes of the river even then in sight. These rafts were dragged to the riverside and then launched, the boatmen having furnished themselves with long poles to push them off the rocks, against which they were sure the current would drive them. De Lussan, who never exaggerates a danger, cannot find words to express the terrors of this stream.

> It springs in the mountains of Segovia, and discharges itself into the North Sea at Cape Gracias à Dios, after having run a long way, in a most rapid manner, across a vast number of rocks of a prodigious bigness, and by the most frightful precipices that can be thought of, besides a great many falls of water, to the number of at least a hundred of all sorts, which it is impossible for a man to look on without trembling, and making the head of the most fearless to turn round, when he sees and hears the waters fall from such a height into those tremendous whirlpools.

To this dangerous river and its merciless falls, these way-worn men trusted themselves on frail rafts, and sank up to their middles in water. Sometimes they were hurried, in spite of all their resistance, into boiling pools, where they were buried with their rafts in the darkness beneath the foam, at others drifted under rocks and against fallen trees. Some tied themselves to their barks. Says Lussan:

> As for those great falls they had, to our good fortunes, at their entrances and goings out, great basins of still water, which gave us the opportunity to get upon the banks of the river, and draw our piperies ashore to take off those things

we had laid on them, which were as wet as we were. These we carried with us, leaping from rock to rock, till we came to the end of the fall, from whence one of us afterwards returned to put our pipery into the water, and let her swim along to him who waited for her below. But if he failed to catch hold (by swimming) of those pieces of wood before they got out of the basin below, the violence of the stream would carry them away to rights, and the men were necessitated to go and pick out trees to make another.

The rafts at first went all together for the sake of mutual assistance; but at the end of three days, finding this dangerous, Ravenau de Lussan advised their going in a line apart, so that, if any were carried against the rocks, they might get off before the next *pipery* arrived, which at first occasioned many disasters. De Lussan, being himself cast away, found much safety in this plan; for, uncording his raft, he straddled upon one piece and his companion upon another, and floated down, till, reaching a place less rapid, they got on land and reconstructed the raft. By his advice, those who went first put up flags at the end of long poles, to give notice on which side to land, not to signal the falls, for their roar could be clearly heard a league off.

During all these dangers the men lived on the bananas that they found growing by the river side, some of which the Indians had sown, and others floated down and self-planted during the inundations. The horse-flesh they had brought the water had spoiled, compelling them to throw it away after two days; and although game abounded on the land, they could kill none, for their arms were continually wet and their ammunition all damaged.

It was at this crisis the conspirators we have before mentioned chose to carry out their cruel plot. Hiding behind some rocks, they killed and plundered five Englishmen, who were known to be rich. Lussan whose raft came last of all, and followed the English float, found their bodies, and thanked God he had given others his treasure to carry. When the buccaneers were all met together, lower down the river, Lussan told them of the murder, of which they had not heard, but the murderers were seen no more. On the 20th of February the river grew wider, slower, and deeper, the falls ceased, but the stream was encumbered with trees and bamboos, drifted together by the floods. These snags frequently overturned the rafts, but the water being, though deeper, much slower, none were drowned. Some leagues further, the stream became gentle and free from all impediment, and they determined for the next sixty leagues to the sea to build canoes.

Dividing themselves into parties of sixty men, they landed and cut down *mapou* trees, and, working with wonderful diligence, built four canoes by the first of March. Leaving 140 men still working, 120 embarked, eager for home, ease, and rest. The English, too impatient to make canoes, had long since reached the sea-shore in their *piperies*.

They here met a Jamaica boat lying at anchor, and attempted to persuade the captain to return, and obtain leave for them to land, as they had no commission. The captain refused to go without receiving £6,000 in advance, which they could not afford, as many of them had lost all by the upsetting of the *piperies*. The sailors, therefore, resolved to remain with the friendly Mosquito Indians, who dwelt about the mouth of this river, and to whom they had often brought trinkets from Jamaica. The English, unable to buy the boat, determined to send word to the French, hoping to get to St. Domingo by their aid. Two Mosquito Indians were despatched in a canoe, forty leagues up the river, to bring down forty Frenchmen, as the vessel was small and short of provision, and could not hold more. But, in spite of all this, 120, instead of forty, hurried down to get on board, waiting five days for the ship that had gone to the Isle of Pearls.

Great was the delight of the French to pass Cape Gracias à Dios, and enter the North Sea.

The Mulattoes that lived on this cape, Lussan says, were descended from the crew of a negro vessel, lost on a shoal. They slept in holes dug in the sand, to avoid the mosquitoes, which stung them till they appeared like lepers. Lussan speaks much of the fiery darts of this mischievous insect. He says:

> It is no small pain to be attacked with them, for, besides that they caused us to lose our rest at night, it was then that we were forced to go naked for want of shirts, when the troublesomeness of these animals made us run into despair and such a rage as set us beside ourselves.

At last the longed-for vessel arrived, and, regardless of lots that had been drawn, fifty of the more vigilant, including Lussan, crowded in, one on the top of the other, and instantly weighed anchor, engaging the master for forty pieces of eight a head to take them to St. Domingo, afraid of venturing to Jamaica. At Cuba they landed, and surprising some hunters, compelled them to sell them food, uncertain whether France and Spain were at war or peace.

On the 4th of April they rode at anchor at Petit Guaves, hoping to hear news from France. De Lussan relates a curious instance here of the effect of habit and instinctive imagination. He says:

> There were some of our people so infatuated with the long miseries we had suffered, that they thought of nothing else but the Spaniards, insomuch that, when from the deck they saw some horsemen riding along the sea-side, they flew to arms to fire upon them, as imagining they were enemies, though we assured them we were now come among those of our own nation.

De Lussan, at once going on shore, demanded of Mons. Dumas, the King's lieutenant, in the Governor Mons. de Cussy's absence, indemnity and protection, by favour of an amnesty granted by the French king to those who, in remote places, had continued to make war on the Spaniards, not hearing of the peace that had been concluded between the two nations. De Lussan relates with much unpretending pathos the feelings of himself and his Ulyssean friends upon once more landing in a friendly country.

> When we all were got ashore, to a people that spoke French, we could not forbear shedding tears for joy that, after we had run so many hazards, dangers, and perils, it had pleased the Almighty Maker of the earth and seas to grant a deliverance, and bring us back to those of our own nation, that at length we may return without any more ado to our own country; whereunto I cannot but further add, that, for my own part, I had so little hopes of ever getting back, that I could not, for the space of fifteen days, take my return for any other than

an illusion, and it proceeded so far with me, that I shunned sleep, for fear when I awaked I should find myself again in those countries out of which I was now safely delivered.

From the preface to De Lussan's book, we learn that he returned to Dieppe, with letters of introduction from De Cussy, the Governor of Tortuga and St. Domingo, to Mons. de Lubert, Treasurer-General of Marine in France. Of the end of this brave man we know nothing. He had many requisites for a great general.

CHAPTER 13

The Last of the Buccaneers

Of all the motley characters of buccaneer history, Montauban appears one of the most extraordinary. His friends describe him to have been as prudent as he was brave, blunt and sincere, relating his own adventures with a free and generous air that convinced the hearer of their truth, and at last consenting to write his story, not from ostentation, but from the simple desire of giving a French minister of state a narrative of his campaigns. He is interesting to us as the latest known buccaneer, and in strict parlance he can scarcely be classed as a buccaneer at all, attacking the English as he did more than the Spanish, and not confining his cruises to the Spanish main. He begins his book with great *naïveté* thus:

> Since I have so often felt the malignant influence of those stars that preside over the seas, and by an adverse fortune lost all that wealth which with so much care and trouble I had amassed together, I should take no manner of pleasure in this place to call to mind the misfortunes that befell me before the conclusion of the last campaign, had not a desire of serving still both the public and particular persons, as well as to let his majesty know the affection and weddedness I have always had for his service, made me take pen in hand to give Mons. de Phelipeaux an account of such observations as I have made; wherein he may also find with what eagerness I have penetrated to the remotest colonies of our enemies, in order to destroy them and ruin their trade. I was not willing to swell up this relation with an account of all the voyages I have made, and all the particular adventures that have be-

fallen me on the coasts of New Spain, Carthagena, Mexico, Florida, and Cape Verd, which last place I had been at twenty years ago, having begun to use the seas at the age of sixteen.

He goes on to say that he will not stop to relate how, in 1691, in a ship called the *Machine*, he ravaged the coasts of New Guinea, and, entering the great Serelion, took a fort from the English and split twenty-four pieces of cannon, but will confine himself simply to his last voyage:

> Some information having been given thereof, by the noise made in France and elsewhere of the burning my ship, and the terrible crack it made in the air.

In the year 1694, having ravaged the coast of Caracca, he went towards St. Croix, to watch for some merchant ships and a fleet expected from Barbadoes and Nevis, bound for England. Sailing towards the Bermudas, expecting good booty, he saw them coming towards him without any apprehension of danger. He at once attacked the convoy (*The Wolf*), and took her and two merchant ships laden with sugar, the rest escaping during the fight. Returning with his prizes to France, he captured an English ship of sixteen guns from Spain and bound for England, which surrendered after a short fight. This last vessel he took to Rochelle and sold it, the Admiralty declaring it good prize; the last he took to Bordeaux and sold to the merchants. Here abandoning themselves to pleasure after a long abstinence, many of his men deserted him, and he supplied their place with youths from the town, who soon became as expert as veterans.

> I made it my continual care and business to teach my men to shoot, and my so frequent exercising of them rendered them in a short time as capable of shooting and handling their arms as the oldest sea freebooters, or the best fowlers by land.

Re-victualling his ship, that carried only thirty-four guns, he left Bordeaux in February, 1695, to cruise on the coast of Guinea. From the Azores he passed the Canary Islands, and sailed for fourteen days in sight of Teneriffe, in hopes of meeting some Dutch vessels, that after all escaped him, and at the Cape de Verd Islands he pursued two English interlopers of thirty guns each, who left behind in the roads their anchors and *shallops*. He then went in search of a Dutch guard-ship, of thirty-four guns, along the neighbouring coast. Decoying the foe by showing Dutch colours, he waited till he got within cannon shot, hoisting the French flag, gave her a signal to strike, and then exchanged broadsides. They fought from early morning till four in the afternoon, without Montauban being able to get the weather-gauge, or approach near enough to use his chief arms—his fusils. Taking advantage of a favourable wind, the Dutchman then anchored under the fort of the Cape of Three-points, where two other Dutch men-of-war lay, one of fourteen and the other of twenty-eight guns. Thinking the three vessels had leagued to fight him, Montauban anchored within a league of the shore, hoping to provoke them out by continued insults, but the guard-ship, already much mauled, would not move. This vessel, he found afterwards, had driven away a French flute. At Cape St. John he took with little difficulty an English ship of twenty guns, carrying 350 negroes, and much wax and elephants' teeth. The English captain had killed some of his blacks in a mutiny, and others had escaped in the *shallop*, which they stole. At Prince's Isle he took a small Bradenburg caper (a pirate), mounted with eight pieces of cannon, and carrying sixty men. He then put into port to careen, and sent his prize to St. Domingo to be condemned and sold, putting the Sieur de Nave and a crew on board, but the ship was taken by some English men-of-war before Little Goara. To keep his men employed during the careening, Montauban fitted up the caper, and with ninety men cruised for six weeks without success, and, then putting into the Isle of St. Thomas, trucked the prize for provisions, and started for the coasts of Angola, hearing that three English men-of-war and a fire-ship were fitting out against him at Guinea. On his way he chased a Dutch interloper, laden with 150 pounds of gold dust, but she ran ashore on the Isle of St. Omer and fell to pieces.

When approaching the coasts of Angola, and not far from the port of Cabinda, he saw an English vessel of fifty-four guns bearing down upon him. To decoy her Montauban hung out Dutch colours, while the English fired guns, as a signal of friendship. The Frenchman, pretending to wait, sailed slow, as if heavy laden or encumbered for want of sails and men.

We kept in this manner from break of day till ten in the forenoon. He gave me a gun from time to time without ball, to assure me of what he was, but finding at last I did not answer him on my part in the same manner, he gave me one again with ball, which made me presently put up French colours, and answer him with another. Hereupon the English captain, without any more ado, gave me two broadsides, which I received without returning him one again, though he had killed me seven men; for I was in hopes, if I could have got something nearer to him, to put him out of condition ever to get away from me. I endeavoured to come within a fusil shot of him and was desirous to give him an opportunity to show his courage in boarding me, since I could not so well do the same by him, as being to the leeward. At last being come by degrees nearer, and finding him within the reach of my fusils, which for that end I kept concealed upon the deck from his sight, they were discharged upon him, and my men continued to make so great a fire with them, that the enemy on their part began quickly to flag. In the mean time, as their ship's crew consisted of above 300 men and that they saw their cannon could not do their work for them, they resolved to board us, which they did with a great shout and terrible threatenings of giving no quarter, if we did not surrender. Their grappling-irons failing to catch the stern of my ship, made theirs run in such a manner, that their stern ran upon my boltsprit and broke it. Having observed my enemy thus encumbered, my men plied them briskly with their small shot, and made so terrible a fire upon them for an hour and a-half, that being unable to resist any longer, and having lost a great many men, they left the sport and ran down between decks, and I saw them presently after make signals with their hats of crying out for quarter. I caused my men therefore to give over their firing, and commanded the English to embark in their *shallops* and come on board of me, while I made some of my crew at the same time leap into the enemy's ship and seize her, and so prevent any surprise from them. I already rejoiced within myself for the taking of such a considerable prize, and so much the more in that I hoped that after having taken this vessel, that was the guard-ship of Angola, and the largest the English had in those seas, I should find myself in a condition still to take better prizes, and attack any man-of-war I should meet with. My ship's crew were also as joyful as myself, and did the work they were engaged in with a great deal of pleasure; but the enemy's powder suddenly taking fire, by the means of a match the captain had left burning on purpose, as hoping he might escape with his two *shallops*, blew both the ships into the air, *and made the most horrible crack that was ever heard.* It is impossible to set forth this horrid spectacle to the life; the spectators themselves were the actors of this bloody scene, *not knowing whether they saw it or not*, and not being able to judge of that which themselves felt. Wherefore leaving the reader to imagine the horror which the blowing up of two ships above 200 fathoms into the air must work in us, where there was formed as it were a mountain of water, fire, wreck of the ships, cordages, cannon, men, and a most horrible clap made, what with the cannon that went off in the air, and the waves of the sea that were tossed up thither, to which we may add the cracking of masts and boards, the rending of the sails and ropes, the cries of men, and the breaking of bones—I say, leaving these things to the imagination of the reader, I shall only take notice of what befell myself, and by what good fortune it was that I escaped.

When the fire first began I was upon the fore-deck of my own ship, where I gave the necessary orders. Now I was carried up on part of the said deck so high, that I fancy it was the height alone prevented my being involved in the wreck of the ships, where I must infallibly have perished, and been cut into a thousand pieces. I fell back into the sea (*you may be sure giddy-headed enough*), and continued a long time under water, without being able to get up to the surface of it. At last falling into a debate with the water, as a person who was afraid of being drowned, I got upon the face of it, and laid hold of a broken piece of a mast that I found near. I called to some of my men whom I saw swimming round about me, and exhorted them to take courage, hoping we might yet save our lives, if we could light upon any one of our *shallops*. But what afflicted me more than my very misfortune, was to see two half bodies, who had still somewhat of life remaining in them, from time to time mount up to the face of the water, and leave the place where they remained all dyed with blood. It was also much the same thing to see round about a vast number of members and scattered parts of men's bodies, and most of them spitted upon splinters of wood. At last one of my men, having met with a whole *shallop* among all the wreck, that swam up and down upon the water, came to tell me that we must endeavour to stop some holes therein, and to take out the canoe that lay on board her.

We got, to the number of fifteen or sixteen of us who had escaped, near unto this *shallop*, every man upon his piece of wood, and took the pains to loosen our canoe, which at length we effected. We went all on board her, and after we had got in saved our chief gunner, who in the fight had had his leg broke. We took up three or four oars, or pieces of board, which served us to that purpose, and when we had done that we sought out for somewhat to make a sail and a little mast, and, having fitted up all things as well as we possibly could, committed ourselves to the Divine Providence, who alone could give us life and deliverance. As soon as I had done working I found myself all over besmeared with blood, that ran from a wound I had received on my head at the time of my fall. We made some lint out of my handkerchief, and a fillet to bind it withal out of my shirt, after I had first washed the wound with urine. The same thing was done to the rest that had been wounded, and our *shallop* in the meanwhile sailed along without our knowing where we were going, and, what was still more sad, without victuals, and we had already spent three days without either eating or drinking. One of our men, being greatly afflicted with hunger and thirst at the same time, drank so much salt water that he died of it.

Most of the men vomited continually, Montauban's body swelled, and he was finally cured of his dropsy by a quartan-ague. All his hair and one side of his face and body were burnt with powder, and he bled as "bombardiers do at sea," at the nose, ears, and mouth.

But this was no time, he says manfully, for a consultation of physicians, while they were dying of hunger, so leaving the English, they forced their way over the bar of Carthersna, an adverse wind preventing their landing at the port of Cabinda. Here they found some oysters sticking to the trees that grew round a pond, and opening them with their clasp knives, which they lent, Montauban says, "charitably and readily to each other," they made a lusty meal.

Having spent two days there, they divided into three small companies, and went up the country, but could find no houses, and see nothing but herds of buffaloes that fled from them. On reaching Cape Corsa they found negroes assembled to furnish ships with wood and water in exchange for brandy, knives, and hatchets.

Montauban, who had often traded in these parts, knew several of the natives, and tried to make them believe he was the man he represented; but disfigured as he was by his late misfortune, they considered him an impostor. In their own language he told them he was dying of famine, but could get nothing but a few bananas to eat.

He then desired them to carry him and his men to Prince Thomas, the son to the king of that country, upon whom he had conferred many favours. But the Prince refused to recognize him, till he showed him the scar of a wound in his thigh which he had once seen when they bathed together. On seeing this the Prince rose and embraced him; commanded victuals to be given to his men; expressed his sorrow for their misfortunes; and quartered them among his negro lords. Montauban he kept at his own expense, and made him eat at his own table. In a few days he took him some leagues up the country in a canoe, to see the king his father, who ruled over a village of 300 huts among the marshes. The high priest was just dead, and during the funeral ceremonies, lasting for seven days, Montauban was regaled with elephant's flesh. The king he found surrounded by women, and guarded by negroes armed with lances and fusils. Flags, trumpets, and drums preceded this monarch of a realm of hunters, who was himself clothed in a robe of white and blue striped cotton. The black prince shook the French captain by the hand, being the first man whose hand he had ever thus honoured. He asked many questions about his brother of France, and when he heard that he sometimes waged war with England and Holland singlehanded, and sometimes with Germany and Spain, the king expressed himself pleased, and, calling for palm wine, said he would drink the French king's health, and as he drank the drums and trumpets sounded, just as they do in Hamlet, and the negro guard discharged their pieces. Prince Thomas then asked the name of the French king who was so powerful, and being told it was Louis le Grand, declared he would give that name to his son, who was about to be baptised, and that Montauban should be godfather. He also expressed his hope that at some future voyage Montauban would carry the child to France, and present him to the brother monarch, and have him brought up in that country. "Assure him," said the same prince, "that I am his friend, and that if he has occasion for my service, I will go myself into France, with all the lances and fusils belonging to the king my father."

The king said, if need were he would go himself in person. At this generous promise the guard discharged their muskets frantically, and the men and women shouted their admiration. The drums and trumpets went to it again, and the spearmen ran from one side to the other, uttering horrible cries, sounding like pain, but expressive of joy. Then the glasses went round faster, and the ceremony concluded by the negro king presenting Montauban with two cakes of wax. The white men now rose in public estimation. Whenever they stirred out, they were followed by crowds of negroes bringing presents of fruits and buffalo flesh, never having seen a white face before, and generally supposing the devil to be of that colour. Sable philosophers begged to be allowed to scrape their skin with knives, till the king issued an edict forbidding any one, under pain, scraping or rubbing the strangers.

The baptism passed off with great *éclat*. There being no priest in the town who knew how to baptize, or remembered the words of the service, a priest was procured from a Portuguese ship lying at the Cape. The freebooter speaks with much unction of his sponsorship. "I did it with so much the more pleasure," quoth he, "in that I was helping to make a Christian and sanctify a soul."

A few days after this ceremony, which afforded so much satisfaction to Montauban's tender conscience, he determined to embark on board an English ship lying at the Cape; but the black king would not have him trust himself into the hands of his enemies, and soon after he set sail in a Portuguese vessel that arrived to barter iron, arms, and brandy, for ivory, wax, and negroes. Two of his men, who had strayed up the country, he left behind. The Portuguese captain turned out to be an old friend, and took him at once to St. Thomas's, and here he stayed a month, the governor of the island showing him a thousand civilities. He then embarked on board an English vessel, with whose captain he contracted an intimate friendship, in spite of the governor's warnings. He gave up his own cabin to Montauban, to use our adventurer's own words:

> ... with all the pleasure and diversion he could think of, for the solacing of my spirits under the afflictions I had from time to time endured.

A tedious sail of three months brought them to Barbadoes. During this time, his provisions running short, the English captain began to regret having taken up his French passengers, and reduced their daily allowance by three-fourths. On arriving at the port, Colonel Russel blamed the captain for having brought such visitors, and forbade him under pain of death to land; but some Jewish physicians declaring that he must die if he did not, the governor consented, keeping a strict watch upon the sick man, and telling him to understand that he and his fellows were prisoners of war. Montauban replied that he had only embarked on the faith of the English captain, on whose friendship he relied. He promised, if liberty were granted, them, he would be ever mindful of the favour, and would either pay the colonel a ransom, or restore at a future time any prisoners belonging to the island.

"No," replied the governor, "I will have neither your ransom nor your prisoners, and you are too brave a man for me to have no compassion upon your many misfortunes. I desire, on the contrary, that you will accept of these forty *pistoles*, which I present you with to supply your present occasions."

A vessel soon after arrived from Martinique, and Montauban went on board with two of his men, all that could be collected. The

English governor, when he thanked him at parting, prayed him to be kind to any English that fell into his hands, and lamented the war regulations that compelled him to severity.

On arriving at Port Royal, at Martinique, Mons. de Blenac, the governor, who was then dying, made him stay at his house, and relate every day his adventure with the English vessel. In the same breath, Montauban praises De Blenac's wisdom, justice, integrity, and knowledge of all the coasts and heights of land in America. In a few days the freebooter embarked in the *Virgin* for Bordeaux, and we lose sight of his stalwart figure and scarred face among the bustling eager crowds that fill the streets of that busy seaport. We have a shrewd suspicion that Sieur de Montauban did not die in a bed, but with his face to the foe and his back on a bloody plank. There is something delightfully sincere and *naïve* in the sort of out-loud thinking with which he concludes his simple "yarn."

> I do not know whether I have bid the sea *adieu*, so much has my last misfortune terrified me, or whether I shall go out again to be revenged on the English, who have done me so much mischief, or go and traverse the seas with a design to get me a little wealth, or rest quiet and eat up what my relations have left me. *There is a strange inclination in men to undertake voyages*, as there is to gaming; whatever misfortunes befall them, they do not believe they will be always unhappy, and therefore will play on. Thus it is as to the sea, whatever accidents befall us, we are in hopes to find a favourable opportunity to make us amends for all our losses. I believe, whoever reads this account will find it a hard task to give me counsel thereupon, or to take the same himself.

Laurence de Graff, our next hero, was a Dutchman by birth, and served first in the service of Spain as a sailor and a gunner. He soon became remarkable as a good shot, and renowned for his address and bravery, his bearing being equally attractive and commanding. Going to America, he carried these talents to the best market, and, being taken prisoner by the corsairs, became a buccaneer, and soon rose to independent command. His name grew so terrible to the Spaniards, that the monks used to pray God in their prayers to deliver them from "Lorençillo," and the whole brotherhood used his name as a war-cry to strike terror. Vessels struck their flag when they heard that shout, and the horsemen fled before it through the savannah. Knowing that the Spaniards would not forgive him the injuries he had inflicted on them, De Graff never fought without strewing powder on the deck, or having a gunner with a lighted match ready to blow up the powder magazine at the first signal. On one occasion the people of Carthagena, knowing that he was sailing near the port in a single small vessel, despatched two frigates to bring him bound to land. Lorençillo, believing himself lost, had already given orders to blow up the vessel, when, making a last desperate effort, he captured both of his enemies. These men were never so formidable as when surrounded by an overwhelming force. On another occasion the admiral and vice-admiral of the galleon fleet had orders to take him at all risks, which they should easily have done, as each of their vessels carried sixty guns. Finding it impossible to escape, Laurence animated his crew, and told them that in victory lay their only hope of life. The gunner was placed as usual ready beside the magazine, and then running boldly between the two vessels, De Graff poured in a volley of musketry and killed forty-eight Spaniards. The action still continued, when a French shot carried away the mainmast of the largest galleon, and her consort, afraid to board, left Lorençillo the conqueror. The report of this victory produced a great sensation both at Paris and Madrid. The French sent the conqueror letters of naturalization and a pardon for the death of Van Horn, and the court of Spain issued orders to cut off the head of their recreant admiral.

At another time Laurence was cruising near Carthagena, in company with the French captains, Michel Jonqué, Le Sage, and Breac. The Spaniards, thinking to catch him alone, sent out two thirty-six gun ships and a small craft of six guns, which overtook him in a bay to leeward of the city. Surprised to see him well guarded, they endeavoured to escape, but Laurence attacked them, and after an eight hours' action, having killed 400 Spaniards, took the admiral's ship, Jonqué's capturing its companion. Laurence's prize, however, was soon after driven ashore, and the prisoners escaped.

Captain Laurence is at this time described as a tall, fair man, with light hair and *moustachios*. He was fond of music, and kept a band of violins and trumpets on board his ship. On one occasion landing in Jamaica, the French levelled the three entrenchments, spiked the cannon, burnt a town, and retreated to their ships—carrying off 3000 negroes, and much indigo and merchandise. The island was saved by the fact of the inhabitants of one corner having fortified all their houses, and turned each into an inaccessible and unscalable fort. In the attack of one of these alone Captain Le Sage and fifty men were killed. The English say that there were 7000 fugitive negroes in the mountains, anxious to join the French, and to escape to St. Domingo, but the French, taking them for enemies, fled at their approach.

Afraid of retaliation, Hispaniola now prepared for defence. Le Sieur de Graff commanded at Cape François, and was to lay ambuscades and throw up entrenchments, and dispute every inch with the Spaniards or the English. If the enemy was too strong he was ordered to spike his cannon, blow up his powder, and fall back to Port de Paix. In 1695 the Spaniards and English landed with 6000 men. Contrary to all expectation, De Graff, perhaps too old for service, wasted eight days in reconnoitring, and abandoned post after post. His men lost all courage when they saw his irresolution. His lieutenant, Le Chevalier de Leon, also deserted his guns without a blow, De Graff merely remarking that it was only twenty-eight cannon lost. A succession of disasters followed, and nothing but climate and the quarrels of the allies saved the desolated colony.

In 1686, De Graff was made major in the French army, and henceforward fought with more or less fidelity for the country that had ennobled him. Not long after this event, the termination of all his glory, being a widower, he married Anne Dieu le Veut, a French lady of indomitable spirit. She was one of those French women brought over by the governor, M. D'Ogeron, to marry to the hunters of Hispaniola. "They grew," says Charlevoix, "perfect Atalantas, and joined in the chase, using the musket and sabre with the best."

From such Amazonian mould came some of the buccaneer chiefs. One day before her marriage, this heroine having received some insult from her husband, drew out a pistol and forced him to unsay what he had uttered. Full of admiration at her courage, and thinking such an Amazon worthy of a hero's bed, he married her.

Both she and her children were taken prisoners by the English, and not released for a long time after the peace. De Graff's first wife was Petroline de Guzman, a Spanish lady.

At the time De Graff's brevet arrived, he was on a reef near Carthagena, having been wrecked while pursuing a bark in a vessel of forty-eight guns and 400 men. With his canoe the wrecked men took the ship, and landing in Darien, lost twenty-five adventurers in an Indian ambuscade. His two prizes he sent to St. Domingo, but his crew obliged him to continue privateering till the letters from De Cussy recalled him. One of the chief reasons why this honour had been bestowed on him was, that, by his great credit with the adventurers, he might draw them to settle on land.

About this time, the Spaniards surprised Petit Guaves, and war commenced. Only the year before, the same nation had seized Breac, the *flibustier* captain, and hung him, with nine or ten of his men. Soon after this, a Spanish officer, whom De Graff, now commandant at the Isle à la Vache, had delivered from some English corsairs, informed him that a Spanish galleon full of treasure was lying wrecked at the Seranillas Islands, but this prize he was obliged to relinquish to the English.

De Graff now became remarkable for his firmness and justice. He encouraged colonization, settled differences between English and French buccaneers, and prohibited all privateering. His name was still so terrible, that on one occasion 2000 Spaniards attacking Hispaniola retreated when they heard that the old chief commanded the militia of the island.

The *flibustier*s were found bad colonists: the French could manage to keep them at a fortified post when a Spanish invasion was expected, but the instant the enemy retreated, the sea grew dark with buccaneer vessels, eager for prizes. Indocile and desperate, they seduced all the youth of Hispaniola from their plantations. At one time the French governor seems to have resolved on their total destruction, but their usefulness as light troops saved them. The descents on Jamaica in search of slaves by the French buccaneers grew soon so numerous, that the English island became known as "little Guinea."

In 1692, a French adventurer named Daviot, with 290 men, landed and pillaged the north of Jamaica. His vessel being driven out to sea by a storm, his men were compelled to remain fifteen days exposed to incessant attacks from their enemies. While waiting for the vessel's return, the dreadful earthquake happened that swallowed 11,000 souls, and destroyed Port Royal. The *flibustiers*, alarmed at the rocking of the earth, embarked 115 sailors and forty prisoners in canoes, but the sea was as convulsed as the land, and they lost all but sixty men, and were driven again on shore. Attacked when he again put out to sea by two English vessels, Daviot beat them off with a loss of seventy-six men, only two of his own being killed. Boarded by the English a second time, his vessel blew up, and he surrendered with twenty-one of his crew. Soon after this, three French vessels, manned with buccaneers, took an English *guarda costa* of forty guns, killing eighteen men.

In 1694, De Graff commanded in a buccaneer invasion of Jamaica, sailing to that island with fourteen vessels and 550 men. He forced the English entrenchments in spite of 1400 musketeers and twelve guns, slew 360 of the defenders, and captured nine ships, losing himself only twenty-two men. He then drove off 260 troopers from Spanish Town, after two hours' combat. The next day De Graff despatched troops to carry off cattle.

In 1696, a process was instituted against De Graff, whom M. Du Casse suspected of intrigues with Spain. The evidence, M. Charlevoix thinks, showed only his extreme fear of falling into the hands of the enemy. It is certain that the Spanish had offered to make him a vice-admiral, but he would not trust their sincerity. The English despised him for this supposed treachery, and when he proposed to the governor of Jamaica to retreat to that island, if he could give him employment, the governor replied, that he had already betrayed three nations, and would not stick at betraying a fourth.

The Spaniards regarded him with fear till his death, and never forgave him the injury he had done them. Says Charlevoix:

> During the next war between France and Spain the Marquis of Cöelogon arriving at Havannah with a French squadron that he commanded in the Mexican Gulf, having De Graff on board, all the town ran to the shore at the news, to see the famous Lorençillo that had so long been the terror of the West Indies, but the Marquis would not let him land for fear of danger.

Deprived of his command, De Graff was appointed captain of a light frigate. This situation suited him better than land service, for which he showed no genius, and he was frequently employed on board the French squadrons, no man knowing better the navigation of the North Pacific. Of his death we know nothing, but it is supposed he lived to a good age.

One of the most important enterprises ever attempted by the French buccaneers, in conjunction with the French government, was the capture of Carthagena in 1697. The fleet of M. de Poincy consisted of eighteen vessels, besides ten *flibustier* craft, carrying 700 adventurers, in addition to his own 4658 men and two companies of negroes. The buccaneer captains were Montjoy, Godefroy, Blanc, Galet, Pierre, Pays, Sales, Macary, and Colong. Their vessels were named *Le Pontchartrain, La Ville de Glamma, La Serpente, La Gracieuse, La Pembrock, Le Cerf Volant, La Mutine, Le Brigantin, Le Jersé*, and *L'Anglais*. The whole force mustered 6,500 men. The adventurers at first refused to embark till a fit share of the booty was promised to them, being accustomed to be deprived of their rights by the French officers. Enraged at not being treated as equals, and finding one of their men imprisoned at Petit Guaves, they invested the fort, and were only appeased by ready concessions. The first scheme of the expedition was to seek the galleons; but this was abandoned, though it appeared afterwards that at that very time they were lying at Porto Bello richer than they had been for fifty years, and laden with 50,000,000 crowns. The second plan was to attack Vera Cruz, and the last to sail to Carthagena.

That most graphic and vigorous of writers, Michael Scott, describes Carthagena as situated on a group of sandy islands, surrounded by shallow water. A little behind the town, on a gentle acclivity, is the citadel of Fort St. Felipe, and on the ship-like hill beyond it the convent of the Popa, projecting like a poop-lantern in the high stern of a ship.

Arrived at that city, the French *galliot* bombarded the whole night; and as this was the first bomb ship ever seen in the West Indies, the splintering of shells produced a great terror in the citizens. Two days after the fleet anchored before Bocca Chica. This fort contained thirty-three guns; had four bastions, and was defended by a dry fosse cut in the rocks. The ramparts were bomb proof and the walls shot proof. Under the fire of the *St. Louis*, the *galliot*, and two bomb vessels, the troops landed and advanced without opposition within a quarter of a league of the fort. By the advice of the buccaneers, accustomed to such marches, 3000 men crossed through a wood by a path so difficult that only one man could pass at a time, and, unobserved, took possession of the road leading from Carthagena to the fort, fortifying themselves on both sides, and cutting off the communication between the fort and the city, taking some negroes prisoners, and losing a few men from the shots of the enemy.

The next morning, at daybreak, the adventurers, finding some boats on the beach, pursued and captured a Spanish *piragua* containing several monks of high rank. One of the priests in vain was sent with a flag of truce and a drummer and trumpeter to summon the governor to surrender. The negroes clearing the road, a battery of guns and mortars opened upon the fort, and the buccaneer sharp-shooters shot down the enemy's gunners, driving back some half galleys that attempted to bring reinforcements. The buccaneers, pursuing the boats, found shelter under the covered way, and killed every man who showed himself on the batteries of the fort. The governor, who saw the adventurers rushing, as he thought, madly to destruction, began to lament that he had employed such people. Warned that if left alone "the brothers" would give a good account of the place, he scornfully laughed and ordered up reinforcements. Thinking the *flibustiers* had only run under the covered way for shelter, he pursued a few who really did turn tail with his cane, and attempted in vain to drive them to the assault. By this time the freebooters had won the drawbridge, and, displaying their colours on the edge of the ditch, demanded means for the escalade. Thirty ladders were placed, and the assault had already commenced, when the Spaniards hung out the white flag, and, shouting "*Viva el rey!*" flung their arms and hats into the ditch. The gate being opened, 100 of the garrison were confined in the chapel; 200 others were found wounded. The governor, handing the keys of the fortress to M. de Poincy, said: "I deliver into your hands the keys of all the Spanish Indies." About forty adventurers were killed, and as many wounded, in this attack.

The next day the fleet entered the harbour, and the Spaniards burned all their vessels to prevent capture. The governor still refusing to surrender, saying he wanted neither men, arms, nor courage, the adventurers embarked to attack the convent of Nuestra Senhora de la Popa, and to occupy the heights. M. du Casse being wounded in the thigh, the *flibustiers* refused to march under the command of M. Galifet, to whom they had a dislike; and on his striking one of them, the man took him by the cravat. The mutineer was instantly tied to a tree and sentenced to be shot, but pardoned at M. Galifet's intercession. M. de Poincy, going on board Captain Pierre's ship, seized him and ordered him to execution, and the revolt then ceased, De Poincy threatening to decimate them on the next outbreak.

The convent stood on a mountain shaped like the poop of a ship, about a gunshot from Carthagena. It had been abandoned by the monks, who had stripped it of every valuable.

The army then marched by sunset to the fort Santa Cruz, suffering much from thirst. The fort mounted sixty guns, was surrounded by a wet ditch, and on the land side accessible only through a morass, but it surrendered without firing a shot. The adventurers then pushed on to within a gunshot of Fort St. Lazarus, which commanded the suburbs on the other side of the city. The French defiled round the fort, while some of their grenadiers carried on a pretended conference with the fort. The next day roads were cut through a hill, and the army were placed within pistol shot of the walls, concealed by an eminence that covered them from the enemy's fire. The Spaniards, losing their commander, abandoned the place in disorder, and their fort, St. Lazarus, being within musket shot of Gezemanie (the suburbs), they opened a fire of ten guns upon the captured batteries, the buccaneer musketry clearing the streets. Thirty men were killed in trying to turn a chapel into a redoubt, and the camp removed behind St. Lazarus, De Poincy having been wounded in the breast.

The three next days several breaching batteries were completed, and the *galliot* and mortars bombarded the city all night. In three days more, the breach was pronounced practicable, and the storming commenced. M. du Casse, although wounded, led the grenadiers, and M. Macharais the adventurers, who set the army an example of daring. Planks were laid over the broken drawbridge, and the troops passed over, under a tremendous fire from the bastion of St. Catherine, one man only being able to cross at a time. The breach and batteries were lined with Spanish lancers, who flung their spears, nine feet long, a distance of twelve or fifteen yards. The French had 250 men killed and wounded, and many officers fell. Vice-admiral the Count de Cöetlogon was mortally hurt; the commander-in-chief's nephew, le Chevalier de Poincy, a young midshipman, had his knee broken, and many were wounded in pursuing the Spaniards to the city.

The French gave no quarter, putting to the sword 200 Spaniards who had thrown themselves into a church. The governor, who had ordered his servants to carry him in his easy chair to the breach to animate his men, fled into Carthagena. The army now advanced to the bridge which led from Gezemanie to the city, and repulsed two sorties of the enemy.

The French threw up entrenchments and erected batteries to breach the walls. Two days were spent in these preparations and in dressing the wounded. There were still great difficulties to encounter. Armies of Indians were approaching. The Spanish garrison had six months' provision and eighty guns mounted on their ramparts. The next day, Carthagena, terrified at the fate of Gezemanie, surrendered. The conditions were, that the churches should not be plundered, that those who chose might leave the city unmolested, and that the inhabitants should surrender half their money on pain of losing all. The governor and troops were to depart with the honours of war. The merchants were to surrender their account books to the French commander. The adventurers instantly occupied the bastions and gate, and the other troops seized the ramparts. The governor, having marched out with 700 men, M. de Poincy proceeded to the cathedral to hear the *Te Deum*, and then repaired to his lodgings at the house where the royal treasure was deposited.

At first the soldiers and sailors were forbidden to enter any house on pain of death, and the admiral's carpenter being caught plundering, and confessing his guilt, had his head cut off on the spot. But a change soon took place. The governor, assembling the heads of religious houses, informed them that the treaty did not spare any convent that had money. Many days were spent in receiving and weighing the crowns. De Poincy declared, that before his arrival the monks had fled with 120 mules laden with gold, and he had obtained barely nine million pieces. Other accounts say he obtained forty million *livres, i.e.,* twenty millions without including merchandise. Every officer had 100,000 crowns, besides his general share of the spoil, before he allowed his soldiers to enter a house. Charlevoix confesses, that the honour the French won by their bravery they lost by their cruelty. The capitulation was broken, churches were profaned, church plate stolen, images broken, virgins violated on the very altars, the monks tortured, and the sick in the hospitals left to starve, or resort to the horrors of cannibalism. Notwithstanding the inhabitants brought in their money, some to the amount of 400,000 dollars, a general search was made throughout the town, and much gold found. A few of the inhabitants hired guards of adventurers, but, in general, these men also turned plunderers, the officers only attempting to keep up appearances.

Anxious to get the adventurers out of the way while he collected the spoil, De Poincy spread a report that 10,000 Indians were approaching, and sent the *flibustiers* to drive them back. After plundering the country for four leagues, they returned with fifty prisoners, a drove of cattle, and 4,000 crowns. During the siege, they had been employed in skirmishing, cutting off supplies, and foraging, and were accustomed to laugh at the sailors, who dragged the guns and called them "white negroes."

Disease breaking out, and carrying off 800 men in six weeks, De Poincy embarked his plunder, and prepared to sail. Eighty-six guns he carried off, and destroyed St. Lazarus and Bocca Chica. The buccaneers, calling out loudly for their share, received only 40,000 crowns. The men instantly shouted—"Brothers, we do wrong to take anything of this dog, our share is left at Carthagena."

This proposal was received with a ferocious gaiety, and they all swore never to return to St. Domingo. They derided M. du Casse's promises to get them justice from the French king, and fired at those vessels that would not follow them. The people of Carthagena shuddered to see them return. Shutting up all the men in the cathedral, they promised to depart on receiving five millions as a ransom. In one day a million crowns were brought, but, this being still inadequate, they broke open the very tombs, and goaded the citizens to the torture, firing off guns, and pretending to put men to death in the neighbouring rooms. Two men, guilty of cruelty, their leaders hanged. Each man received about 1,000 crowns; and having spent four days in collecting and dividing the gold and silver, they appointed the Isle à la Vache as a rendezvous to divide the slaves and merchandise.

The retribution was at hand. They had not sailed thirty leagues when they fell in with the combined English and Dutch fleets. *Le Christ*, with 250 men, and more than a million crowns, was taken by the Dutch, *Le Cerf Volant* by the English, a third was driven on shore and burnt near St. Domingo, a fourth, running on land near Carthagena, was taken, and her crew employed in rebuilding the fortifications they had destroyed. Of De Poincy's plunder, 120,000 *livres* were carried off by an English foray on Petit Guaves. Admiral Neville, who failed to overtake the French deep-laden and weakly manned fleet, died of a broken heart at Virginia.

Du Casse was rewarded with the cross of St. Louis for his services, and orders arrived from France to distribute 1,400,000 of De Poincy's spoil among the freebooters, very little of which, however, reached them. A curse, says Charlevoix, rested on the whole enterprise.

In 1698, a French fleet, under the command of Count d'Estrees, on its way to attack the Dutch island of Curaçoa, was lost on the Aves Islands, a small cluster of rocks surrounded by breakers. Attracted by the distress-guns fired by the first ship that ran aground, its companions, believing that it had been attacked by the enemy, hurried pell-mell to its assistance, and, blinded by the fog, ran one by one on destruction. Eighteen of them were lost. Of this disaster, Dampier, who visited the island about a year afterwards, gives a very interesting account. The buccaneer part of the crew (for the buccaneers took an active part in these wars), quite accustomed to such chances, scrambled to shore, and proceeded to save all they could from the wreck; but a few of them, breaking into the stores of a stranded vessel, floated with her out to sea, drinking and cursing on the poop, and holding up their flasks, shouting and laughing to the drowning men around them. Every soul of them perished.

Several *flibustier* vessels were lost at the same time, about 800 buccaneers having joined the expedition at Tortuga. About 300 of these perished with the wrecks. Dampier describes the islands as strewn with shreds of sail, broken spars, masts, and rigging. For some years, in consequence, the Aves became the resort of buccaneer captains, who careened and refitted here, employing their crews in diving for plate, and in attempts to recover guns and anchors.

To console themselves for this failure, M. de Poincy led 800 buccaneers to attack Santiago, first touching at Tortuga for reinforcements. They landed unseen, taking advantage of a bright moonlight night. The vanguard wound their way round the base of a mountain that barred their approach to the town, and, instead of advancing, worked round till they met their rearguard, whom they mistook for the enemy, and furiously attacked. They discovered their mistake at last by their mutual cries of *"Tue, tue."* But it was now late; all hopes of surprise were over; the Spaniards, alarmed, put themselves on their defence, and at daybreak drove back the freebooters to their ships with an irresistible force of 4000 men. Another party, more successful, plundered Port au Prince, St. Thomas's, and Truxillo on the mainland.

Grammont, during this time, had been left behind on the Aves Islands, to collect all that was valuable from the wreck, and to careen the surviving vessels. Having completed this, and finding himself short of provisions, and the season being favourable for an excursion to the Gulf of Venezuela, Grammont decided upon a visit to Maracaibo. Arriving at the fort of the bar, mounted with twelve guns and garrisoned by seventy men, he commenced an attack. The French had opened a trench, had already pushed it within cannon shot, and were preparing the ladders to scale, when the governor surrendered on condition of obtaining the honours of war. Passing on to the town, Grammont found it abandoned. Gibraltar also made little resistance. From the lake he carried off three vessels, and also took a prize of value, cannonading it with his guns, and at the same time boarding it with a swarm of canoes. Being now master of the whole lake, he visited all the places where his prisoners told him he was likely to find gold hidden, defeating the Spaniards wherever he met them.

Then, collecting all his scattered plunderers, Grammont prepared to attack Torilla, making a detour of forty-five leagues in order to take it by surprise. Arriving near the town, the buccaneers came to the banks of a rapid river, with only one ford, which they had the good fortune to find, crossing over under shelter of a hot fire that the rearguard kept up upon the Spaniards, who lay entrenched upon the opposite bank. The moment they had crossed, their enemies fled, and Torilla was their own. The prize, however, proved not worth the winning, for the town was abandoned, and the treasure hid. The buccaneer rule, indeed, was that no place was worth sacking which was taken without a blow, as the Spaniards always fought best when they had most to fight for. The buccaneers departed with little booty; their 700 men having taken three towns, and conquered a province, with the loss of only seventy men, and these chiefly by illness.

In 1680 Grammont made another expedition to the coast of Cumana. Having collected twenty-five *piraguas*, he ascertained from some prisoners that there were three armed vessels anchored under the forts of Gonaire, and these he determined to cut out. He embarked all his 180 men in a single bark, and left orders for the others to sail up to Gonaire at a given signal. He landed with a few men at night, and surprised four watchmen, who, however, had still time left to fire, and alarm the town, before they could be overpowered. Gonaire leaped instantly from its sleep. The bells rang backward; the guns fired; the musketeers hurried to the market-place; doors were barred; and the women and children fled in tears to the altars. Grammont, doubling his speed, arrived at the east gate, his drums beating, trumpets sounding, and colours flying. Although it was defended by twelve guns, he took it with the hot fierceness of a Caesar, pushed on at once to a fort about a hundred yards distant, and commenced a vigorous attack. At the head of his crew he entered the embrasures, killing twenty-six out of its thirty-eight defenders. Planting his colours on the wall, the men shouted *"Vive le Roi!"* with such unanimity and fierceness that at the very sound the whole garrison of the neighbouring fort at once surrendered, and forty-two men instantly laid down their arms. These successes were obtained with only forty-seven men—a mere handful being able to keep up in the rapid and headlong charge. Grammont, rallying his men, then placed garrisons in the forts, razed the embrasures, spiked the cannon, and then proceeded to entrench himself in a strong position. The next day he entered the town, making several vigorous sorties on the enemy, who now began to gather in round him on all sides. Being informed that 2000 men were advancing to meet him from Caragua, he gave orders for embarkation, the buccaneers seldom fighting when no booty was to be obtained. Remaining last upon the shore to cover the retreat of his men, withstanding for nearly twenty-four hours the onslaught of 300 Spaniards, he was at last dangerously wounded in the throat, and one of his officers had his shoulder broken.

Grammont took with him the Governor of Gonaire, and 150 other prisoners, the usual resource of the buccaneers when a town either furnished no booty, or gave them no time to collect it. This daring enterprise was achieved with the loss of only eight men. On his way home to be cured of a wound which his vexation and impatience had rendered dangerous, he was wrecked near Petit Guaves, and his own vessel and his prize both lost.

About the next adventure of this chivalrous corsair some doubts are thrown, although it is related boastingly by Charlevoix, who says:

> He then took an English vessel of thirty guns, which had defied the Governor of Tortuga, and beaten off a buccaneer bark. This ship, armed with fifty guns, and navigated by a crew of 300 men, Grammont is reported to have boarded, killing every Englishman on board but the captain, whom he reserved to carry in triumph to shore.

Grammont was born in Paris of a good family. His mother being left a widow, her daughter was courted by an officer who treated Grammont, then a student, as a rude boy. They fought, and the lover received three mortal stabs. Obtaining the dying man's pardon, the young duellist entered the marines, eventually commanded a privateer frigate, and took, near Martinique, a Dutch flute, containing 400,000 *livres*. Having spent all this in gaiety at St. Domingo, the young captain turned buccaneer. Charlevoix notices his manners and address, which were as fascinating as those of De Graff. The writer describes *"Sa bonne grâce, ses manières honnêtes, et je ne sçais quoi d'aimable qui gagnoit les coeurs."*

We have described already his surprise of Maracaibo, and his expedition to Vera Cruz. His expedition to Campeachy was against the wish of the French Governor of St. Domingo. On their way home he quarrelled and separated from De Graff. Says Charlevoix:

With all the talent that can raise man to command, he had, all the vices of a corsair. He drank hard, and abandoned himself to debauchery, with a total disregard of religion.

In 1686 Grammont, at the recommendation of M. de Cussy, Governor of St. Domingo, was made Lieutenant de Roi, Cussy intending to make him Protector of the south coast. But Grammont, elated at his new title, and anxious to show that he deserved it, armed a ship, manned by 180 buccaneers, to make a last cruise against the Spaniards, and was heard of no more.

Chapter 14
Fall of the Floating Empire

The English were the first to attempt to put down Buccaneering, but the last to succeed in doing it. When the freebooters had served their purpose, the English government would have thrown them by as a soldier would his broken sword. In 1655, after Morgan returned from Panama, Lord John Vaughan, the new governor of Jamaica, had strict orders to enforce the treaty concluded with Spain in the previous year, but to proclaim pardon, indemnity, and grants of land to all buccaneers who would turn planters. By royal proclamation, all cruising against Spain was forbidden under severe penalties. To avoid this irksome imprisonment to a plot of sugar canes, many of the English freebooters joined their brethren at Tortuga, or turned cow-killers and logwood cutters in the Bay of Campeachy. In the next year the war broke out between England and Holland, and many fitted out privateers.

The unwise restrictions of France, and home interference with colonial administration, once more fostered "the people of the coast." Annoying prohibitions and vexatious monopolies drove the planters to sea.

In 1690 a royal proclamation granted pardon to all English buccaneers who should surrender themselves. The French *flibustiers* continued to flourish during the war which followed the accession of William III. to the throne of England.

In 1698 the knell of the brotherhood was finally rung by the joy bells that announced the peace of Ryswick. The English and Dutch made great complaints to the Governor of St. Domingo of the French *flibustiers*, and demanded compensation, which was granted. A colony was established at the Isle à la Vache in hopes of carrying on a trade with New Spain, by orders of the French king the church plate brought from Carthagena was returned, and Buccaneering prohibited.

The government advised that force should be resorted to to induce those *flibustiers* to turn planters who were not willing to avail themselves of the amnesty. Those who had settled in Jamaica, seeing in 1702 a new war likely to break out between England and France, and determined not to take arms against their own country, passed over to the mainland, and settled in Bocca Toro. As soon as the war broke out, however, a great many French buccaneers, persecuted at St. Domingo, joined the English under Benbow. In 1704, M. Auger, a new governor, coming to St. Domingo, and seeing the false step his predecessors had taken, recalled the *flibustiers*, and made peace with the Bocca Toro Indians. M. d'Herville led 1,500 of them to the Havannah, and died there. He held the buccaneers of Hispaniola far beyond those of Martinique, and, had he lived, would have united them all under his flag.

In 1707 Le Comte de Choiseul Beaupré, the new governor, attempted to revive Buccaneering as the only hope of saving French commerce in the Indies, the English privateers carrying off every merchant ship that approached the shores of St. Domingo. The French government approved of all his plans, and gave him unlimited power to carry them out. He issued an amnesty to all *flibustiers* who had settled among the Indians of Sambres and Bocca Toro. The greater part of those who had joined the English returned; and those who had joined in the last expedition against Carthagena received their pay. The Brothers were restored to all their ancient privileges. The Count intended to guard the coast with frigates while his smaller vessels harassed Jamaica, but in the midst of these immature projects he was killed, in 1710, in a sea engagement.

The buccaneers, gathered from every part, now turned planters. Thus, says Charlevoix, ended the "*Flibuste de Saint Domingue*," which only required discipline and leaders of ambition to have conquered both North and South America. Undisciplined and tumultuous as it has been, without order, plan, forethought, or subordination, it has still been the astonishment of the whole world, and has done deeds which posterity will not believe.

Attachment to old habits and difficulty in finding employment made many turn pirates. Proscribed now by all nations, with no excuse for plunder, and with no safe place of refuge, they sailed over the world, enemies to all they met. Many frequented the Guinea coast, others cruised off the coast of India, and New Providence island, one of the Bahama group, was now the only sanctuary. Here the memorable Blackbeard, Martel, and his associates, were at last hunted down, about 1717.

The last achievement related of the *flibustiers* is in 1702, when a party of Englishmen having a commission from the Governor of Jamaica, landed on the Isthmus of Darien, near the Samballas isles, and were joined by some old *flibustiers* who had settled there, and 300 friendly Indians. With these allies they marched to the mines, drove out the Spaniards according to Dampier's plan, and took seventy negroes. They kept these slaves at work twenty-one days, but obtained, after all, only eighty pounds' weight of gold.

CHAPTER 15

The Pirates of New Providence & the Kings of Madagascar

The last refugee buccaneers turned pirates, and settled in the island of New Providence.

The African coast, and not the main, was now their cruising ground, and Madagascar was their new Tortuga. They no longer warred merely against the Spaniard—their hands were raised against the world. Their cruelty was no longer the cruelty of retaliation, but arose from a thirst of blood, never to be slaked, and still unquenchable. There was no longer honour among the bands, and they grew as cowardly as they were ferocious. Flocks of trading vessels were scuttled, but no town attacked. We waste time even to detail their guilt, and only append the terrible catalogue as a *finis* to our narrative. The following articles, signed by Roberts's crew, may furnish a fair example of the ordinary rules drawn up by pirate captains:

> Every man has a vote in affairs of moment, and an equal title to the fresh provisions or strong liquors at any time seized; which he may use at pleasure, unless a scarcity make it necessary for the good of all to vote a retrenchment.
>
> Every man shall be called fairly in turn by list on board the prizes, and, over and above their proper share, shall be allowed a change of clothes. Any man who defrauds the company to the value of a dollar in plate, jewels, or money, shall be marooned. If the robbery is by a messmate, the thief shall have his ears and nose slit, and be set on shore at the place the ship touches at.
>
> No man shall play at cards or dice for money.

The lights and candles to be put out at eight o'clock at night. If any of the crew, after that hour, still remain inclined for drinking, they are to do it on the open deck.

Every man shall keep his piece, pistols, and cutlass clean, and fit for service.

No woman to be allowed on board. Any man who seduces a woman, and brings her to sea disguised, shall suffer death.

Any one deserting the ship, or leaving his quarters during an engagement, shall be either marooned or put to death.

No man shall strike another on board, but the disputants shall settle their quarrel on shore with sword or pistol.

No man shall talk of breaking up the company till we get each £100. Every man losing a limb, or becoming a cripple in the service, shall have 800 dollars, and for lesser hurts proportional recompense.

The captain and quartermaster shall receive two shares of every prize. The master, boatswain, and gunner one share and a-half, and all other officers one and a-quarter.

The musicians to rest on Sundays, but on no other days without special favour.

From another set of articles we find, that

He that shall be found guilty of taking up any unlawful weapon on board a prize so as to strike a comrade, shall be tried by the captain and company, and receive due punishment.

All men guilty of cowardice shall also be tried.

If any gold, jewels, or silver, to the value of a piece of eight, be found on board a prize, and the finder do not deliver it to the quartermaster within twenty-four hours, he shall be put to his trial.

Any one found guilty of defrauding another to the value of a shilling, shall be tried.

Quarter always to be given when called for.

He that sees a sail first, to have the best pistols or small arms on board of her.

One of the most cruel of their punishments was "sweating," an ingenuity probably invented by the London rakes and "scourers" of Charles the Second's reign. They first stuck up lighted candles circularly round the mizenmast, between decks, and within this circle admitted the prisoners one by one. Outside the candles stood the pirates armed with penknives, tucks, forks, and compasses, and the musicians playing a lively dance, they drove the prisoner round, pricking him as he passed. This could seldom be borne more than ten minutes, at the end of which time the wretch, maddened with fear and pain, generally fell senseless.

Their diversions were as strange as their cruelties. On one occasion some pirates captured a ship laden with horses, going from Rhode Island to St. Christopher's. The sailors mounted these beasts, and rode them backwards and forwards, full gallop, along the decks, cursing and shouting till the animals grew maddened. When two or three of these rough riders were thrown, they leaped up and fell on the crew with their sabres, declaring that they would kill them for not bringing boots and spurs, without which no man could ride.

In dress the pirates were fantastic and extravagant. Their favourite ornament was a broad sash slung across the breast and fastened on the shoulder and hip with coloured ribbons. In this they slung three and four pairs of pistols, for which, at the sales at the mast, they would often give £40 a pair. Gold-laced cocked hats were conspicuous features of their costume.

For small offences, too insignificant for a jury, the quartermaster was the arbitrator. If they disobeyed his command, except in time of battle, when the captain was supreme, were quarrelsome or mutinous, misused prisoners, or plundered when plundering should cease, or were negligent of their arms, as the master he might cudgel or whip them. He was, in fact, the manager of all duels, and the trustee of the whole company, returning to the owners what he chose (except gold and silver), and confiscating whatever he thought advisable. The quartermaster was, in fact, their magistrate, the captain their king.

The captain had always the great cabin to himself, and was often voted parcels of plate and china. Any sailor, however, might use his punch-bowl, enter his room, swear at him, and seize his food, without his daring to find fault, or contest his rights. The captain was generally chosen for being "pistol proof," and in some cases had as privy council a certain number of the elder sailors, who were called "lords."

The captain's power was uncontrollable in time of chase or battle: he might then strike, stab, or shoot anybody who disobeyed his orders. The fate of the prisoner depended much upon the captain, who was oftener inclined to mercy than his crew.

Their flags were generally intended to strike terror. Roberts's was a black silk flag, with a white skeleton upon it, with an hourglass in one hand, and cross-bones in the other, underneath a dart, and a heart dripping blood. The pennon bore a man with a flaming sword in one hand, standing on two skulls, one inscribed A. B. H. (a Barbadian's head), and the other, A. M. H. (a Martiniquian's head).

Blackbeard

Edward Teach, *alias* Blackbeard, was born in Bristol, and at a seaport town all daring youths turn sailors. He soon became distinguished for daring and courage, but did not obtain any command till 1716, when a Captain Benjamin Hornigold gave him the command of a sloop, and became his partner in piracy, till he surrendered.

In the spring of 1717, the pair sailed from their haunt in New Providence towards the Spanish main, and taking by the way a *shallop* from the Havannah, laden with flour, supplied their own vessels. From a ship of Bermuda they obtained wine, and from a craft of Madeira they got considerable plunder.

Careening on the Virginian coast, they returned to the West Indies, and capturing a large French Guinea-man, bound for Martinique, Teach went aboard as captain, and started for a cruise. Hornigold, returning to New Providence, surrendered to proclamation, and gave himself up to Governor Rogers.

Blackbeard had in the meantime mounted his prize with forty guns, and christened her the *Queen Anne's Revenge*. Cruising off St. Vincent, he captured the *Great Allan*, and having plundered her, and set the men on shore, fired the ship, and let her drift to sea.

A few days after, Teach was attacked by the *Scarborough* man-of-war, who, finding him well manned, retired to Barbadoes, after a cannonade of some hours. On his way to the mainland, Teach was joined by Major Bonnet, a gentleman planter, turned pirate, who joined with him, commanding a sloop of ten guns. Finding he knew nothing of naval affairs, Teach soon deposed him, and took him on board his own ship, on pretext of relieving him from the fatigues and cares of such a post, wishing him, as he said, to live easy and do no duty.

While taking in water near the Bay of Honduras, they surprised a sloop from Jamaica, which surrendered without a blow, striking sail at the first terror of the black flag. The men they took on board Teach's vessel, and manned it for their own use.

At Honduras they found a ship and four sloops, some from Jamaica, and some from Boston. The Americans deserted one vessel, and escaped on shore, and the pirates burnt it in revenge. The other vessel they also burnt, because some pirate had been lately hung at Boston. The three sloops they allowed to depart.

Taking turtles at the Grand Caiman's islands, they sailed to the Havannah, and from the Bahamas went to Carolina, capturing a brigantine and two sloops. For six days they lay off the bar of Charlestown, taking many vessels, and a brigantine laden with negroes. The people of Carolina, who had not long before been visited by the pirate Vane, were dumb with terror. No vessel dared put out, and the trade of the place stood still. To add to these misfortunes, a long and expensive war with the natives, only just concluded, had much impoverished the colony.

Teach detained all the ships and prisoners, and being in want of medicines, sent a boat's crew of men ashore, with one of the prisoners, to ask the governor to supply him with the drugs. The pirates were insolent in their demands, and, swearing horribly, vowed, if any violence was offered to them, that their captain would murder all the prisoners, send their heads to the governor, and then fire the vessels and slip cable. These rude ambassadors swaggered through the streets, insulting the inhabitants, who longed to seize them, but dared not, for fear of endangering the town. The governor did not deliberate long, for one of his brother magistrates was in the murderer's hands, and at once sent on board a chest, worth about £400, which the pirates returned with in triumph. Blackbeard then released the prisoners, having first taken about £1,500 out of the ships, besides provisions.

From the bar of Charlestown the kingly villains sailed to North Carolina, where Teach broke up the partnership, objecting to any division of money, preferring all the risk and all the profit. Running into an inlet to clean, he purposely grounded his ship, and Hands, another captain, coming to his assistance, ran ashore by his side. He then with forty men took possession of the third vessel, and marooned seventeen other men upon a sandy island, about a league from the main, where neither herb grew nor bird visited. Here they would have perished, had not Major Bonnet taken them off two days after.

Teach then surrendered himself, with twenty of his men, to the Governor of North Carolina, and received certificates and pardons from him, having soon crept into his favour. Through the governor's permission, the *Queen Anne's Revenge*, though avowedly the property of English merchants, was forfeited by an Admiralty Court, as a Spaniard, and declared the property of Teach. Before setting out again to sea Blackbeard married his fourteenth wife, twelve more being still alive. The governor, who seems to have been half a pirate, and wholly a rogue, performed the ceremony.

In June, 1718, he steered towards Bermudas, and meeting several English vessels, plundered them of provisions. He also captured two French vessels, one of which was loaded with sugar and cocoa, and bound to Martinico. The loaded vessel he brought home, and the governor, calling a court, condemned it as a derelict, and divided the plunder with Teach, receiving sixty hogsheads of sugar as his dividend, and his secretary twenty. For fear the vessel might still be claimed, Teach declared it was leaky, and burnt her to the water's edge. He now spent three or four months in the river, lying at anchor in the coves, or sailing from inlet to inlet, bartering his plunder with any ship he met, giving presents to the friendly, and ransacking those who resisted. His nights he spent in revelries with the planters, to whom he made presents of rum and sugar, sometimes, when he grew moody, laying them under contribution, and even bullying his confederate, the villainous governor.

The plundered sloops, finding no justice could be obtained in Carolina, determined with great secrecy to send a deputation to the Governor of Virginia, and to solicit a man-of-war to destroy the pirates.

The governor instantly complied with their request. The next Sunday a proclamation was read in every church and chapel in Virginia, and by the sheriffs at their country houses. For Blackbeard's head £100 was offered, if brought in within the year, for his lieutenant's £20, for inferior officers £10, and for the common sailors £10. The *Pearl* and *Lime*, men-of-war, lying in St. James's river, manned a couple of small sloops, supplied by the governor. They had no guns mounted, but were well supplied with small arms and ammunition. The command was given to Lieutenant Robert Maynard, of the *Pearl*, a man of courage and resolution.

On the 7th of November the lieutenant sailed from Picquetan, and on the evening of the 21st reached the mouth of the Ollereco inlet, and sighted the pirates. Great secrecy was observed: all boats and vessels met going up the river were stopped to prevent Blackbeard knowing of their approach. But the governor contrived to put him on his guard, and sent back four of his men, whom he found lounging about the town.

Blackbeard, frequently alarmed by such reports, gave no credit to the messenger, till he saw the sloops. He instantly cleared his decks, having only twenty-five of his forty men on board. Having prepared for battle with all the coolness of an old desperado, he spent the night in drinking with the master of a trading sloop, who seemed to be in his pay.

Maynard, finding the place shoal and the channel intricate, dropped anchor, knowing there was no reaching the pirate that night. The next morning early he weighed, sent his boat ahead to sound, and, coming within gunshot of Teach, received his fire. The lieutenant then, boldly hoisting the king's colours, made at him with all speed of sail and oar, part of his men keeping up a discharge of small arms. Teach then cut cable and made a running fight, discharging his big guns. In a little time the pirate ran aground, and the royal vessel drawing more water anchored within half a gunshot. The lieutenant then threw his ballast overboard, staved all his water, and then weighed and stood in for the enemy.

Blackbeard, loudly cursing, hailed him. "D—— you villains, who are you? From whence come you?"

The lieutenant replied, "You see by our colours we are no pirates."

Teach bade him send a boat on board that he might know who he was. Maynard answered that he could not spare his boat, but would soon board with his sloop. Whereupon Blackbeard, drinking to him, cried, "Devil seize my soul if I give you quarter or take any." Maynard at once replied, "He should neither give nor take quarter."

By this Blackbeard's sloop floated, and the royal boats were fast approaching.

The sloops being scarcely a foot high in the waist, the men were exposed as they toiled at the sweeps. Hitherto few on either side had fallen. Suddenly Blackbeard poured in a broadside of grape, and killed twenty men on board one ship and nine on board the other; his vessel then fell broadside to the shore to keep its one side protected, and the disabled sloop fell astern. The Virginia men still kept to their oars, however exposed, because otherwise, there being no wind, the pirate would certainly have escaped.

Maynard finding his own sloop had way, and would soon be on board, ordered his men all down below, for fear of another broadside, which would have been his total destruction. He himself was the only man that kept the deck, even the man at the helm lying down snug; the men in the hold were ordered to get their pistols and cutlasses ready for close fighting, and to come up the companion at a moment's signal. Two ladders were placed in the hatchway ready for the word. As they boarded, Teach's men threw in grenades made of case-bottles, filled with powder, shot, and slugs, and fired with a quick match. Blackbeard, seeing no one on board, cried out, "They are all knocked on the head except three or four, and therefore I will jump on board and cut to pieces those that are still alive."

Under smoke of one of the fire-pots he leaped over the sloop's bows, followed by fourteen men. For a moment he was not heard, during the explosion, nor seen for the smoke. Directly the air cleared Maynard gave the signal, and his men, rising in an instant, attacked the pirates with a rush and a cheer.

Blackbeard and the lieutenant fired the first pistols at each other, and then engaged with sabres till the lieutenant's broke. Stepping back to cock his pistol, Blackbeard was in the act of cutting him down, when one of Maynard's men gave the pirate a terrible gash in the throat, and the lieutenant escaped with a small cut over his fingers.

They were now hotly engaged, Blackbeard and his fourteen

men—the lieutenant and his twelve. The sea grew red round the vessel. The ball from Maynard's first pistol shot Blackbeard in the body, but he stood his ground, and fought with fury till he received twenty cuts and five more shot. Having already fired several pistols (for he wore many in his sash), he fell dead as he was cocking another. Eight of his fourteen companions having now fallen, the rest, much wounded, leaped overboard and called for quarter, which was granted till the gibbet could be got ready.

The other vessel now coming up attacked the rest of the pirates, and compelled them to surrender. So ended a man that in a good cause had proved a Leonidas.

With great guns the lieutenant might have destroyed him with less loss, but no large vessel would have got up the river, so shallow, that, small as it was, the sloop grounded a hundred times. The very broadside, although destructive, saved the lives of the survivors, for Blackbeard, expecting to be boarded, had placed a daring fellow, a negro named Caesar, in the powder room, with orders to blow it up at a given signal. It was with great difficulty that two prisoners in the hold dissuaded him from the deed when he heard of his captain's death.

The lieutenant cutting off Blackbeard's head, hung it at his boltsprit end, and sailed into Bath Town to get relief for his wounded men. In rummaging the sloop, the connivance of the governor was detected; the secretary, falling sick with fear, died in a few days, and the governor was compelled to refund the hogsheads.

When the wounded men began to recover, the lieutenant sailed back into James's river, with the black head still hanging from the spar, and bringing fifteen prisoners, thirteen of whom were hung.

Of the two survivors, one was an unlucky fellow captured only the night before the engagement, who had received no less than seventy wounds, but was cured of them all and recovered. The other was the master of the pirate sloop, who had been shot by Blackbeard, and put on shore at Bath Town. His wound he received in the following way: one night, drinking in the cabin with the mate, a pilot, and another sailor, Blackbeard, without any provocation, drew out a small pair of pistols and cocked them under the table. The sailor, perceiving this, said nothing, but got up and went on deck. The pistols being ready, Blackbeard blew out the candle, and, crossing his hands under the table, discharged the pistols. The master fell shot through the knee, lamed for life, the other bullet hit no one. Being asked the meaning of this cruelty, Blackbeard answered, by swearing that if he did not kill one of them now and then, they would forget who he was.

This man was about to be executed, when a ship arrived from England with a proclamation prolonging the time of pardon to those who would surrender. He pleaded this, was released, and ended his days as a beggar in London.

It is a singular fact that many of Blackbeard's captors themselves eventually turned pirates.

Teach derived his nickname from his long black beard, which he twisted with ribbons into small tails, and turned about his ears. This beard was more terrible to America than a comet, say his historians. In time of action he wore a sling over his shoulders, with three brace of pistols hanging to it in holsters like bandoliers. He then stuck lighted matches under his hat, and this, with his natural fierce and wild eyes, gave him the aspect of a demon.

His frolics were truly satanic, and only madness can furnish us with any excuse for such crimes. Pre-eminent in wickedness, he was constantly resorting to artifices to maintain that pre-eminence. One day at sea, when flushed with drink, "Come," said he, "let us make a hell of our own, and try how long we can bear it."

He then, with two or three others, went down into the hold, and, closing up all the hatches, lighted some pots of brimstone, and continued till the men, nearly suffocated, cried for air and pushed up the hatches. Blackbeard triumphed in having held out longest.

The night before he was killed, as he was drinking, one of his men asked him, if anything should happen to him, if his wife knew where he had buried his money. He answered that nobody but himself and the devil knew where it was, and the longest liver should have all.

These blasphemies had filled the crew with superstitious fears, and perhaps unnerved their arms in the last struggle. The survivors declared that, once upon a cruise, a man was found on board more than the crew, sometimes below and sometimes above. No one knew whence he came and who he was, but believed him to be the devil, as he disappeared shortly before their great ship was cast away.

In Blackbeard's journal were found many entries illustrating the fear and misery of a pirate's life. For instance:

3rd June, all rum out; our company somewhat sober; rogues a plotting; great talk of separation; so I looked sharp for a prize.

5th June, took one with a great deal of liquor on board, so kept the company hot, d—— hot; then all things went well again.

Some sugar, cocoa, indigo, and cotton were found on board the pirate sloops, and some in a tent on the shore. This, with the sloop, sold for £2,500. The whole was divided amongst the crews of the *Lime* and *Pearl*, the brave captors getting no more than their dividend, and that very tardily paid, as such things usually are by English governments.

Captain England

Captain England began life as mate of a Jamaica sloop, and being taken by a pirate named Winter, before Providence was turned into a freebooter fortress, became master of a piratical vessel. He soon became remarkable for his courage and generosity.

When Providence was taken by the English, England sailed to the African coast, a hot place, but not too hot for him, like the shores of the main. He here took several ships, among others the *Cadogan*, bound from Bristol to Sierra Leone—Skinner, master. Some of England's crew had formerly served in this ship, and, having proved mutinous, had been mulcted of their wages and sent on board a man of war, from whence deserting to a West Indian sloop, they were taken by pirates, and eventually joined England and started for a cruise.

As soon as Skinner struck to the black flag, he was ordered on board the pirate. The first person he saw was his old boatswain, who addressed him with a sneer of suppressed hatred. "Ah, Captain Skinner," said he, "is that you? the very man I wished to see. I am much in your debt, and will pay you now in your own coin."

The brave seaman trembled, for he knew his fate, and shuddered as an ox does when it smells the blood of a slaughter-house. The boatswain, instantly shouting to his companions, bound the captain fast to the windlass. They then, amidst roars of cruel laughter, pelted him with glass bottles till he was cut and gashed in a dreadful manner. After this, they whipped him round the deck till they were weary, in spite of his prayers and entreaties. At last, vowing that he should have an easy death, as he had been a good master to his men, they shot him through the head. England then plundered the vessel and gave it to the mate and the crew of murderers, and they sailed with it till they reached death's door, and the port whose name is terrible.

Taking soon after a ship called the *Pearl*, England fitted her up for his own use, and re-christened her the *Royal James*. With her they took several vessels of various nations at the Azores and Cape de Verd Islands.

In 1719 the rovers returned to Africa, and, beginning at the river Gambia, sailed all down the torrid coast as far as Cape Corso. In this trip they captured the *Eagle Pink*, six guns, the *Charlotte*, eight guns, the *Sarah*, four guns, the *Wentworth*, twelve guns, the Buck, two guns, the *Castanet*, four guns, the *Mercury*, four guns, the *Coward*, two guns, and the *Elizabeth* and *Catherine*, six guns. Three of these vessels they let go, and four they burnt. Two they fitted up as pirates, and calling them the *Queen Anne's Revenge* and the *Flying King*, many of the prisoners joined their bands.

These two ships sailed to the West Indies, and careening, started for Brazil, taking several Portuguese vessels, but were finally driven off by a Portuguese man-of-war. The *Revenge* escaped, but soon after went down at sea; the *Flying King* ran ashore; twelve of the seventy men were killed, and the rest taken prisoners. Thirty-two English, three Dutch, and two Frenchmen of these were at once hung.

But to return to England. In going down the coast, he captured two more vessels, and detained one, releasing the other. Two other ships, seeing them coming, got safe under the guns of Cape Corso castle. The pirates, turning their last prize into a fire-ship, resolved to destroy both the fugitives, but, the castle firing hotly upon them, they retreated, and at Whydah road found Captain la Bouche, another pirate, had forestalled their market.

Here England fitted up a Bristol galley for his own use, calling it the Victory. Committing many insolences on shore, the negroes rose upon them and compelled them to retire to their ship, when they had fired one village, and killed many of the natives.

They now put it to the vote what voyage to take, and, deciding for the East Indies, arrived at Madagascar (1720), and, taking in water and provisions, sailed for the coast of Malabar, in the Mogul's territory. They took several Indian vessels, and one Dutch, which they exchanged for one of their own, and then returned to Madagascar. England now sent some men on shore, with tents, powder, and shot, to kill hogs, and procure venison, but they searched in vain for Avery's men.

Cleaning their ships, they then set sail for Panama, falling in with two English ships, and one Dutch, all Indiamen. Fourteen of La Bouche's crew boarded the Englishmen in canoes, declaring that they belonged to the *Indian Queen*, twenty-eight guns, which had been lost on that coast, and that their captain, with forty men, was building a new vessel. The two English captains, Mackra and Reily, were about to sink and destroy these castaways, when England's two vessels, of thirty-four and thirty-eight guns, stood in to the bay. In spite of all promises of aid, the *Ostender* and *Kirby* deserted Mackra, a breeze admitting of their escape, while the pirate's black and bloody flags were still flaunting the air. Mackra, undaunted by their desertion, fought desperately for three hours, beating off one of the pirates, striking her between wind and water, and shooting away their oars, when they put out their sweeps and tried to board. Mackra being wounded in the head, and most of his officers killed, ran ashore, and England following, ran also aground, and failed in boarding. The engagement then commenced with fresh vigour, and, had Kirby come up, the pirates would have been driven off. England, obtaining three boats full of fresh men, was now in the ascendant, and soon after Kirby stood out to sea, leaving his companion in the very jaws of death. Mackra, seeing death inevitable, lowered the boats and escaped to land, under cover of the smoke, and the pirate, soon after boarding, cut three of their wounded men in pieces. The survivors fled to Kingstown, a place twenty-five miles distant.

England offered 10,000 dollars for Mackra's head, but the king and chief people being in his interest, and a report being spread of his death, he remained safe for ten days, then obtaining a safe conduct from the pirate, Mackra had an interview with their chief. England and some men who had once sailed with Mackra protected him from those who would have cut him to pieces, with all who would not turn rovers. Finding that they talked of burning their own ships, and refitting the English prize, Mackra prevailed on them to give him the shattered ship, the *Fancy*, of Dutch build, and 300 tons burden, and also to return 129 bales of the Company's cloth.

Fitting up jury masts, Mackra sailed for Bombay, with forty-five sailors, two passengers, and twelve soldiers, arriving after much suffering, and a passage of forty-three days, frequently becalmed between Arabia and Malabar. In the engagement he had thirteen men killed and twenty-four wounded, and killed nearly a hundred of the pirates. If Kirby had proved staunch, he might have destroyed them both, and secured £100,000 of booty. Opposed to him were 300 whites and eighty blacks. We are happy to record that this brave fellow was well rewarded, and honoured with fresh command.

Nothing but despair could have driven Mackra, he said in his published account, to throw himself upon the pirates' mercy, still wounded and bleeding as they were. He did not either seem to know how friendly the Guiana people were to the English, so much so, that there was a proverb, *"A Guiana man and an Englishman are all one."*

When he first came on board, England took him aside and told him that his interest was declining among his crew, that they were provoked at his opposition to their cruelty, and that he should not be able to protect him. He advised him, therefore, to win over Captain Taylor, a man who had become a favourite amongst them by his superiority in wickedness. Mackra tried to soften this wretch with a bowl of punch, and the pirates were in a tumult whether to kill him or no, when a sailor, stuck round with pistols, came stumping upon a wooden leg up the quarterdeck and asked for Captain Mackra, swearing and vapouring, and twirling a tremendous pair of whiskers. The captain, expecting he was his executioner, called out his name. To his delight, the bravo seized him by the hand, and, shaking it violently, swore he was d——d glad to see him. "Show me the man," cries he, "that dares offer to hurt Captain Mackra, for I'll stand by him; he's an honest fellow, and I know him well."

This put an end to the dispute. Taylor consented to give the ship, and fell asleep on the deck. Mackra put off instantly, by England's advice, lest the monster should awake and change his mind.

This clemency soon led to England's deposition, and on a rumour that Mackra was fitting out a force against them, he was marooned with three more on the island of Mauritius, and making a boat of drift wood, escaped to Madagascar.

The pirate, detaining some of Mackra's men, set sail for the Indies. Seeing two ships which they supposed to be English, they commanded one of their prisoners to show them the Company's private signals, or they would cut him in pound pieces. On approaching, they proved to be Moorish ships from Muscat, loaded with horses. They rifled the ships and put the officers to the torture, and left them without sails and with the masts cut through.

The next day they fell in with the Bombay fleet of eight vessels and 100 men, despatched to attack Angria, a Malabar chief. Afraid to show their fear, the pirates attacked the fleet and destroyed two laggers, torturing the crew and sending them adrift. The commodore of the fleet would not fight the pirates without orders, which so enraged the governor of Bombay, that he appointed Mackra the commander, and enjoined him to pursue and engage England wherever he met him. Some time after this, the same fleet, aided by the Viceroy of Goa, landed 10,000 men at Calabar, Angria's stronghold, but were compelled to retreat.

The next day between Goa and Carwar the pirates drove two grabs under the guns of India-diva castle, and would have taken the island but for the delay. At Carwar they took a ship, and sent in a prisoner to demand water and provisions, for which they offered to surrender their prize. Failing in this they sailed for the Laccadeva islands, and landing at Melinda, violated the women, destroyed the cocoa trees, and burnt the churches. At Tellechery they heard of Mackra's expedition, and cursed his ingratitude. Some wished to hang the dogs who were left, but the majority agreed to keep them alive to show their contempt and revenge.

At Calicut they attempted to take a large Moorish ship in the roads, but were prevented by some guns mounted on the shore. One of Mackra's men they obliged to tend the braces on the booms amid all the fire. When he refused, they threatened to shoot him or loaded him with blows. His old tormentor, Captain Taylor, being gouty, could not hold a cudgel. Some interceded for him, but Taylor declared if he was let go he would disclose all their plans.

They next arrived at Cochin, and, sending on shore a fishing boat with a letter, ran into the road, saluting the fort. At night boats came off with provisions and liquor. The governor sent a boat full of arrack and sixty bales of sugar, and received in return a present of a table clock, and a gold watch for his daughter. The boatmen they paid some £7000, and threw them handfuls of *ducatoons* to scramble for. The fiscal brought out cloths and piece goods for sale, but the fort opened fire when they chased a vessel under its shelter. They were soon after chased by five tall ships, supposed to be Mackra's, but escaped. Their Christmas for three days they spent in a carouse, using the greater part of their fresh provisions, so that in their voyage to the Mauritius they were reduced to a bottle of water and two pounds of beef a day for ten men.

Fitting up at Mauritius, they sailed again in two months, leaving this inscription on one of the walls: *"Left this place the 5th of April, to go to Madagascar for limes."*

At the island of Mascarius they fell upon a great prize, finding the Viceroy of Goa in a Portuguese ship of seventy guns, lying dismasted on the shore. Of diamonds alone she had a cargo worth four millions of dollars. The viceroy coming calmly on board, taking them for English, was captured with all his officers, and ransomed for 2,000 dollars. To the leeward of the island they found an Ostend vessel, which they sent to Madagascar to prepare masts for the prize, and followed soon after with a cargo of 2,000 Mozambique negroes. When they reached Madagascar they found that the Dutch crew had made the pirates drunk, and sailed back to Mozambique, and from thence to Goa with the governor.

They now divided their plunder, most of them receiving forty-two small diamonds as their share. The madman, who obtained one large one, broke it in a mortar, swearing he had got now a better share than any of them, for he had forty-three sparks.

Some of the pirates now gave up their wild life and settled in *matelotage* at Madagascar, on the tontine principle of the longest liver inheriting all.

The two prizes were then burnt, and Taylor sailed for Cochin to sell his diamonds to the Dutch, and thence to the Red and China Seas, to avoid the English men-of-war.

The pirates, about this time, had 11 sail and 1500 men in the Indian seas, but soon separated for the coast of Brazil and Guinea, or to settle and fortify themselves at Madagascar, Mauritius, Johanna, and Mohilla. A pirate named Condin, in a ship called the *Dragon*, took a vessel from Mocha with thirteen *lacs* of *rupees* (130,000 half-crowns), and burning the ship settled at Madagascar. The commander of the English fleet, still in pursuit of these pirates, attempted to prevail on England to serve him as spy and pilot, but in vain.

Taylor, resolving to sail to the Indies, but hearing of the four men-of-war, started for the African main, and put into Delagoa, destroying a small fort of six guns. This fort belonged to the Dutch East India Company, but its 150 men had been deserted, and left to pine away and starve; sixteen turned pirates, but the rest, being Dutch, were left to die. They stayed in this den of fever three months, and having careened, paid the Dutch with bales of muslins and chintzes.

Some now left, and returned to settle in Madagascar. The rest sailed for the West Indies, and, escaping the fangs of two English men-of-war, surrendered themselves to the Governor of Porto Bello. Eight of them afterwards passed to Jamaica as shipwrecked sailors, and shipped for England. Captain Taylor entered the Spanish service, and commanded the man-of-war that afterwards attacked the English logwood-cutters in the bay of Honduras, and caused the Spanish war.

Captain Avery

Captain Avery was a more remarkable man than England, and his ambition of a wider kind. He was a native of Plymouth, and served as mate of a merchant vessel in several voyages. Before the peace of Ryswick, the French of Martinique carried on a smuggling trade with the natives of Peru, in spite of the Spanish *guarda costa*s. The Spaniards, finding their vessels too weak for the French, hired two Bristol vessels of thirty guns and 220 men, which were to sail first to Corunna or the Groine, and from thence to the main.

Of one of these ships, the *Duke*, Gibson was commander, and Avery first mate. Avery, planning with the boldest and most turbulent of the crew, plotted to run away with the vessels, and turn pirates on the Indian coasts.

The captain, a man much addicted to drink, had gone to bed, when sixteen conspirators from the other vessel, the *Duchess*, came on board and joined the company. Their watchword was, "Is your drunken boatswain on board?" Securing the hatches, they slipped their cable and put to sea, without any disorder, although surrounded by vessels. A Dutch frigate of forty guns refused to interrupt their progress, although offered a reward.

The captain, awoke by the motion of the ship and the noise of working the tackle, rang his bell, and Avery and two others entered the cabin. The captain, frightened and thinking the ship had broken from her anchors, asked, "What was the matter?"

Avery replied coolly, "Nothing."

The captain answered, "Something has happened to the ship; does she drive? what weather is it?"

"No, no," said Avery, "we're at sea with a fair wind and good weather."

"At sea?" said the captain, "how can that be?"

Upon which Avery told him to get up and put on his clothes, and he could tell him a secret, for he (Avery) was captain, and that was his cabin, and that he was on his way to Madagascar to make his fortune and that of all the brave fellows who were with him.

Avery then bade the captain not to be afraid, for if he was sober and minded his business, he might in time make him one of his lieutenants. At his request, however, he sent him on shore with six others.

On reaching Madagascar they found two sloops lying at anchor, which the men had run away with from the West Indies, and who, taking his vessel for a frigate, fled into the woods and posted themselves in a strong place with sentinels. Discovering their mistake, after some cautious parleying, they united together and sailed for the Arabian coast. Near the river Indus they espied a sail and gave chase, believing they had caught a Dutch East Indian ship, but found it to be one of the Great Mogul's vessels, carrying his daughter with pilgrims and offerings to Mecca. The sloops boarded her on either side, and she at once struck her colours. The Indian ship was loaded with treasure, the slaves and attendants richly clad and covered with jewels, and all having vessels of gold and silver, and large sums of money to defray their expenses in the land journey.

Taking all the treasure, they let the princess go, and the ship put back for India. The Mogul, on learning it, threatened to drive the English from India with fire and sword, but the Company contrived to pacify him by promising to deliver up to him the pirate ship and her crew.

The rumours of this adventure occasioned a report at Wapping that Jack Avery had married the Great Mogul's daughter, founded an empire, and purchased a fleet.

Avery, having secured his prize, determined to return to Madagascar, build a fort and magazine where he could leave a garrison to overawe the natives when he was absent on a cruise. A fresh scheme suggesting itself, he resolved to plunder his friends the sloops, and return to New Providence. He began by sending a boat on board each of his allies, desiring their captain to come and attend a general council. At this meeting he represented to them that if they were separated in a storm they must be taken, and the treasure would then be lost to the rest. He therefore proposed, as his ship was so strong that it could hold its own against any vessel they could meet with on those seas, to put the treasure on board in his care, in a chest sealed with three seals, and that a rendezvous should be appointed in case of separation. The two captains at once agreed to the proposal as manifestly for the common good.

That day and the next the weather was fair, and they all kept company. In the mean time Avery persuaded his men to abscond with the plunder, and escape to some country where they might spend the rest of their days in splendour and luxury. Taking advantage of a dark night, they steered a new course, and by morning had lost sight of the outwitted sloops.

Avery now resolved to steer for America, change his name, purchase a settlement, and die in peace and charity with all the world—a calm, rich Christian. They first visited New Providence, afraid that they might be detected in New England as the deserters from the Groine expedition. Avery, pretending that his vessel was a privateer that had missed her mark and was sold by the owners, disposed of her to good advantage, and bought a sloop.

In this vessel he touched at several parts of the American coast, giving his men their dividends, and allowing those who chose to leave the ship. The greater part of the diamonds he had concealed at the first plunder of the vessel. Some of his men settled at Boston; but he, afraid of selling his diamonds in New England, betook himself with a few companions to Ireland, putting into one of the northern ports, and avoiding St. George's Channel. The sailors now dispersed. Some went to Dublin, and some to Cork, to obtain pardons from King William.

Avery, still afraid of being apprehended as a pirate if he offered his diamonds for sale, passed over to England, and sent for some Bristol friends to Bideford. They agreed, for a commission, to put the stones into the hands of Bristol merchants who, being men of wealth and credit, would not be suspected. The merchants, after some negotiation, visited him at Bideford, and, after many protestations of honour and integrity, received several packets of diamonds and some vessels of gold to dispose of. They gave him some money for his present necessities and departed. Changing his name Avery continued to live at Bideford, visited by those relations to whom he confided his secret. The merchants, after many letters and much importunity, sent him small supplies of money, scarce sufficient to pay his debts and buy him bread. Weary of this life, he ventured over privately to Bristol, and to his dismay, when he desired them to come to an account with him, they threatened to proclaim him as a pirate, for men who had been robbed by him could be found on the 'Change, in the docks, or in any street.

Afraid of their threats (for he never showed much personal courage), or detected by some sailor, he fled to Ireland, and from thence again solicited the merchants, but in vain, for a supply. In a short time reduced to beggary, he resolved to throw himself upon their throats, and obtain money or revenge, and, working his passage on board a trading vessel to Plymouth, travelled on foot to Bideford. In a few days he fell sick and died, and was buried at the expense of the parish.

To return to the deserted crews of the sloops. They, believing the separation an accident, sailed at once to the rendezvous, and then discovering the cheat, and having no more fresh provisions, resolved to establish themselves on land. They therefore made tents of their sails, and unloaded their vessels. On shore they were joined by the crew of a privateer which had been despatched by the government of Bermuda to take the French factory of Goree, in the river Gambia, and had turned pirates by the way, Captain Tew, their captain, capturing a large Arabian vessel in the strait of Babelmandel, in spite of its crew and 300 soldiers. By this prize his men gained £3,000 a-piece, and but for the cowardice and mutiny of the quartermaster and some others would have captured five other ships. This leading to a quarrel, the band left off pirating, and retired to Madagascar. Captain Tew sailed to Rhode Island, and obtained a pardon.

The pirates lived at Madagascar like little princes, each with his harem, and with large retinues of slaves, whom they employed in fishing, hunting, and planting rice. The English sided with some of the negro princes in their wars, and struck such terror in their adversaries by their fire-arms, that whole armies fled at the sight of two or three of the white faces. At first, these piratical chieftains waged war on each other, but at last, alarmed by a revolt of the negroes, united in strict union.

Before this they tied their slaves to trees, and shot them to death for the smallest offence; and at last the negroes, uniting in a general conspiracy, resolved to murder them all in one night. As they lived apart, this would undoubtedly have been done, had not one of their black concubines run nearly twenty miles in three hours to discover the plot. They instantly, upon this alarm, flocked together in arms, and compelled the advancing negroes to retire. This escape made them very cautious. They therefore fomented war between the native tribes, but henceforward remained neutral. All murderers and outlaws they took under their protection, and turned into bodyguards, whilst the vanquished they defended. By this diplomacy, worthy of the most civilized people, they soon grew so powerful and numerous as to be compelled to branch out in colonies, parting into tribes, each with their wives and children.

They had now all the power and all the fears of despotism. Their houses were citadels, and every hut a fortress. They generally chose a place overgrown with wood, and situated near a spring or pool. Round this spot they raised a rampart, encircled by a fosse. This wall was straight and steep, could not be ascended without scaling ladders, and had but one entrance. The hut was so hidden that it might not be seen at a distance. The passage that led to it was intricate, labyrinthine, and narrow, so that only one person could walk it abreast, and the path wound round and round, with so many cross-paths, that any one uninitiated might search for hours and not find the cabin. All along the sides of the path, huge thorns peculiar to the island were stuck into the ground, with points uppermost, like *chevaux-de-frise*, sufficient to impale the assailant who ventured by night.

These men were found in this state by Captain Woods Rogers, when he visited Madagascar in the *Delicia* (40 guns), wishing to buy slaves, to sell to the Dutch of New Holland. The men he met had been twenty-five years on the island, and had not seen a ship for seven years. The petty kings of the bush were covered with untanned skins, and were savage wretches, overgrown with beard and hair. They bartered slaves for cloths, knives, saws, powder, and ball. They went aboard the *Delicia* and examined her with care, and, talking familiarly with the men, invited them on shore, intending to surprise the ship by night when there was a slender watch kept, having plenty of boats and arms. They wanted the men to surprise the captain, and clap those who resisted under hatches. At a given signal, the negroes were to row on board, and then all would start as pirates and roam round the world. The captain, observing the intimacy, would not suffer his men to even speak with the islanders, choosing an officer to negotiate with them for slaves.

These pirate kings were all foremast men, and could read no more than their chief secretaries could write. The chief prince of this Newgate paradise had been a Thames waterman, who had committed a murder on the river.

As even a few years since an old sailor at Minehead was known as the "King of Madagascar," we suppose divine right and hereditary succession still continue in that Eden of gaol-birds.

During the time of war the pirates diminished in number and turned privateersmen, but increased at the peace of Utrecht, when the disbanded privateersmen again turned thieves for want of excitement and some more honest employment.

About 1716, Captain Martel appeared as commander of a pirate sloop of eight guns and eighty men, that, cruising off Jamaica, captured a galley and another small vessel, from the former of which he plundered £1000. In their way to Cuba they took two more sloops, which they rummaged and let go, and off Cavena hoisted the black flag, and boarded a galley of twenty guns, called the *John and Martha*. Part of the men they put ashore and part enrolled in the crew.

The cargo of logwood and sugar they seized, and, taking down one of the ship's decks, mounted her with twenty-two guns and 100 men, and proceeded to cruise off the Leeward Islands, capturing a sloop, a brigantine, and a Newfoundland vessel of twenty guns.

They soon after plundered a Jamaica vessel, and two ships from Barbadoes, detaining all the best men, and from a Guinea galley they stole some gold dust, elephants' teeth, and forty slaves.

In 1717, they put into Santa Cruz to clean and refit with a small piratical fleet of five vessels, warping up a little creek, very shallow, but guarded by rocks and sands. They then erected a battery of four guns on the island, and another of two guns near the road, while a sloop with eight guns protected the mouth of the channel.

In November, 1716, the commander-in-chief of all the Leeward islands sent a sloop to Barbadoes for the *Scarborough*, of thirty guns and 140 men, to inform her of the pirate. The captain had just buried twenty men, and having forty sick could scarcely put out to sea. However, putting on a bold heart, he left his sick behind and beat up for recruits at all the islands he passed. At Antigua he took in twenty soldiers, at Nevis ten, and the same number at St. Christopher's.

Unable to find the pirate, he was on the point of putting back, when a boat from Santa Cruz informed him of a creek where he had seen a vessel enter. The *Scarborough* instantly sailed to the spot and discovered the pirates, but the pilot refused to enter. The pirates all this while fired red-hot shot from the shore; but at length the ship anchored alongside the reef and cannonaded the vessels and batteries. The sloop in the channel soon sank, and the larger vessel was much punished, but the *Scarborough*, fearing the reef, stood off and on for a day or two and blockaded the creek. The pirates, endeavouring to warp out and slip away, ran aground, and, seeing the *Scarborough* again standing in, fired the ship and ran ashore, leaving twenty negroes to perish. Nineteen escaped in a sloop, and the captain and twenty other negroes fled to the woods, where it is supposed they perished, as they were never heard of again.

Captain Charles Vane

Captain Charles Vane, our next Viking, is known as one of the men who helped to steal the silver which the Spaniards had fished up from their sunk galleons in the gulf of Florida.

When Captain Rogers with his two men-of-war conquered Providence, and pardoned all the pirates who submitted, Vane slipped his cable, fired a prize in the harbour, hoisted the black flag, and, firing a broadside at one of the men-of-war, sailed boldly away. Capturing a Barbadoes vessel, he manned it with twenty-five hands, and, unloading an interloper of its pieces of eight, careened at a key, and spent some time in a revel.

In the next cruise they captured some Spanish and New England vessels, and one laden with logwood. The crew of the latter they compelled to throw the lading overboard, intending to turn her into a pirate vessel, but in a fit of caprice suddenly let the men go and the ship with them. The prize captain, offended at Vane's arrogance, left him, and surrendered himself and 90 negroes to the governor of Charlestown, receiving a free pardon. Vane saluted the runaway with a broadside as he left, and lay wait for some time for him, but without success. Soon after this two armed sloops started in pursuit of Vane, and, failing in the capture, attacked and took another pirate vessel that was clearing at Cape Fear.

In an inlet to the northward Vane met Blackbeard, and saluted him, according to piratical etiquette, with a discharge of his shotted guns. Off Long Island he attacked a vessel that proved to be a French man-of-war, and gave chase; Vane was for flight, but many of the men, in spite of the enemy's weight of metal and being twice their force, were for boarding. A pirate captain in all cases but that of fighting was controlled by a majority, but in this case had an absolute power; Vane refused to fight, and escaped.

The next day Vane was branded by vote as a coward and deposed, and Rackham, his officer, elected captain. Vane and the minority were turned adrift in a sloop. Putting into the bay of Honduras, Vane captured another sloop, and fitted it up as a pirate vessel, and soon after captured two more. Vane was soon after shipwrecked on an island near Honduras, and most of his men drowned; he himself being supported by the turtle fishermen. While in this miserable state, a Jamaica vessel arrived, commanded by a buccaneer, an old acquaintance, to whom he applied to help him. The man refused, declaring Vane would intrigue with his men, murder him, and run off as a pirate. On Vane expressing scruples about stealing a fisherman's boat from the beach, the buccaneer declared that if he found him still there on his return he would take him to Jamaica and hang him.

Soon after his friend's departure a vessel put in for water, and, not knowing Vane to be a pirate, took him on board as a sailor. On leaving the bay the buccaneer met them and came on board to dine. Passing to the cabin he spied Vane working in the hold, and asked the captain if he knew that that was Vane, the notorious pirate. The other then declared he would not have him, and the buccaneer, sending his mate on board with at loaded pistol, seized Vane and took him to Jamaica, where he was soon after hung.

Rackham, after a cruise among the Caribbee islands, spent a Christmas on shore, and when the liquor was all gone put to sea. Their first prize was an ominous one, a ship laden with Newgate convicts bound for the plantations, which was soon after retaken by an English ship of war. Two others of his prizes were also recaptured while careening at the Bahama islands by Governor Rogers, of New Providence.

They then sailed to the back of Cuba, where Rackham had a settlement, and there spent their plunder in debauchery. As they were fitting out for sea, they were attacked by a Spanish *guarda costa* that had just captured an English interloper. Rackham being protected by an island, the Spaniards warped into the channel at dusk and waited for day. The pirates, roused to despair, boarded the Spanish prize with pistols and cutlasses in the dead of the night, and, threatening the crew with death if they spoke, captured her almost without a blow, and slipping the cable stood out to sea. When day broke the Spaniards opened a tremendous fire upon the deserted pirate vessel, but soon discovered their mistake.

1720 was spent in small cruises about Jamaica, their crew being still short; they then swept off some fishing boats from Harbour Island, and landing in Hispaniola, carried off some wild cattle and several French hunters.

He then captured several more vessels, and was joined by the crew of a sloop in Dry Harbour Bay. But their end was at hand. The governor of Jamaica despatched a sloop in pursuit of them, who found the pirates carousing with a boat's crew from Point Negril, and they were soon overpowered.

A fortnight after sentence of death was passed upon nine of them at a court of admiralty held at St. Jago de la Vega. Five of them were executed at Gallows Point in Port Royal, and the four others the day after at Kingston. Rackham and two more were afterwards taken down and hung in chains, one at Plumb Point, one at Buskkey, and the other at Gun-key. By the terrible Draconic laws of Jamaica, the nine boatmen from Port Negril were also hung by their side. After such justice, can we wonder at the crimes to which despair too often drove the pirates?

Among these "unfortunate brave," as Prior generously calls them, two female pirates are not to be forgotten. The first of these, Mary Reed, was the daughter of a sailor, whose wife having after his death given birth to an illegitimate girl, palmed it off as a boy, in order to excite the compassion of her husband's mother. Being reduced in circumstances she put the girl out as a foot-boy, but she soon after ran to sea, and entered on board a man-of-war. Quitting the sea service Mary Reed wintered over in Flanders and obtained a cadetship in a regiment of foot, behaving herself in many actions with a great deal of bravery, and finally entering a regiment of horse. Here she fell in love with a comrade, a young Fleming, whom she eventually married, and set up an eating-house at Beda, called the Three Horse-Shoes. Her husband dying, and the peace ruining her trade, Mary went into Holland, and joined a regiment quartered on a frontier town, but, finding preferment slow, she shipped herself on board a vessel bound for the West Indies.

The vessel was taken by English pirates, and the Amazon, being the only English sailor, was detained. A pardon soon afterwards being issued, the crew surrendered themselves, but Mary Reed sailed for New Providence, and joined a privateer squadron fitting out there against the Spaniards. The crews, who were pardoned pirates, soon rose against their commander, and resumed their old trade, and Mary Reed among them. Abhorring the life of a pirate, she still was the first to board, and was as resolute as the bravest. By chance Anne Bonny, another disguised woman, being with the crew, discovered her sex, and soon after she fell in love with a sailor whom they took prisoner, and was eventually married to him. Her husband hated his new profession as much as herself, and they were about to quit it when they were both taken prisoners.

On one occasion Mary Reed, to prevent her husband fighting a duel, challenged his opponent to meet her on a sand island near which their ship lay, with sword and pistol, and killed him on the spot.

At the trial she declared that her life had been always pure, and that she had never intended to remain a pirate. When they were taken, only she and Anne Bonny kept the deck, calling to those in the hold to come up and fight like men, and when they refused firing at them, killing one and wounding several. In prison she said the fear of hanging had never driven her from piracy, for but for the dread of that there would be so many pirates that the trade would not be worth following.

Great compassion was evinced for her in the court, but she was still found guilty, though being near her pregnancy, her execution was respited. She might have been pardoned, but a violent fever coming on soon after her trial she died in prison.

Her companion, Anne Bonny, was the illegitimate daughter of a Cork attorney. Her father, disguising the child as a boy, pretended it was a relative's son, and bred it up for a clerk. Becoming ruined he emigrated to Carolina, and turning merchant bought a plantation. Upon her mother's death Anne Bonny succeeded to the housekeeping. She was of a fierce and ungovernable temper, and was reported to have stabbed an English servant with a case-knife. Marrying a penniless sailor, her father turned her out of doors, and she and her husband fled to New Providence, where he turned pirate. Here she was seduced by Captain Rackham, and ran with him to sea, dressed as a sailor, and accompanied him in many voyages. The day that Rackham was executed she was admitted to see him by special favour, but she only taunted him and said that she was sorry to see him there, but that if he had fought like a man he would not have been hung like a dog.

Becoming pregnant in prison she was reprieved, and, we believe, finally pardoned.

Captain Howel Davis

Captain Howel Davis, our next sea king, was a native of Milford, who, being taken prisoner by England, was appointed captain of the vessel of which he had been chief mate. At first, he declared he would rather be shot than turn pirate, but eventually accepted sealed orders from England, to be opened at a certain latitude. On opening them, he found they directed him to make the ship his own, and go and trade at Brazil. The crew, refusing to obey Davis, steered for Barbadoes, and put him in prison, but he was soon discharged.

Starting for New Providence, the pirates' nest, he found the island had just surrendered to Captain Woods Rogers. He here joined the ships fitting out for the Spanish trade, and at Martinique joined in a conspiracy, secured the masters, and started on a cruise against all the world. At a council of war, held over a bowl of punch, Davis was unanimously elected commander, and the articles he drew up were signed by all the crew.

They then sailed to Coxon's-hole, at the east end of Cuba, to clean, that being a narrow creek, where one ship could defend itself against a hundred, and, having no carpenter, they found some difficulty in careening. On the north side of Hispaniola, they fell in with a French ship of twelve guns, which they took, and sent twelve men on board to plunder, being now very short of provisions. They had scarcely leaped on deck before another French vessel of twenty-four guns and sixty men hove in sight. This vessel Davis proposed to attack, quite contrary to the wish of his crew, who were afraid of her size. When Davis approached, the Frenchmen bade him strike, but giving them a broadside, he said he should keep them in play till his consort arrived, when they should have but hard quarters. At this moment came up all the prisoners, having been dressed in white shirts, and forced on deck, and a dirty tarpaulin was hoisted for a black flag. The French captain, intimidated, instantly struck, and was at once, with ten of his hands, put in irons.

The guns, small arms, and powder in the small ship were then removed, and the prize crew sent on board the larger vessel. Part of the prisoners were put in the smaller and now defenceless bark. At the end of two days, finding the French prize a dull sailor, Davis restored her to the captain, minus her ammunition and cargo. The Frenchman, vexed at being so outwitted, would have destroyed himself had not his men prevented him.

Davis then visited the Cape de Verd islands, and left some of his men as settlers among the Portuguese. They also plundered many vessels at the Isle of May, obtained many fresh hands, and fitted one of their prizes with twenty-six guns, and called her the King James. At St. Jago the governor accused them of being pirates, and Davis resolved to resent the affront by surprising the fort by night. Going on shore well armed, they found the guard negligent, and took the place, losing only three men. The fugitives barricaded themselves in the governor's house, into which the pirates threw grenades. By daybreak the whole country was alarmed, and poured down upon them, but they, unwilling to stand a siege, dismounted the fort guns and fought their way to their ships.

Mustering their hands, and finding themselves still seventy strong, they proposed to follow Davis' advice, and attack Gambia castle, where a great deal of money was always kept, for they had now such an opinion of Davis' courage and prudence that they would have followed him anywhere.

Having come within sight of the place, he ordered all his men below but such as were absolutely necessary for the working of the vessel, that the people on shore might take her for a trader. He then ran close under the fort, anchored, and ordering out the boat, manned her with six plain-dressed men, himself as the master, and the rest attired as merchants. The men were instructed what to say.

At the landing-place they were received by a file of musketeers, and led to the governor, who received them civilly. They said they were from Liverpool, bound to the river of Senegal to trade for gums and ivory, but being chased to Gambia by two French men-of-war, were willing to trade for slaves; their cargo, they said, being all iron and plate. The governor, promising them slaves, asked for a hamper of European liquor, and invited them to stay and dine. Davis himself refused to stay, but left his two companions.

On leaving he observed there was a sentry at the entrance, and a guard-house near, with the arms of the soldiers on duty thrown in one corner. Going on board he assured his men of success, desired them to keep sober, and when the castle flag struck to send twenty hands immediately ashore. He then seized a sloop that lay near, for fear the crew should discern their preparations.

He put two pairs of loaded pistols in his pocket, and made all his crew do the same, bidding them get into conversation with the guard, and when he fired a pistol through the governor's window, leap up and secure the piled arms.

While dinner was getting ready, the governor began to brew a bowl of punch, when Davis, at a whisper of the coxswain who had been reconnoitring the house, suddenly drew out a pistol, and, clapping it to the governor's breast, bade him surrender the fort and all his riches, or he was a dead man. The governor, taken by surprise, promised to be passive. They then shut the door, and loaded the arms in the hall, while Davis fired his piece through the window. The men, hearing this signal, cocked their pistols, got between the soldiers and the arms, and carried them off, locking up the men in the guard-room, and guarding it without. Then striking the flag, the rest of the crew tumbled on shore, and the fort was their own without the loss of a man. Davis at once harangued the soldiers, and persuaded many to join him, and those who resisted he sent on board the sloop, which he first unrigged. The rest of the day they spent in salutes—ship to castle and castle to ship, and the next day plundered. Much money had been lately sent away, so they found only £2,000 in bar gold, and many rich effects. They then dismounted the guns, and demolished the fortifications.

A French pirate of 14 guns, and sixty-four men, half French, half negroes, soon joined Davis, and they sailed down the coast together. They soon after met another pirate ship, of 24 guns, and spent several days in carousing. They then attacked in company the fort of Sierra Leone, and the garrison, after a stiff cannonade, surrendered the place and fled. Here they spent seven weeks careening; and, capturing a galley, La Bouce, the second captain, cut her half deck, and mounted her with 24 guns. They now sailed together, and appointed Davis commodore, but, like men of a trade, soon quarrelled, and parted company. Off Cape Apollonia Davis took several vessels, and off Cape Points Bay attacked a Dutch interloper, of 30 guns, and ninety men. After many hours' fighting the Dutchman surrendered to the black flag, having killed nine of Davis' men at one broadside. This vessel Davis called the *Rover*, fitted with 32 guns and 27 swivels, and, sailing to Anamaboe, captured several ships laden with ivory, gold dust, and negroes, saluting the fort, and then started for Prince's island, a Portuguese settlement near the same coast.

They here captured a Dutchman, a valuable prize, having the governor of Acra and £150,000, besides merchandise, on board, and recruited their force with thirty-five hands. The *King James* springing a leak, they deserted her and left her to sink. At the isle of Princes Davis passed himself off for an English man-of-war in search of pirates, and was received with great honours by the governor, who approved of his openly plundering a French vessel which he accused of piracy. A few days after Davis and fourteen of his men attempted to carry off the chief men's wives from a small village in which they lived, but failed in the attempt. But Davis had determined to plunder the island by means of the following stratagem. He resolved to present the governor with a dozen negroes in return for his civilities, and afterwards to invite him with the friars and chief men of the island to an entertainment on board his ship. He would then clap them in irons, and not release them under a ransom of £40,000.

This plot proved fatal to him. A Portuguese negro, swimming ashore at night, disclosed the whole. The governor dissembled and professed to fall into the snare. The next day Davis went himself on shore to bring the governor on board, and was invited to take some refreshment at the government house. He fell at once into the trap. A prepared ambuscade rose and fired a volley, killing every pirate but one, who, running to the boat, got safely to the ship. Davis, though shot through the bowels, rose, made a faint effort to run, drew out his pistols, fired at his pursuers, and fell dead.

Upon Davis' death, Bartholomew Roberts was at once chosen commander, in preference to many other of the *lords* or head seamen. The sailors said, that any captain who went beyond their laws should be deposed, but that they must have a man of courage and a good seaman to defend their commonwealth. One of the lords, whose father had suffered in Monmouth's rebellion, swore Roberts was a Papist. In spite of all, Roberts, who had been only taken prisoner six weeks before, was chosen commander. He told them that, "since he had dipped his hands in muddy water, and must needs be a pirate, he would rather be commander than mere seaman."

Their first thought was to avenge Davis' death, for he had been much beloved for his affability and good nature. Thirty men were landed, and attacked the fort in spite of the steep hill on which it was situated. The Portuguese deserted the walls, and the pirates destroyed the guns. Still unsatisfied, they would have burnt the town, had it not been protected by a thick wood, which furnished a cover to the enemy. They, however, mounted the French ship with twelve guns, running into shoal water, battered down several houses, and then sailed out of the harbour by the light of two ships to which they set fire. Having taken two more vessels and burnt one of them, they started by general consent for Brazil.

Cruising here for nine weeks and taking no prize, the pirates grew quite discouraged, and resolved to steer for the West Indies, but soon after fell in with forty-two sail of Portuguese ships laden for Lisbon, and lying off the bay of los Todos Santos, waiting for two men-of-war of seventy guns each for their convoy. Stealing amongst them, Roberts hid his men till he had closed upon the deepest of them, threatening to give no quarter if the master was not instantly sent on board. The Portuguese, alarmed at the sudden flourish of cutlasses, instantly came. Roberts told him they were gentlemen of fortune, and should put him to death if he did not tell them which was the richest vessel of the fleet. The trembler pointed out a ship of forty guns and 150 men, more force than Roberts could command; but Roberts, replying "They are only Portuguese," bore down at once upon it. Finding the enemy was aware of their being pirates, Roberts poured in a broadside, grappled, and boarded. The dispute was short and warm. Two of the pirates fell, and many of the Portuguese. By this time it was pretty well seen that a fox had got into the poultry-yard. Signals of topgallant sheets were flying, and guns fired to bring up the convoy that still rode at anchor. Roberts, finding his prize sail heavy, waited for the first man-of-war, which, basely declining the duel, lingered for its consort till Roberts was out of sight. The prize proved exceedingly rich, being laden with sugar, skins, tobacco, and 4,000 *moidors*, besides many gold chains and much jewellery. A diamond cross, which formed part of this spoil, they afterwards gave to the governor of Caiana. Elated with this spoil, they fixed on the Devil's Islands, in the Surinam river, as a place for a revel, and, arriving there, found the governor ready to barter.

Much in want of provision, Roberts threw himself, with forty men, into a prize sloop, in hopes of capturing a brigantine laden with provision from Rhode Island, which was then in sight, and was kept at sea by contrary winds for eight days. Their food ran short, and failing in securing the prize, they despatched their only boat to bring up the ship.

Landing at Dominica, Roberts took on board thirteen Englishmen, the crews of two New England vessels that had been seized by a French *guarda costa*. At this island they were nearly captured by a Martinique sloop, but contrived to escape to the Guadanillas. Sailing for Newfoundland they entered the harbour with their black colours flying, their drums beating, and trumpets sounding. The crews of twenty-two vessels fled on shore at their approach, and they proceeded to burn and sink all the shipping and destroy the fisheries and the houses of the planters. Mounting a Bristol galley that he found in the harbour with sixteen guns, Roberts destroyed nine sail of French ships, and carried off for his own use a vessel of twenty-six guns. From many other prizes they pressed men and got plunder. The passengers on board the *Samuel*, a rich London vessel, he tortured, threatening them with death if they did not disclose their money. His men tore up the hatches, and, entering the hold with axes and swords, cut and ripped open the bales and boxes. Everything portable they seized, the rest they threw overboard, amidst curses and discharges of guns and pistols. They carried off £9,000 worth of goods, the sails, guns, and powder. They told the captain "They should accept of no act of grace. The king might be d—— with their act of grace for them: they weren't going to Hope Point to be hung up sun-drying like Kidd's and Braddish's company were; and if they were overpowered they would set fire to the powder, and go all merrily to hell together."

While debating whether to sink or burn the prize, they espied a sail, and left the *Samuel* tumultuously to give chase. It proved to be a Bristol vessel, and hating Bristol men because the Martinique sloops were commanded by one, he used him with barbarous cruelty.

Their provisions growing scarce, Roberts put into St. Christopher's, and, being refused succours, fired on the town and burnt two ships in the road. They then visited St. Bartholomew, where they were well received. Sailing for Guinea, weary of even debauchery, they captured a rich laden vessel from Martinique, and changed ships. By some extraordinary ignorance of navigation, Roberts, in trying to reach the Cape Verd islands, got to leeward of his port, and, obliged to go back again with the trade wind, returned to the West Indies, steering for Surinam, 700 leagues distant, with one hogshead of water for 124 souls.

Great suffering followed their pleasures in the islands of the Sirens; each man obtained only one mouthful of water in twenty-four hours. Many drank their urine or the brine and died fevered and mad; others wasted with fluxes. The rest had but an inch or two of bread in the day, and grew so feeble they could hardly reef and climb. They were all but dying, when they were suddenly brought into soundings, and at night anchored in seven fathoms water.

Thirsty in the sight of lakes and streams, and maddened with hunger, Roberts tore up the floor of the cabin, and, patching together a canoe with rope yarn, paddled to shore and procured water. After some days, the boat returned with the unpleasant intelligence that the lieutenant had absconded with the vessel.

This Lieutenant Kennedy's sail into Execution Dock we will give before we return to Roberts. Upon leaving Caiana Roberts's treacherous crew determined to abandon piracy. Their Portuguese prize they gave to the master of the prize sloop, a good-natured man, whose quiet philosophy under misfortune had astonished and pleased them. Off Barbadoes Kennedy took a Quaker's vessel from Virginia, the captain of which allowed no arms on board, and his equanimity so attracted the pirates that eight of them returned with him to Virginia. These men rewarded the sailors and gave £250 worth of gold dust and tobacco to the peaceful captain. At Maryland the treacherous Quaker surrendered his friends, who were all hung on the evidence of some Portuguese Jews whom they had brought from Brazil.

Off Jamaica Kennedy captured a flour vessel from Boston, in which himself and many others embarked. This Kennedy had been a pickpocket and a housebreaker, could neither read nor write, and had been only elected captain for his cruelty and courage.

His crew, at first afraid of his treachery, would have thrown him overboard, but relented, on his taking solemn oaths of fidelity. Of all these men only one knew anything of navigation, and he was so ignorant that, trying to reach Ireland, he ran them ashore on Scotland. Landing they passed at first for shipwrecked sailors; seven of them reached London in safety, the rest were seized at Edinburgh and hung, having attracted attention by rioting and drunken squandering. Two others were murdered on the road.

Kennedy turned robber, and some years after was arrested as a pirate by the mate of a ship he had plundered, turned king's evidence, but was hung in 1721.

We must now return to Roberts, whom we left swearing and vapouring on the coast of Newfoundland. He began by drawing up a code of laws and establishing stricter discipline, and then steered for the West Indies, capturing several vessels by the way, and was soon after pursued by a Bristol galley of twenty guns and eighty men, and a sloop of ten guns and forty men, despatched by the governor of Barbadoes. Roberts, taking them for traders, attempted to board, but was driven off by a broadside, the king's men huzzaing as they fired. Roberts, crowding all sail, took to flight and escaped, after a galling pursuit, by dint of throwing overboard his guns and heavy goods. He was henceforward particularly severe to Barbadian vessels, so deeply established were the principles of justice and compensation in the mind of this great man.

In the morning, they saw land, but at a great distance, and despatching a boat, it returned late at night with a load of water: they had reached Surinam. The worst blasphemer heard the words, and fell upon his knees to thank a God whom he had so often denied. They swore that the same Providence which had given them drink would bring them meat.

Taking provisions from several vessels, Roberts touched at Tobago, and then sailed to Martinique to revenge himself on the governor. Adopting the custom of the Dutch interlopers, he hoisted a jack and sailed in as if to trade. He was soon surrounded by a swarm of sloops and smacks; then sending all the crews on shore on board one vessel, minus their money, he fired twenty others. His new flag bore henceforward a representation of himself trampling on the skulls of a Barbadian and Martinique man. At Dominica he took several vessels, and several others at Guadaloupe, and then put into a key off Hispaniola to clean and refit.

While here, the captains of two piratical sloops visited him, having heard of his fame and achievements, to beg from him powder and arms. After several nights' revel, Roberts dismissed them, hoping "the Lord would prosper their handy works." Three of their men, who had long excited suspicion by their reserve and sobriety, deserted, but being recaptured were put upon their trial. The jury sat in the steerage, before a bowl of rum punch; the judge on the bench smoked a pipe. Sentence was already passed, when one of the jury, with a volley of oaths, swore Glashby (one of the prisoners) should not die. "He was as good a man as the best of them, and had never turned his back to a man in his life. Glashby was an honest fellow in spite of his misfortune, and he loved him. He hoped he would live and repent of what he had done; but d——if he must die, he would die along with him," and as he spoke he handled a pair of loaded pistols, and presented them at two of the judges, who, thinking the argument good, at once acquitted Glashby. The rest, allowed to choose their executioners, were tied to the mast and shot.

Amply stocked with provision, they now sailed for Guinea to buy gold dust, and on their passage burnt and sank many vessels. Roberts, finding his crew mutinous and unmanageable, assumed a rude bearing, offering to fight on shore any one who was offended, with sword or pistol, for he neither feared nor valued any. On their way to Africa they were deserted by a prize, a brigantine, which they had manned. Roberts being insulted by a drunken sailor, killed him on the spot. His messmate returning from shore declared the captain deserved the same fate. Roberts hearing this stabbed him with his sword, but in spite of the wound the seaman threw him over a gun and gave him a beating. A general tumult ensued, which was appeased by the quartermaster, and the majority agreeing that the captain must be supported at all risks, the sailor received two lashes from every man on board as soon as he recovered from his wound. This man then conspired with the captain of the brigantine and his seventy hands, and agreed to desert Roberts, as they soon after did on the first opportunity.

Near the river of Senegal the pirates were chased by two French cruisers of ten and sixteen guns, who mistook him for one of those interlopers for whom they were on the look-out. The pair surrendered, however, with little resistance on the first shot of the Jolly

Roger, and with these prizes they put into Sierra Leone. About thirty retired buccaneers and pirates lived here, one of whom, who went by the name of Crackers, kept two cannon at his door to salute all pirate ships that arrived.

They found that the *Swallow* and *Weymouth* men-of-war, fifty guns, had just been there, and would not return till Christmas; so, after six weeks' debauch, they put out again to sea, plundering along the coast. They exchanged one of their vessels for a French frigate-built ship, pressing the sailors, and allowing some soldiers on board to sail with them for a quarter share.

They found an English chaplain on board, and wanted him to go with them to make punch and say prayers, but as he refused they let him go, detaining nothing of the property of the church but three prayer-books and a corkscrew. This ship they altered by pulling down the bulkheads and making her flush. They then christened her the *Royal Fortune*, and mounted her with forty guns.

They next proceeded to Calabar, where a shoal protected the harbour. Enraged at the negroes refusing to trade, they landed forty men under protection of the ships' fire, drove back a party of 2000 natives, and then burnt their town. Still unable to obtain provisions, they returned to Cape Apollonia. Here they took a vessel called the *King Solomon*, boarding her from the long boat in spite of a volley from the ship, the pirates shouting defiance. The captain would have resisted, but the boatswain made the men lay down their arms and cry for quarter. They then cut her cable, and rifled her of everything. They next cut the mast of a Dutch vessel, and strung the sausages they found on board round their necks, killing the fowls, and inviting the captain to drink from his own but, singing obscene French and Spanish songs from his Dutch prayer-book.

Going too near the land they alarmed the coast, and the English and Dutch factories spread signals of danger.

Entering Whydah with St. George's ensign and a black flag flying, eleven ships instantly surrendered without a blow; most of the crews being, in fact, ashore. Each captain ransomed his cargo for 8 lbs. of gold dust, upon which they gave him acquittals, signed with sham names, as "Whiffingpin" and "Tugmutton." One vessel full of slaves refusing to give any ransom, he set fire to it, and burnt eighty negroes who were chained in the hold; a few leaped overboard to avoid the flames, and were torn to pieces by the sharks that swarmed in the road.

Discovering from an intercepted letter that the *Swallow* was after him, Roberts put back to the island of Anna Bona, but the wind failing steered for Cape Lopez. The cruiser had lost 100 men from sickness in a three weeks' stay at Prince's island, and, unable to return to Sierra Leone, turned to Cape Corso, unknown to Roberts, who was ignorant of the causes that had led to their return. Receiving many calls for help, and finding the trade of the whole coast disturbed, the *Swallow* sailed for Whydah. The crew were impatient to attack the pirates, learning that they had an arms' chest full of gold, secured by three keys. Recruiting thirty volunteers, English and French, the *Swallow* reached the River Gaboon, and soon discovered the pirates, one of whom gave them chase, believing her a Portuguese sugar vessel, and the sugar for their punch now ran short.

The pirates were cursing the wind and the sails that kept them from so rich a prey, when the *Ranger* suddenly brought to and hauled up her lower ports, while the first broadside brought down their black flag. Hoisting it again, they flourished their cutlasses on the poop, but tried to escape. Some prepared to board, but, after two hours' firing, their maintop came down with a run, and they struck, having had ten men killed and twenty wounded. The *Swallow* did not lose one. The *Ranger* carried thirty-two guns, and was manned by sixteen Frenchmen, seventy-seven English, and ten negroes. Their black colours were thrown overboard. As the *Swallow* was sending a boat to board, an explosion was heard, and a smoke poured out of the great cabin. It appeared that half a dozen of the most desperate had fired some powder, but it was too little to do anything but burn them terribly.

The commander, a Welshman, had had his leg shot off, and had refused to allow himself to be carried below. The rest were gay and brisk, dressed in white shirts and silk waistcoats, and wearing watches.

An officer said to a man whom he saw with a silver whistle at his belt—"I presume you are boatswain of this ship." "Then you presume wrong," said the pirate, "for I am boatswain of the *Royal Fortune*—Captain Roberts, commander."

"Then, Mr. Boatswain, you'll be hanged," said the officer.

"That is as your Honour pleases," said the man, turning away.

The officer asking about the explosion, he swore "they are all mad and bewitched, for I have lost a good hat by it." He had been blown out of the cabin gallery into the sea.

"But what signifies a hat, friend?" said the officer.

"Not much," he answered.

As the sailors stripped off his shoes and stockings, the officer asked him if all Robert's crew were as likely men as himself? He answered, "There are 120 of them as clever fellows as ever trod shoe-leather; would I were with them."

"No doubt on't," said the officer.

"It's naked truth," said the man laughing, as he looked down at his bare feet.

The officer then approached another man, black and scorched, who sat sullenly alone in a corner. He asked him how it happened.

"Why," said he, "John Morris fired a pistol into the powder, and if he had not done it I would."

The officer said he was a surgeon, and offered to dress his wounds, which he bore without a groan. He swore it should not be done and he would tear off the dressing, so he was then overpowered and bandaged. At night he grew delirious and raved about "brave Roberts," who would soon release him. The men then lashed him down to the forecastle, as he resisted with such violence to his burnt sore flesh that he died next day of mortification. The other pirates they fettered, and sent the shattered ship, scarcely worth preserving, into port.

The next day Roberts appeared in sight with a prize, and his men ran to tell him of the cruiser as he was dining in the cabin with the prisoner captain. Roberts declared the vessel was his own returning, or nothing but a Portuguese or French slave ship, and laughed at the cowards who feared danger, offering to strike the most apprehensive. As soon as he discovered his mistake he slipped his cable, got under sail, and ordered his men to arms, declaring it was "a bite."

He appeared on deck dressed in crimson damask, with a red feather in his cocked hat, a gold chain and diamond cross round his neck, a sword in his hand, and two pairs of pistols hanging pirate-fashion from a silk sling over his shoulders. His orders were given in a loud voice and with unhesitating boldness. Informed by a deserter that the *Swallow* sailed best upon a wind, he resolved to go before it, if disabled to run ashore and escape among the negroes, or if, as many of his men were drunk, everything else failed, to board and blow up both vessels.

Exchanging a broadside he made all sail he could crowd, but steering ill was taken aback and overtaken. At this critical moment a grapeshot struck him on the throat, and he sat calmly down on the tackle of a gun and died. The man at the helm running to his assistance, and not seeing a wound, thought his heart had failed him, and bade him stand up and fight it out like a man, and remember the *Jolly Roger*. Discovering his mistake the rough sailor burst into tears, and prayed the next shot might strike him. The pirates then threw their captain overboard, with all his arms and ornaments, as he had often requested in his life. When Roberts fell the men deserted their quarters and fell into a torpor, till their mainmast being shot away compelled them to surrender. Some of the crew lit matches and tried to blow up the magazine, but the rest prevented them. The black flag, crushed under the fallen mast, they had no time to destroy.

The *Royal Fortune* was found to have forty guns and 157 men, forty-five of them being negroes. Only three were killed in the action, and the *Swallow* did not lose a man. She had upwards of £2,000 of gold dust in her. From the other vessel the same quantity was embezzled by an English captain, who sailed away before the *Swallow* arrived.

The prisoners were mutinous under restraint, and cursed and upbraided each other for the folly that had brought them into that trap. For fear of an outbreak they were manacled and shackled in the gun-room, which was strongly barricaded, and officers with pistol and cutlass placed to guard it night and day.

The pirates laughed at the short commons, and swore they should be too light to hang. Those who read and prayed were sneered at by the others

"Give me hell," said one blasphemer; "it is a merrier place than heaven, and at my entrance I'll give Roberts a salute of thirteen guns." The whole of the prisoners made a formal complaint against "the wretch with a prayer-book," as a common disturber.

A few of the more violent conspired, having loosened their shackles, to rise, kill the officers, and run away with the ship. A mulatto boy who attended them, conveyed messages from one to the other, but the very evening of the outbreak two prisoners heard the whispers, and warned the officers. They were then treated rougher, and heavier chains put on.

The negroes and surgeon on board the other ship also contrived a conspiracy, the surgeon knowing a little of the Ashantee language. They were betrayed by a traitor, all re-chained, and brought to Cape Corso castle to be tried. Here they grew chap-fallen, forgot to jest, and begged for good books. Some joined in prayers, and others sang psalms. Brawny, sunburnt, scarred men were seen spelling out hymns, and, through the blood-red haze of a thousand crimes, trying with moistened eyes to look back to calm Sunday evenings when fond mothers had first taught them the words of long since forgotten prayers.

When the ropes were fitting only one appeared dejected, and he had been ill with a flux. A surgeon of the place was charitable enough to offer himself as chaplain, and represented to them the urgent need of repentance and the tender forgiveness of a Saviour. They hardly listened to him, but some begged caps of the soldiers, for the sun was burning on their bare heads. Others asked for a single draught of water. When they were pressed to speak of religion, they burst into curses, and imprecated vengeance on their judge and jury, saying they were hung as poor rogues, but many worse escaped because they were rich.

He then implored them to be in charity with all the world, and asked their names and ages. They said, "What is that to you? we suffer the law, and shall give no account but to God." One cursed a woman in the crowd for coming to see him hung, and another laughed at their tying his hands behind him, "for he had seen many a good fellow hung, but never that done before." A third said, the sooner the better, so he might get out of pain.

Nine others showed much penitence. One obtained a short reprieve, and devoted it to prayer, singing the thirty-first Psalm at the foot of the gallows. Another (the deserter) exhorted the seamen to a good life, and sang a psalm. The next instant a gun was fired, and he swung from the fore-yard-arm. Bunce, the youngest of them all, made a pathetic speech, and begged forgiveness of God and all mankind. Seeing the gallows standing on a rock above the sea, he took a last look at the element which he had so often braved, and saying, he stood "as a beacon on a rock to warn mariners of danger," was turned off by the hangman.

Captain Worly

Captain Worly, the next adventurer, embarked in an open boat, with eight other men, from New York in 1718, captured a *shallop* up the Delaware river, and soon took many other vessels, pursuing an English cruiser from Sandy Hook. He had now twenty-five men and six guns, and his crew had taken an oath to receive no quarter. While careening in an inlet in North Carolina he was attacked by two government sloops. These cruisers boarded him on either side, and the pirates fought so desperately that only the captain and another man were taken prisoners, and being much wounded were hung the next day for fear they should die, and the law not have its due.

Captain George Lowther

Captain George Lowther was originally second mate on board a vessel carrying soldiers to a fort of the Royal African Company's on the river Gambia, the very one that had been destroyed by Davis. Captain Massey, who commanded these men, offended at the arrogance of the merchants, plotted with Lowther, who had been ill-treated by his captain, to run away with the vessel. They then started as pirates—their vessel, the *Delivery*, having fifty men and sixteen guns. The worthy partners soon quarrelled, Massey knowing nothing of the sea and Lowther nothing of the land. Massey wished to land with thirty men and attack the French in Hispaniola, but Lowther refused his consent; and when Lowther resolved to scuttle a ship, Massey interposed in its behalf. Massey, soon after this, being put on board a prize with ten malcontents, gave himself up at Jamaica, and was sent to cruise in search of his old partner. Massey wrote to the African Company, and prayed to be forgiven, or at least shot as a soldier, and not hung as a pirate. He then came to London, gave himself up, and was soon after hung.

Off Hispaniola Lowther captured two vessels—one of them a Spaniard, the crew of which, in consideration of their being also pirates, and having just boarded an English ship, were drifted off in their own launch, but the English sailors were enrolled in their own crew. They then put into a key, cleaned, and spent some time in revelry. Starting again about Christmas, at the Grand Caimanes they met with a small pirate vessel, commanded by a captain named Low, who now became Lowther's lieutenant. The old ship they sank, and soon after attacked a Boston vessel, the *Greyhound*, which, though only 200 tons, refused to bring to in answer to Lowther's gun, and held out for an hour before she struck her ensign, seeing resistance hopeless. The pirates whipped, beat, and cut these men cruelly, and at last set fire to their vessel, and left them to burn and perish. They soon after burnt and sank several New England sloops; a vessel of Jamaica they generously sent back to her master, and two other vessels they fitted up for their own use, mounting one with eight carriage and ten swivel guns.

With this little fleet, Admiral Lowther, in the *Happy Delivery*, went to the gulf of Matique to careen, carrying ashore all their sails and stores, and putting them in tents on the beach. While the ships, however, were on the keel, and the men busy heaving, scrubbing, and tallowing, they were attacked by a large body of the natives. Burning the *Happy Delivery*, their largest ship, and leaving all their stores behind, they then turned one sloop adrift, and all embarked in the other, the *Ranger*. This disaster, and the shortness of provisions, soon produced mutiny and mutual recrimination.

In May 1721 they went to the West Indies, capturing a brigantine, which they plundered and sank, and then started for New England. Low and Lowther always quarrelling, at last parted, Low taking forty-four hands in the brigantine, and leaving the same number in the sloop to Lowther. The latter for some time captured nothing but fishing vessels, and a New England ship with a cargo of sugar from Barbadoes. Off the coast of South Carolina, being pursued by an English vessel that he had imprudently attacked, he was driven on shore in his attempts to escape. The English captain, in attempting to board, was shot, and his mate declined the combat. The pirate sloop soon put again to sea, but much shattered, and with many of the crew killed and wounded. The winter Low spent in repairing, in an inlet of North Carolina, where his men pitched tents, and lived on the wild cattle they shot in the woods, while in very cold nights they slept on board the ship.

After a cruise round Newfoundland the pirates sailed for the West Indies, and put into a creek in the island of Blanco, not far from Tortuga, to careen. Here they were attacked by the *Eagle* sloop of Barbadoes, belonging to the South Sea Company. She fired a gun first to make Lowther show his colours, and then boarded. Lowther and twelve of his crew made their escape out of a cabin window after their vessel had struck. The master of the *Eagle*, with twenty-five men, spent five days in search of the fugitives, and, capturing eight only of them, returned to Cumana.

The Spanish governor applauding the *Eagle* condemned the sloop, and sent a small vessel with twenty-five hands to scour the patches of *lignum vitae* trees that covered the low level island, and took four pirates, but Lowther and three men and a boy still escaped. It is supposed he then destroyed himself, as he was found soon after by some sailors dead, beside a bush, with a burst pistol by his side. Of his companions nine were hung at St. Christopher's, two pardoned, and five acquitted; four the Spaniards condemned to slavery for life, three to the galleys, and the others to the Castle of Arraria.

Captain Spriggs was another of this same gang, having been quartermaster to Lowther. In 1723 Spriggs, with eighteen men, sailed by night from the coast of Guinea, in the *Delight* (a man-of-war) taken by Low, for they had quarrelled as to the punishment of a pirate who had murdered another. Low was for mercy and Spriggs for the yard-arm.

They then chose Spriggs captain, hoisted the black flag, and fired all their guns to honour his inauguration. In their voyage to the West Indies they plundered a Portuguese bark, tortured the crew, set them adrift in a boat with a small quantity of provisions, and then burnt the vessel. The crew of a Barbadoes sloop they cut and beat for refusing to serve with them, and turned them off like the Portuguese. They next rummaged a logwood ship from Jamaica, cut the cable, broke the windows, destroyed the cabins, and when the mate refused to go with them, every man in the vessel gave him ten lashes, which they called "writing his discharge" in red letters flaring on his back. George the Second's birthday they spent in roaring out healths, shouting, and drinking, expecting that there would be an amnesty at his accession, and vowing, if they were excepted, to murder every Englishman they met. They next gave chase to a vessel (supposed to be a Spaniard), till the crew made a lamentable cry for quarter, and they discovered it was the logwood vessel they had turned off three days before, not worth a penny. Enraged at this, fifteen of them flew at the captain and cut him down, though his mate, who had joined the pirates, interceded for his life. It being midnight, and nearly all, as usual at such an hour, drunk, it was unanimously agreed to make a bonfire of the Jamaica ship. They then called the bleeding captain down into the cabin to supper, and made him, with a sword and pistol at his breast, eat a dish of candles, treating all the crew in the same way. Twenty days afterwards they landed the captain and a passenger on a desert island in the Bay of Honduras, giving them powder, ball, and one musket. Here they supported life for fifteen days, till two marooned sailors coming in a canoe paddled them to another island, where they got food and water. Espying a sloop at sea, they made a great smoke and were taken off after nineteen days' more suffering. Spriggs, while laying wait to take his revenge on the *Eagle*, was pursued by a French man-of-war from Martinique, and then went to Newfoundland to obtain more men and attack Captain Harris, who had lately taken another pirate vessel. Of their future fate we hear nothing. Let us hope they sailed on till they reached Gallows Point and there anchored.

John Gow

John Gow was one of the crew of an Amsterdam galley, who in 1724, in a voyage to Barbary, plotted to murder the captain and seize the vessel. Having first cut his throat they tried to throw him overboard, but as he grappled with them Gow and the second mate and gunner shot him through the body. They then murdered the chief mate and the clerk, who was asleep in his hammock; the latter, handing the key of his chest, begged for time to say his prayers, but a sailor shot him as he knelt, with a pistol that burst as he fired.

The murders being over, one of the red-handed men came on deck, and, striking a gun with his cutlass, cried "You are welcome, Captain Gow, to your new command."

Gow then swore that if any whispered together or refused to obey orders, they should go the same way as those that had just gone. They plundered a French fruit vessel and some others, but were soon after stranded on the Orkney coast, where they had intended to clean, were apprehended by a gentleman named Fea, and brought up to London.

Gow obstinately refusing to plead, his thumbs were tied with whipcord till they broke. As he still remained silent he was ordered by the Draconic law of those days to be pressed to death. When the preparations were completed Gow's courage failed him, he sullenly pleaded not guilty, and was soon after, with nine of his crew at the same time, executed.

Captain Weaver

Captain Weaver, of the *Good Fortune*, brigantine, which had taken some sixty sail off the banks of Newfoundland, on his return from thence came to Bristol, and passed himself off as a sailor who had escaped from pirates, walking openly about the town. Here he was met by a captain whom he had once plundered, and who invited him to share a bottle in a neighbouring tavern, telling him he had been a great sufferer by the loss of his ship, but that for four hogsheads of sugar he would never mention the affair again. Unable to obtain this compensation he arrested Weaver, who was soon after hung.

Captain Edward Low

Captain Edward Low, our last commodore, was originally a London thief, the head of a gang of Westminster boys, and a gambler among the footmen in the lobby of the House of Commons. One of his brothers was the first thief who stole wigs by dressing as a porter, and carrying a boy on his head in a covered basket. He ended his days at Tyburn.

Low was originally a logwood cutter at Honduras, but quarrelling with his captain, and attempting his life, put off to sea with twelve companions, and taking a sloop, hoisted a black flag, and declared war against the world. Of his adventures with Lowther we have already made mention. In May, 1722, while off Rhode Island, the governor ordered a drum to beat up for volunteers, and fitted out two sloops with 140 men to pursue him, but Low contrived to escape, and soon after running into Port Rosemary, seized thirteen vessels at one stroke, arming a schooner of ten guns for his own use, putting eighty men on board, and calling her the Fancy. He was soon after beaten off by two armed sloops from Boston. Low waiting too long for his consort, a brigantine, to come up, in steering for the Leeward Islands, they were overtaken by a dreadful storm, the same which drowned 400 people at Jamaica, and nearly destroyed the town of Port Royal. The pirates escaped by dint of throwing over all their plunder and six of their guns, and put into one of the Caribbees to refit, buying provisions of the natives. In this storm it was that forty sail of ships were cast away in Port Royal harbour.

Once refitted, Low sailed into St. Michael's road, and took seven sail, threatening with present death all who dared to resist. Being without water, he sent to the governor demanding some, and declaring that if none were sent he would burn all his prizes. On the governor's compliance he released six, and fitted up the seventh for himself. Another one they burnt. The crews they compelled to join them, all but one French cook, who was so fat that they said he would fry well. They then bound him to the mast, and allowed him to burn with the ship. The crew of another galley they cruelly cut and mangled, and two Portuguese friars they tied up to the yard-arm, pulling them up and down till they were dead. A Portuguese passenger looking sorrowfully on at these brutalities, one of the pirates cried out that he did not like his looks, and cut open his belly with his cutlass, so that he fell down dead. Another of the men, cutting at a prisoner, slashed Low across the upper lip, so as to lay the teeth bare. The surgeon was called to stitch up the wound, but the medical man being drunk, Low cursed him for his bungling. He replied by striking Low a blow in the mouth that broke the stitches, telling him to sew up his chops himself.

Off Madeira, they seized a fishing boat, and obtained water by a threat of hanging the fishermen. While careening at the Cape Verd Islands, after making many prizes, Low sent a sloop to St. Michael's in search of two vessels, but his crew were seized and condemned to slavery for life.

In careening his other ship, it was lost, and Low had now to fall back on his old schooner, the *Fancy*, which he sailed in with a hundred men. Proceeding to the West Indies, they captured, after some resistance, a rich Portuguese vessel called the *Nostra Signora de Victoria*, bound home from Bahia. Several of the crew they tortured till they confessed that during the chase their captain had hung a bag of 11,000 *moidors* out of the cabin window, and when the ship was taken dropped it into the sea. The pirates, in a fury at this, cut off his lips, broiled them before his face, and then murdered him and thirty-two of his crew. In the next month they seized four vessels, burning all those from New England.

In the Bay of Honduras Low boarded a Spanish sloop of six guns and seventy men, that had that morning captured five English vessels. Finding out this from the prisoners in the hold, these butchers proceeded to destroy the whole crew, plunging among them with pole-axes, swords, and pistols. Some leaped into the hold and others into the sea. Twelve escaped to shore: the rest were knocked on the head in the water. While the pirates were carousing on land, one wounded wretch, fainting with his wounds, came to them and begged in God's name for quarter, upon which a brutal sailor replied, he would give him good quarters, and, forcing him down on his knees, ran the muzzle of his gun down his throat, and shot him. They then burnt the vessel, and forced the English prisoners to return to New York, and not to Jamaica.

Hating all men of New England, Low cut off the ears of a gentleman of that nation, and tied burning matches between the fingers of some other prisoners. The crew of a whaler he whipped naked about the deck, and made the master eat his own ears with pepper and salt.

On one occasion, the captain of a Virginian vessel refusing to pledge him in a bowl of punch, he cocked a pistol and compelled him to drain the whole quart. Off South Carolina, his consort was taken by a cruiser, but Low basely deserting him, escaped, and off Newfoundland took eighteen ships, and in July, 1723, he fitted up a prize called the *Merry Christmas*, with thirty-four guns, and assumed the title of admiral, hoisting a black flag, with the figure of death in red. At St. Michael he cut out of the road a London vessel of fourteen guns, which the men refused to defend. The ears of the captain Low cut off, for daring to attempt resistance, and giving him a boat to escape in, burnt his ship.

He then visited the Canaries, Cape de Verd Islands, and lastly, the coast of Guinea. At Sierra Leone he captured the *Delight*, of twelve guns, which he supplied with sixteen guns, and sixty men, appointing Spriggs, his quartermaster, as captain, who two days after deserted him, and sailed for the West Indies.

Of the end of this detestable monster we know nothing, but if there is any truth in old adages, he could not have well perished by a mere storm.

★ ★ ★ ★ ★

The best account of a pirate's life extant is to be found in Captain Roberts's Narrative of the Loss of his Vessel in 1721, preserved in Astley's amusing Collection of Voyages, four dusty quartos, that contain a mine of "auld warld" information.

This Captain Roberts, it appears, contracted with some London merchants to go to Virginia, to fit out a sloop, named the *Dolphin*, with a cargo "to slave with" on the coast of Guinea, and then to return to trade at Barbadoes. Arriving at that island, in 1722, he was discharged, and upon that bought the *Margaret* sloop, and started again for the African coast. At Curisal he turned up to procure a supply of wood and water, and the next morning after his arrival, it being calm as day broke, he looked out and espied three sail of ships off the bay, and making one of them plain with his glass, observed that she was full built and loaded, and supposed that she and her companions wanted water, as they first brought to, then edged away without making any signals.

As soon as the day broke clean and they made his ship, one of them stood right in towards her, and as the sun rose and the wind freshened, tacked more to the eastward. As she drew nigher, Roberts found her by his glass to be a schooner full of hands, all in white shirts; and when he saw a whole tier of great guns grinning through the portholes, he began to suspect mischief. But it was now too late to escape, as it held calm within the bay, and the three ships came crowding in as fast as the wind, flaunting out an English ensign, jack, and pendant. Roberts then hoisted his ensign. The first of the three that arrived had 8 guns, 6 *patereroes*, 70 men, and stretching ahead hailed him. Roberts said he was of London, and came from Barbadoes. They answered, with a curse, that they knew that, and made him send a boat on board.

The pirate captain, John Lopez, a Portuguese, who passed himself off as John Russel, an Englishman, from the north country, asked them where their captain was. They pointed him out Roberts, walking the deck. He instantly called out, "You dog, you son of a gun, you speckled shirt dog!" for Roberts had just turned out, wore a speckled Holland shirt, and was slipshod, without stockings. Roberts, afraid if he showed contempt by continued silence they would put a ball through him, thought it best to answer, and cried "Holloa!" upon which Russel said, "You dog you, why did you not come aboard with the boat? I'll drub you within an inch of your life, and that inch too."

Roberts meekly replied that only the boat being commanded aboard, he did not think he had been wanted, but if they would please to send the boat, he would wait upon him. "Ay, you dog you," said the Portuguese, "I'll teach you better manners."

Upon this eight of the pirates boarded, and took possession of the ship, and as soon as Roberts came alongside, the pirate began again to threaten to drub him for daring to affront him; and when he declared he meant no offence, cried out, "D—n you, you dog, don't stand there to chatter, come aboard," and stood with a cutlass ready drawn to receive him.

While still hesitating, the gunner, who wore a gold-laced hat, looked over the side, and said, "Come up, master, you shan't be abused."

When he got up, the pirate raised his sabre as if to cut him down, asking what a dog deserved for not coming aboard when the boat was first sent. Roberts replied, if he had done amiss, it was through ignorance, as he did not know what they were.

"Curse you," said the pirate, "who do you think we are?"

Roberts now trembled for fear, for having once been captured by pirates at Newfoundland, he knew—one wrong word and the knife was at his throat. After a short pause, he said, "I believed you were gentlemen of fortune belonging to the sea."

At this the Portuguese, a little pacified, said, "You lie, we are pirates."

After vapouring for some time, the pirate asked, in a sneering tone, why Roberts had not put on his clothes to visit gentlemen. Roberts replied, that he did not know of the visit when he dressed, and, besides, came in such a fright on account of their threats, that he had very little thought or stomach to change clothes, still, if it would please them to grant him the liberty, he would go and put on better clothes, hoping it was not yet too late.

"D—n you," said the pirate, "yes, it is too late; what clothes you took you shall keep, but your sloop and what is in her is ours."

Roberts said, he perceived it was, but hoped, as he lay at their mercy, they would be so generous as to take only what they had occasion for and leave him the rest.

The Portuguese said, "that was a company business, and he could say nothing about that yet."

He then bade him give an account of his cargo and money, and of everything aboard his sloop, for if upon rummaging they found the least article concealed, they would burn the vessel and him in her. The pirates standing by also begged him to make a full discovery of all money, arms, and ammunition, which were the chief things they sought after, for it was their way to punish liars and concealers very severely. Roberts then drew up an account from memory, and asked to see his ship's papers that he might complete it. Russel said, "No, he would take care of the papers, and if anything was found missing in the inventory he must look out for squalls." During this time the pirates were rummaging the sloop, but found nothing but a ring and a pair of silver buckles not inserted in the list.

During the capture a Portuguese priest and six black fishermen, taken on board at the Isle of Sal, who had been sent on shore, escaped to the hills. Russel, seeing them, told Roberts that he had captured the fishing sloop to which the fugitives belonged, but one of his gang had run away with it, carrying off £800 in cash, in addition. Russel then slipped cable and made Roberts pilot them to Paraghisi, in company with their other vessel, the *Rose Pink*, of thirty-six guns, commanded by Edmund Loe, their commodore. At Paraghisi they landed thirty-five men and captured the fugitive priest, five negroes, and the old governor's son. Russel on his return was received with great ceremony by his commander, the gunner acting as master of the ceremonies and presenting Roberts.

Captain Loe welcomed him aboard with the usual compliments, "It's not my desire, captain," he said, "to meet with any of my countrymen (but rather foreigners), excepting some few whom I want to chastise for their roguishness; but, however, since fortune has ordered it so that you have fallen into our hands, I would have you be of good cheer and not cast down."

Roberts replied, "I am very sorry, sir, that I chanced to fall in your way, but I feel I am still in the hands of gentlemen of honour and generosity, in whose power it is still to make my capture no misfortune."

Loe said, "It does not lie singly in my breast, for all business of this nature is determined by a majority of votes in the whole company, and though neither I nor, I believe, any of the rest desire to meet with any of our nation, yet when we do it cannot well be avoided to take as our own what Providence sends us; and, as we are gentlemen who depend entirely on fortune, we durst not be so ungrateful to her as to despise any of her favours, however mean, for fear that she might withdraw her hand and leave us to perish for lack of those very things we had slighted."

After this philosophical utterance, the great man, who sat astride on a great gun, and not, like other potentates, in a chair of state, without moving from his place, begged Roberts, with much condescension, to make himself at home, requesting to know what he would drink.

The broken-spirited man, still trembling for his life, replied, "He did not care then much for drinking, but out of a sense of the honour they did him in asking he would drink anything he chose."

Loe told him "Not to be cast down, it was the fortune of war: d———, sir, care killed the cat, and fretting thinned the blood and was d—— bad for the health. To please the company he should be brisk and cheerful and he would soon have better fortune."

He then rang the bell and bade one of the *valets de cabin* bring in a bowl of punch. This was brought and mixed in a rich silver bowl holding two gallons. He then called for some wine, and two bottles of claret being brought, Roberts sipped at the claret while

Loe drained the bowl with his usual philosophy and contentment. As he grew warm with the fragrant draught, he told Roberts that he was a d——d good fellow, and he would do him all the favours he could, but wished he had had the good fortune to have been captured ten days earlier, when they had taken two Portuguese outward bound Brazilmen, laden with cloth, woollens, hats, silk, and iron, for he believed he could have prevailed on his company to have loaded Roberts's ship.

"But now unfortunately," he added, as he put down the empty bowl, "we have no goods at all, having flung all the Brazil stuffs into David Jones's locker (the sea)."

He did not know, however, but he might meet Roberts again (such things did come round), and then if it lay in his way he would make Roberts a return for his loss, for he might depend on his readiness to serve him as far as his power or interest could reach. To this outburst of sympathy Roberts replied by bowing and sipping his unrelished glass of claret.

While they were talking word was brought that Quartermaster-General Russel had arrived with the prisoners, and the commodore, ordering the empty bowl to be removed, bade them come in. Russel, the chief officers, and the prisoners then crowded into the cabin, and to the question of "How goes the game?" Russel gave an account of his expedition.

On landing they had at once seized two blacks, who had been sent by the governor as heralds, and used them as guides. Though the road was uneven and rocky they reached the town, twelve miles distant, that night, surprising the governor and priest. Russel told them, that hearing they had great stores of dollars hoarded up, he had come to share it with them, as it was one rule of his trade to keep money moving and circulation brisk. The priest said they had none, and the island was barren and uncultivated. Russel said he had only two senses, seeing and feeling, which could convince him the information was false. The priest then lit a number of consecrated wax-candles, and allowed them to search. They found, however, nothing but twenty dollars, which he did not think worth taking. The men then lay down to sleep, keeping their arms loaded and their pistols slung, and setting a watch. The next morning he carried the prisoners to the boats.

Upon this tame conclusion, Loe, who had been sitting patient and quiet as a judge, started up and said, interrupting Russel, "Zounds! what satisfaction is this to me or the company? We did not want these black fools, d——n them! No, we wanted their money, and if they had none, they might have stayed ashore or gone to the devil."

Russel, nettled at this rebuke, replied fiercely, "I have as much interest in getting the money as any of the company, and did as much to find it: I don't believe there was more than we saw, and that wouldn't have been sixpence a head, a trifle not worth having our name called in question for. For my part, I am for something that is worth taking, and if I can't light on such, I never will give the world occasion to say that I am a poor sneaking rogue and mean-spirited fellow. No, I will rob for something of value, or not at all, especially among these people, where, if our company breaks, we may look for a place of refuge; and I boldly affirm that it is a fool's act to draw on us their odium by such peddling thefts, that would be by all men accounted a narrow-souled, beggarly action, and would be cursed to all futurity by this fraternity, who might suffer for its effects."

Captain Loe, abashed by the murmur of approval that followed this speech, said, "it was all very true, and carried a deal of reason with it, that he was satisfied with Russel's judgment and courage in the affair; but come," says he, "let us do nothing rashly"—and filling a bumper, drank to Russel, wishing Roberts better success in his next voyage.

Russel then went on shore again, and, finding the priest had escaped to the mountains, told the governor, an old negro, that he should burn the town to ashes if he was not brought in in three hours' time. The governor said the thing was impossible, that he lay at their mercy, and hoped he would not destroy the innocent for the guilty. Russel declared the doom should not be deferred, but promised the priest should not be killed if he surrendered himself. While parties of blacks were on the hunt, Russel ordered an ox to be roasted for his men, and a pipe of wine to be broached; and on the priest being captured, treated all the natives at their Christian minister's expense, leaving him to extract it from them again in tithes.

The priest and governor, when they heard they were to be taken on board, to assure Loe of their poverty, prayed not to be detained as slaves. Russel told them he was a Catholic, and no harm should be done them. They were soon afterwards released. Loe then ordered a hammock for Roberts, till his own and ship's fate were decreed by the company, telling him generously, in language rather metaphorical than strictly accurate, that everything in the ship was at his command, and begging him not to vary his usual course of hours, drinking, or company.

Next morning about eight, as Roberts was pacing unemployed and melancholy on the deck, three pirates came up to him, and said that they had once sailed with him on board the *Susannah*, in 1718. They expressed sorrow for his ill luck, and promised to do something for him. They said they had fifty pieces of white linens, and eight of silk, and that when the company had agreed to restore him his ship, they would make interest to load it. Then looking about as if wishing to tell him a secret, and seeing the deck clear, which it seldom was in pirate vessels, with much concern they informed him that if he did not take abundance of care, he would be forced to stay with them, for their mate had found that he knew the coast of Brazil, whither they were bound after they had scoured that of Guinea, and they would take him as pilot.

Then enjoining him to secrecy (for their lives depended upon it), they said they had been in close consultation as to his fate, and had almost agreed to take him as a forced prisoner. They had praised him as kind to his men, and a good paymaster, and, knowing the pirate law that no married man could be forced to join their ships, swore at a hazard that he was married, and had four children. His mate had turned informer, but he was as yet ignorant of their articles, which they never showed till they were signed. His only chance of escape was to keep up to their story. Russel, one of the council, had been in favour of breaking through the law in this special case, and keeping Roberts at all events till they could catch another guide, but Loe was opposed to it, telling them it would be an ill precedent and of bad consequence, for that if once they took the liberty of breaking their articles and oath, nothing would be sure. They added that most of the company being of Loe's opinion, Russel was vexed and determined if possible to break the articles.

Soon after they were gone, Loe came on deck, and bidding him good morrow, with many compliments, ordered the flag, the signal for consultation, to be hoisted. This they called "the green trumpeter," and was a green silk flag, with the figure of a trumpeter in yellow, and hoisted on the mizen peak. Upon this all came on board to breakfast, crowding both cabin and steerage.

After breakfast Loe asked Roberts, as if casually, if he was married and had children. The latter answered he had five and perhaps six, for one was on the stocks when he came away. He then asked him, if he had left them well provided for. Roberts replied, he had left his wife in such indifferent circumstances, having met with recent misfortunes, that the greater part of his substance was in that ship and cargo, and if that failed they would want even for bread.

Loe then turned to Russel and said, "It won't do, Russel."

"What won't do?" replied the quartermaster.

"You know what I mean," said Loe; "it must not and it shall not be, by——"

"It must and shall be, by——" replied Russel; "'Self-preservation is the first law of nature,' and 'Necessity knows no law,' says the adage."

"Well," says Loe, "it shall never be by my consent."

The rest of the company then declared it was a pity, and ought to be seriously weighed and put to the vote. Loe said, indeed it ought, and that there was no time like the present to determine the matter. The rest all cried, "Ay, it is best to end it now."

Loe then ordered all hands upon deck, and bade Roberts stay in the cabin. In about two hours (awful hours for Roberts, to sit listening for shouts or cries), Loe came down, and asked him how he did.

Russel said, with a frown, "Master, your sloop is very leaky."

Roberts replied it was, wishing to depreciate its value.

"Leaky," said Russel, "I don't know what you could do with her if we gave her you, for all your hands now belong to us." Russel then continued to taunt him for his want of cargo and provision, as if to give a keener edge to his misery.

At last, "Come, come," said Loe, "let us toss the bowl about, and call a fresh course."

They then proceeded to carouse and talk of their past transactions at Newfoundland, the Western Islands, the Canaries, &c., and at dinner tore their food one from the other, thinking such ferocity looked martial.

Next morning one of the three men contrived to speak to Roberts, and apologized for his caution, as they had an article making it death to hold any secret correspondence with a prisoner. He then informed him that his own mate was his great enemy, and seemed likely to turn rogue and enter with them, leaving him only a boy and a child to manage the sloop. Both he and his companions heartily wished to join him, but found it would be death even to mention it, as they had an article that any of the company advising or merely speaking of separation should be shot to death by the quartermaster's order, without even court-martial. Russel had been Roberts' friend till the mate had told him of his captain's knowledge of Brazil, and had even planned a gathering for him nearly equal in value to what they had taken, for it was a custom in pirate vessels to keep a spare stock of linen, silk, gold lace, and clothes, to give to any prisoner whom they took a liking to or had known before. Loe was his friend, the sailor assured him, but that he could do little against Russel, who had really more power and sway than anyone else.

Some time after this man left him, Captain Loe turned out, and, passing the usual compliments, sent for some rum, and discoursed on many indifferent subjects. Upon all of these Roberts was obliged to appear interested, dreading this sea-despot's displeasure. Perhaps a button-holder, like this Trunnion, never had so attentive an auditor, or so hearty an applauder of anecdotes, good or bad.

About ten o'clock Russel, the evil genius, came on board, and accosted Roberts in an agreeable manner, trying to conciliate him into consenting to his proposal. He said, he had been considering Roberts's scheme, and did not see how he could carry it through. He believed Roberts was a man of understanding, but in this case was directed by sheer desperation rather than reason. For his part he did not think it would stand with the credit or reputation of the company to put it into his power to throw himself wilfully away, as he seemed determined to do. Wishing him indeed well, he had been thinking all night upon a scheme which, without exposing him to danger, would turn out more to his advantage than anything he could expect by getting the sloop. (Here Roberts's eye brightened.) He had resolved to sink or burn the sloop, and detain Roberts as a prisoner, all the company promising to give him the first prize they took, or to allow him to join their crew. This would be the making of him, and enable him to soon leave off sea, and live ashore if he were so inclined.

Roberts thanked him, but said he thought he should gather no advantage from such a plan, for he could not dispose of a ship or cargo without a lawful power to sell, and if the owners heard of it, he should be either obliged to make restitution, or be thrown into prison, and run the hazard of his own life.

Russel replied that his objections were frivolous, and could easily be evaded. To avoid detection, they would make him a bill of sale, and give him powers in writing that would answer any inquiry. As for the owners, they would take care from the ship's writings, which they always first seized, to let him know who were the owners of the cargo, and where they lived. These writings should be made in a false name, which Roberts could assume till all were sold.

Roberts said there was abundant address in his contrivance and much plausibility in the whole. But were he even sure that all would turn out well, he had a still stronger motive than any he had yet mentioned, and that was his dread of the continual sting and accusation of his conscience. He then with more courage than he had hitherto shown, began to expatiate on the duty of restitution, and tried to awaken his hearers to some sense of the sin of piracy.

Many said, with a laugh, he would do well to preach a sermon, and would make a good chaplain. Others shouted that they wanted no preaching there. "Pirates had no god but money, no saviour but their muskets." A few approved of what he said, and declared that if a little goodness, or at least rude humanity, was in practice among them, their reputation would be a little better both with God and man.

A short silence followed, which captain Russel broke by employing some Jesuitical sophistry, to persuade Roberts that it would be no sin for him merely to accept what they had stolen, since he had no hand in the theft, and was their constrained prisoner.

"Suppose," he said, "we should still resolve to sink or burn your sloop, unless you will accept of her. Now, where I pray, is the owner's property when the ship is sunk or burnt. I think the impossibility of his ever having her again cuts it off to all intents and purposes, and our power was the same, notwithstanding our giving her to you, if we had thought fit to make use of it."

Loe and the rest here burst out laughing, declared it was as good as a play to hear the two argue, and that Roberts was a match for Russel, though few could generally stand up to him in a fight with mere words.

Roberts not allowing this praise to over-balance his prudence, would not drive Russel further, seeing him vexed at their applause. He merely said that he knew he was absolutely in their power to dispose of as they pleased, but that having hitherto been treated so generously by them, he could not doubt of their future goodness to him. That if they would please to give him his sloop again, it was all he requested at their hands, and that, he doubted not, by his honest endeavours he should be able to retrieve his present loss.

Upon this Captain Loe said, "Gentlemen, the master, I must needs say, has spoke nothing but what I think is very reasonable, and I think he ought to have his sloop. What do you say, gentlemen?"

The majority cried out with one voice, "Ay, ay, by G—— let the poor man have his sloop again, and go in God's name and seek a living in her for his family."

In the evening Russel insisted on treating Roberts on board his own schooner before his departure. All passed off well till after supper, when a bowl of punch and half a dozen of claret were put on the table. The captain first took a bumper, wishing success to the undertaking, and this toast passed round, Roberts not daring to refuse to drink. The next health was, "Prosperity to our trade." The third, "Health to the King of France." Russel then proposed "The King of England's health," and all drank it, some repeating his words, others saying, "the aforesaid health." Just before it came to Roberts, Russel poured two bottles of claret into the punch, and his prisoner disliking this mixture, begged to pledge the health in a bumper of claret.

At this heresy, Russel, who had laid his trap, flew into a passion, "D——" he said, "you shall drink in your turn a full bumper of that sort of liquor the company does."

"Well then, gentlemen," said Roberts, "rather than have words, I will drink, though it is in a manner poison to me."

"Curse you," said Russel; "if it be in a manner or out of a manner, or really rank poison, you shall drink as much and as often as anyone here, unless you fall down dead, dead."

Then Roberts, dreading a quarrel with his old enemy, took the glass, which held about three-quarters of a pint, and filling a bumper, said, "The aforesaid health."

"What health is that?" said Russel.

"Why," answered Roberts, "the health you have all drank—the King of England's health."

"Who is king of England?" said Russel.

"In my opinion," said Roberts, "he that wears the crown is certainly king of England."

"Well," argued his opponent, "and who is that?" Upon his saying King George, he swore at him, and said the English had no king.

Roberts replied, laughing, "He wondered he should begin and drink a health to a person who was not in being."

At this quip, Russel drew a pistol from his sash, and would have shot his unoffending enemy dead, had not the gunner snatched it out of his hand. At this Russel, who was a Roman Catholic and a Jacobite, grew still more maddened, and fired another at Roberts, saying, "The Pretender is the only lawful king."

The master striking down the barrel, the pistol went off without doing mischief.

High words then arose between Russel and the gunner, and the latter, addressing the company, said, "Well, gentlemen, if you have a mind to maintain these laws, made, established, and sworn to by us all, as I think we are obligated by the strongest ties of reason and self-interest to do, I assure you my opinion is that we ought to secure John Russel, so as to prevent his breaking our constitution."

When Russel attempted, still in a passion, to defend his conduct, the gunner declared, "That no man's life should be taken away in cold blood till the company, under whose care he was, had so decreed it." Then accusing him of hating Roberts, merely because he had been prevented from breaking the articles by detaining him, he left the spot.

Russel's arms were next taken away, and Roberts, being guarded during the night, was sent to the commodore in the morning, there being a law among them to receive no boats aboard after nine o'clock at night.

About four in the afternoon Russel came to Loe, with Spriggs, the commander of the other ship, and told him that Roberts's mate was willing to join them as a volunteer. Loe said, in that case Roberts would have no one but a child to help him; and he thought, in reason, they could not give him less than the mate and two boys.

Russel said he could not help that, "the mate was a brisk lusty young fellow, and had been upon the account before. He had declared he would not go in the sloop unless forced; that when he first came to Barbadoes his resolve had been to ship himself on board the first pirate he met with."

Loe replied, "That to give the master a vessel without men was only putting him to a lingering death, and they had better knock him on the head at once."

Russel replied, "as for that they might do as they pleased; he spoke for the good of the company and according to articles, and he should like to see or hear the man who dared to gainsay it. He was quartermaster, and by the authority of that office should at once enter the mate, and had a pistol and a brace of bullets for any who opposed him."

Loe said he would not argue against law and custom, but he thought if they kept the mate they should substitute another man.

Russel said, with an oath, grinding his teeth, "No, the sloop's men were enrolled already in his books, and he should rub no names out." Then turning to Roberts, he added, "The company, master, has decreed you your sloop, and you shall have her; you shall have your two boys, that's all: but you shall have neither provisions nor anything else more than she has now. And, as I hear some of the company design to make a gathering for you, that also I forbid, by the authority of my office, because we are not certain but we may have occasion ourselves for those very things before we get more. And I swear by all that's good and bad, if I know anything that's carried or left on board the sloop against my order, or without my knowledge, I will set her on fire that very instant, and you with her."

After a little more dispute and feeble and intimidated resistance to this violence, Russel's stern resolution and heartless villainy carried the day, and about dusk they parted, each to his own ship, several professing kindness to Roberts, but none giving him anything. When Russel was ready, he sent Roberts into his boat, and bringing him to his own ship, ordered supper for him, and bottles, and pipes and tobacco, being set on the table, he invited Roberts and his officers into his cabin.

His revenge was now accomplished and the wretch, now resolved to make Roberts taste the tortures of death, by anticipation, addressed him with a sneer worthy of the applause of hell.

"Captain Roberts," he said, "you are very welcome, and I pray you eat and drink heartily, for you have as tedious a voyage to go through as Elijah in his forty days' journey to Horeb, and, as far as I know, without a miracle, it must be only by the strength of what you now eat, for you shall have neither eatables nor drinkables with you in the sloop."

Roberts replied, "I hope not so," but Russel answered he would find it certainly true.

Roberts then said, that rather than be put on board the sloop in that manner, when there was no possibility of escaping but by a miracle, he should be glad to be sent ashore on some island off the coast of Guinea, or even to tarry on board till an opportunity occurred to land where he pleased, for he would yield to anything else they should think fit to do with him, except entering into their service.

Russel answered with an oath, the usual prelude of a pirate's harangue, that it had been once in his power to have been his own friend, but as he chose to slight their proffered favours, and had made that choice, he must now take it, as all apologies were too late; and he thought he had proved himself a better friend than Roberts could have expected, since he had caused him to have more differences with his company than he had ever had before.

Roberts pleaded the innocence of his intentions, and entreated Russel and all the gentlemen present to consider him an object rather of pity than vengeance. But his tormentor, more inexorable than a headsman, said: "All your whining arguments, you dog, are now too late. You not only refused our commiseration when it was offered, but ungratefully despised it. Your lot is cast, and you have nothing to do but to go through your chance with a good face. Fill your belly with victuals and good drink, and strengthen yourself for three days or so, or have some brandy and die drunk, and be happy. This is your last meal in this world, so fail not to make the most of it. Yet, perhaps, such a conscientious man as you pretend to be may have a miracle worked for you, but for my own part I don't believe God himself, if there is one, could help you. I pity the boys, and have a great mind, Roberts, to keep them on board, and let the miracle be worked on you alone."

The master and governor said they heard the boys were willing to take their chance with the master, let it be what it would. "Nay, then," said Russel, "it is fit the young devils should, and I suppose the master has made them as religious and conscientious as himself. However, master," he cried, "eat and drink heartily; this is your last supper, as the priests call it, and don't try to change your allotted fate, or it may provoke us to treat you worse."

"Gentlemen," said Roberts, with a resignation that would have touched any other man, "I have done; you can do no more than God is pleased to permit you, and I own for that reason I ought to take it patiently. God forgive you."

"Well, well," said Russel, "if it is done by God's permission, you need not fear He will permit any harm to befall one of his peculiar elect."

About ten at night, in order that darkness might add to his dismay, some of Russel's partisans brought the sloop's boat. In answer to an inquiry as to whether they had cleared the vessel as he had ordered, they replied with an oath, "Ay, ay, she has nothing on board except ballast and water."

"Zounds," said Russel, stamping on the deck, "did I not bid you stave all the casks that had water in them?"

"So we have," was the reply; "the water we mean is salt water leaked in, and now above the ballast, for we have not pumped her, we don't know when."

He asked if they had brought away the sails. They said they had, all but the mainsail that was bent, for the other old mainsail was so rotten it was only fit to cut up for parcelling, and was so torn it could not be brought to, and was past mending.

"Zounds," said Russel, "we must have it, for I want it to make us a mainsail. The same miraculous Power that brings the rogue provisions will bring him sails."

"What a devil! is he a conjuror?" said one.

"No, no!" replied Russel, "but he expects miracles to be wrought for him, or he would never have chosen what he has."

"Nay, nay, if he be such a one, he will do well enough."

"But I doubt," cried another, "if he be such a mighty conjuror, for if he was, how the devil was it that he did not conjure himself clear of us?"

"Pish!" cried a third, "may be his conjuring books were all shut up."

"Ay," said a fourth, "now we have all his conjuration books over board, I doubt he'll be hard put to it."

The gunner alone seemed to retain any trace of humanity, he bade Russel take care he had not this to answer for some day when he would be sorry for it.

"Howsum-dever," he said, "you've got the company's assent, I can't tell how, and, therefore, I shall say no more, only that I, and I believe most of the gentlemen came here to get money, but not to kill, except in fight, much less in cold blood, or for private revenge. And I tell you, Jack Russel, if ever such cases as these be any more practised, my endeavours will be to leave this company as soon as convenient."

Russel made no answer, but ordered his men to fetch the mainsail from the sloop. He then gave Roberts an old worm-eaten musket, a damp cartridge, and two half pounds of tobacco "as a parting present." His victim was then conducted with great ceremony over the side into his own boat, and put on board with his two boys.

As their boat was putting away, Roberts thought he heard his mate's voice, so he called to him and said, "Arthur! what, are you going to leave me?"

A voice replied, for it was pitch dark, "Ay."

"What!" said Roberts, "do you do it voluntarily, or are you forced?"

He answered faintly, "I am forced, I think!"

Roberts answered "Very well."

The mate then called out and asked Roberts, if he ever had an opportunity, to write and give his brother an account of him. Roberts asked where he lived, and the mate replied at Carlingford, in Ireland. Now this mate the captain had picked up at Barbadoes, a naked shipwrecked man, who had served in a New England sloop. He had bought him clothes and instruments, and treated him with sympathy and kindness. He was a rigid Presbyterian, a great arguer on theological points, and a loud inveigher against the Church of England. Although he had never before been heard to utter an oath, as soon as Russel persuaded him to join the pirate crew, he became constantly drunk, and outdid them all in blasphemy and wickedness, but he had told his new companions so much of Roberts's kindness, that but for Russel they would not have allowed him to join them.

Next morning Roberts proceeded to rummage the sloop, and sweeping out the bread lockers, he found about his hat crown full of biscuit crumbs, some broken pipes, and a few screws of tobacco. They had left his fore-staff, but took his bedding, although they generally lay upon deck, or against a gun carriage. In the hold, the more merciful had left ten gallons of rum in one hogshead, and thirty pounds of rice in another, with three pints of water and a little flour, together with some needles and twine, sufficient to repair his rotten sails. A day or two afterwards they caught a shark, which they boiled for several dinners, using the shark's liver, melted, for oil. He soon after reached Curisal, obtained a negro crew, was wrecked, built a boat, and was eventually taken home by an English ship.

★ ★ ★ ★ ★

Scarcely less interesting than this narrative of Roberts is that of Captain William Snelgrave, who was engaged in the slave trade on the Guinea coast in 1738. Having escaped one of the dreaded Salee rovers, he was taken at Sierra Leone by Captain Cocklyn of the *Rising Sun*, a pirate commanding three vessels and a gang of eighty men. He had been marooned by a man named Moody, but had gradually collected men, and captured, in a short time, ten English vessels. Moody's crew, soon after Cocklyn's departure, disliking their captain's cruelty, put him and twelve more in an open boat, which they had taken from the Spaniards off the Canary Islands, and chose a Frenchman named Le Bouce as their commander, who instantly put back and joined Cocklyn, whom they liked because he was fierce and brutal, being resolved to have no more gentlemanlike captains like Moody.

The next day Davis, the pirate, arrived with 150 well disciplined men, the black flag flying at his mast head.

The evening Snelgrave entered the river, he observed a suspicious smoke on land, but his mate said it was only travellers roasting oysters, and it appeared afterwards that he was a traitor. On standing in for the river's mouth, the pirate vessels appeared in sight. Towards dusk he heard a boat approaching, so he ordered twenty men to get ready their firearms and cutlasses. Lanterns being brought and the boat hailed, the pirates fired a volley at the ship, being then within pistol shot distance, a daring act for twelve men, who were attacking a ship of sixteen guns and forty-five men.

When they began to near, the captain called out to fire from the steerage port-holes. This not being done, he went below, and found his people staring at each other, and declaring they could not find the arm chest. The pirates instantly boarded, fired down the steerage, shooting a sailor in the loins, and throwing hand grenades amongst them. On their calling for "mercy," the quartermaster, who always headed the pirate boarders, came down from the quarterdeck and inquired for the captain, asking how he dared to fire. On Snelgrave saying it was his duty to defend his ship, the quartermaster presented a pistol at his breast, but he parried it, and the bullet passed under his arm. The wretch then struck him on the head with the butt end, bringing him on his knees. On his getting up and running to the quarterdeck, the pirate boatswain made a blow at his head with his broad sword, swearing no quarter should be offered to any captain who dared to defend his vessel. The blow missed him, but the blade cut an inch deep in the quarterdeck rail, and there broke.

The pirate's pistols being all unloaded, he then struck at him with the butt end of one of them till the crew cried out for his life, and said they had never sailed with a better man. One of the crew, however, had his chin cut off; another fell for dead on the deck. The quartermaster who came up, told him he should be cut to pieces if his men did not recover the pirate's boat that had run adrift. On recovering this, he took him by the hand, and declared his life was safe if none of his crew complained of him. The pirate then fired several volleys for joy at their recovery, but forgetting to hail their companions, were fired on by the other ships. When Snelgrave questioned the quartermaster why he did not use his speaking trumpet, he asked him angrily whether he was afraid of going to the devil by a great shot, "for that he hoped to be sent to hell by a cannon ball some time or other."

The pirates now prepared for dinner by cramming geese, turkeys, fowls, and ducks, all unpicked, into the furnace, with some Westphalia hams, and a large sow in pig, which they only bowelled, leaving the hair on. Soon after this, a sailor came to Snelgrave to ask him what o'clock it was, and on the captain's presenting him with his watch, laid it on the deck, and kicked it about, saying it would make a good football. One of the pirates then caught it up, and said it should go into the common chest, and be sold at the mast.

Snelgrave was soon after carried on board the pirate ship. The commander told him he was sorry for the bad usage he had met with, but it was the fortune of war, and that if he did not answer truly every question he would be cut into even ounces, but that if he told the truth they would make it the best voyage he had ever taken. One of them asked if his ship sailed well on wind, and on his saying, "Very well," Cocklyn threw up his hat, saying she would make a brave pirate man-of-war. A tall fellow, with four pistols in his belt, and a broadsword in his hand, then came up and claimed him as an old schoolfellow, and told him secretly that he was a forced man, having been mate in a Bristol vessel lately captured, and was obliged to go armed. He told him also that at night, when the pirates drank hard, was the time of most danger for prisoners.

A bowl of punch was then ordered, and the men, going into the great cabin, sat on the floor cross-legged, for want of seats, drinking the Pretender's health by the name of "King James the Third." At midnight they gave Snelgrave a hammock, and his old schoolfellow kept guard over him with a drawn sword, but he could not sleep for the songs and cursing. About two o'clock the pirate boatswain came on board, and hearing Snelgrave was asleep, declared he would slice his liver for daring to fire at the boat, and refusing to give up his watch. Griffin threatened to cleave him if he came nearer, and struck at him with his sword. In the morning, when all were sober, the sentinel complained of the boatswain for infringing the pirate law, "that no ill usage be offered to prisoners when quarter has once been given."

The crew proposed the offender should be whipped, but Snelgrave prudently begged him off. Soon after, his own first mate came to tell him that, being badly off and having a scolding wife, he had joined the pirates. He found out afterwards that he had hid the arm-chest, and dissuaded the men from resistance.

The pirate then began to rummage the vessel, and, not caring for anything but money, threw overboard, before night, about £4,000 worth of Indian bales. They broke up his escritoires, and destroyed his chests of books, swearing there was "jaw work enough for a whole nation." Against all religious books they exercised a strict censorship, for fear of any of the crew being roused to qualms of conscience, or taking a dislike to the profession. The wine too began to be passed freely round, and the pirates grew merciful, and good-humouredly made up a bundle of clothes for the prisoners.

At this moment one of Davis' crew, a pert young fellow of 18, broke open a chest for plunder, and on the quartermaster complaining, replied "that they were all equal, and he thought he was in the right."

The quartermaster then struck at him with his sword, and pursued him into Davis' cabin, where he thrust at him, and ran him through the hand, wounding the captain as well. Davis vowed revenge, saying that if his man had offended, no one had a right to punish him, and especially in his presence. He then instantly went on board his own ship, and bore down upon Cocklyn, who finally consented to make the quartermaster beg pardon for his fault.

Snelgrave was sitting in the cabin with the carpenter and three or four other pirates, when the boatswain came down very drunk, and beginning to abuse him was turned out of the place. Soon after a puff of wind put out the candle, and the boatswain returning, declared Snelgrave had put it out, with the design of going into the powder-room and blowing up the ship; and in spite of the carpenter declaring it was done by accident, he drew a pistol and swore he would blow out the dog's brains. In rising to blow in the candle Snelgrave and the carpenter had, unknown to the boatswain, changed places. The pistol flashing in the pan, the carpenter saw by the light that he must have been shot if it had gone off, and in a rage ran in the dark to the boatswain, wrenched the pistol from his hand and beat him till he was nearly dead. The noise alarmed the ship, and the disturber was carried off to bed.

The next morning Davis' crew came on board to divide the wines and liquors. They hoisted on deck a great many half hogsheads of claret and French brandy, knocked out their heads and dipped out cans and bowls full, throwing them at each other, and washing the decks with what was left. The bottles they took no trouble to mark, but "nicked" them, as they called it, by striking off their necks with a cutlass, spilling the contents of about one in every three. The eatables were wasted in the same way. Three drunken pirates coming into the cabin, and tumbling over Snelgrave's bundles of clothes, threw three of the four overboard. A fourth pirate, more sober than the rest, opened the remaining bundle, and taking out a black suit and a wig, put them on and strutted on deck, throwing them over in an hour when the crew had drenched him with claret. When Snelgrave mildly expostulated with him on this robbery, he struck him on the shoulder with the flat of his sword, whispering at the same time a caution never to dispute the will of a pirate for fear he might get his skull split for his impudence.

When night came on, Snelgrave had nothing left of four bundles of clothes but a hat and a wig, and these were soon after put on by a drunken man, who staggered into the cabin, saying he was "one of the most respectable merchants on the African coast." As he was leaving the room, a sailor came in and beat him severely for taking what he had no right to, and thinking he was one of the crew. The interposer then comforted Snelgrave, and promised to recover what he had lost, while others of the crew brought him food.

Next day, Davis, ordering all the crews on the quarter-deck, made a speech in Snelgrave's behalf, persuading them to give him a ship and several thousand pounds' worth of miscellaneous plunder. One of the men proposed they should take him with them down the Guinea coast, and if they took a Portuguese vessel, to give him a cargo of slaves. Down the coast he might sell his goods for gold dust, and then, sailing for St. Thomas's, sell his ship and the slaves to the Danes, and return to London a rich man. Snelgrave demurring to this, they grew angry, thinking their gift would have been legal, but Davis kindly said, "I know this man and can easily guess his thoughts, he thinks he would lose his reputation. Now, I am for allowing everybody to go to the devil in their own way, so beg you to give him the remains of his own cargo and let him do as he thinks fit."

This they granted, but of his own adventure not more than £50 worth was now left. The sailors had taken rolls of fine Holland and opened them to lie down in on the deck. Then when the others came and flung buckets of claret over them, they flung the stained parcels overboard. In loading, the pirates always dropped the bales over, if they were not passed as quickly as they expected. The Irish beef they threw away, Cocklyn saying Snelgrave had horsebeans enough to last his crew six months.

Soon after this the brutal quartermaster fell sick of a fever, and sent to Snelgrave to beg his forgiveness, for having attempted to shoot him. He said he had been a wicked wretch, and that his conscience tormented him, for he feared he should roll in hell fire. When Snelgrave preached repentance he declared his heart was hardened, but he would try, and he ordered Snelgrave to take any necessaries he wanted from his chest, but died that night in terrible agonies and cursing God.

This so affected many of the new recruits that they begged Snelgrave to get them off, and promised not to be guilty of murder or other cruelty. In the cabin the pirates found some proclamations, and being unable to read asked the prisoner to do it for them. He then read His Majesty's proclamation for a pardon to all pirates that should surrender themselves at any of the British plantations by the 1st of July, 1719. The next was the declaration of war against Spain. When they heard the latter, some said they wished they had known it before they left the West Indies, as they might have turned privateersmen, and have enriched themselves. Snelgrave told them it was not yet too late, there being still three months left of the term prescribed. But when they heard the rewards offered for the apprehension of pirates, a buccaneer who had been guilty of murder, treated the proclamation with contempt, and tore it in pieces.

Amongst other men that consulted Snelgrave was a sailor named Curtis, who, being sick, walked about the deck wrapped in a silk gown. He had sailed with Snelgrave's father.

Among other spoil the three pirate captains had found a box with three second-hand embroidered coats, which they seized and put on. The longest falling to Cocklyn's share, who was a short man, it reached to his ankles, but Le Bouce and Davis refused to change with him, saying that as he was going on shore where the negro ladies knew nothing of white men's fashions, it did not matter, and moreover, as his coat was scarlet embroidered with silver, he would be the bravest of them all.

These clothes being taken contrary to law, and without the quartermaster's leave, the crew were offended, declaring that if they suffered such things, the captains would assume a new power, and soon take whatever they liked. The next morning when their captains returned, the coats were taken from them, and put into the common chest; and it having been reported that Snelgrave had advised the costume, many of the men turned against him, one of them threatening to cut him to pieces. A sailor who stood near told Snelgrave not to be frightened at the man's threat, for he always spoke in that way, and advised him to call him "captain" when he came on board, for the fellow had once been commander of a pirate sloop, did not like the post of quartermaster, and loved to be called by his old title.

On entering the ship, Snelgrave said softly to him, "Captain Williams, pray hear me on the point you are so offended about."

Upon this Williams gave him a playful blow on the shoulder with the flat of his sword, and said "I have not the heart to hurt thee." He then explained the affair, drank a glass of wine with him, and they were friends ever after.

The pirates next captured a French ship that they had at first taken for a forty-gun ship in pursuit of them. The men drunk and newly levied, might at this time have easily been cut off, and the hundred sail of ships they afterwards destroyed saved. When some of the men cried out that they had never seen a gun fired in anger, Cocklyn caned them, telling them they should soon learn to smell gunpowder. The French captain they hung at the yard-arm for not striking at their first shot. When they had pulled him up and down several times till he was almost dead, Le Bouce interfered for his countryman, protesting he would sail no longer with such barbarous villains. They then gave him the French ship, first destroying her cargo, cutting her masts by the board, and running her on shore, as old and useless.

Snelgrave's ship being now fitted up by the pirates, he was invited to its christening. The officers stood round the great cabin, holding bumpers of punch in their hands; and on Captain Cocklyn saying, "God bless the Wyndham galley," they drank the liquor, broke their glasses, and the guns thundered a broadside.

The new ship being galley built with only two flush decks, the powder-room scuttle was in the chief cabin, and at that time stood open. One of the guns blowing at the touch-hole, set fire to some cartouche boxes that held small arm cartridges, the shot of which flew about, filling the room with smoke. When it was over, Davis remarked on the great danger they had been in, the scuttle having been all the time open, and 20,000 lb. weight of powder lying under. Cocklyn replied with a curse, "I wish it had taken fire, for it would have been a noble blast to have gone to hell with."

The next day the pirate captains invited Snelgrave to dinner, and during supper a trumpeter and other musicians, who had been taken from various prizes, played and sang. About the middle of supper there was a sudden cry of fire, and a sailor boy, running in, with a pale face, said the main hatchway was on fire. The crew were then nearly drunk, and many of them leaped into the boats, leaving the officers and the fifty prisoners. On Snelgrave remarking to Davis the danger they were in, being left without a boat, Davis fired a great gun at the fugitives, and brought them back. The gunner then put wet blankets on the bulk head of the powder-room, and so saved it from destruction. This immense store of powder had been collected from various prizes, as being an article in great request with the negroes. Snelgrave took one of the quarterdeck gratings and lowered it over the ship's side with a rope, in case he should be obliged to leave the ship, and all this time the drunken sailors were standing on the quarterdeck, to the horror of the prisoners, shouting, "Hurrah for a quick passage to hell!"

About ten o'clock the master, a brisk and courageous man, who, with fifteen more, had spared no pains to conquer the flames, came up miserably burnt, and calling for a surgeon, declared the danger was now all over. The fire had arisen from the carelessness of a negro, who being sent to pump out some rum, held his candle so near the bung-hole of the hogshead that a spark caught the spirit. This soon fired another tub, and both their heads flew off with the report of a cannon; but though there were twenty casks of rum, and as many of pitch and tar in the store, all the rest escaped.

Before morning, the gunner's mate having spoken in favour of Snelgrave's conduct during the fire, the crew sent for him to attend the sale of his effects on board the Wyndham galley. Some promised to be kind to him; and the captain offered to buy his watch. As they were talking, a mate, half drunk, proposed that Snelgrave should be kept as a pilot till they left the coast, but Davis caned him off the quarter deck.

Two days after this the pirates took a small vessel belonging to the African Company. Snelgrave's first mate then told them that he had been once very badly served by this company, and begged that they would burn the vessel in revenge. This was about to be ordered when Stubbs, a quick-witted sailor, stood up and said, "Pray, gentlemen, hold, and I will prove to you that the burning of this ship will only advance the company's interests. The vessel has been out two years; is old, crazy, and worm-eaten; her stores are worth little, and her cargo consists only of red wood and pepper, the loss of which will not harm the company, who will save the men's wages, which will be three times the value of the cargo."

This convinced the crew, who at once spared the vessel, and returned her to the captain.

A few days afterwards, Snelgrave's things were sold at the mast, many of the men returning him their purchases, his old school-fellow in particular begging hard on his behalf. When the fiercer men observed the great heap of things he had collected, they swore the dog was insatiable, and said it would be a good deed to throw them overboard. Hearing this, Snelgrave loaded his canoe, and, by the advice of his friends, returned to shore. Soon after he left, his watch was put up for sale, and run to £100 in order to vex Davis, who, however, bought it at that enormous price. One of the sailors, enraged at this, tried the case on a touch-stone, and, seeing it looked copperish from the alloy in the gold, swore it was bad metal. They then declared Snelgrave was a greater rogue than any of them, since he had cheated them all. Russel laughed at this, and then vowed to whip him when he came next. Upon the advice of his friends, Snelgrave hid in the woods till the pirates left the river, and soon after returned with several other ruined men to England.

★ ★ ★ ★ ★

Of the Madagascar pirates some scanty record in Hamilton's Account of the East Indies, published in 1726. He mentions the fact that the pirates had totally destroyed the English slave trade in that island, in spite of several squadrons of men-of-war sent against them. To use the author's own rather ambiguous words:

> A single ship, commanded by one Millar, did more than all the chargeable fleets could do, for, with a cargo of strong ale and brandy, which he carried to sell them in 1704, he killed about 500 of them by carousing, though they took his ship and cargo as a present from him, and his men entered, most of them, into the society of the pirates.

Commodore Littleton lent them blocks and tackle-falls to careen, and, for some secret reasons, released some of their number. The author concludes in the following manner:

> Madagascar is environed with islands and dangerous shoals both of rocks and sand. St. Mary's, on the east side, is the place which the pirates first chose for their asylum, having a good harbour to defend them from the weather, though in going in there are some difficulties. But hearing the squadrons of English ships were come in quest of them, they removed to the main island for more security, and there they have made themselves free denizens by marriage.

And the author is of opinion it will be no easy matter to dispossess them. In 1722 Mr. Matthews went in search of them, but found they had deserted St. Mary's Island, leaving behind them some marks of their robberies, for in some places he found pepper strewed a foot thick on the ground. The commodore went, with his squadron, over into the main island, but the pirates had carried their ships into rivers or creeks, out of danger of the men-of-war, and to burn them with their boats would have been impracticable, since they could have easily distressed the crews from the woods. The commodore had some discourse with several of them, but they stood on their guard, ready to defend themselves in case any violence had been offered them.

The 11th and 12th of William III., and the 8th George I., are both statutes against piracy, and are indications of the years in which their ravages were peculiarly felt. By the first, any natural-born subject committing an act of hostility against any of his Majesty's subjects, under colour of a commission from any foreign power, could be tried for piracy. And further, any commander betraying his trust, and running away with the ship, or yielding it up voluntarily to a pirate, or any one confining his captain to prevent him fighting, was adjudged a pirate, felon, and robber, and was sentenced to death.

The later acts make it piracy even to trade with known pirates.

Commanders or seamen wounded, or their widows slain in piratical engagements, were entitled to a bounty not exceeding one-fiftieth part of the value of the cargo, and wounded men received the pension of Greenwich Hospital. If the commander behaved cowardly, he was to forfeit all his wages, and suffer six months' imprisonment.

★ ★ ★ ★ ★

Such are a few of the facts connected with the almost unrecorded and uncertain history of the pirates of New Providence and Madagascar, the most loathsome wretches that perhaps, since Cain, have ever washed their hands in human blood. Ferocious yet often cowardly, they were subtle and cruel, with none of the frequent generosity of outlaws, and little of the enterprise of the military adventurers. Long ago have their bones crumbled from the dark gibbets on the lonely sand islands of the Pacific, and they remain without monument or record, except in prison chronicles and forgotten voyages. We have reviewed their history simply as the natural sequel of our annals, and as an illustration of the character of the English seaman in its most brutal and satanic aspect.

ALSO FROM LEONAUR
AVAILABLE IN SOFTCOVER OR HARDCOVER WITH DUST JACKET

A HISTORY OF THE FRENCH & INDIAN WAR *by Arthur G. Bradley*—The Seven Years War as it was fought in the New World has always fascinated students of military history—here is the story of that confrontation.

WASHINGTON'S EARLY CAMPAIGNS *by James Hadden*—The French Post Expedition, Great Meadows and Braddock's Defeat—including Braddock's Orderly Books.

BOUQUET & THE OHIO INDIAN WAR *by Cyrus Cort & William Smith*—Two Accounts of the Campaigns of 1763-1764: Bouquet's Campaigns by Cyrus Cort & The History of Bouquet's Expeditions by William Smith.

NARRATIVES OF THE FRENCH & INDIAN WAR: 2 *by David Holden, Samuel Jenks, Lemuel Lyon, Mary Cochrane Rogers & Henry T. Blake*—Contains The Diary of Sergeant David Holden, Captain Samuel Jenks' Journal, The Journal of Lemuel Lyon, Journal of a French Officer at the Siege of Quebec, A Battle Fought on Snowshoes & The Battle of Lake George.

NARRATIVES OF THE FRENCH & INDIAN WAR *by Brown, Eastburn, Hawks & Putnam*—Ranger Brown's Narrative, The Adventures of Robert Eastburn, The Journal of Rufus Putnam—Provincial Infantry & Orderly Book and Journal of Major John Hawks on the Ticonderoga-Crown Point Campaign.

THE 7TH (QUEEN'S OWN) HUSSARS: Volume 1—1688-1792 *by C. R. B. Barrett*—As Dragoons During the Flanders Campaign, War of the Austrian Succession and the Seven Years War.

INDIA'S FREE LANCES *by H. G. Keene*—European Mercenary Commanders in Hindustan 1770-1820.

THE BENGAL EUROPEAN REGIMENT *by P. R. Innes*—An Elite Regiment of the Honourable East India Company 1756-1858.

MUSKET & TOMAHAWK *by Francis Parkman*—A Military History of the French & Indian War, 1753-1760.

THE BLACK WATCH AT TICONDEROGA *by Frederick B. Richards*—Campaigns in the French & Indian War.

QUEEN'S RANGERS *by Frederick B. Richards*—John Simcoe and his Rangers During the Revolutionary War for America.

AVAILABLE ONLINE AT **www.leonaur.com**
AND FROM ALL GOOD BOOK STORES

ALSO FROM LEONAUR
AVAILABLE IN SOFTCOVER OR HARDCOVER WITH DUST JACKET

JOURNALS OF ROBERT ROGERS OF THE RANGERS by *Robert Rogers*—The exploits of Rogers & the Rangers in his own words during 1755-1761 in the French & Indian War.

GALLOPING GUNS by *James Young*—The Experiences of an Officer of the Bengal Horse Artillery During the Second Maratha War 1804-1805.

GORDON by *Demetrius Charles Boulger*—The Career of Gordon of Khartoum.

THE BATTLE OF NEW ORLEANS by *Zachary F. Smith*—The final major engagement of the War of 1812.

THE TWO WARS OF MRS DUBERLY by *Frances Isabella Duberly*—An Intrepid Victorian Lady's Experience of the Crimea and Indian Mutiny.

WITH THE GUARDS' BRIGADE DURING THE BOER WAR by *Edward P. Lowry*—On Campaign from Bloemfontein to Koomati Poort and Back.

THE REBELLIOUS DUCHESS by *Paul F. S. Dermoncourt*—The Adventures of the Duchess of Berri and Her Attempt to Overthrow French Monarchy.

MEN OF THE MUTINY by *John Tulloch Nash & Henry Metcalfe*—Two Accounts of the Great Indian Mutiny of 1857: Fighting with the Bengal Yeomanry Cavalry & Private Metcalfe at Lucknow.

CAMPAIGN IN THE CRIMEA by *George Shuldham Peard*—The Recollections of an Officer of the 20th Regiment of Foot.

WITHIN SEBASTOPOL by *K. Hodasevich*—A Narrative of the Campaign in the Crimea, and of the Events of the Siege.

WITH THE CAVALRY TO AFGHANISTAN by *William Taylor*—The Experiences of a Trooper of H. M. 4th Light Dragoons During the First Afghan War.

THE CAWNPORE MAN by *Mowbray Thompson*—A First Hand Account of the Siege and Massacre During the Indian Mutiny By One of Four Survivors.

BRIGADE COMMANDER: AFGHANISTAN by *Henry Brooke*—The Journal of the Commander of the 2nd Infantry Brigade, Kandahar Field Force During the Second Afghan War.

BANCROFT OF THE BENGAL HORSE ARTILLERY by *N. W. Bancroft*—An Account of the First Sikh War 1845-1846.

AVAILABLE ONLINE AT www.leonaur.com
AND FROM ALL GOOD BOOK STORES

ALSO FROM LEONAUR
AVAILABLE IN SOFTCOVER OR HARDCOVER WITH DUST JACKET

AFGHANISTAN: THE BELEAGUERED BRIGADE *by G. R. Gleig*—An Account of Sale's Brigade During the First Afghan War.

IN THE RANKS OF THE C. I. V *by Erskine Childers*—With the City Imperial Volunteer Battery (Honourable Artillery Company) in the Second Boer War.

THE BENGAL NATIVE ARMY *by F. G. Cardew*—An Invaluable Reference Resource.

THE 7TH (QUEEN'S OWN) HUSSARS: Volume 4—1688-1914 *by C. R. B. Barrett*—Uniforms, Equipment, Weapons, Traditions, the Services of Notable Officers and Men & the Appendices to All Volumes—Volume 4: 1688-1914.

THE SWORD OF THE CROWN *by Eric W. Sheppard*—A History of the British Army to 1914.

THE 7TH (QUEEN'S OWN) HUSSARS: Volume 3—1818-1914 *by C. R. B. Barrett*—On Campaign During the Canadian Rebellion, the Indian Mutiny, the Sudan, Matabeleland, Mashonaland and the Boer War Volume 3: 1818-1914.

THE KHARTOUM CAMPAIGN *by Bennet Burleigh*—A Special Correspondent's View of the Reconquest of the Sudan by British and Egyptian Forces under Kitchener—1898.

EL PUCHERO *by Richard McSherry*—The Letters of a Surgeon of Volunteers During Scott's Campaign of the American-Mexican War 1847-1848.

RIFLEMAN SAHIB *by E. Maude*—The Recollections of an Officer of the Bombay Rifles During the Southern Mahratta Campaign, Second Sikh War, Persian Campaign and Indian Mutiny.

THE KING'S HUSSAR *by Edwin Mole*—The Recollections of a 14th (King's) Hussar During the Victorian Era.

JOHN COMPANY'S CAVALRYMAN *by William Johnson*—The Experiences of a British Soldier in the Crimea, the Persian Campaign and the Indian Mutiny.

COLENSO & DURNFORD'S ZULU WAR *by Frances E. Colenso & Edward Durnford*—The first and possibly the most important history of the Zulu War.

U. S. DRAGOON *by Samuel E. Chamberlain*—Experiences in the Mexican War 1846-48 and on the South Western Frontier.

AVAILABLE ONLINE AT **www.leonaur.com**
AND FROM ALL GOOD BOOK STORES

ALSO FROM LEONAUR
AVAILABLE IN SOFTCOVER OR HARDCOVER WITH DUST JACKET

THE 2ND MAORI WAR: 1860-1861 *by Robert Carey*—The Second Maori War, or First Taranaki War, one more bloody instalment of the conflicts between European settlers and the indigenous Maori people.

A JOURNAL OF THE SECOND SIKH WAR *by Daniel A. Sandford*—The Experiences of an Ensign of the 2nd Bengal European Regiment During the Campaign in the Punjab, India, 1848-49.

THE LIGHT INFANTRY OFFICER *by John H. Cooke*—The Experiences of an Officer of the 43rd Light Infantry in America During the War of 1812.

BUSHVELDT CARBINEERS *by George Witton*—The War Against the Boers in South Africa and the 'Breaker' Morant Incident.

LAKE'S CAMPAIGNS IN INDIA *by Hugh Pearse*—The Second Anglo Maratha War, 1803-1807.

BRITAIN IN AFGHANISTAN 1: THE FIRST AFGHAN WAR 1839-42 *by Archibald Forbes*—From invasion to destruction-a British military disaster.

BRITAIN IN AFGHANISTAN 2: THE SECOND AFGHAN WAR 1878-80 *by Archibald Forbes*—This is the history of the Second Afghan War-another episode of British military history typified by savagery, massacre, siege and battles.

UP AMONG THE PANDIES *by Vivian Dering Majendie*—Experiences of a British Officer on Campaign During the Indian Mutiny, 1857-1858.

MUTINY: 1857 *by James Humphries*—Authentic Voices from the Indian Mutiny-First Hand Accounts of Battles, Sieges and Personal Hardships.

BLOW THE BUGLE, DRAW THE SWORD *by W. H. G. Kingston*—The Wars, Campaigns, Regiments and Soldiers of the British & Indian Armies During the Victorian Era, 1839-1898.

WAR BEYOND THE DRAGON PAGODA *by Major J. J. Snodgrass*—A Personal Narrative of the First Anglo-Burmese War 1824 - 1826.

THE HERO OF ALIWAL *by James Humphries*—The Campaigns of Sir Harry Smith in India, 1843-1846, During the Gwalior War & the First Sikh War.

ALL FOR A SHILLING A DAY *by Donald F. Featherstone*—The story of H.M. 16th, the Queen's Lancers During the first Sikh War 1845-1846.

AVAILABLE ONLINE AT www.leonaur.com
AND FROM ALL GOOD BOOK STORES

ALSO FROM LEONAUR
AVAILABLE IN SOFTCOVER OR HARDCOVER WITH DUST JACKET

THE FALL OF THE MOGHUL EMPIRE OF HINDUSTAN by H. G. Keene—By the beginning of the nineteenth century, as British and Indian armies under Lake and Wellesley dominated the scene, a little over half a century of conflict brought the Moghul Empire to its knees.

LADY SALE'S AFGHANISTAN by Florentia Sale—An Indomitable Victorian Lady's Account of the Retreat from Kabul During the First Afghan War.

THE CAMPAIGN OF MAGENTA AND SOLFERINO 1859 by Harold Carmichael Wylly—The Decisive Conflict for the Unification of Italy.

FRENCH'S CAVALRY CAMPAIGN by J. G. Maydon—A Special Correspondent's View of British Army Mounted Troops During the Boer War.

CAVALRY AT WATERLOO by Sir Evelyn Wood—British Mounted Troops During the Campaign of 1815.

THE SUBALTERN by George Robert Gleig—The Experiences of an Officer of the 85th Light Infantry During the Peninsular War.

NAPOLEON AT BAY, 1814 by F. Loraine Petre—The Campaigns to the Fall of the First Empire.

NAPOLEON AND THE CAMPAIGN OF 1806 by Colonel Vachée—The Napoleonic Method of Organisation and Command to the Battles of Jena & Auerstädt.

THE COMPLETE ADVENTURES IN THE CONNAUGHT RANGERS by William Grattan—The 88th Regiment during the Napoleonic Wars by a Serving Officer.

BUGLER AND OFFICER OF THE RIFLES by William Green & Harry Smith—With the 95th (Rifles) during the Peninsular & Waterloo Campaigns of the Napoleonic Wars.

NAPOLEONIC WAR STORIES by Sir Arthur Quiller-Couch—Tales of soldiers, spies, battles & sieges from the Peninsular & Waterloo campaingns.

CAPTAIN OF THE 95TH (RIFLES) by Jonathan Leach—An officer of Wellington's sharpshooters during the Peninsular, South of France and Waterloo campaigns of the Napoleonic wars.

RIFLEMAN COSTELLO by Edward Costello—The adventures of a soldier of the 95th (Rifles) in the Peninsular & Waterloo Campaigns of the Napoleonic wars.

AVAILABLE ONLINE AT **www.leonaur.com**
AND FROM ALL GOOD BOOK STORES

ALSO FROM LEONAUR
AVAILABLE IN SOFTCOVER OR HARDCOVER WITH DUST JACKET

AT THEM WITH THE BAYONET by *Donald F. Featherstone*—The first Anglo-Sikh War 1845-1846.

STEPHEN CRANE'S BATTLES by *Stephen Crane*—Nine Decisive Battles Recounted by the Author of 'The Red Badge of Courage'.

THE GURKHA WAR by *H. T. Prinsep*—The Anglo-Nepalese Conflict in North East India 1814-1816.

FIRE & BLOOD by *G. R. Gleig*—The burning of Washington & the battle of New Orleans, 1814, through the eyes of a young British soldier.

SOUND ADVANCE! by *Joseph Anderson*—Experiences of an officer of HM 50th regiment in Australia, Burma & the Gwalior war.

THE CAMPAIGN OF THE INDUS by *Thomas Holdsworth*—Experiences of a British Officer of the 2nd (Queen's Royal) Regiment in the Campaign to Place Shah Shuja on the Throne of Afghanistan 1838 - 1840.

WITH THE MADRAS EUROPEAN REGIMENT IN BURMA by *John Butler*—The Experiences of an Officer of the Honourable East India Company's Army During the First Anglo-Burmese War 1824 - 1826.

IN ZULULAND WITH THE BRITISH ARMY by *Charles L. Norris-Newman*—The Anglo-Zulu war of 1879 through the first-hand experiences of a special correspondent.

BESIEGED IN LUCKNOW by *Martin Richard Gubbins*—The first Anglo-Sikh War 1845-1846.

A TIGER ON HORSEBACK by *L. March Phillips*—The Experiences of a Trooper & Officer of Rimington's Guides - The Tigers - during the Anglo-Boer war 1899 - 1902.

SEPOYS, SIEGE & STORM by *Charles John Griffiths*—The Experiences of a young officer of H.M.'s 61st Regiment at Ferozepore, Delhi ridge and at the fall of Delhi during the Indian mutiny 1857.

CAMPAIGNING IN ZULULAND by *W. E. Montague*—Experiences on campaign during the Zulu war of 1879 with the 94th Regiment.

THE STORY OF THE GUIDES by *G.J. Younghusband*—The Exploits of the Soldiers of the famous Indian Army Regiment from the northwest frontier 1847 - 1900.

AVAILABLE ONLINE AT www.leonaur.com
AND FROM ALL GOOD BOOK STORES

ALSO FROM LEONAUR
AVAILABLE IN SOFTCOVER OR HARDCOVER WITH DUST JACKET

ZULU:1879 *by D.C.F. Moodie & the Leonaur Editors*—The Anglo-Zulu War of 1879 from contemporary sources: First Hand Accounts, Interviews, Dispatches, Official Documents & Newspaper Reports.

THE RED DRAGOON *by W.J. Adams*—With the 7th Dragoon Guards in the Cape of Good Hope against the Boers & the Kaffir tribes during the 'war of the axe' 1843-48'.

THE RECOLLECTIONS OF SKINNER OF SKINNER'S HORSE *by James Skinner*—James Skinner and his 'Yellow Boys' Irregular cavalry in the wars of India between the British, Mahratta, Rajput, Mogul, Sikh & Pindarree Forces.

A CAVALRY OFFICER DURING THE SEPOY REVOLT *by A. R. D. Mackenzie*—Experiences with the 3rd Bengal Light Cavalry, the Guides and Sikh Irregular Cavalry from the outbreak to Delhi and Lucknow.

A NORFOLK SOLDIER IN THE FIRST SIKH WAR *by J W Baldwin*—Experiences of a private of H.M. 9th Regiment of Foot in the battles for the Punjab, India 1845-6.

TOMMY ATKINS' WAR STORIES: 14 FIRST HAND ACCOUNTS—Fourteen first hand accounts from the ranks of the British Army during Queen Victoria's Empire.

THE WATERLOO LETTERS *by H. T. Siborne*—Accounts of the Battle by British Officers for its Foremost Historian.

NEY: GENERAL OF CAVALRY VOLUME 1—1769-1799 *by Antoine Bulos*—The Early Career of a Marshal of the First Empire.

NEY: MARSHAL OF FRANCE VOLUME 2—1799-1805 *by Antoine Bulos*—The Early Career of a Marshal of the First Empire.

AIDE-DE-CAMP TO NAPOLEON *by Philippe-Paul de Ségur*—For anyone interested in the Napoleonic Wars this book, written by one who was intimate with the strategies and machinations of the Emperor, will be essential reading.

TWILIGHT OF EMPIRE *by Sir Thomas Ussher & Sir George Cockburn*—Two accounts of Napoleon's Journeys in Exile to Elba and St. Helena: Narrative of Events by Sir Thomas Ussher & Napoleon's Last Voyage: Extract of a diary by Sir George Cockburn.

PRIVATE WHEELER *by William Wheeler*—The letters of a soldier of the 51st Light Infantry during the Peninsular War & at Waterloo.

AVAILABLE ONLINE AT **www.leonaur.com**
AND FROM ALL GOOD BOOK STORES

ALSO FROM LEONAUR
AVAILABLE IN SOFTCOVER OR HARDCOVER WITH DUST JACKET

OFFICERS & GENTLEMEN *by Peter Hawker & William Graham*—Two Accounts of British Officers During the Peninsula War: Officer of Light Dragoons by Peter Hawker & Campaign in Portugal and Spain by William Graham.

THE WALCHEREN EXPEDITION *by Anonymous*—The Experiences of a British Officer of the 81st Regt. During the Campaign in the Low Countries of 1809.

LADIES OF WATERLOO *by Charlotte A. Eaton, Magdalene de Lancey & Juana Smith*—The Experiences of Three Women During the Campaign of 1815: Waterloo Days by Charlotte A. Eaton, A Week at Waterloo by Magdalene de Lancey & Juana's Story by Juana Smith.

JOURNAL OF AN OFFICER IN THE KING'S GERMAN LEGION *by John Frederick Hering*—Recollections of Campaigning During the Napoleonic Wars.

JOURNAL OF AN ARMY SURGEON IN THE PENINSULAR WAR *by Charles Boutflower*—The Recollections of a British Army Medical Man on Campaign During the Napoleonic Wars.

ON CAMPAIGN WITH MOORE AND WELLINGTON *by Anthony Hamilton*—The Experiences of a Soldier of the 43rd Regiment During the Peninsular War.

THE ROAD TO AUSTERLITZ *by R. G. Burton*—Napoleon's Campaign of 1805.

SOLDIERS OF NAPOLEON *by A. J. Doisy De Villargennes & Arthur Chuquet*—The Experiences of the Men of the French First Empire: Under the Eagles by A. J. Doisy De Villargennes & Voices of 1812 by Arthur Chuquet.

INVASION OF FRANCE, 1814 *by F. W. O. Maycock*—The Final Battles of the Napoleonic First Empire.

LEIPZIG—A CONFLICT OF TITANS *by Frederic Shoberl*—A Personal Experience of the 'Battle of the Nations' During the Napoleonic Wars, October 14th-19th, 1813.

SLASHERS *by Charles Cadell*—The Campaigns of the 28th Regiment of Foot During the Napoleonic Wars by a Serving Officer.

BATTLE IMPERIAL *by Charles William Vane*—The Campaigns in Germany & France for the Defeat of Napoleon 1813-1814.

SWIFT & BOLD *by Gibbes Rigaud*—The 60th Rifles During the Peninsula War.

AVAILABLE ONLINE AT www.leonaur.com
AND FROM ALL GOOD BOOK STORES

ALSO FROM LEONAUR
AVAILABLE IN SOFTCOVER OR HARDCOVER WITH DUST JACKET

ADVENTURES OF A YOUNG RIFLEMAN by Johann Christian Maempel—The Experiences of a Saxon in the French & British Armies During the Napoleonic Wars.

THE HUSSAR by Norbert Landsheit & G. R. Gleig—A German Cavalryman in British Service Throughout the Napoleonic Wars.

RECOLLECTIONS OF THE PENINSULA by Moyle Sherer—An Officer of the 34th Regiment of Foot—'The Cumberland Gentlemen'—on Campaign Against Napoleon's French Army in Spain.

MARINE OF REVOLUTION & CONSULATE by Moreau de Jonnès—The Recollections of a French Soldier of the Revolutionary Wars 1791-1804.

GENTLEMEN IN RED by John Dobbs & Robert Knowles—Two Accounts of British Infantry Officers During the Peninsular War Recollections of an Old 52nd Man by John Dobbs An Officer of Fusiliers by Robert Knowles.

CORPORAL BROWN'S CAMPAIGNS IN THE LOW COUNTRIES by Robert Brown—Recollections of a Coldstream Guard in the Early Campaigns Against Revolutionary France 1793-1795.

THE 7TH (QUEENS OWN) HUSSARS: Volume 2—1793-1815 by C. R. B. Barrett—During the Campaigns in the Low Countries & the Peninsula and Waterloo Campaigns of the Napoleonic Wars. Volume 2: 1793-1815.

THE MARENGO CAMPAIGN 1800 by Herbert H. Sargent—The Victory that Completed the Austrian Defeat in Italy.

DONALDSON OF THE 94TH—SCOTS BRIGADE by Joseph Donaldson—The Recollections of a Soldier During the Peninsula & South of France Campaigns of the Napoleonic Wars.

A CONSCRIPT FOR EMPIRE by Philippe as told to Johann Christian Maempel—The Experiences of a Young German Conscript During the Napoleonic Wars.

JOURNAL OF THE CAMPAIGN OF 1815 by Alexander Cavalié Mercer—The Experiences of an Officer of the Royal Horse Artillery During the Waterloo Campaign.

NAPOLEON'S CAMPAIGNS IN POLAND 1806-7 by Robert Wilson—The campaign in Poland from the Russian side of the conflict.

AVAILABLE ONLINE AT www.leonaur.com
AND FROM ALL GOOD BOOK STORES

ALSO FROM LEONAUR
AVAILABLE IN SOFTCOVER OR HARDCOVER WITH DUST JACKET

OMPTEDA OF THE KING'S GERMAN LEGION *by Christian von Ompteda*—A Hanoverian Officer on Campaign Against Napoleon.

LIEUTENANT SIMMONS OF THE 95TH (RIFLES) *by George Simmons*—Recollections of the Peninsula, South of France & Waterloo Campaigns of the Napoleonic Wars.

A HORSEMAN FOR THE EMPEROR *by Jean Baptiste Gazzola*—A Cavalryman of Napoleon's Army on Campaign Throughout the Napoleonic Wars.

SERGEANT LAWRENCE *by William Lawrence*—With the 40th Regt. of Foot in South America, the Peninsular War & at Waterloo.

CAMPAIGNS WITH THE FIELD TRAIN *by Richard D. Henegan*—Experiences of a British Officer During the Peninsula and Waterloo Campaigns of the Napoleonic Wars.

CAVALRY SURGEON *by S. D. Broughton*—On Campaign Against Napoleon in the Peninsula & South of France During the Napoleonic Wars 1812-1814.

MEN OF THE RIFLES *by Thomas Knight, Henry Curling & Jonathan Leach*—The Reminiscences of Thomas Knight of the 95th (Rifles) by Thomas Knight, Henry Curling's Anecdotes by Henry Curling & The Field Services of the Rifle Brigade from its Formation to Waterloo by Jonathan Leach.

THE ULM CAMPAIGN 1805 *by F. N. Maude*—Napoleon and the Defeat of the Austrian Army During the 'War of the Third Coalition'.

SOLDIERING WITH THE 'DIVISION' *by Thomas Garrety*—The Military Experiences of an Infantryman of the 43rd Regiment During the Napoleonic Wars.

SERGEANT MORRIS OF THE 73RD FOOT *by Thomas Morris*—The Experiences of a British Infantryman During the Napoleonic Wars-Including Campaigns in Germany and at Waterloo.

A VOICE FROM WATERLOO *by Edward Cotton*—The Personal Experiences of a British Cavalryman Who Became a Battlefield Guide and Authority on the Campaign of 1815.

NAPOLEON AND HIS MARSHALS *by J. T. Headley*—The Men of the First Empire.

ALSO FROM LEONAUR
AVAILABLE IN SOFTCOVER OR HARDCOVER WITH DUST JACKET

COLBORNE: A SINGULAR TALENT FOR WAR *by John Colborne*—The Napoleonic Wars Career of One of Wellington's Most Highly Valued Officers in Egypt, Holland, Italy, the Peninsula and at Waterloo.

NAPOLEON'S RUSSIAN CAMPAIGN *by Philippe Henri de Segur*—The Invasion, Battles and Retreat by an Aide-de-Camp on the Emperor's Staff.

WITH THE LIGHT DIVISION *by John H. Cooke*—The Experiences of an Officer of the 43rd Light Infantry in the Peninsula and South of France During the Napoleonic Wars.

WELLINGTON AND THE PYRENEES CAMPAIGN VOLUME I: FROM VITORIA TO THE BIDASSOA *by F. C. Beatson*—The final phase of the campaign in the Iberian Peninsula.

WELLINGTON AND THE INVASION OF FRANCE VOLUME II: THE BIDASSOA TO THE BATTLE OF THE NIVELLE *by F. C. Beatson*—The final phase of the campaign in the Iberian Peninsula.

WELLINGTON AND THE FALL OF FRANCE VOLUME III: THE GAVES AND THE BATTLE OF ORTHEZ *by F. C. Beatson*—The final phase of the campaign in the Iberian Peninsula.

NAPOLEON'S IMPERIAL GUARD: FROM MARENGO TO WATERLOO *by J. T. Headley*—The story of Napoleon's Imperial Guard and the men who commanded them.

BATTLES & SIEGES OF THE PENINSULAR WAR *by W. H. Fitchett*—Corunna, Busaco, Albuera, Ciudad Rodrigo, Badajos, Salamanca, San Sebastian & Others.

SERGEANT GUILLEMARD: THE MAN WHO SHOT NELSON? *by Robert Guillemard*—A Soldier of the Infantry of the French Army of Napoleon on Campaign Throughout Europe.

WITH THE GUARDS ACROSS THE PYRENEES *by Robert Batty*—The Experiences of a British Officer of Wellington's Army During the Battles for the Fall of Napoleonic France, 1813 .

A STAFF OFFICER IN THE PENINSULA *by E. W. Buckham*—An Officer of the British Staff Corps Cavalry During the Peninsula Campaign of the Napoleonic Wars.

THE LEIPZIG CAMPAIGN: 1813—NAPOLEON AND THE "BATTLE OF THE NATIONS" *by F. N. Maude*—Colonel Maude's analysis of Napoleon's campaign of 1813 around Leipzig.

AVAILABLE ONLINE AT **www.leonaur.com**
AND FROM ALL GOOD BOOK STORES

ALSO FROM LEONAUR
AVAILABLE IN SOFTCOVER OR HARDCOVER WITH DUST JACKET

BUGEAUD: A PACK WITH A BATON by *Thomas Robert Bugeaud*—The Early Campaigns of a Soldier of Napoleon's Army Who Would Become a Marshal of France.

WATERLOO RECOLLECTIONS by *Frederick Llewellyn*—Rare First Hand Accounts, Letters, Reports and Retellings from the Campaign of 1815.

SERGEANT NICOL by *Daniel Nicol*—The Experiences of a Gordon Highlander During the Napoleonic Wars in Egypt, the Peninsula and France.

THE JENA CAMPAIGN: 1806 by *F. N. Maude*—The Twin Battles of Jena & Auerstadt Between Napoleon's French and the Prussian Army.

PRIVATE O'NEIL by *Charles O'Neil*—The recollections of an Irish Rogue of H. M. 28th Regt.—The Slashers—during the Peninsula & Waterloo campaigns of the Napoleonic war.

ROYAL HIGHLANDER by *James Anton*—A soldier of H.M 42nd (Royal) Highlanders during the Peninsular, South of France & Waterloo Campaigns of the Napoleonic Wars.

CAPTAIN BLAZE by *Elzéar Blaze*—Life in Napoleons Army.

LEJEUNE VOLUME 1 by *Louis-François Lejeune*—The Napoleonic Wars through the Experiences of an Officer on Berthier's Staff.

LEJEUNE VOLUME 2 by *Louis-François Lejeune*—The Napoleonic Wars through the Experiences of an Officer on Berthier's Staff.

CAPTAIN COIGNET by *Jean-Roch Coignet*—A Soldier of Napoleon's Imperial Guard from the Italian Campaign to Russia and Waterloo.

FUSILIER COOPER by *John S. Cooper*—Experiences in the 7th (Royal) Fusiliers During the Peninsular Campaign of the Napoleonic Wars and the American Campaign to New Orleans.

FIGHTING NAPOLEON'S EMPIRE by *Joseph Anderson*—The Campaigns of a British Infantryman in Italy, Egypt, the Peninsular & the West Indies During the Napoleonic Wars.

CHASSEUR BARRES by *Jean-Baptiste Barres*—The experiences of a French Infantryman of the Imperial Guard at Austerlitz, Jena, Eylau, Friedland, in the Peninsular, Lutzen, Bautzen, Zinnwald and Hanau during the Napoleonic Wars.

AVAILABLE ONLINE AT **www.leonaur.com**
AND FROM ALL GOOD BOOK STORES

ALSO FROM LEONAUR
AVAILABLE IN SOFTCOVER OR HARDCOVER WITH DUST JACKET

CAPTAIN COIGNET by Jean-Roch Coignet—A Soldier of Napoleon's Imperial Guard from the Italian Campaign to Russia and Waterloo.

HUSSAR ROCCA by Albert Jean Michel de Rocca—A French cavalry officer's experiences of the Napoleonic Wars and his views on the Peninsular Campaigns against the Spanish, British And Guerilla Armies.

MARINES TO 95TH (RIFLES) by Thomas Fernyhough—The military experiences of Robert Fernyhough during the Napoleonic Wars.

LIGHT BOB by Robert Blakeney—The experiences of a young officer in H.M 28th & 36th regiments of the British Infantry during the Peninsular Campaign of the Napoleonic Wars 1804 - 1814.

WITH WELLINGTON'S LIGHT CAVALRY by William Tomkinson—The Experiences of an officer of the 16th Light Dragoons in the Peninsular and Waterloo campaigns of the Napoleonic Wars.

SERGEANT BOURGOGNE by Adrien Bourgogne—With Napoleon's Imperial Guard in the Russian Campaign and on the Retreat from Moscow 1812 - 13.

SURTEES OF THE 95TH (RIFLES) by William Surtees—A Soldier of the 95th (Rifles) in the Peninsular campaign of the Napoleonic Wars.

SWORDS OF HONOUR by Henry Newbolt & Stanley L. Wood—The Careers of Six Outstanding Officers from the Napoleonic Wars, the Wars for India and the American Civil War.

ENSIGN BELL IN THE PENINSULAR WAR by George Bell—The Experiences of a young British Soldier of the 34th Regiment 'The Cumberland Gentlemen' in the Napoleonic wars.

HUSSAR IN WINTER by Alexander Gordon—A British Cavalry Officer during the retreat to Corunna in the Peninsular campaign of the Napoleonic Wars.

THE COMPLEAT RIFLEMAN HARRIS by Benjamin Harris as told to and transcribed by Captain Henry Curling, 52nd Regt. of Foot—The adventures of a soldier of the 95th (Rifles) during the Peninsular Campaign of the Napoleonic Wars.

THE ADVENTURES OF A LIGHT DRAGOON by George Farmer & G.R. Gleig—A cavalryman during the Peninsular & Waterloo Campaigns, in captivity & at the siege of Bhurtpore, India.

AVAILABLE ONLINE AT **www.leonaur.com**
AND FROM ALL GOOD BOOK STORES

ALSO FROM LEONAUR
AVAILABLE IN SOFTCOVER OR HARDCOVER WITH DUST JACKET

THE LIFE OF THE REAL BRIGADIER GERARD VOLUME 1—THE YOUNG HUSSAR 1782-1807 *by Jean-Baptiste De Marbot*—A French Cavalryman Of the Napoleonic Wars at Marengo, Austerlitz, Jena, Eylau & Friedland.

THE LIFE OF THE REAL BRIGADIER GERARD VOLUME 2—IMPERIAL AIDE-DE-CAMP 1807-1811 *by Jean-Baptiste De Marbot*—A French Cavalryman of the Napoleonic Wars at Saragossa, Landshut, Eckmuhl, Ratisbon, Aspern-Essling, Wagram, Busaco & Torres Vedras.

THE LIFE OF THE REAL BRIGADIER GERARD VOLUME 3—COLONEL OF CHASSEURS 1811-1815 *by Jean-Baptiste De Marbot*—A French Cavalryman in the retreat from Moscow, Lutzen, Bautzen, Katzbach, Leipzig, Hanau & Waterloo.

THE INDIAN WAR OF 1864 *by Eugene Ware*—The Experiences of a Young Officer of the 7th Iowa Cavalry on the Western Frontier During the Civil War.

THE MARCH OF DESTINY *by Charles E. Young & V. Devinny*—Dangers of the Trail in 1865 by Charles E. Young & The Story of a Pioneer by V. Devinny, two Accounts of Early Emigrants to Colorado.

CROSSING THE PLAINS *by William Audley Maxwell*—A First Hand Narrative of the Early Pioneer Trail to California in 1857.

CHIEF OF SCOUTS *by William F. Drannan*—A Pilot to Emigrant and Government Trains, Across the Plains of the Western Frontier.

THIRTY-ONE YEARS ON THE PLAINS AND IN THE MOUNTAINS *by William F. Drannan*—William Drannan was born to be a pioneer, hunter, trapper and wagon train guide during the momentous days of the Great American West.

THE INDIAN WARS VOLUNTEER *by William Thompson*—Recollections of the Conflict Against the Snakes, Shoshone, Bannocks, Modocs and Other Native Tribes of the American North West.

THE 4TH TENNESSEE CAVALRY *by George B. Guild*—The Services of Smith's Regiment of Confederate Cavalry by One of its Officers.

COLONEL WORTHINGTON'S SHILOH *by T. Worthington*—The Tennessee Campaign, 1862, by an Officer of the Ohio Volunteers.

FOUR YEARS IN THE SADDLE *by W. L. Curry*—The History of the First Regiment Ohio Volunteer Cavalry in the American Civil War.

AVAILABLE ONLINE AT www.leonaur.com
AND FROM ALL GOOD BOOK STORES

ALSO FROM LEONAUR
AVAILABLE IN SOFTCOVER OR HARDCOVER WITH DUST JACKET

LIFE IN THE ARMY OF NORTHERN VIRGINIA by *Carlton McCarthy*—The Observations of a Confederate Artilleryman of Cutshaw's Battalion During the American Civil War 1861-1865.

HISTORY OF THE CAVALRY OF THE ARMY OF THE POTOMAC by *Charles D. Rhodes*—Including Pope's Army of Virginia and the Cavalry Operations in West Virginia During the American Civil War.

CAMP-FIRE AND COTTON-FIELD by *Thomas W. Knox*—A New York Herald Correspondent's View of the American Civil War.

SERGEANT STILLWELL by *Leander Stillwell*—The Experiences of a Union Army Soldier of the 61st Illinois Infantry During the American Civil War.

STONEWALL'S CANNONEER by *Edward A. Moore*—Experiences with the Rockbridge Artillery, Confederate Army of Northern Virginia, During the American Civil War.

THE SIXTH CORPS by *George Stevens*—The Army of the Potomac, Union Army, During the American Civil War.

THE RAILROAD RAIDERS by *William Pittenger*—An Ohio Volunteers Recollections of the Andrews Raid to Disrupt the Confederate Railroad in Georgia During the American Civil War.

CITIZEN SOLDIER by *John Beatty*—An Account of the American Civil War by a Union Infantry Officer of Ohio Volunteers Who Became a Brigadier General.

COX: PERSONAL RECOLLECTIONS OF THE CIVIL WAR--VOLUME 1 by *Jacob Dolson Cox*—West Virginia, Kanawha Valley, Gauley Bridge, Cotton Mountain, South Mountain, Antietam, the Morgan Raid & the East Tennessee Campaign.

COX: PERSONAL RECOLLECTIONS OF THE CIVIL WAR--VOLUME 2 by *Jacob Dolson Cox*—Siege of Knoxville, East Tennessee, Atlanta Campaign, the Nashville Campaign & the North Carolina Campaign.

KERSHAW'S BRIGADE VOLUME 1 by *D. Augustus Dickert*—Manassas, Seven Pines, Sharpsburg (Antietam), Fredricksburg, Chancellorsville, Gettysburg, Chickamauga, Chattanooga, Fort Sanders & Bean Station.

KERSHAW'S BRIGADE VOLUME 2 by *D. Augustus Dickert*—At the wilderness, Cold Harbour, Petersburg, The Shenandoah Valley and Cedar Creek..

AVAILABLE ONLINE AT **www.leonaur.com**
AND FROM ALL GOOD BOOK STORES

ALSO FROM LEONAUR
AVAILABLE IN SOFTCOVER OR HARDCOVER WITH DUST JACKET

THE RELUCTANT REBEL *by William G. Stevenson*—A young Kentuckian's experiences in the Confederate Infantry & Cavalry during the American Civil War..

BOOTS AND SADDLES *by Elizabeth B. Custer*—The experiences of General Custer's Wife on the Western Plains.

FANNIE BEERS' CIVIL WAR *by Fannie A. Beers*—A Confederate Lady's Experiences of Nursing During the Campaigns & Battles of the American Civil War.

LADY SALE'S AFGHANISTAN *by Florentia Sale*—An Indomitable Victorian Lady's Account of the Retreat from Kabul During the First Afghan War.

THE TWO WARS OF MRS DUBERLY *by Frances Isabella Duberly*—An Intrepid Victorian Lady's Experience of the Crimea and Indian Mutiny.

THE REBELLIOUS DUCHESS *by Paul F. S. Dermoncourt*—The Adventures of the Duchess of Berri and Her Attempt to Overthrow French Monarchy.

LADIES OF WATERLOO *by Charlotte A. Eaton, Magdalene de Lancey & Juana Smith*—The Experiences of Three Women During the Campaign of 1815: Waterloo Days by Charlotte A. Eaton, A Week at Waterloo by Magdalene de Lancey & Juana's Story by Juana Smith.

TWO YEARS BEFORE THE MAST *by Richard Henry Dana. Jr.*—The account of one young man's experiences serving on board a sailing brig—the Penelope—bound for California, between the years 1834-36.

A SAILOR OF KING GEORGE *by Frederick Hoffman*—From Midshipman to Captain—Recollections of War at Sea in the Napoleonic Age 1793-1815.

LORDS OF THE SEA *by A. T. Mahan*—Great Captains of the Royal Navy During the Age of Sail.

COGGESHALL'S VOYAGES: VOLUME 1 *by George Coggeshall*—The Recollections of an American Schooner Captain.

COGGESHALL'S VOYAGES: VOLUME 2 *by George Coggeshall*—The Recollections of an American Schooner Captain.

TWILIGHT OF EMPIRE *by Sir Thomas Ussher & Sir George Cockburn*—Two accounts of Napoleon's Journeys in Exile to Elba and St. Helena: Narrative of Events by Sir Thomas Ussher & Napoleon's Last Voyage: Extract of a diary by Sir George Cockburn.

AVAILABLE ONLINE AT **www.leonaur.com**
AND FROM ALL GOOD BOOK STORES

ALSO FROM LEONAUR
AVAILABLE IN SOFTCOVER OR HARDCOVER WITH DUST JACKET

ESCAPE FROM THE FRENCH *by Edward Boys*—A Young Royal Navy Midshipman's Adventures During the Napoleonic War.

THE VOYAGE OF H.M.S. PANDORA *by Edward Edwards R. N. & George Hamilton, edited by Basil Thomson*—In Pursuit of the Mutineers of the Bounty in the South Seas—1790-1791.

MEDUSA *by J. B. Henry Savigny and Alexander Correard and Charlotte-Adélaïde Dard*—Narrative of a Voyage to Senegal in 1816 & The Sufferings of the Picard Family After the Shipwreck of the Medusa.

THE SEA WAR OF 1812 VOLUME 1 *by A. T. Mahan*—A History of the Maritime Conflict.

THE SEA WAR OF 1812 VOLUME 2 *by A. T. Mahan*—A History of the Maritime Conflict.

WETHERELL OF H. M. S. HUSSAR *by John Wetherell*—The Recollections of an Ordinary Seaman of the Royal Navy During the Napoleonic Wars.

THE NAVAL BRIGADE IN NATAL *by C. R. N. Burne*—With the Guns of H. M. S. Terrible & H. M. S. Tartar during the Boer War 1899-1900.

THE VOYAGE OF H. M. S. BOUNTY *by William Bligh*—The True Story of an 18th Century Voyage of Exploration and Mutiny.

SHIPWRECK! *by William Gilly*—The Royal Navy's Disasters at Sea 1793-1849.

KING'S CUTTERS AND SMUGGLERS: 1700-1855 *by E. Keble Chatterton*—A unique period of maritime history-from the beginning of the eighteenth to the middle of the nineteenth century when British seamen risked all to smuggle valuable goods from wool to tea and spirits from and to the Continent.

CONFEDERATE BLOCKADE RUNNER *by John Wilkinson*—The Personal Recollections of an Officer of the Confederate Navy.

NAVAL BATTLES OF THE NAPOLEONIC WARS *by W. H. Fitchett*—Cape St. Vincent, the Nile, Cadiz, Copenhagen, Trafalgar & Others.

PRISONERS OF THE RED DESERT *by R. S. Gwatkin-Williams*—The Adventures of the Crew of the Tara During the First World War.

U-BOAT WAR 1914-1918 *by James B. Connolly/Karl von Schenk*—Two Contrasting Accounts from Both Sides of the Conflict at Sea During the Great War.

AVAILABLE ONLINE AT www.leonaur.com
AND FROM ALL GOOD BOOK STORES

ALSO FROM LEONAUR
AVAILABLE IN SOFTCOVER OR HARDCOVER WITH DUST JACKET

IRON TIMES WITH THE GUARDS by An O. E. (G. P. A. Fildes)—The Experiences of an Officer of the Coldstream Guards on the Western Front During the First World War.

THE GREAT WAR IN THE MIDDLE EAST: 1 by W. T. Massey—The Desert Campaigns & How Jerusalem Was Won---two classic accounts in one volume.

THE GREAT WAR IN THE MIDDLE EAST: 2 by W. T. Massey—Allenby's Final Triumph.

SMITH-DORRIEN by Horace Smith-Dorrien—Isandlwhana to the Great War.

1914 by Sir John French—The Early Campaigns of the Great War by the British Commander.

GRENADIER by E. R. M. Fryer—The Recollections of an Officer of the Grenadier Guards throughout the Great War on the Western Front.

BATTLE, CAPTURE & ESCAPE by George Pearson—The Experiences of a Canadian Light Infantryman During the Great War.

DIGGERS AT WAR by R. Hugh Knyvett & G. P. Cuttriss—"Over There" With the Australians by R. Hugh Knyvett and Over the Top With the Third Australian Division by G. P. Cuttriss. Accounts of Australians During the Great War in the Middle East, at Gallipoli and on the Western Front.

HEAVY FIGHTING BEFORE US by George Brenton Laurie—The Letters of an Officer of the Royal Irish Rifles on the Western Front During the Great War.

THE CAMELIERS by Oliver Hogue—A Classic Account of the Australians of the Imperial Camel Corps During the First World War in the Middle East.

RED DUST by Donald Black—A Classic Account of Australian Light Horsemen in Palestine During the First World War.

THE LEAN, BROWN MEN by Angus Buchanan—Experiences in East Africa During the Great War with the 25th Royal Fusiliers—the Legion of Frontiersmen.

THE NIGERIAN REGIMENT IN EAST AFRICA by W. D. Downes—On Campaign During the Great War 1916-1918.

THE 'DIE-HARDS' IN SIBERIA by John Ward—With the Middlesex Regiment Against the Bolsheviks 1918-19.

AVAILABLE ONLINE AT **www.leonaur.com**
AND FROM ALL GOOD BOOK STORES

ALSO FROM LEONAUR
AVAILABLE IN SOFTCOVER OR HARDCOVER WITH DUST JACKET

FARAWAY CAMPAIGN *by F. James*—Experiences of an Indian Army Cavalry Officer in Persia & Russia During the Great War.

REVOLT IN THE DESERT *by T. E. Lawrence*—An account of the experiences of one remarkable British officer's war from his own perspective.

MACHINE-GUN SQUADRON *by A. M. G.*—The 20th Machine Gunners from British Yeomanry Regiments in the Middle East Campaign of the First World War.

A GUNNER'S CRUSADE *by Antony Bluett*—The Campaign in the Desert, Palestine & Syria as Experienced by the Honourable Artillery Company During the Great War .

DESPATCH RIDER *by W. H. L. Watson*—The Experiences of a British Army Motorcycle Despatch Rider During the Opening Battles of the Great War in Europe.

TIGERS ALONG THE TIGRIS *by E. J. Thompson*—The Leicestershire Regiment in Mesopotamia During the First World War.

HEARTS & DRAGONS *by Charles R. M. F. Crutwell*—The 4th Royal Berkshire Regiment in France and Italy During the Great War, 1914-1918.

INFANTRY BRIGADE: 1914 *by John Ward*—The Diary of a Commander of the 15th Infantry Brigade, 5th Division, British Army, During the Retreat from Mons.

DOING OUR 'BIT' *by Ian Hay*—Two Classic Accounts of the Men of Kitchener's 'New Army' During the Great War including *The First 100,000* & *All In It*.

AN EYE IN THE STORM *by Arthur Ruhl*—An American War Correspondent's Experiences of the First World War from the Western Front to Gallipoli-and Beyond.

STAND & FALL *by Joe Cassells*—With the Middlesex Regiment Against the Bolsheviks 1918-19.

RIFLEMAN MACGILL'S WAR *by Patrick MacGill*—A Soldier of the London Irish During the Great War in Europe including *The Amateur Army*, *The Red Horizon* & *The Great Push*.

WITH THE GUNS *by C. A. Rose & Hugh Dalton*—Two First Hand Accounts of British Gunners at War in Europe During World War 1- Three Years in France with the Guns and With the British Guns in Italy.

THE BUSH WAR DOCTOR *by Robert V. Dolbey*—The Experiences of a British Army Doctor During the East African Campaign of the First World War.

AVAILABLE ONLINE AT **www.leonaur.com**
AND FROM ALL GOOD BOOK STORES

ALSO FROM LEONAUR
AVAILABLE IN SOFTCOVER OR HARDCOVER WITH DUST JACKET

THE 9TH—THE KING'S (LIVERPOOL REGIMENT) IN THE GREAT WAR 1914 - 1918 *by Enos H. G. Roberts*—Mersey to mud—war and Liverpool men.

THE GAMBARDIER *by Mark Severn*—The experiences of a battery of Heavy artillery on the Western Front during the First World War.

FROM MESSINES TO THIRD YPRES *by Thomas Floyd*—A personal account of the First World War on the Western front by a 2/5th Lancashire Fusilier.

THE IRISH GUARDS IN THE GREAT WAR - VOLUME 1 *by Rudyard Kipling*—Edited and Compiled from Their Diaries and Papers—The First Battalion.

THE IRISH GUARDS IN THE GREAT WAR - VOLUME 1 *by Rudyard Kipling*—Edited and Compiled from Their Diaries and Papers—The Second Battalion.

ARMOURED CARS IN EDEN *by K. Roosevelt*—An American President's son serving in Rolls Royce armoured cars with the British in Mesopatamia & with the American Artillery in France during the First World War.

CHASSEUR OF 1914 *by Marcel Dupont*—Experiences of the twilight of the French Light Cavalry by a young officer during the early battles of the great war in Europe.

TROOP HORSE & TRENCH *by R.A. Lloyd*—The experiences of a British Lifeguardsman of the household cavalry fighting on the western front during the First World War 1914-18.

THE EAST AFRICAN MOUNTED RIFLES *by C.J. Wilson*—Experiences of the campaign in the East African bush during the First World War.

THE LONG PATROL *by George Berrie*—A Novel of Light Horsemen from Gallipoli to the Palestine campaign of the First World War.

THE FIGHTING CAMELIERS *by Frank Reid*—The exploits of the Imperial Camel Corps in the desert and Palestine campaigns of the First World War.

STEEL CHARIOTS IN THE DESERT *by S. C. Rolls*—The first world war experiences of a Rolls Royce armoured car driver with the Duke of Westminster in Libya and in Arabia with T.E. Lawrence.

WITH THE IMPERIAL CAMEL CORPS IN THE GREAT WAR *by Geoffrey Inchbald*—The story of a serving officer with the British 2nd battalion against the Senussi and during the Palestine campaign.

AVAILABLE ONLINE AT www.leonaur.com
AND FROM ALL GOOD BOOK STORES

www.ingramcontent.com/pod-product-compliance
Lightning Source LLC
Chambersburg PA
CBHW031306150426
43191CB00005B/95